Indexed in

EGLI   1991

HAUNTED JOURNEYS

William Hodges, *Oaitepeha Bay*; also called *Tahiti Revisited*.
Courtesy of National Maritime Museum, London.

Haunted Journeys

DESIRE AND TRANSGRESSION IN EUROPEAN TRAVEL WRITING

Dennis Porter

PRINCETON UNIVERSITY PRESS

PRINCETON, NEW JERSEY

Copyright © 1991 by Princeton University Press
Published by Princeton University Press, 41 William Street,
Princeton, New Jersey 08540
In the United Kingdom: Princeton University Press, Oxford

Library of Congress Cataloging-in-Publication Data
Porter, Dennis, 1933–
Haunted journeys : desire and transgression in European travel
writing / Dennis Porter.
p. cm.
Includes index.
ISBN 0-691-06850-X (acid-free paper)
1. European literature—History and criticism. 2. Authors,
European—Journeys. 3. Travel in literature. 4. Exoticism
in literature. I. Title.
PN56.T7P6 1991
910.4—dc20 90-37224

This book has been composed in Linotron Baskerville

Princeton University Press books are printed on
acid-free paper, and met the guidelines for permanence and
durability of the Committee on Production Guidelines for
Book Longevity of the Council on Library Resources

Printed in the United States of America by
Princeton University Press
Princeton, New Jersey

1   3   5   7   9   10   8   6   4   2

For three of my favorite travelers

Gregory, Thomas, Benjamin

The only true travelers are those who leave
For leaving's sake.
Baudelaire, "Le Voyage"

. . . like those who set out on a journey to see a desired city with their own eyes, imagining that one can
enjoy in reality the spell of a dream.
Proust, *In Search of Lost Time*

Perhaps he merely hungered after the unusual. We
can only imagine that he desired something, the fulfillment of some personal and private dream, to
which he pinned his life.
Barry Lopez, *Artic Dreams*

CONTENTS

ACKNOWLEDGMENTS

IT HAS BEEN some years since I first began to read widely and think seriously about the literature of travel. In that time I have incurred many debts to the writers themselves, to thinkers, scientists, scholars in various fields, family, friends, and students, all of whom reminded me that there was always something else to be read. Literary scholarship, like travel writing itself, is a collective enterprise, and I would be hard put to know now where many of my ideas came from. Under the circumstances, I would simply like to thank by name those who have made the most direct and obvious contribution to the composition of this book in its final form. Michael Holquist was kind enough to read the first overlong version of the manuscript and make helpful suggestions for change. Princeton University Press's original reader gave the work a scrupulous and well-informed reading that was also of great help. Murray Schwartz has been supportive in a number of ways during the years since he came to Amherst, and my friend Harlan Sturm has given generously of his time in taking me through the ABC of the computer age.

I am grateful to the American Council of Learned Societies for a research fellowship that enabled me to complete a first draft. Finally, I would like to thank Robert E. Brown for his support and Charles B. Purrenhage for his precise editorial eye.

Unless otherwise indicated, all translations from the French or German are my own.

HAUNTED JOURNEYS

AT BEST that heterogeneous corpus of works I am calling European travel writing has been an effort to overcome cultural distance through a protracted act of understanding. At worst it has been the vehicle for the expression of Eurocentric conceit or racist intolerance. Yet, in either case, one thing is certain. From the narratives of youthful grand tourists or the journals of circumnavigators of the globe in the eighteenth century to the impressionistic sketches of nineteenth-century aesthetes or the field studies of contemporary ethnographers, written accounts of foreign places and their peoples are of interest for an important reason. They have traditionally been the vehicle by which our knowledge of things foreign has been mediated. As such they merit a more sustained, less belletristic attention than has frequently been accorded them.

Like all verbal artifacts, the reports of travelers constitute a changing yet always conventionalized extension of language. And it is one that furnishes a particularly rich field of inquiry for anyone interested in the way we conceptualize and represent the world, categorize its peoples according to a variety of overlapping schemas, affirm the relationships between them, and perceive our own (apparently central) place within this imaginary global geography. Above all, they bring into sharp focus that illuminating moment when two cultures are brought into sudden proximity. Yet it is only over the past decade or so that, in the various fields engaged in cross-cultural representation, we have come to appreciate just how problematic such cultural "earth-writing" (geo = earth; graphy = writing) is. The issues are complex enough to require some preliminary theoretic ground-clearing of a kind that will also enable me to define my own approach and delimit my concerns.

My own effort to think through the problems posed by the vast literature of travel began, in fact, when I first read Edward Said's important book, *Orientalism*.[1] The implications of the discourse theory deployed there by Said are such that if he were right, no alternative to Orientalism, or its equivalent for other areas of the globe, is conceivable in the West.

[1] (New York: Vintage Books, 1978). Said defines "Orientalism" as "a Western style for dominating, restructuring, and having authority over the Orient" (p. 5) or a Western hegemonic discourse dependent on "a distribution of geopolitical awareness into aesthetic, scholarly, historical, and philosophical texts" (p. 120). For a thoughtful extension of Said's approach in the direction of "Africanism," see Christopher L. Miller's *Blank Darkness: Africanist Discourse in French* (Chicago: University of Chicago Press, 1985).

If articulate language is a collective enterprise of the kind Said describes, then the individual is not free to write against the discursive grain, but is bound by an already constituted system of utterances. In short, in all our representations of things foreign, a knowledge—as opposed to an ideology—of the Other is impossible.

Behind Said's formulation of the issues in connection with several hundred years of Western representations of the Near and Far East, there stands, of course, the formidable theoretic project of Michel Foucault. And behind Foucault is the radical skepticism of Nietzsche's counter history or genealogy.[2] What Foucault, in effect, did in works from "The Discourse on Language" and *The Order of Things* through *Discipline and Punish* was reformulate the thought of the philosopher of power in the light of modern linguistic theory and of a new, more philosophically informed history of science. Discourse was defined as a form of violence done to the world and its inhabitants, including notably its human inhabitants. Thus, more systematically than Nietzsche, Foucault asserted not the traditional opposition between truth and politics, knowledge and power, but a complicity. And in his detailed, historical studies of "the dubious sciences" in particular, he showed how such complicity was maintained through material as well as discursive practices and their institutional supports. It was out of such a critique that there emerged the fused concept "power/knowledge."

Yet, in spite of the frequent brilliance and explanatory power of Foucault's thought, prolonged contact with the literature of travel has convinced me of the relative coarseness of discourse theory when applied to the literary field and of its own structural limitations. This is not because I am concerned to reaffirm a faith in some kind of existentialist freedom of choice or of representation, but because the human subject's relation to language is such that he or she is never merely a passive reflector of collective speech. We leave our individual mark in our written and spoken utterances in ways of which we are frequently aware, if at all, only after the fact. Not only are the uses of an inherited language invariably overdetermined at the level of the individual, but natural languages themselves provide the resources to loosen the constraints they also impose. In short, the limitations inherent in discourse theory are of a kind that frequently limit an understanding of the complex and problematic character of the works of my corpus.

As far as the representation of foreign places is concerned, the greatest problem to which a strict interpretation of discourse theory gives rise is

[2] "Nothing in man—not even his body—is sufficiently stable to serve as the basis for self-recognition or for understanding other men." "Nietzsche, Genealogy, History," in *Language, Counter-memory, Practice: Selected Essays by Michel Foucault*, ed. Donald F. Bouchard (Ithaca: Cornell University Press, 1977), p. 153.

the implication that there is no way out of cultural solipsism. Even granted the differences in the traditional relations of geopolitical power between the colonizing West and the colonized East, it is difficult to imagine how from a theoretical point of view our Orientalism would look very different from the Occidentalism of other parts of the globe. One may piously wish for alternatives to Orientalism, but how these would emerge in the context of a theory dominated by the concept of power/knowledge is by no means clear.[3]

Foucault himself made a theoretical opening in a more positive direction in such late works as the second and third volumes of *The History of Sexuality, The Use of Pleasure* and *The Care of the Self*, and in "On the Genealogy of Ethics."[4] In his reflections on the possibility of a modern ethics, he, in effect, came to advocate a form of living that was an experimentation at and beyond established limits. In place of that obliteration of otherness, which is implied by radical discourse theory, he came to argue for exploration and self-transformation through a dialogic engagement with alien modes of life. The important prerequisite for such a dialogue is the acknowledgment that there is always a "surplus" beyond that which, at any one time or place, we are in a position to perceive and record, and that one must devise strategies in order to illuminate some part of this surplus. Hence it is a major premise of the present work that the most interesting writers of nonfictional travel books have managed to combine explorations in the world with self-exploration. They submitted themselves to the challenge of travel and, in the process, managed if not always to make themselves over, then at least to know themselves differently.

[3] "Perhaps the most important task of all would be to undertake studies in contemporary alternatives to Orientalism, to ask how one can study other cultures and other peoples from a libertarian, or a nonrepressive and nonmanipulative perspective." *Orientalism*, p. 24.

[4] "On the Genealogy of Ethics" is to be found in Hubert L. Dreyfus and Paul Rabinow, *Michel Foucault: Beyond Structuralism and Hermeneutics* (Chicago: University of Chicago Press, 1982). For an updated account of Said's views and a cogent survey of new approaches to the question of colonial and neocolonial discourse, see his "Representing the Colonized: Anthropology's Interlocutors," *Critical Inquiry* 15 (Winter 1989). Said concludes there with a statement that is closer to the approach I will be developing here: "Exile, immigration, and the crossing of boundaries are experiences that can provide us with new narrative forms or, in John Berger's phrase, *other* ways of telling" (p. 225). My point is that those "*other* ways of telling" were already available in the heterogeneity of a great many multilayered texts. One of the more theoretically sophisticated analysts of colonial discourse, Homi Bhaba, has also suggested in his more recent writings that there is ambivalence and a potential for subversion in such discourse. See, for example, "Signs Taken for Wonders: Questions of Ambivalence and Authority Under a Tree Outside Delhi," in *Race, Writing, and Difference*, ed. Henry Louis Gates, Jr. (Chicago: University of Chicago Press, 1986).

It is also important to my argument throughout to note that the direction taken by Foucault's reflections on ethics are related in significant ways to the developing theory of literature that extends from the Russian Formalists down through Roland Barthes and beyond. In opposition to discourse theory stands the theory of textuality, or of "writing" in the strong modern sense.

By promulgating the opposition between the "poetic" and the "practical" functions of language, the Formalists were the first to identify systematically some of the defining characteristics of the domain of non-practical language use. They insisted from the beginning on the patterning, "roughening", and retarding mechanisms of various literary genres. Yet, in spite of the accusation of "Formalism," they related such formal devices to a purpose in the world that is of a particular relevance to a work on travel writing. "Poetic" language was deemed important because of its power to renew perception, to release the hold of stereotypes and make the world strange again. The emphasis is placed on a perpetual "re-visioning" of the external world, as Victor Shklovsky affirmed in a celebrated essay—"[an image] creates a 'vision' of the object instead of serving as a means for knowing it."[5]

The "defamiliarizing" activity is chiefly associated by the Formalists with high art and with the literary modernism of their times. By collapsing genre distinctions and by concentrating on the play of language wherever it is deployed, the French theorists of Roland Barthes's generation acknowledged the "poetic" function of language as a potential of all verbal artifacts under the rubric of "writing." "Practical language" can never wholly suppress its "poetic" twin. In a paper presented as the inaugural lesson of his chair of literary semiology at the Collège de France, Barthes outlined his conception of semiology as a critical, oppositional practice that corrects discourse theory by insisting on "the Text" as "the very index of powerlessness (dépouvoir)": "it thrusts aside to an unclassable, so to speak atopic space, far from the topoi of political culture, 'that obligation to form concepts, species, forms, ends, laws . . . the world of identical cases' to which Nietzsche refers."[6]

Having recognized after Foucault that the *libido dominandi* is located in one way or another in every discursive operation, Barthes goes beyond the Formalists in concluding that "literature" is precisely a sphere of language use that resists the exercise of power encoded within it. "Literature" is a form of "trickery" with and against language: "That salutary trickery, that art of evasion, that magnificent deception, which allows one

[5] "Art as Technique," in *Russian Formalist Criticism: Four Essays*, trans. Lee T. Lemon and Marion J. Reis (Lincoln: University of Nebraska Press, 1965), p. 18.

[6] *Leçon inaugurale de la chaire de sémiologie littéraire du Collège de France* (Paris: Le Seuil, 1978).

to hear out-of-power language in the splendor of a permanent revolution of language, is what I call 'literature' " (*Leçon*, p. 16). And it will be frequently apparent in the following chapters that such literary cunning even inhabits texts of a determined scientific sobriety, often in spite of themselves.

Barthes also shared with a great many others in recent times the notion of "the ubiquity of language," a notion that is of obvious consequence for a study such as the present one. On the one hand, it raises serious doubts about the status of the kind of texts with which I am dealing, because it rejects the correspondence theory of truth: namely, that it is possible to produce verbal statements which are held in some sense to be in correspondence with a pregiven reality. In Richard Rorty's radical formulation, the new skepticism gives rise to the conclusion that "there is no way to compare descriptions of the world in respect of adequacy."[7] On the other hand, the same skepticism also affirms that there is no metalanguage which one might have recourse to, no "final vocabulary" that enables one to produce the truth of a corpus of texts themselves.

As a consequence, that body of theory which has been particularly concerned with the ubiquity of language and that has gone under the name of deconstruction has also helped to focus critical attention on the ideological presuppositions of ordinary as well as philosophic language. Even more important in this context is the way in which it has highlighted those oppositional categories by means of which we organize and represent the world. Thus, we are no longer inclined to take for granted the apparently given identities or fixed positionalities of our discourses that have traditionally defined, for example, the differences between the races and the sexes or between us and them, East and West, North and South, in our various cultures. All that dismantling of texts which has taken place in so many books and articles over the past decade or so has at least managed to demonstrate, in Barbara Johnson's phrase, that "the differences *between* entities (prose and poetry, man and woman, literature and theory, guilt and innocence) are . . . based on a repression of differences *within* entities, ways in which an entity differs from itself."[8]

It is a lesson that should lead us back to a reflection on the verbal representations of alien life as a "writing" or as "transgressions" with relation to a given discursive regime. Consequently, the word "writing" in my subtitle is to be read as both with and without quotation marks, as discourse and antidiscourse, or, in the idiom of Mikhail Bakhtin, as official and unofficial language. What interests me is the stepping (*gradi* = to step)

[7] *Consequences of Pragmatism* (Minneapolis: University of Minnesota Press, 1982), p. XLIII.

[8] *The Critical Difference: Essays in the Contemporary Rhetoric of Reading* (Baltimore: Johns Hopkins University Press, 1980), pp. x–xi.

across (*trans*) borders on a number of levels. The concept of "transgression" along with "desire" is, on the other hand, also used in a broadly psychoanalytic sense.

o   o   o

IN a way, Foucault had already prepared the ground for a more historically informed and critical psychoanalysis. Crucial to his late thought on a modern ethics is the notion of the creation of the self through a dialogic encounter with others. However, Foucault's preoccupation with the heterogeneity that is masked by hegemonic affirmations of identity and with the otherness within is characteristic of his inquiry from the very beginning. The genealogical project was centrally an effort to illuminate the normative processes of subjection and the production of human subjects in order to make possible the liberation of repressed impulses or marginalized elements within the individual as well as within the social body. From *Madness and Civilization* on, Foucault celebrated insubordinate behaviors and transgressive activities, not least on the level of the human subject. The so-called self is not unified but divided, the human body a locus of differences. At the core of Foucault's critical philosophy one finds, therefore, the notion that human beings are condemned to living the opposition between normalization and resistance to it that, through taking thought, they also struggle to transcend. And far from the relatively homogeneous products posited by discourse theory, the works of travel literature to be discussed here will reveal the tensions and contradictions that such a theory implies. In short, in some respects Foucault's thought had more in common with psychoanalysis than he usually cared to acknowledge.

In the first place, Freudian theory turns out to be particulary helpful in understanding some of the motivations for travel and the characteristic ambivalence voiced by many of the travelers to be discussed. Thus, "desire" in my subtitle is used both in its commonly accepted and in its specifically psychonanalytic sense. That is, it refers to conscious as well as unconscious desire. With reference to the latter it derives from Freud's notion of the libido as updated by Lacan; it embodies the notion of a dynamic but obscure energy within a human subject that insists on satisfactions of a kind the world of objects cannot supply. It is that which we as speaking animals are structurally obliged both to repress and express obliquely through our insertion into language.[9]

[9] For the most cogent discussion of the issue, see Jacques Lacan, "The Agency of the Letter in the Unconscious or Reason since Freud," in *Ecrits: A Selection*, trans. Alan Sheridan (New York: Norton, 1977). Two of the most important books in English to explore the whole problematic opened up by the Lacanian concept of desire in the literary sphere are Tony Tanner, *Adultery in the Novel: Contract and Transgression* (Bal-

Yet, at one level, most forms of travel at least cater to desire: they seem to promise or allow us to fantasize the satisfaction of drives that for one reason or another is denied us at home. As a result, not only is travel typically fueled by desire, it also embodies powerful transgressive impulses. If, as anthropologists have long since taught us, borders of all kinds are perceived as dangerous as well as exciting places, and are associated with taboos, this is no less true of territorial borders, of tribal or national frontiers.[10] Moreover, something of such an attitude no doubt contributes to the frequent ambivalence to be found in so many works of travel literature. In connection with some of the travelers I shall be concerned with, the notions of guilt and duty are almost as important as desire and transgression. The acknowledgment of law and obligation, resistance to them and a pervasive sense of guilt, recur with a symptomatic frequency.

The practice of psychoanalysis is also of special interest to students of texts of all kinds because it promotes preeminently the attentive listening to insistences of individual speech. Moreover, the focus of its listening is neither a sociolect, as in discourse theory, nor the submerged metaphysics of a given rhetoric, as in deconstructionism, but the verbal behavior of a specific writer. If one learns anything from a close reading of a variety of travel writings, in fact, it is precisely that although there are both cultural and historically specific fantasies concerning our various Others, there are also markedly idiosyncratic ones. All that my colleague Paul Hollander lumps together under the wonderfully broad, oppositional categories of "alienation" and "utopian-seeking," in his study *Political Pilgrims*,[11] is shattered in a number of ways as soon as one begins to listen

timore: Johns Hopkins University Press, 1979), and Peter Brooks *Reading for the Plot: Desire and Intention in Narrative* (New York: Knopf, 1984).

[10] The British historian Richard Cobb touches on the ambivalent pleasures of frontiers in his own life—the quickening of the senses he associates with them along with a promise of freedom—in two passages from the autobiographical sections of *A Sense of Place* (London: Duckworth, 1975). The first passage concerns his frequent crossings at one stage in his life between France and Belgium: "The entry of the kingdom was epitomised by the rich cigar smell emanating from the *buffet de la gare* at Baisieux, as well as by the feeling of solid comfort contained in any Belgian cafe: potted plants, solid brasswork, *Le Soir*, an old-fashioned looking newspaper attached to a stick. . . . *Le passage de la frontière*, even though repeated almost weekly, would thus appear as a perpetual *renouvellement*" (p. 3). The second passage evokes the hills in the Welsh border country that were visible from his public school at Shrewsbury: "the Breiddens with an even more compelling and mysterious message, hinting at Wales, a foreign land, just over a couple of valleys . . . the biblical land that could be seen, rising and falling, in lines of blue and tawny hills, from the school playing fields, a reminder that freedom lay to the west" (p. 28).

[11] *Political Pilgrims: Travels of Western Intellectuals to the Soviet Union, China, and Cuba* (New York: Harper Colophon, 1983), pp. 11–12.

closely to the writings of individual travelers and to analyze the peculiar psychic investments they make on their chosen journeys.

The ostensible motivations for Europeans to travel outside their countries or their continent since the Renaissance are, of course, multiple, and they change somewhat over the two and a half centuries that interest me; they range from exploration, conquest, colonization, diplomacy, emigration, forced exile, and trade to religious or political pilgrimage, aesthetic education, anthropological inquiry, and the pursuit of a bronzer body or a bigger wave.

In a way, the narrator of Laurence Sterne's *A Sentimental Journey Through France and Italy* gives a more accurate categorization of travelers known to his age by focusing satirically on the humors and manias they display in the course of peregrination rather than on a declared mission:

> Idle Travellers
> Inquisitive Travellers
> Lying Travellers
> Proud Travellers,
> Vain Travellers,
> Splenetic Travellers,
>   Then follow
> The Travellers of Necessity,
> The delinquent and felonious Traveller,
> The unfortunate and innocent Traveller,
> The simple Traveller,
> And last of all (if you please) The Sentimental Traveller
> (meaning thereby myself) . . .[12]

Thus the public motive does not preclude in a traveler the kind of personal investments referred to above. As the travel supplements of our Sunday newspapers remind us every week, in our time at least the association between travel and pleasure is firmly entrenched in the culture. And such pleasure was, if anything, at least as familiar to those sons of the British upper classes as they departed on their continental grand tours in the eighteenth century—although one does not immediately connect it with the circumnavigators and with scientific exploration.

Moreover, as Boswell's travel journals make particularly clear, the notion of duty was equally familiar. And for a long time much of the tension experienced by male travelers, at least, tends to be focused on reconciling the call to pleasure in a foreign land with the demands of duty emanating from home. Central to Diderot's search for a universal moral code derived from nature—as his *Supplement to Bougainville's Voyage* makes

[12] (London: J. M. Dent, 1927), pp. 11–12.

clear—is, in fact, the urge to conflate the opposition, to make a duty of desire. In the travel literature of the romantic period, however, a third notion begins to emerge that is neither duty nor pleasure as traditionally conceived. Travel becomes self-consciously an end in itself, in a way that is often difficult to explain fully in terms of pleasure. The phenomenon begins with Byron but is most apparent in the Oriental journey of a Flaubert, where it appears in the lurid colors of the "romantic agony" as an orientation to death.

In retrospect, when reading such works it is difficult to avoid thinking in terms of the theory of instincts that Freud developed in *Beyond the Pleasure Principle*, a theory in which the early opposition between the reality principle and the pleasure principle is radically reformulated in order to take into account the impulse to autodestruction that he dubbed the death drive. Without such a concept in any case, especially as updated in Jacques Lacan's demanding reflections on *jouissance*, one has trouble explaining what is going on in certain of the works of travel I will be discussing. In the same celebrated Baudelairean poem from which I took the first of my epigraphs, "Le Voyage," it is for example difficult to avoid reading into the repeated demand for the new, the desire for an end. Death, it will be remembered, is hailed as an "old captain" in the last section, a modern and benevolent Charon with whom the poet will embark for his final voyage into the unknown.

Psychoanalysis also helps us to understand the strength of the investments individuals make in this country or that through the theory of the transference. Unconscious desire, as Lacan frequently reminded us, insists on reproducing itself in scenarios of our adult life that are retransfigurations of early fantasmatic scenarios, Thus, as is clear in many of the texts to be discussed here, decisions concerning flight or exile from the "homeland" along with the embracing or rejection of the countries through which one travels, often derive from identifications dependent less on objective factors than on the projection of early prototypes onto geographic space. The positive and negative transferences people make on countries are frequently just as powerful and just as "irrational" as are those they make on individuals. Moreover, with countries, as in a classic essay Freud suggests is the case with people, it is virtually impossible to distinguish "transference-love" from the real thing.[13] The longing to leave one's homeland, like the longing to return is the expression of a

---

[13] "Transference-love has perhaps a degree less of freedom than the love which appears in ordinary life and is called normal; it displays its dependence on the infantile pattern more clearly and is less adaptable and capable of modification; but that is all, and not what is essential." "Observations on Transference Love," in *The Standard Edition of the Complete Psychological Works* (London: Hogarth, 1955), vol. 12, p. 168; hereafter, referred to as *S.E.*

subject's desire that is as insatiable as it is as unlikely ever to find final satisfaction.

In a radical formulation of his celebrated essay "The Uncanny," Freud both connects the question with the search for origins and reverses our usual understanding of it by implying that love of "place" is prior to love for a human object, that it is, in fact, homesickness for the lost world of prenatality: " 'Love is home-sickness'; and whenever a man dreams of a place or a country and says to himself, while he is still dreaming: 'this place is familiar to me. I've been here before,' one may interpret the place as being his mother's genital or her body."[14] If in an important way we can be said to be always in language, it is just as true that there is a sense in which our desire to leave a given home is at the same time the desire to recover an original lost home. As several texts will reveal, there is a *déjà vu* of travel that is to be understood in part through the theory of the uncanny. The lands we pass through are haunted even if the ghosts do not always manifest themselves directly.

Many of the works I shall be discussing may be said to be haunted in other respects. Alongside refigurations of forgotten encounters, one also frequently comes across a sense of belatedness in a traveler, especially in a traveler who decides to give a written account of his travels. The vast majority of the places visited in the centuries that concern me, especially in Europe, were already familiar through a great many representations in various media. Under the circumstances, the challenge thrown down to the traveler is to prove his self-worth by means of an experience adequate to the reputation of a hallowed site. If he is a writer, he will be in the even more exposed position of having to add something new and recognizably his own to the accumulated testimony of his predecessors. To the anxiety of travel itself is added the anxiety of travel writing. It may, of course, be resolved by choosing to play the iconoclast rather than the rhapsodist, that is to say, by denigrating what others had praised.

Finally, in extra-European travel writing at least, one often comes across a sense of the return of the past that either has to do with the reemergence of a previously abandoned system of belief, in writers from Diderot to Naipaul, or is racial in the broadest sense of the word. From Captain Cook to Lévi-Strauss the traveler reports on the sensation of coming face to face in a remote place with the apparent past of the human race in its pristineness or menace. For pre-twentieth-century Europeans, the shock of such encounters with naked or seminaked peoples of color seems to reside in the perception of similarity within radical difference. Although the human past may have been deliberately sought out

[14] "The Uncanny," *S.E*, vol.17, p. 245.

as part of the quest for origins, it often returns in a way that nothing in their culture had quite prepared them for.

At the beginning of *Sea and Sardinia* D. H. Lawrence asks, "Why can't one sit still?"[15] in order to suggest the mysterious and unbidden quality of the impulse that impels one at a given moment to go somewhere where one is not required to go. It is a question to which the works here under discussion will provide a variety of answers. Since the narrative of a journey gives an author great freedom to focus on whatever it is in an unfamiliar land that "strikes his fancy," it invites a form of self-disclosure that is only partially conscious, but that is in any case different from what one finds in other forms of writing precisely because of the stimulus of *dépaysement*. There is a sense in which a foreign country constitutes a gigantic Rorschach test; it stimulates free association of a kind that is not reproducible in other ways.

As a result, in their writings travelers put their fantasies on display often in spite of themselves. In one way or another, they are always writing about lives they want or do not want to live, the lost objects of their desire or the phobias that threaten to disable them. Thus the literature of travel reminds us, among other things, of how dissatisfied most people are much of the time, of how the promise of other lands and other cultures is often that of demands fulfilled or of richer, more sensuous lives.[16] It is often difficult to ignore the possibility that the satisfactions represented in a great deal of travel writing are hallucinated satisfactions like those of dreams.[17]

Finally, as far as psychoanalysis is concerned, it will be seen that not

[15] (New York: Viking Press, 1963). In his final travel book, the late Bruce Chatwin refers to "the nature of human restlessness" as "the question of questions." And he goes on to summarize Pascal on the issue: "Why, he asked, must a man with sufficient to live on feel drawn to divert himself on long sea voyages? To dwell in another town? To go off in search of a peppercorn? Or to go off to war and break skulls?" *The Songlines* (New York: Viking Penguin, 1988), p. 161.

[16] Henri Baudet speaks of the "fundamental duality" that has characterized Westerners' approaches to the non-Western world: "There was, on the one hand, the actual physical outside world which could be put to political, economic, and strategic use; there was also the outside world onto which all identification and interpretation, all dissatisfaction and desire, all nostalgia and idealism seeking expression could be projected." *Paradise on Earth: Some Thoughts on European Images of Non-European Man* (New Haven: Yale University Press, 1965), p. 55. In our representations, of course, such a separation is more apparent than real.

[17] In an MLA panel entitled "Men in Feminism: Men and Feminist Theory," Stephen Heath asserted: "All representation, we know, is transferential. Representation is at once an image given, an argument made and a deputation established, a construction of object, me and other. Representation, to put it another way, includes my position, my desire and its vicissitudes." In *Critical Exchange* 18 (Spring 1985), ed. Paul Smith, p. 11.

only does Freud's general theory furnish concepts for an understanding of many of the psychic operations occurring in travel writing, but he himself also reflected briefly yet specifically on travel itself. Freud's comments on a range of topics—including his reflections on his avoidance of Rome, the guilt relative to his father that he experienced on first standing on the Acropolis, the heroism of travel, "derealization," and "the dissatisfaction with home and family" that so often motivates a traveler—turned out to be wonderfully suggestive openings for the reading of many of the works I discuss. In brief, Freud's autoanalyses and commentaries shed some light on the question of travel as desire and transgression, and on the strategies we devise to deny that fact.

Yet psychoanalysis, too, has its inherent limitations for my purpose, chiefly because it is both ahistorical and apolitical. That is in part why my chapter on Freud is located in the body of this book and does not form part of its introduction. As comments made above were designed to suggest, psychonanalysis is only one of the bodies of contemporary theory that have seemed to me to be particularly helpful in analyzing travel writing. Moreover, Freud's observations on travel need themselves to be located in the cultural and historical context of late-nineteenth- and early-twentieth-century Austria. His embryonic "theory of travel" is part of that tradition in European travel writing on which it also sheds an interesting light.

In fact, even the theory of transference cannot be taken over without modification. The difference between transferential relations between individuals and those between a subject and the world's countries is that the latter have macropolitical consequences of one kind or another and the former usually do not. Given the object of the representation, even the most apparently apolitical of travel narratives have something of the character of a political intervention. Not the least interest of many of the works to be discussed here, in fact, is that they have played a crucial role in the political and ideological debates of their time, from Bougainville's descriptions of noble savages in the South Seas for Enlightenment France and Stendhal's reflections on Restoration Europe in the early nineteenth century to André Gide's account of Soviet communism between the two world wars and V. S. Naipaul's reports on postcolonial societies in our own time.

Nowhere perhaps as much as in the field of travel writing, in fact, is the fundamental ambiguity of "representation" more apparent. To represent the world is a political as well as an aesthetic-cognitive activity. It is an effort both to put something alien into the words of a shared language for someone else at home and to put oneself in the Other's place abroad in order to speak on its behalf. One is at the same time *represen-*

tator and *representative*, reporter and legislator. And in all that one writes one also inevitably (re)presents, however imperfectly, oneself.[18]

○   ○   ○

GIVEN the inevitable theoretic orientation of this introduction, it is perhaps appropriate to point out that the analyses that follow involve for the most part relatively close readings of a limited number of more or less disparate works. Considering the nature of my corpus and the theoretic bias of the age, it seemed to me that if I had to err in choosing between an abundance of coruscating detail and a controlling, overshapely theory, I would on this occasion choose the detail. What in *English Hours*[19] Henry James refers to as "the bits"—those quaint and curious features of English civilization that speak to him in unforeseeable ways—should not be instantly recuperated by "a subject supposed to know," even if that subject is the author of a critical work. Some form of bold cartoon outline is essential, as James himself acknowledged, but it means something only if it is open to the resistances in its raw material and is filled out with richly suggestive detail.

The most rewarding kind of travel writing is often that which manages to surprise its reader with images that are startlingly new or with the extravagance of an idea that can no longer be thought. Consequently, any study of that literature should communicate some sense of the quirks and disturbances to be found there. In this respect, the example of Foucault is once again suggestive. In the preface to the second volume of *The History of Sexuality*, he notes: "The object was to learn to what extent the effort to think one's own history can free thought from what it silently thinks, and so enable it to think differently."[20]

In any case, the quality of most of the works here under discussion should at least ensure the stimulation of an unusual kind of anthology, if the choice of quotations is judicious. There is even a noble, if neglected, precedent for volumes of quotation and commentary in that earlier hu-

---

[18] See Raymond Williams's discussion of the complex development of the concept in English, under the heading "Representative" in *Keywords: A Vocabulary of Culture and Society* (New York: Oxford University Press, 1976).

[19] (Oxford: Oxford University Press, 1981).

[20] *The Use of Pleasure* (New York: Pantheon Books, 1978), p. 9. It is interesting that a cultural historian like Robert Darnton uses the imagery of travel and of a reverse conversion in order to insist on the strangeness to us of the *mentalités* of *ancien régime* France. He has, it seems, "gone native" in the French eighteenth century: "One is always running up against mysteries—not simply ignorance (a familiar phenomenon) but the unfathomable strangeness of life among the dead. Historians return from that world like missionaries who once set out to conquer foreign cultures and then come back converted, won over to the otherness of others." *The Kiss of Lamourette: Reflections in Cultural History* (New York: Norton, 1990), p. XIV.

manist tradition, which achieved its fullest elaboration in the *Essays* of Montaigne and which expressed in its own way a distrust of those metalinguistic systems that overlook their own discursive nature. As Montaigne himself might well have acknowledged, there is more power than honesty or pleasure in too constraining a theory in such a sphere.

As a consequence, the present work is organized as "a study" and not as a history. It in no sense claims to be a comprehensive history of European travel writing over the past two and a half centuries, but focuses deliberately on a limited number of specific works. It is about the travel writers and the writing as well as about what at different historical moments that writing itself is about. If I speak of "a study" rather than "studies," that is because although the different chapters are by and large independent and could be read separately, there are certain overarching concerns and questions that are illuminated through the comparison and contrast of works written at different historical moments. The surprise for me, in fact, was in the discovery of substantial continuity in the themes and engagements of travel writing from Boswell to Naipaul or from Diderot to Lévi-Strauss and Barthes.

The broad outline that I intend to fill in with commentary—James's cartoon—will then be a limited number of travel writings, chiefly by British and French male authors, that were written between the mid-eighteenth century and the present. My corpus is composed almost entirely of works that at least claim to be nonfictional, works that were chosen to some extent at random from a vast body of material that no individual could hope to control. Nevertheless, the works have for the most part been recognized by others before me for their intrinsic or representative value, and they have seemed to me significant in a variety of ways for literary or historical reasons. They have in common the fact that they are in one way or another examples of what might be called "critical travel." That is to say, whether they are the work of men known primarily as men of letters, philosophes, natural scientists, social scientists, navigators, or novelists, they pose or cause to be posed questions of central significance for European society in their time.

Whatever else it is, the present study is clearly not a monograph with the kind of intense focus on a limited field that that implies. As a result, in the cases of some authors I do not claim to be comprehensive in my reading of even their travel works. Any effort to be exhaustive here, even more than in most scholarly endeavors, is particularly vain.

The decision to focus solely on male authors came at a fairly late stage in my own writing. It was taken not out of any desire to reaffirm a maledominated canon; nor is it a reflection of the fact that European women over the centuries have left their homelands less frequently than men. In this respect, although Barthes is correct in declaring that from the beginning of the French literary tradition, from the *chansons de toile*, the female role is to experience absence as she waits at home—"Woman is sedentary, Man hunts, journeys; Woman is faithful (she waits), Man is fickle (he sails away, he cruises)."[21]—it is by no means true that women did not travel or even that they did not report on their travel. Mary B. Campbell begins her recent study of premodern accounts of travel outside Europe, *The Witness and the Other World: Exotic European Travel Writing, 400–1600*, with the *Peregrinato* by the obscure late-fourth-century woman Egeria.[22] And there has recently begun to appear a whole secondary literature that details the exploits of more recent women travelers.[23] My decision to focus exclusively on male writers was rather the consequence of the surprising discovery, surprising to me at least, that the father/son relationship was a central, though often submerged, topos of so many of the texts I am concerned with. To deal adequately with the complex motivations that drive women to travel or at least to write about it would, therefore, require a separate book that would have to be theorized differently. My own work might be regarded as in part a contribution to "masculinist studies"; in an important sense, it turns out to be an extended commentary on a question Freud never explicitly asked because, from the theory of the Oedipus complex on, he assumed he had already answered it: namely, "What does man want?"

As the table of contents suggests, I have deliberately included accounts of journeys undertaken for a wide variety of purposes and addressed to different audiences. It goes without saying that although I frequently rely on the work of specialists of different periods and authors, I do not in the great majority of cases pretend to such knowledge myself. Nor do I claim to master all the secondary literature, especially where it relates to controversies around such major nonliterary figures as Captain Cook, Darwin, or Lévi-Strauss, whose works I have perhaps recklessly reduced—or should it be elevated?—to the status of "writing." My assumption is that if a study such as this has any interest, it is precisely because it collapses categories and in its synoptic sweep sets up a fascinating play of echoes as well as contrasts.

The mid-eighteenth century seemed to me an appropriate point of departure for more than one reason. The age of the Enlightenment on the whole saw itself as the triumphant culmination of some two thousand

---

[21] *A Lover's Discourse: Fragments*, trans. Richard Howard (New York: Farrar, Straus, and Giroux, 1978), pp. 13–14.

[22] (Ithaca: Cornell University Press, 1988).

[23] See, for example, Dorothy Middleton, *Victorian Lady Travellers* (New York: E. P. Dutton, 1965); Catherine Barnes Stevenson, *Victorian Women Travel Writers in Africa* (Boston: Twayne, 1982); and Dea Birkett, *Spinsters Abroad: Victorian Lady Explorers* (Oxford: Basil Blackwell, 1989).

years of European cultural development, the age in which the progress of science and civilization had clearly resolved the quarrel between the Ancients and the Moderns to the satisfaction of the latter. Moreover, one consequence of that progress was the extension and consolidation of European power over the course of the century to the remotest regions of the globe. It was, as commentators both then and since have never ceased to acknowledge, preeminently an "age of discovery" in which the exploring and mapping in geographic space was connected in a variety of ways to the spread of the Newtonian scientific revolution to a wide range of fields.[24]

The voyages of world travelers, who were professional sailors, natural philosophers, naturalists, and artists, were therefore integrally connected to the project of the Enlightenment in all kinds of ways. In this connection, not the least interest of the travel writing of the period is, as Michèle Duchet has shown, that in an intellectual culture dominated by the thought of the philosophes it contributed in crucial ways to the progressive emergence of anthropology as a general science of man.[25] And along with it came that special kind of collective guilt which European travelers with a philosophic cast of mind have frequently experienced when contemplating the impact of their civilization on peoples less developed than their own. For these and for other reasons, the vogue of travel literature of all kinds in the eighteenth-century—factual and fictional, speculative, utopian, satirical, scientific, artistic, improving or sentimental—was unprecedented.[26]

Although the present study is not a history, then, the historical dimension is as important as the scope of my corpus because I am concerned to illuminate change as well as continuity in Europeans' attitudes both toward themselves and toward extra-European countries and peoples, from the era of European global hegemony to the present moment when relative European military and economic power have significantly de-

---

[24] In her carefully researched study of European illustrated travel accounts, Barbara Maria Stafford comments: "In the eighteenth century, as during the renaissance, great explorations abruptly widened the cultural and geographic horizon. The world of realities in which men lived changed, growing broader, richer in possibilities, and ultimately limitless. The eighteenth century undertook and largely achieved a heroically vast description of the sensible universe that moved from discovery to discovery." And, she adds two pages later, "The entire age was dominated by travelers." *Voyage into Substance: Art, Science, Nature, and the Illustrated Travel Account, 1760–1840* (Cambridge: MIT Press, 1984), pp. 18 and 20.

[25] *Anthropologie et histoire au siècle des lumières: Buffon, Voltaire, Rousseau, Helvétius, Diderot* (Paris: Maspéro, 1971).

[26] J. H. Plumb has noted that during the 1720s and 1730s in England "the output of travel books was second only to theology." *England in the Eighteenth Century* (London: Penguin Books, 1963).

clined. It is important to my comparative purpose that accounts of journeys undertaken outside Europe be contrasted with narratives of intra-
European travel; as will become clear, in the geopolitical imaginary of
Europeans down to relatively recent times at least, there is a hegemonic
geometry of center and periphery that conditions all perceptions of self
and the Other. Thus, the grand tour may stand as a paradigm of travel
undertaken to the center of a self-confident cultural tradition for the
purposes of self-cultivation and the reaffirmation of a common civilized
heritage. As a result, it stands in a relationship of complementarity to the
eighteenth-century voyages of global circumnavigation that mapped and
described unknown lands and peoples, and in the process produced
them as objects of an essentially European knowledge.

A decade or so ago, for ideological as well as aesthetic reasons, it would
have been harder to justify a book-length critical study of travel literature.[27] There was a firmer sense then of what in the literary canon was
central and what was marginal, and a general agreement on what came
under the category of the "literary" and what was relegated to the domain of "nonliterary" writings.[28] Thus, although there were a certain
number of recognized minor classics in what can only loosely be referred
to as a genre, the great majority of the works falling under the heading
of "travel writings" have been granted not much more than an informa-
tional or curiosity value. One of the positive results of the poststructuralist critique, however, has been that we no longer fetishize so-called creative writing as something essentially separate from and superior to
writing of other kinds.

The hierarchy of genres that during the romantic period came to replace that of the preceding classical age and went relatively unchallenged
down to the 1960s may still be integral to the ideology of literature found
in departments of creative writing or in Sunday journalism, but it no
longer commands universal respect. Lyric poetry and the novel do not
seem anymore to be the only vehicles for all that is most serious and
probing in current literary activity. Hence my own interest in what after
Foucault might even be called "ignoble genres," or works that (like the
literary products of mass culture itself) were once considered marginal
to the activities of the literary critic, if not of historical scholarship.

[27] I must admit to finding misguided certain relatively recent efforts to isolate "literary travel" from other kinds, to define the characteristics of the genre, and to for-
mulate a poetics.

[28] Clifford Geertz has discussed the breakdown of traditional institutional boundaries and theoretic self-understanding in the social sciences in a way that is already familiar in the sphere of literary studies. See, for example, "Blurred Genres: The Re-
figuration of Social Thought," in *Local Knowledge: Further Essays in Interpretive
Anthropology* (New York: Basic Books, 1983).

Such an interest is also in line with my own sense that the role played in our society by what, until recently at least, was called "the literary critic" is a debilitatingly narrow one. It is bound up, of course, with the cultural and institutional history that led to the creation of departments of modern (as opposed to classical) literature in Western universities, and with the subsequent emergence of a kind of scholar who was a specialist reader of the literary works of a national canon. Yet, as Terry Eagleton has pointed out,[29] there is an important case to be made for a return to the pre-romantic practice of the eighteenth century, to Addison and Steele, and what might loosely be called "culture criticism." As Eagleton sees it, the study of literature was important in their time precisely because it had not yet come to be defined as "an autonomous specialist discourse," but simply as "one sector of a general ethical humanism, indissoluble from moral, cultural and religious reflection" (*Function*, p. 18). And whatever one might think of the concept of humanism or the need for religious thought in our time, it seems to me difficult to argue against Eagleton's general point. If they are to retain any importance for contemporary society, literary studies should once again be integrated into historical and cultural studies. The goal is to work "back and forth between text and context."[30]

Finally, two considerations concerning travel literature that such a broader perspective suggests to me right off are, first, that the will to represent the world masks the effort to control it with the ideological fixity associated with Lacan's imaginary order and, second, that we all become historical much more rapidly than we normally care to believe. From the beginning, writers of travel have more or less unconsciously made it their purpose to take a fix on and thereby fix the world in which they found themselves; they are engaged in a form of cultural cartography that is impelled by an anxiety to map the globe, center it on a certain point, produce explanatory narratives, and assign fixed identities to regions and the races that inhabit them. Such representations are always concerned with the question of place and of placing, of situating oneself once and for all vis-à-vis an Other or others. They are also an integral

---

[29] *The Function of Criticism: From the Spectator to Poststructuralism* (London: Verso Editions and NLB, 1984).

[30] The phrase is Robert Darnton's. See *The Great Cat Massacre and Other Episodes in French Cultural History* (New York: Vintage Books, 1985), p. 262. The kind of cultural history practiced by Darnton at the border of a number of academic disciplines and subdisciplines—including the history of *mentalités*, the social history of ideas, the history of books, and the history of reading—suggests a variety of possibilities for literary studies proper that have yet to be explored. It has less in common with the New Historicism than might be assumed from a similar interest in anthropological method and cultural anecdote. See *The Literary Underground of the Old Regime* (Cambridge: Harvard University Press, 1982) as well as *The Great Cat Massacre* and *The Kiss of Lamourette*.

part of the ideological practice of every social formation that becomes aware of the existence of more or less remote lands and neighboring peoples.[31]

Yet, owing to a variety of causes, individuals within a culture have found ways to resist such normative readings. In any case, not the least interest of adopting a long view, even within the relatively homogeneous cultural traditions of European travel literature, is then because it demonstrates for our discomfort or pleasure how various writers at different historical moments fixed their world differently.

What also becomes apparent in more recent examples of European travel writing is the speed at which even the immediate past rushes away from us. In the attitudes and values they embrace and in the problematics of their discourses, my contemporaries tell me in books a decade or two old that we have become historical together. Under such circumstances, it is not difficult to agree with Claude Lévi-Strauss that we should be at least as impressed by what the Renaissance navigators to the New World saw as by what they managed to miss-see.[32] We do not stand in the place of truth any more than they did. We, too, will have to wait for future generations to tell us what it was that we mistook for our equivalent of mermaids in the ocean or sheep-trees on land.

In a manner that is inimitably his own, Jorge Luis Borges has made the point in a way that connects travel with all the commerce between a human subject and its world: "To discover the unknown is not a prerogative of Sinbad, of Eric the Red, or of Copernicus. Each and every man is a discoverer. He begins by discovering bitterness, saltiness, concavity, smoothness, harshness, the seven colors of the rainbow and the twenty-some letters of the alphabet; he goes on to visages, maps, animals and stars. He ends with doubt or with faith, and the almost total certainty of his own ignorance."[33] In short, that desire to reach out and discover which characterized preeminently eighteenth-century European culture has a universal dimension—as does the sense of doubt that so often overcomes the traveler once his journey is done.

---

[31] See J. B. Harley's valuable discussions of mapmaking from a Foucauldian perspective: "Maps, Knowledge, and Power," in *The Iconography of Landscape*, eds. Denis Cosgrove and Stephen Daniels (Cambridge: Cambridge University Press, 1988); and "Silences and Secrecy: the Hidden Agenda of Cartography in Early Modern Europe," in *Imago Mundi* (King's College, London, 1988). Direct comments on these questions by Foucault himself are to be found in "Questions on Geography," in *Power/Knowledge: Selected Interviews and Other Writings, 1972–1977*, ed. Colin Gordon (New York: Pantheon, 1980).

[32] See *Tristes Tropiques* (Paris: Plon, 1955), p. 84.

[33] Borges in collaboration with Maria Kodama, *Atlas* (New York: E. P. Dutton, 1985), p. 8.

PART ONE

Enlightenment Europe
and Its Globe

Chapter I

USES OF THE GRAND TOUR: BOSWELL AND HIS CONTEMPORARIES

BY THE TIME the young James Boswell undertook his grand tour in the 1760s, the quantity and scope of European travel writing had become a widely attested phenomenon of the age. In the wake of the discovery, exploration, conquest and colonization of the New World in particular, writers from the Renaissance on had spawned a wide variety of literary forms that were centered on travel well beyond the confines of Europe as well as within it. And the New Science of the seventeenth century stimulated a fresh vogue of discovery and speculation that gave rise to further kinds of voyage literature. Thus, alongside the nonfictional but frequently fanciful accounts of the navigators, conquistadores, freebooters, or diplomatic emissaries, there developed down through the sixteenth and seventeenth and into the eighteenth centuries an often marginal but popular literature composed of romances, tales of exotic adventure, voyages that are alternatively defined as imaginary, fantastic, extraordinary, extraterrestial or as "robinsonades," and journeys of a utopian, critical, and satirical cast.[1]

As a result of the quest for increasingly exact knowledge of the planet and its creatures, or of the newly discovered variety of human racial types, a more determined critical effort was made, beginning early in the

---

[1] Among the many standard works on this literature not mentioned in the Introduction are Boies Penrose, *Travel and Discovery in the Renaissance: 1420–1620* (New York: Atheneum, 1975); Geoffrey Atkinson, *The Extraordinary Voyage in French Literature before 1700* (New York: Columbia University Press, 1920), *Les Relations de voyages du XVIIe siècle: Contribution à l'étude de la formation de l'esprit du XVIIe siècle* (Paris: Champion, 1924); Philip Babcock Gove, *The Imaginary Voyage in Prose Fiction* (New York: Columbia University Press, 1941); René Pintard, *Le Libertinage érudit dans la première moitié du XVIIe siècle* (Paris: Boivin, 1943); John Lough, *France Observed in the Seventeenth Century by British Travellers* (Stocksfield: Oriel Press, 1985); Frank E. Manuel, *The Eighteenth Century Confronts the Gods* (Cambridge: Harvard University Press, 1959); Frank E. Manuel and Fritzie P. Manuel, *French Utopias: An Anthology of Ideal Societies* (New York: The Free Press, 1966); Percy G. Adams, *Travelers and Travel Liars: 1660–1800* (Berkeley: University of California Press, 1962), id., *Travel Literature and the Evolution of the Novel* (Lexington: University of Kentucky Press, 1983); and Ralph-Rainer Wutherow, *Die Erfahrene Welt: Europäische Reiseliteratur im Zeitalter der Aufklärung* (Frankfurt am Main: Insel Verlag, 1980).

eighteenth century, to separate out the factual from the fabulous, to distinguish between genres, and to condemn those "fireside travelers" whose fabrications complicated the task of acquiring accurate information about remoter regions of the globe. At the same time, the increasing possibilities for travel, especially in the continental European countries and the British Isles, meant that men and women of letters, philosophers, naturalists, and amateurs of the arts or of exotic landscapes undertook to report on their journeys to an educated reading public that was eager to be informed and diverted by such accounts.[2] Voyages of discovery came to be better equipped with appropriately trained personnel and scientific instruments as the century progressed. And, closer to home, the more inhospitable regions of Europe from the Swiss Alps to the Hebrides and Corsica were the focus of a new curiosity.

Moreover, the centrality of travel writing meant that at one time or another it engaged the attention of most of the important writers and thinkers of the age. A great many of them published major works in one or another of the genres in which travel and travelers played a central role. On the English side of the channel, one thinks immediately of Addison, Defoe, Swift, Johnson, Boswell, Fielding, Smollett, and Sterne. And in France more than one generation of missionaries, libertines, freethinkers, moralists, philosophes, or plain *honnêtes hommes*, from Jean-Baptiste Tavernier, Louis Armand de Lahontan, Cyrano de Bergerac, Fontenelle, and Fénelon to Montesquieu, Voltaire, Diderot, De Brosses, and Louis-Sébastien Mercier, found in different forms of travel writing appropriate outlets for their critical explorations of the natural and social world of their time.[3]

At the same time, it was widely assumed throughout Europe that travel within the boundaries of the Continent was indispensable to the education of an enlightened man of the world. In part as a consequence of the classical literary tradition in which they were educated and, in part, out of a sense that modern European society since the Renaissance had developed an advanced form of civilized life that needed to be observed at

[2] Charles L. Batten, Jr., comments that by the end of the eighteenth century in England, travel accounts had "won a readership second only to novels." *Pleasurable Instruction: Form and Convention in Eighteenth-Century Travel Literature* (Berkeley: University of California Press, 1978), p. 1.

[3] The crucial role played by eighteenth-century voyage literature in the development of Enlightenment thought is emphasized by Michèle Duchet. The inventories of the private libraries of the philosophes is testimony to the range of their readings in the field. And one of the century's major scientific treatises, Buffon's multivolume *Histoire naturelle, générale et particulière*, would have been impossible without the rich data furnished him in Paris by travelers' journals, reports, and letters from the field. See Duchet, *Anthropologie et histoire au siècle des lumières: Buffon, Voltaire, Rousseau, Helvétius, Diderot* (Paris: Maspéro, 1971).

first hand, the grand tour or its equivalent in continental countries was taken to be the proper culmination of the education of a young gentleman. Yet such a view did not go unchallenged. In Britain especially the debate on the value of the grand tour was a matter of lively controversy throughout the century, for reasons that concern one of the central themes of this study: namely, the implicitly transgressive character of a great deal of travel.

Richard Hurd's 1763 essay "On the Uses of Foreign Travel"[4] is representative of the tenor of the debate insofar as it takes the form of a dialogue between two older men concerning the value of travel for young men. John Locke and Lord Shaftesbury are the interlocutors who discuss the grand tour in connection with "the education of a young man of rank and quality." But briefly, at the end, Locke is made to introduce the idea of a very different kind of journey; he contrasts the dubious value for young men of travel within Europe in a philosophic age with the importance of voyages around the globe for the proper study of the human species. The opposition is between travel for the sake of education and travel for the sake of the emerging science of man.

In any case, Shaftesbury is made a foil for the elderly Locke's disquisition on the goals of education, on the one hand—"the business of education is to form the UNDERSTANDING and regulate the HEART ("Uses," p. 138)—and on the moral and intellectual malleability of boys, on the other. "Knowledge of the world" for Bishop Hurd's Locke concerns, not "virtuososship," but "the study and contemplation of men" ("Uses," p. 122). And it is acquired not by "sauntering within the circle of the grand Tour" in the company of "shallow, servile, and interested governors" ("Uses," p. 104), but by patient nurturing and a discreet surveillance at home. An education that produces "useful and able men" ("Uses," p. 149) presupposes the benevolent authoritarianism of family life.

Granted the ubiquity of vice and temptation in England as well as abroad, Locke affirms: "I should still imagine our youth to be safer from the infection at home, under the eye and wing of their own parents and families, than wandering at large in foreign countries" ("Uses," p. 103). In short, travel more often than not corrupts, unless, of course, one is already fully formed and something of a "citizen of the world," in which case it is not Europe but the globe that one should visit. The philosopher argues that "the tour of *Europe* is a paltry thing: a tame, uniform, unvaried prospect." Instead, "to study HUMAN NATURE to purpose, a traveller must enlarge his circuit beyond the bounds of Europe. He must go, and catch her undressed, nay quite naked, in *North America*, and at the Cape of *Good Hope*" ("Uses," p. 197). And that, of course, was what, as the cen-

---

[4] *The Works of Richard Hurd, D.D.* (London: T. Caddell and L. Davis, 1881), vol. 4.

tury progressed, increasing numbers of Europeans were doing in North and South America, Africa, South East Asia, and the South Seas.

Whether the benefits of foreign travel outweighed its disadvantages for the young is, then a recurring topic of debate throughout the eighteenth century. And the reason why is clear from Boswell's journal of his continental tour; there he expresses passionately and energetically the point of view of one of the young grand tourists in opposition to the voice of paternal authority adopted by Hurd's Locke.

In this respect, it is significant that in his introduction to the second half of *Boswell on the Grand Tour*, which is devoted to Italy, Corsica, and France, Frank Brady comments: "James Boswell's main concerns during the period of his life covered by this volume were sex, religion, and politics—the three subjects of conversation forbidden in polite society" (*Italy*, p. IX).[5] I would add, first, that those concerns preoccupy, to varying degrees and in more or less explicit ways, a great many of the writers of travel books and, second, that what at bottom those same concerns have in common in the question of happiness. In their different ways the apparently disparate spheres of sex, religion, and politics are invested with movements of a personal or a collective desire that individual human subjects find it easy to identify with. Leaving home always has an element of promise as well as danger, of pleasurable adventure and of risk, that either solidifies the traveler's faith in inherited norms and values or puts them to the seductive test of difference—something that Locke in Hurd's dialogue, concerned with producing educated men and future "senators" for English public life identifies as a threat.

To travel through the world is to gather a series of impressions and to make a succession of more or less conscious notations on the superiority or inferiority of other societies, when compared with one's own, in respect of the satisfactions they afford their members, mostly in this world but occasionally in the next. To go on to ask why it is we are not happy all the time and to wonder whether perpetual happiness has been achieved by others at other times and places is to raise the ancient question of paradise or of that version of paradise which emerged in the speculative thought of the Renaissance, utopia. Whether or not the question of the perfect society is raised in an explicit way, however, what the religious beliefs, political institutions, and sexual practices of a given society make possible or deny in the way of happiness or personal gratification

[5] All references to *Boswell's London Journal, 1762–1763, Boswell in Holland, 1763–1764, Boswell on the Grand Tour: Germany and Switzerland, 1764*, and *Boswell on the Grand Tour: Italy, Corsica, and France, 1765–1766* are to the editions by Frederick A. Pottle and by Frank Brady and Frederick A. Pottle, respectively (New York: McGraw-Hill, 1950, 1953, and 1955).

is a crucial and enduring preoccupation of most travel writers since long before the eighteenth century.

Yet, as Henri Baudet has noted, it was not until the Enlightenment and the emergence of critical philosophy that European travelers began to make systematic comparisons between their homeland and non-European societies: "The problem of whether our civilization was heading in the right direction was a subject of debate throughout the century. Speculation like this is, of course, a common phenomenon that may be found in almost any period. But the practice of making comparisons with non-Western peoples did not play a major role until the advent of the eighteenth century."[6] Such comparisons will be the topic of my chapter on cicumnavigation. Comparisons between one's European homeland and other European societies present and past, on the other hand, have a much older history and will be the focus of this chapter and the next. In many ways, they constituted much of the *raison d'être* of grand tour literature since the Renaissance.

I do not, of course, intend to imply any uniformity in the manner in which questions of sex, religion, and politics come to be formulated or the pursuit of happiness fantasized. On the contrary, a great deal of the interest of the works under discussion lies in the way national, period, class, sexual, and generational differences as well as specific familial dynamics often give rise to radically contradictory representations of the way the world is or ought to be. Boswell's travel journals, therefore, manage to be both representative and unique. At the same time, because they are wonderfully candid and often more wide-ranging, elliptical, and less studied than many later works, they allow me to bring into immediate focus the tensions and recurring problematics of travel writing.

As Charles L. Batten has reminded us, for a long time in eighteenth-century England the model for accounts of the grand tour was Addison's *Remarks on Several Parts of Italy*, published in 1705. It was characterized by its sobriety, the relative absence of narrative elements, and the concentration on the sites and artistic monuments of Italy. But such is, for the most part, far from the case with Boswell's journal. If according to the critical commentary of the century the aim in travel writing was for a long time the neoclassical balance implied by the Horatian notion of *utile dulce*, then more often than not it is an aim that Boswell fails to achieve. By Addison's standards the focus is too often on the traveler, rather than on his observations. Boswell is altogether too confessional and anecdotal or, something the reviewers of travel writings of the age denounced almost as much as they berated fictional travel passed off as fact, too

[6] Henri Baudet, *Paradise on Earth: Some Thoughts on European Images of Non-European Man* (New Haven: Yale University Press, 1965), p. 39.

"egotic."[7] Yet, from the point of view of a modern reader, such liberties taken with the conventions of the genre constitute much of the journal's vitality.

Maturer points of view than Boswell's on the significance of the grand tour for the education of eighteenth-century English gentlemen are to be found in the works of Edward Gibbon and Tobias Smollett. And some limited attention will be paid to the *Autobiography* and *Travels Through France and Italy*, respectively, further on in this chapter in order to suggest the context in which Boswell wrote. In addition, it is important to note that the continental travels on which the relevant portions of the works I am concerned with depend, occurred in the 1760s. So we have three British, upper-class, male travelers who were yet positioned differently and who, within the limits imposed by the regularities and exclusions of eighteenth-century discourse, yield three different articulations of the experience of continental travel.

o   o   o

BETWEEN November 1762 and February 1766, James Boswell produced an extensive body of writings that in the Yale editions of the Private Papers have been published as four volumes, of which the first three are of interest here: namely, *Boswell's London Journal, 1762–1763, Boswell in Holland, 1763–1764* and *Boswell on the Grand Tour, 1764–1766*, parts 1 and 2. The period of time covered by these works runs from the moment of Boswell's arrival in London from his native Scotland, for his second visit at age twenty-two—this time with his father's acquiescence—to his return to London after two and a half years on the Continent, when he was in his twenty-fifth year. As the title of the first of these volumes suggests, there is a sense in which all these writings have the character of journals. If one can also make the claim that they belong to the literature of travel, it is because their focus is outward as well as inward. The young Scot, who had been struggling for a number of years to escape from the paternal home and homeland, finally found himself free and financially equipped to face a wider and more brilliant world than the one he had been used to. And he made full use of the leisure afforded him to record the way he indulged his curiosity and put himself to the test by exploring the fashions and manners, pleasures, sexual behavior, taste, institutions, morals, and beliefs of the different societies through which he passed, beginning with mid-eighteenth-century London.

Boswell on the Grand Tour is one of the most representative accounts of

---

[7] "Too little autobiographical information would cause the writer to be suspected as a 'fireside,' 'whirlwind,' or 'forgetful' traveler; too much would make him seem either an egotist or a writer of fiction." Batten, *Pleasurable Instruction*, p. 76.

the significance of the tour for the eighteenth-century in more than one sense. Its author was not one of the major writers or thinkers of his age; nor at the time of his journey did he have a specific vocation or passionate interest of a kind that concentrated his thinking and perceptions. He was not a painter, poet, musician, art historian, diplomat, merchant, soldier, collector, or even a passionate amateur of the *beaux arts* insofar as one can tell from the journal, in spite of occasional dutiful notations on famed sites, buildings, sculpture, and paintings.

He was, on the contrary, a representative *fils de famille*,[8] an intelligent young man with a solid classical education and a developed taste for letters and the theater. He was still young enough to be enthralled by the variety of life's possibilities and pleasures, still in search of a career and of a place in the world, still uncertain of his abilities and given to alternating moods of self-assurance and self-doubt, still undecided as to whether he was at heart merely "a man of pleasure" or one who was morally and intellectually destined for a nobler role. He was sufficiently well-off to travel decently and with a servant, but not in luxury: "I do not intend to travel as a *milord anglais*," he notes apropos of his projected Italian journey, "but merely as a scholar and a man of elegant curiosity" (*Germany*, p. 75). He was not an aristocrat, but was from an ancient Scottish landowning family and well enough connected to have an entrée into the courts and upper-class circles of most European countries. He was, finally, enough of a critical observer of his life and times to recognize intellectual distinction and to seek out some of the major thinkers and men of letters of the age, from David Hume, David Garrick, Dr. Johnson, and Oliver Goldsmith in Britain to Rousseau and Voltaire in Switzerland and France, respectively.

As far as Boswell is concerned, there is to begin with something exemplary in the fragmentation of texts that are, if anything, reinforced by a scholarly tradition in editorship that has added a variety of interesting ancillary material to the actual journals Boswell left behind. The "Boswell" we construct largely on the basis of his own written works is a Boswell whose "identity" or "true nature" posed a problem for the narrator who records his own comings and goings, solicitations and impulses, from one day to the next over several years. Boswell's travel writings are exemplary in a second sense, therefore. Because a journal form draws attention to the moment and activity of writing, the reader is rarely wholly distracted from an awareness of the narrator in the interest of

---

[8] In one of his earlier exercises in self-evaluation during the time of his courtship of the actress "Louisa," he describes himself as "a young fellow of spirit and fashion, heir to a good fortune, enjoying the pleasures of London, and now making his addresses in order to have an intrigue with that delicious subject of gallantry, an actress." *London*, p. 94.

"pure narrative." If in travel writings, as elsewhere, one encounters the polarity Emile Benveniste first established between deictic discourse and story proper, Boswell's practice, like that of his contemporary Sterne in fiction, is closer to the discursive pole.

Symptomatic of that split between the man who writes, and the man who is written, between the "I" of utterance and the "I" of the uttered, is Boswell's occasional shift out of the first person "I" into the second person "you" to refer to himself. In any case, the Boswell we are familiar with is a textual Boswell. It is in the writings that record his encounters with different European countries that we recognize the repetitions of which he is composed.

The first three volumes of the Yale edition are made up of a variety of material, including fully written journals, letters by and to Boswell, memoranda in telegram style, and part of his book on Corsica that was published in 1768. The first–person narratives of Boswell's journeys that result often have the pace and flavor of eighteenth-century picaresque with a highborn hero. They have a similar richness of anecdote and wide range of characters—from maids, servants, and innkeepers to duchesses, ministers, ambassadors, philosophes, and even a king—and similar representations of contemporary manners. There is a similar frequent change of scene and location, and even more sudden changes of tone. Something of the astringent as well as the sentimental comedy of the developed genre, as well as its flashes of cruelty and plunges into melancholy, are suggested in some of the quick transitions characteristic of the journal notations. Thus, in the space of twenty lines, the young diarist records the "extreme mortification" of a rejection by a certain Mme. S——, the consolation received from a Fellow of the Royal Society, a bungled public execution in which the incompetent hangman ends up strangling the victim with his feet, and a moment of religious fervor in a church: "Here then I felt three successive scenes: raging love—gloomy horror—grand devotion. The horror indeed I only *should* have felt. I jogged slowly on with my vetturino, and had a grievous inn at night" (*Italy*, p. 41).[9]

At the same time, taken together the three works of travel have a kind of inner unity that one does not associate with the picaresque genre. They follow the progress of a young man through the world. Efforts at

---

[9] In discussing "the unaccountable nature of the human mind," which is one of his favorite themes, Boswell as narrator figures himself as the hero of a travel narrative in the classic tradition precisely on account of his abrupt changes of mood: "I am now well and gay. Let me consider that the hero of a romance or novel must not go uniformly along in bliss, but the story must be chequered with bad fortune. Aeneas met with many disasters in his voyage to Italy, and must not Boswell have his rubs?" *London*, p. 206.

self-education and moral improvement alternate with endeavors to make his way in the world and indulge his sexual appetite for a variety of women—his overimpetuous pursuit of Italian "ladies of fashion," one of whom was over fifty, involves an episode characteristic of the comedy of seduction from Restoration theater to the novels of Stendhal. Thus, the journals constitute in their way a sentimental and sexual as well as a moral and political education. Although they by no means have that concentrated focus on the maturation of an inner life, which one associates with the turn-of-the-century *Bildungsroman*, the wayward story Boswell tells does constitute his *Wanderjahre*. Boswell's grand tour turns out to be the narrative of a young man on the make who was also attentive enough to some of the contradictory impulses within him to suggest the processes that, in his time, went into the making of male subjectivity.

Since Vladimir Propp first identified the opening moves of his corpus of folk fairy tales with an interdiction and a transgression that causes a lack, it has been easy enough to recognize that some such exciting force is to be found at the beginning of all narratives. And the narrator of Boswell's travel journals does leave home under a cloud, only to return there after a lengthy and complex journey, more fully self-possessed, if not chastened and reconciled.

While still in Germany, Boswell affirms the "originality" of the figure he cuts in the world and admonishes himself to assert the imaginary fullness of an identity that finds confirmation in a proper name: "Let me then be Boswell and render him as fine a fellow as possible" (*Germany*, p. 29). By the end of the tour the narrator/hero boasts of the growth in his knowledge of the world as well as in self-knowledge and self-confidence. His journey in space and time has turned him into a mature man, "enlarged and broadened by travel" (*Italy*, p. 284).

For long stretches in the narratives of both the German/Swiss and Italian/French journeys, Boswell's grand tour seems so representative because he occupies himself in all the familiar and conventional ways. In his telling descriptions, moreover, people and objects remain in relative balance with the narrative of events and actions. In Germany he evokes the courts of different principalities where he is received and tells of dinners, balls, concerts, operas, and military parades. He also reports on visiting the libraries, galleries, or cabinets of curiosities of aristocratic and royal patrons, on taking riding and music lessons, on reading widely but without particular focus, and on engaging in conversation with a variety of men and women of greater or lesser social standing and knowledge. And in Italy Boswell does for the most part what other young men of his class and nation had practiced on their grand tour—"learning the language, studying the genius, and absorbing the thought of the Italian people" (*Italy*, p. 8).

Preeminently, of course, this included visiting the sites and monuments of ancient Rome, viewing the arts and antiquities, and responding with appropriate enthusiasm. He is filled with "sublime and melancholy emotions" (*Italy*, p. 60) after visiting the Forum and the Coliseum, and he experiences "the true, venerable enthusiasm" (*Italy*, p. 68) as he studies ancient artifacts. Boswell's adjectives here—sublime and melancholy," "the true, venerable"—already suggest the way in which the journey to Rome had the character of a summons; to see its monuments was an interpellation that confirmed one's own subjecthood. As Louis Althusser once reminded us after Pascal, it is often the ritual that produces the faith and not vice versa. For many a grand tourist, therefore, to arrive in Rome and walk its famous sites was sufficient to induce a kind of belief.

Boswell's grand tour also typically included seeking an audience with the pope, circulating in Italian polite society, going to the opera, and pursuing sexual conquests of Italian women, who in the male cosmopolitan world of the grand tourists had a reputation for compliant ways: "My desire to know the world made me resolve to intrigue a little while in Italy, where the women are so debauched that they are hardly to be considered as moral agents, but as inferior beings" (*Italy*, p. 28).

In short, Boswell behaves (as he himself noted) like "a tourist" in Rome and "a libertine" in Naples. In other Italian cities he ranges somewhere between these two poles. For the most part, his self-representations suggest an elegant dilettante of taste, curiosity, and an unassuaged sexual appetite who seeks to combine self-improvement with the various pleasures associated with German eighteenth-century court life or Italy's city-states. Yet, alongside all this there are other features of these travel writings that may be representative in a profounder sense but that are by no means conventional. For example: the fact of keeping a journal itself, the problem of his faith, the fits of melancholy and the "hypochondria" of which he frequently complains,[10] the visit to and enthusiasm for Rousseau, and the journey to Corsica and sojourn with its "freedom fighters."

The fact that Frank Brady identifies sex, religion, and politics as the main concerns of Boswell's Italian, French, and Corsican journals already suggests the conflictual impulses in the writer's psyche. It implies that there is in Boswell's travel journals a mixture of worldliness and moral aspiration, of openness to his own desire and search for the solidification of an inherited faith, as well as for the kind of political institutions most consistent with human well-being. Far more than in the travel journals or related writings of such major writers and thinkers of the eighteenth-

[10] "Melancholia" was a frequent complaint of British travelers. Among the best known of those who gave an account of travels undertaken when they were suffering serious ill-health are Fielding, Smollett, and Samuel Sharp.

century as Addison, Voltaire, Diderot, Winckelmann, Fielding and Goethe, or even Smollett, one finds in Boswell the impressions and confessions of a *jeune homme moyen sensuel* recorded in their fragmentation and dispersion more or less from day to day. As a result, the significance of the grand tour as a cultural practice of the North European upper classes during the age of Enlightenment is seen in a particularly ambivalent light.

The grand tour was, as noted above, regarded as the final stage in the education of young men of the world before they embarked on the serious business of life. Consequently, it was less bookish than "worldly" in the broad sense of that term—although, as is the case with the Lord Mountstuart with whom Boswell traveled for a time in Italy, the young tourist was often accompanied by a tutor as well as a "governor." It was a question of learning about life in those European countries with which one's homeland had a variety of military, diplomatic, and commercial relations, and of how to conduct oneself in polite society at home and abroad in view of the future public role one would be called upon to play. At the same time, one was also intended to learn something of the principal European languages, to see the sights, admire the monunents and works of art of the Western tradition, and become acquainted with the taste and guiding ideas of the classical past along with the latest refinements of the modern age.

The idea was that one's moral, literary, and aesthetic education would be completed at the same time that one's experience of the world would be substantially broadened; the knowledge of men and manners was to complement such theoretical knowledge as one had acquired from a formal classical instruction. Thus formed, one might, if one were British, return home, marry a young heiress from a good family, pursue a seat in Parliament, take up a diplomatic career, or enter one of the professions. From the point of view of society, the grand tour can be seen to be an instrument of social reproduction. And from the point of view of the individual, it has the character of a rite of passage following upon which one accepts the responsibilities of the well-born male to family, class, and nation. One prepared for the time when one would assume one's father's place.

Laurence Sterne put the case for the grand tour in a sermon on the prodigal son:

> the advantages are worth the pursuit;—the chief of which are—to learn the languages, the laws and customs, and understand the governments and interest of other nations,—to acquire an urbanity and confidence of behaviour, and fit the mind more easily for conversation and discourse—to take us out of the company of our aunts and

grandmother, and from the track of nursery mistakes; and by showing us new objects, or old ones in new lights, to reform our judgments—by tasting perpetually the varieties of nature, to know what
is *good*—and by observing the address and arts of man to conceive
what is *sincere*—and by seeing the difference of so many various hu-
mours and manners—to look into ourselves and form our own.[11]

On the other hand, the risk that the grand tour might turn into a continental rake's progress for young men of sixteen to twenty, who were
fresh out of public school or university, was taken with equal seriousness
by the age, as some celebrated lines from Pope's *Dunciad* remind us:

> Led by my hand, he saunter'd Europe round,
> And gather'd ev'ry vice on Christian ground;
> Saw ev'ry court, heard ev'ry king declare
> His royal sense of Op'ras or the Fair;
> The Stews and Palace equally explored
> Intrigu'd with glory and with spirit w——.
>
>   [IV, 311–316]

As far as Boswell is concerned, starting in London the journals make
clear that the impulse to travel was situated somewhere between these
two poles; the pursuit of pleasure was at least as important as personal
enlightenment and preparation for a fitting future. The goal of completing an education is overlaid with the determination to celebrate an emancipation. His first journey to London was carried out against his father's
will, and a form of paternal prohibition hovers over all his subsequent
travels. Thus, Boswell's departure on his grand tour was itself contingent

---

[11] Quoted by William Edward Mead, *The Grand Tour in the Eighteenth Century* (Boston:
Houghton Mifflin, 1914), p. 386. Mead quotes both Sterne and Pope, along with many
more witnesses, in a chapter entitled "Contemporary Comment on the Grand Tour."
Sterne's narrator in *A Sentimental Journey* comments that the fate of "the poor Traveller" involves "sailing and posting through the politer kingdoms of the globe, in pursuit
of knowledge and improvements." But he wonders skeptically whether the traveler
should not "prevail upon himself to live contented without foreign knowledge or foreign improvements, especially if he lives in a country that has no absolute want of
either." *A Sentimental Journey Through France and Italy* (London: J. M. Dent, 1927), pp.
12–13.

The most devastating satirical portrait of the youthful British grand tourist (in verbal
form) is probably Smollett's, however: "I have seen in different parts of Italy raw boys,
whom Britain seemed to have poured forth on purpose to bring her national character
into contempt: ignorant, petulant, rash, and profligate, without any knowledge or experience of their own, without any director to improve their understanding, or super-
intend their conduct. One engages in play with an infamous gamester, and is stripped
perhaps in the very first partie: another is poxed and pillaged by an antiquated canta-
trice: a third is dubbed by a knavish antiquarian; and a forth is laid under contribution
by a dealer in pictures." *Travels Through France and Italy* (Oxford: Oxford University
Press, 1981), p. 241.

on the license reluctantly granted to sow his wild oats and try out styles of living of which his father deeply disapproved. The note is already sounded early in the *London Journal*: "To get away from home, where I lived as a boy, was my great object. It was irksome beyond measure to be a young laird in the house of a father much different from me, of a mind perfectly sound, and who thought that if I was not a man of business, I was good for nothing" (*London*, p. 78).

Boswell's father, Lord Auchinleck, a distinguished Scottish judge from a family line of lawyers, was probably rather typical of certain *bien pensant* milieus, as Bishop Hurd's dialogue suggests, in his suspicion of the value of foreign travel for his son, even though the grand tour had by then the authoritative status of an institution. In any case, the theme of travel as escape from paternal authority and the dictates of the paternal Law recurs from time to time throughout the various travel journals. And it is reinforced in the Yale edition as a result of the insertion of occasional exchanges of letters between father and son.

What the paternal Law meant for a stern Presbyterian father and why the grand tour represented a threat to it, at least as much as it was a support, can hardly be better expressed than in the letter of admonition that Lord Auchinleck addressed to his son toward the end of his stay in Italy. He reproached him for not writing, for spending too much money, and for remaining too long away. It was, he wrote,

> now necessary, to put an end to peregrination. You have had full opportunity to be satisfied that pageantry, civil and ecclesiastic, gives no entertainment to thinking men, and that there is no end nor use of strolling through the world to see sights before unseen, whether of men, birds, or things, and I hope are, with the poet, saying "Utinam remeare liceret ad veteres casas,"[12] and will return with a proper taste and relish for your own country. For if that were not to be your disposition, I should most heartily repent that ever I agreed to your going abroad, and shall consider the money spent in the tour you have made as much worse than thrown away. But I choose to banish all such gloomy suspicions, and hope to my infinite satisfaction to see you on your return a man of knowledge, of gravity and modesty, intent upon being useful in life. If this be so, your travelling will be a little embellishment to the more essential talents, and enable you to make a better figure in your own country, which is the scene of action Providence has pointed out for you. [*Italy*, p. 211]

More than anything else, Lord Auchinleck's letter makes the classic case of a serious-minded, upper-class paterfamilias against foreign travel, finding there nothing more than "a little embellishment to the more es-

[12] "I wish I could go back to the old dwelling."

sential talents."[13] He warns, in turn, against being taken in by the pageantry or mere spectacle of social life, against an idle curiosity for the new, and against the misuse of money. As for those "more essential talents" to which travel makes virtually no contribution, on the testimony of the letter they seem to include a proper fund of knowledge, "gravity," "modesty," a patriotic love of one's homeland, and the capacity to be of use there in a manner preordained by divine Law.

Such notions are, of course, by no means alien to Boswell's own thought. The problem is that he was also driven by impulses that are contradictory to such goals. Consequently, much of the interest and pleasure of reading Boswell's travel journals is to be found in the continuing struggle between his early moral education and his desire, between an alternating indulgence and abstinence that generate a series of self-reproaches and self-recriminations. "What a curious, inconsistent thing is the mind of man!" he notes in a characteristically discursive aside after hearing a sermon at St. James's Church. "In the midst of divine service I was laying plans for having women, and yet I had the most sincere feelings of religion." In this piece of self-representation he, in effect, casts himself in the dual role of rake and sentimentalist. And he endeavors to find inner consistency in such apparent contradiction by reference to his "warm heart" and "vivacious fantasy"—"I am therefore given to love, and also to piety or gratitude to God, and to the most brilliant and showy methods of public worship" (*London*, p. 54). One recognizes in such autoanalysis the eighteenth-century confessional vein that Rousseau had already popularized in his epistolary novel of seduction and redemption, *La Nouvelle Héloïse* of 1761, and had begun to mine more directly in his *Confessions* at the time when Boswell was still traveling on the Continent.

To undertake the grand tour was also for a young gentleman of Boswell's time the fashionable thing to do, and there is no doubt that he aspired for a long time to be a fashionable young man about town. He clearly enjoyed the social life of aristocratic salons along with that of the opera and theater, and of London's eighteenth-century coffee and chop houses. Yet the fact that he particularly sought out literary and theatrical people, even while he was still seeking to acquire a commission in the Foot Guards, and that he kept a journal is a sign of another and potentially more interesting level of his self.

The reasons why anyone keeps a journal are rarely simple. First of all, in Boswell's case, there is undoubtedly an element of worldliness and lit-

---

[13] Lord Auchinleck had already made clear his opinions of travel while his son was in Utrecht: "Travelling about from place to place is a thing extremely little improving except where one needs to rub off bashfulness, which is not your case." *Holland*, p. 325. In another letter, he even goes so far as to affirm that a journey to Italy is "altogether useless." *Italy*, p. 215.

erary ambition; he wanted to follow his own progress through society and record his encounters with leading social figures as well as with some of the literary lions of his day. Second, there is a mixture of narcissism and exhibitionism—if not precisely designed for publication, the *London Journal* was at least communicated directly to his friend John Johnston, and all the works under discussion here were written for the reader in himself. And third, one also finds an inculcated Protestant habit of self-examination and self-accounting overlaid with the new preoccupation with self associated with the age of sensibility. Although Rousseau's *Confessions* were not published until a long time after Boswell had completed his grand tour, the Presbyterian Scot was as open to the painful pleasures of the practice of sincerity as the citizen of Calvinist Geneva.

Accounting, in Boswell's case, is to be understood in both its meanings, since a journal is a way of drawing up the moral and spiritual balance sheet of one's life, of setting down one's accomplishments in the credit column and of contrasting them with the debit of one's failures to live up to prescribed, self-improving goals. The schemes Boswell occasionally draws up for the management of his financial affairs find their equivalent in resolutions for the future conduct of his life. Among the latter, the "Inviolable Plan" he drew up early in his stay in Utrecht with the purpose of breaking with the dissipations of his London life is characteristic. "Read your Plan regularly at breakfast," he exhorts himself. "And when you travel, carry it in your trunk" (*Holland*, p. 47)—not, it should be noted, in "your pocket."

The journal form also gives rise to a characteristic focus on what, in opposition to the narrative itself, is now referred to as "the instance of narration": namely, on the mediating presence of a narrator who records, judges, hesitates. In reformulating the conventional distinction of Anglo-American narrative theory between "showing" and "telling," Gérard Genette has demonstrated that even the mimetic mode of nineteenth-century naturalism, with its "transparent narrator," is a form of "telling" in which one makes maximum use of the referential function of language and elides as far as possible the activity of telling. As a result, he concludes that "the quantity of information and the presence of the informant are in inverse ratio, mimesis being defined by a maximum of information and a minimum of the informer, diegesis by the opposite relation."[14]

Among all the travel writings under discussion in this book, Boswell's probably go as far as any in the direction of diegesis as defined by Genette. So much of the interest relates to the young traveler's encounter

[14] *Narrative Discourse: An Essay in Method*, trans. Jane E. Lewin (Ithaca: Cornell University Press, 1980), pp. 166–167.

with foreign places and peoples and the complex, contradictory impulses they excite. And it is, in part, this foregrounding of a youthful recording consciousness that in Boswell's case goes a long way toward problematizing the representations of an inherited discourse.

Such a focus illuminates a central moral contradiction of the journals: the foreign cities he visits not only afford opportunities for the expansion of his knowledge and for his maturation, they also promise new forms of distraction and pleasure. Consequently, Boswell exhibits the behavior pattern of a classic obsessional neurotic to the extent that, again and again, he puts himself in situations where he finds it particularly difficult to live up to the high standards he imposes on himself. He finds on his return to London in 1762 that during his previous visit he had been "a heedless, dissipated, rattling fellow" and, as such, "a character very different from what God intended me and I myself chose" (*London*, p. 62). Although he struggles to produce moral order and to do what is demanded of him, he struggles in vain. He does not, in fact, need his father's letters to remind him of what he should do, since no matter how far he travels from Edinburgh, his father is always with him.

His neurotic disposition explains a related peculiarity of his behavior that is well-documented by the various travel journals: namely, the propensity to seek out models to imitate and paternal mentors whom he seeks to make responsible for the conduct of his life. Patronage was, of course, an important social institution of British eighteenth-century life and was indispensable to those "schemes of rising in the world" (*London*, p. 174) in which Boswell engaged from time to time throughout his journals. But there is more in his search for models and pursuit of mentors than paying court and seeking preferment, although as a man of his time Boswell by no means neglected to seek out the protection of the powerful. A reference to Addison suggests what he looked for in a model, especially when the temptation to live as a rake seemed about to overwhelm his "native dignity." Yet, his ambivalence emerges in a wonderfully naive formulation which emphasizes that Addison alone is perhaps too demanding an ego ideal: "Mr. Addison's character in sentiment, mixed with a little of the gaiety of Sir Richard Steele and the manners of Mr. Digges, were the ideas which I aimed to realize" (*London*, p. 62).

The moral eclecticism apparent in such efforts to fabricate an ego ideal called simply "James Boswell" is less evident in his choice of successive mentors. Boswell himself articulates this as a need for moral guardianship. What from our post-Freudian point of view can also be read into it is the will to identify with a series of powerful father figures. The male figures involved are patently surrogate fathers of the kind that, as Freud suggested in "Family Romances," a child dissatisfied with his given paternity might well fantasize for himself. In visibly transferential relations with figures from James Lord Somerville, Thomas Sheridan, Sir David Dalrymple, and Dr. Johnson to Rousseau, Voltaire, and the leader of the Corsican independence movement, Pascal Paoli, Boswell is patently appealing to a living embodiment of wisdom and right conduct in his time, to a subject supposed to know, the fullness of whose knowledge is ratified by his fame.

The sudden memory, when he is in Brunswick, of Johnson back home in London is typical of the power of such positive transference: "I glowed with reverence and affection, and a romantic idea filled my mind. To have a certain support at all times, I determined to write to this great man, and beg that he might give me a 'solemn assurance of perpetual friendship,' so that I might march under his protection while I lived, and after his death, imagine that his shade beckoned me to the skies. Grand, yet enthusiastic idea" (*Germany*, p. 54).[15] This solemn vow of loyalty and submission to a paternal will differs from a number of similar ones only in that it refers to the next world as well as to this. Here as elsewhere it is a way of conjuring anxiety that in psychoanalytic theory has been conceptualized as castration anxiety. The protection it demands, in exchange for acceptance of the father's Law, is above all protection from paternal power itself.

If on his journey from Edinburgh to London and the principal cities of Western Europe Boswell gives a new meaning to the notion of "head hunter," then it is as a consequence of his impulse to please and to be approved of. That is why he finds the experience of failing to gain an audience with Frederick the Great during his stay in Prussia as particularly mortifying. Such a failure may be rare in his experience, but it is nonetheless registered as a sign of personal unworthiness. The pleasure he took in the receptions accorded him by Rousseau and Voltaire, as well as by Dr. Johnson, seems to have been inspired in great measure by what, in his essay on Rousseau's contemporary readers, Robert Darnton describes as "the new cult of the writer that Rousseau was helping to create."[16] The goal of a communion of souls that Darnton associates with

---

[15] In an earlier letter to Sir David Dalrymple, Boswell made a similar appeal: "I wanted to be rationally happy, yet easy and gay, and hoped he would take charge of me; would let me know what books to read, and what company to keep, and how to conduct myself." *London*, p. 188.

[16] "Readers Respond to Rousseau," in *The Great Cat Massacre and Other Episodes in French Cultural History* (New York: Vintage Books, 1985). Aspects of the self-portrait Boswell paints in the course of his travels confirm the increasing appeal of the career of author or philosophe for talented and worldly young men from the mid-eighteenth century on. With reference to the preeminent fame of Voltaire, in particular, in the final decades of the *ancien régime*, Robert Darnton writes: "How many youths in the late eighteenth century must have dreamt of joining the initiates, of lecturing monarchs, rescuing outraged innocence, and ruling the republic of letters from the Acadé-

"the reading revolution" of the second half of the eighteenth century—and the example of *La Nouvelle Héloïse*, in particular—is something that Boswell pursued beyond the printed page into the very presence of the authors that inspired him.

The encounters with such authors were in any case enough to convince him of the superior qualities of his nature. At a characteristic moment of self-accounting after his visit to Voltaire, he acknowledges the uniqueness of his character, concluding with a reflection on his power to charm: "What a singular being do I find myself! Let this my journal show what variety my mind is capable of. But am I not well received everywhere? Am I not particularly taken notice of by men of the most distinguished genius?" And he finds the reason for the triumphant spectacle that is himself in his "remarkable knowledge of human nature. . . . What is really Man I think I know pretty well" (*Germany*, p. 304).

Self-congratulation is no less common than self-reproach in the travel journals. The object of Boswell's look here is not the world but himself. The scopophilia one finds elsewhere is turned back narcissistically upon himself; the pleasure he takes in this and similar passages throughout is in the making of such a superior, morally sensitive being as "Boswell."

Moreover, there is something peculiarly Lacanian about the way in which the recognition of desire at such moments is bound up with the desire of recognition. His general amiability and impulse to be accepted into all levels of society derive from the desire to locate himself in the place of the Other. Hence the court he plays to virtually all those he comes into contact with, from his Downing Street landlord who lowers the rent—"I do think this a very strong proof of my being agreeable" (*London*, p. 59)—to Dr. Johnson—"I must say indeed that if I excel in anything, it is in address and in making myself easily agreeable" (*London*, p. 288). Such notations have a disarming innocence that should not conceal their underlying sadness. The triumph is in the fact that we owe one of the most famous biographies in the language to Boswell's impulse to place himself at the disposal of another, especially when that other is a loving as well as powerful father.

Boswell clearly gained great satisfaction, then, from the perception that his presence was agreeable to others, particularly others who were important because of their distinction of mind, their social and political power or, in the case of women, their beauty. If the pleasures of travel turn out to be for Boswell chiefly the pleasures of making fresh conquests in different countries and in a variety of languages, then it is of no surprise that the seduction of women turns out to be at least as important to him as the seduction of famous men.

---

mie *Française* or a chateau like Ferney." *The Literary Underground of the Old Regime* (Cambridge: Harvard University Press, 1982), p. 3.

As noted above, one of the main justifications for undertaking the grand tour was summed up in the formula that it enlarged one's "knowledge of men and manners." The ambivalence with which it might be regarded in certain quarters, however—in the ancestral home of the Boswell's at Auchinleck, for example—resides in large part in the ambiguity of the generic use of the word "men" in that formula. Although "women" are by convention understood to be included, given one important meaning attached to the notion of "knowledge" of a woman, they are also conveniently suppressed. Whereas Lord Auchinleck would undoubtedly have approved of his son's enlarging his knowledge of men and their manners, he would with some reason have been deeply suspicious of the consequences of an enlarged knowledge of women and their manners in his eldest son and heir. And this would be especially true of continental women.

There was no ambiguity on this score in James Boswell's own mind, however. For the young Scottish traveler who had first been initiated into the sexual pleasures of London at age twenty, by Lord Eglinton, and who made a habit of "low street debauchery" (*London*, p. 241) as well as of more genteel affairs throughout his stay in the British capital, the grand tour was, in spite of attacks of conscience and periods of abstinence, also a sexual grand tour. No century has been more explicit than the eighteenth in associating eroticism with travel. And Boswell's travel journals are as much a representative text in this respect as they are in recording the struggle between paternal interdiction and filial emancipation. He records, sometimes in the most perfunctory of fashions and sometimes with considerable circumstantiality, his encounters with whores and servant girls, *blanchisseuses*, actresses, a pregnant soldier's wife, Venetian courtesans, or with Genoese, Roman, and Sienese society ladies and women of fashion. Sometimes he just pays court, at others he flirts, vigorously pursues in the expectation of a sexual conquest, or seeks immediate satisfaction with a bought girl.

Boswell's pursuit of sexual connections across Europe is, in an important sense, emblematic of that metonymy of desire which pushes the tourist on from city to city with the promise of new and richer satisfactions to come. The tourist's relation not just to other members of his own or the opposite sex, but to all the objects he looks forward to seeing, hearing, feeling, tasting, or smelling with more or less discrimination is a function of appetites that psychoanalysis has theorized in the concept of "drives." Why else do the travel supplements of Sunday newspapers present themselves as the gourmet magazines of all our organs?[17]

[17] Roland Barthes's complaint about China in the 1970s was that it afforded "no opportunities for erotic, sensual or sentimental investment." See "What are Intellectuals For?" in *Le Grain de la voix* (Paris: Le Seuil, 1981), p. 250.

Moreover, Boswell as traveler confirms in his journals that the two drives which are an important part of Jacques Lacan's contribution to the theory of psychoanalysis, the scopic and invocatory drives, are equally as demanding as the original oral, anal, and genital drives of Freud. On the one hand, before the age of the Baudelairean *flâneur*, Boswell reveals himself throughout his travel journals to be enamored of "sauntering" and "strolling" so as to take in the sights of the city at his leisure. His gaze is stimulated by "the hurry and bustle of life," by "the variety of brilliant scenes," by the pleasure gardens of Vauxhall and London's royal parks, by exhibitions of paintings, by the pomp of high church ceremony, or by the colorful spectacle of parades in an age of military glamor. On the other hand, he also enjoys the parallel aural pleasures of hearing and overhearing. He is drawn by city sounds, by discussions overheard in coffee houses and taverns, by *conversazioni*, the theater, the opera, music. Finally, it will be no accident if he should prove to be remarkably adept at learning the languages of the countries he passes through. There is pleasure in novel sounds produced by human vocal organs as well as in their successful reproduction in one's own mouth.[18]

The occasion when Boswell comes closest to being tempted to arrest his forward progression for more than a few weeks is during his stay in Siena. From the point of view of happiness, in fact, the high point of Boswell's grand tour is Siena and his love affair with Girolama Piccolomini. Having failed to make a conquest of Lord Mounstuart's former mistress, the thirty–five–year–old Porzia Sansedoni, he turns with characteristic impetuosity to the thirty–seven–year–old woman whom he learns to call "Moma." And here his assiduity is rewarded in excess of his expectations. As he notes in a letter to Rousseau—it is as if the reader of Rousseau's great epistolary novel had learned how to bare his soul, in writing to its author, from the behavior of its characters—since he found that in Siena people lived "in a completely natural fashion, making love as their inclinations suggested," he adopted temporarily the customs of the people among whom he lived: "I did not wish to be more profound than the others. To enjoy was the thing. Intoxicated by that sweet delirium, I gave myself up, without self-reproach and in complete serenity, to the charms of irregular love" (*Italy*, p. 15). With his Moma he "enjoyed," in that stronger sense which the word has in recent years recovered, "the exquisite pleasure of Italian gallantry, whose enchantments I had heard so much of" (*Italy*, p. 17). Yet, after a time, the sense of lack that drove

---

[18] In recent times, it was Barthes who was particularly conscious of the pleasures of language savored in its materiality as pure sound. He notes the pleasure he took in Japan in "the voluptuous immersion in a language . . . whose sounds I don't understand." "Intellectuals," p. 249.

him to Italy in the first place makes itself felt once again, and he moves on.

That Boswell went on to seek out a variety of satisfactions in further intimate relations with the opposite sex after he left Siena is well documented in those parts of his tour which precede and follow the visit to Corsica. The seduction of Rousseau's longtime companion and mother of his children, Thérèse Le Vasseur, on their trip from Paris to London together is only the most notable and most problematic of such conquests, as even the surviving references to it in the journal suggest.[19] One can only speculate on the emotions Boswell must have felt. Although *La Nouvelle Héloïse* is mostly about the piquant delights associated with the practice of virtue in circumstances of great temptation, it did begin with the succumbing to temptation of the kind Boswell engaged in on that London journey. The evidence of his journals taken as a whole suggests that, like Saint-Preux with Julie, Boswell was prepared to repent, provided, of course, that he first had the opportunity to sin.

Travel in any case has always provided the opportunity for illicit liaisons, and Boswell went out of his way to take advantage of such opportunities. What the affair with Thérèse Le Vasseur suggests, along with all his other erotic activities, is that there was, in the eighteenth century as in the twentieth, a micropolitics of sex of a Foucauldian kind. To be successful in one's relations with the opposite sex was to have proof of one's charm, of one's powers of seduction, and of the potency on which male self-worth has traditionally been founded.

In enjoying the mistress of a revered mentor (and the eighteenth century's best-known moral and political philosopher in any case), Boswell's transgression and the proof of his worth were complete. The seduction of Thérèse was the other face of the seduction of Rousseau. It can be read as a deeply ambiguous act: at one and the same time it allowed him, so to speak, to live in a fiction that was the rage throughout educated Europe, to usurp the older man's place in what was, in effect, a marriage bed and to displace a repressed homoerotic desire onto the same female body where they both met. Yet, Boswell might well have found justification for his behavior in Rousseau's own novel. Had not the latter's curious triangle of an elderly husband, a wife, and her former lover living in perfect harmony already pointed the way to a kind of *ménage à trois* that was more perfect than the couple and transcended the flesh? Was not the utopian dream of *La Nouvelle Héloïse* to overcome gender and sexual antimonies in a redefined family appropriate to the age of sensibility? Given

---

[19] Some twelve pages of manuscript, which narrated the progress of Boswell's affair with Thérèse Le Vasseur, were apparently destroyed shortly before the papers were purchased by Colonel Isham in the late 1920s. See the "Editor's Note," *Italy*, p. 277.

the significance of the encounter, it is not surprising if Boswell declares himself to be so upset by his failure of potency at the first attempt.[20] And his male narcissism receives a further blow when, in spite of the return of vigor, he learns from the older woman that he is too precipitate a lover. To be a lesser man than one's father in the arms of one's mother is not envisaged in the myth of Oedipus, but it risks being the cruelest wound of all to male self-esteem.

Nevertheless, what Boswell's periodic bouts of whoring, his sexual pursuit of a variety of women, or even his seduction of Thérèse Le Vasseur do not raise in quite the same way as his affair in Siena is the question of happiness and its relation to manners. In its own way, in fact, the experience of Siena suggests the possibility of an alternative society equally as much as the Corsican independence movement that is the object of Boswell's enrapt attention during his visit to the Mediterranean island. Although his commentary on the delights of Tuscany in general, and of Siena in particular, is not explicitly political, it proved to be an occasion for raising familiar eighteenth-century questions about the relationship between individual happiness and the social order as well as between climate and institutions, on the one hand, or institutions and manners, on the other.

It also led Boswell to reflect on the need for and limits of man-made laws, on the Golden Age of civilization apparently once achieved in classical Rome, or on the best possible life Boswell himself could look forward to on returning to Scotland. The reveries that he evokes in a letter to John Wilkes from Mantua or the conditions for his future personal happiness that he outlines in his "Sienese Reflections" provide important clues to what Boswell looked for in the amenities, manners, and pleasures, if not precisely the organization and institutions, of the ideal society.

The fact of finding himself in the place where Virgil had lived is enough to stimulate Boswell's imagination into speculating on a qualitatively nobler way of life—"I really see nothing improbable in supposing that beings of finer substance than we inhabit such scenes as I now behold"—and into evoking that lost Golden Age of classical Rome: "Time rolls back his volume. I am really existing in the age of Virgil, when man had organs framed for manly enjoyment and a mind unbroken by dreary speculation" (*Italy*, p. 110). Boswell's underlying theme here, of course, is that of progressive degeneration, that of the classical myth of a world slowly completing a descending cycle that had begun so nobly: "Is it pos-

[20] In narrating his affair with Louisa, the actress, Boswell adopts the discourse of eighteenth-century gallantry in declaring himself "proud" of his "godlike vigour." *London*, p. 139.

sible for us to regain those clear and keen sensations, that bright and elegant fantasy, that firm and elegant soul which they [the Romans] certainly had? Bountiful Nature seems as kind as ever. Man alone is degenerated" (*Italy*, pp. 109–110). It is a theme that, in spite of the apparent self-confidence of the age, preoccupied a number of important Enlightenment thinkers, including Buffon, Rousseau, and Diderot, as will be clearer from the following chapters. And it returns in a somewhat different guise in Lévi-Strauss's *Tristes Tropiques* in the form of entropy.

Yet, even given such a loss of vigor and sharpness of sensation in the species, Boswell does, in fact, imply that the Virgilian model of the good life, the model of the *Eclogues* and the *Georgics* rather than of the *Aeneid*, might be transposed from pagan Rome to eighteenth-century Scotland. In a rare moment of "homesickness" in the midst of his Sienese happiness, he even offers a sketch of the idyllic future that a morally responsible grand tourist of his class and social circumstances could look forward to on his return home. Moreover, in the expression of his homesickness Boswell manages to combine the original repressed desire for the mother's body referred to by Freud with the imagery of classical literature.

If, as has been often noted, the way of life of Europe's upper classes did not change radically between the age of classical Rome and the eighteenth century, Boswell's hope that he could live the classic life in imitation of Latin models certainly confirms that view: "If I were now in the romantic woods of Auchinleck my happiness would be complete. I would see myself in the very place where Providence has established my residence, where I can honour the memory of my worthy ancestors, live happily cultivating my lands, doing good to my tenants, and showing a cordial hospitality to my neighbors. This is how I shall wish to live when my travels are over. In winter I shall go to London or Edinburgh, and in the summer I shall stay at my country-house and think many, many times of beautiful Italy" (*Italy*, p. 133).[21]

On the one hand, the place fantasized is his father's place in the absence of his father ("my worthy ancestors," "my lands," "my tenants," "my neighbours"); Boswell accepts in the future the male role in generational

---

[21] At a spirited moment during his stay in London, Boswell had given a more emphatically naive expression to a similar ambition: "Surely I am a man of genius. I deserve to be taken notice of. O that my grandchildren might read this character of me: 'James Boswell, a most amiable man. He improved and beautified his paternal estate of Auchinleck; made a distinguished figure in Parliament; had the honour to command a regiment of footguards, and was one of the brightest wits in the court of George the Third." *London*, p. 181. For a discussion of the topos of the happy man, see the helpful introduction to *The Genius of the Place: The English Landscape Garden, 1620–1820*, ed. John Dixon Hunt and Peter Wills (Cambridge: MIT Press, 1988).

succession. On the other hand, the passage is the classical topos derived from Latin models, including Pliny the Younger and Horace as well as Virgil, of *beatus ille*, of happy the man who lived the good, well-regulated life in a noble villa on a country estate. Although there is also perhaps the same Rousseauist subtext as before—Auchinleck as a substitution for Clarens—the passage reminds us that one of the official functions of the grand tour was to suggest how, upon one's return to Britain, one might practice what one had seen as well as read about, and live as a patrician Roman in a way that was yet adapted to eighteenth-century British circumstances and the genius of British place.

If Boswell, in fact, manages to sound like his father as he anticipates his future life and future memories of Italy—a Lord Auchinleck whose sterner morality has been sweetened and aestheticized by his grand tour and more extensive readings in Latin literature as well as Rousseau—this should come as no surprise. The identification with his father and the desire to please him seem in Boswell's case to have been just as urgent as the impulse to escape his father's prohibitions to pursue happiness in his own way. At the very moment when he was imagining the good yet socially responsible life for himself back in Scotland, he was also enjoying in Siena the greatest love affair of his young life with a married woman a dozen years his senior.

o   o   o

UP TO the point where he quits the Italian mainland for his visit to Corsica, Boswell's grand tour does not differ significantly from that of the great majority of other young, North European males. To go to Corsica with the intention of penetrating to the interior of what was considered a wild and remote island in order to meet patriots fighting for the independence of their homeland was something else again. Charles L. Batten has noted that "the most common stance assumed by the eighteenth-century traveler is that of the philosopher, collecting and commenting on such information as will be of use to readers back home" (*Pleasurable Instruction*, p. 72). Yet, such is only intermittently the case in Boswell's travel journals up to his departure for Corsica.

His interest in the philosophes is, of course, evident throughout his writings, as noted above. And his veneration for Rousseau and his visit to Motiers, in particular, provided the impetus for his journey to the Mediterranean island. It is nevertheless something of a surprise to realize that the first substantial publication of the man who is known in English letters primarily as the biographer of Dr. Johnson was a *History and Journal of Corsica* that was a self-conscious political intervention—the Yale editors refer to it as "a finished piece of propaganda" (*Italy*, p. 146). When the work appeared in 1768, its goal was clearly in part to force the repeal of the British government's 1763 proclamation, which condemned the Corsican patriots as rebels and forbade British subjects to aid them.

This does not mean that Boswell's work is nothing more than a local political pamphlet. It is, on the contrary, a reflective and journalistic piece of writing in the best sense. It takes its time in describing the values, attitudes, and way of life of the Corsicans and, in what would now be called interviews with their leader, in reporting on their political positions and aspirations. Nowhere more than in his sympathies for the alternative society that the Corsican patriots claim they are seeking to build, in fact, does Boswell show himself to be a man of his time. The young grand tourist was trying his hand at political philosophy. "One of the constant dreams of civilized man," note the editors of the Yale edition, "is to alter the state in which he lives, either by re-establishing a natural, harmonious society whose existence he discerns at one point or another in the past, or by working towards an ideal commonwealth of the future" (*Italy*, p. 143). And the prerevolutionary eighteenth century looked back for such inspiration to the classical age or beyond Europe to countries still in the process of being discovered by European explorers.

As the tone of the opening paragraph of "The Journal of a Tour to Corsica" makes clear, Boswell was fully aware that he was departing from the relatively fixed itinerary and purposes of the grand tour when he visited that Mediterranean island. Given that he went there as a self-conscious, eighteenth-century "political pilgrim," the young Scot shows himself to be more adventurous as well as more intellectually serious and politically curious than his writings to that point would allow one to suppose: "I wished for something more than just the common course of what is called the tour of Europe, and Corsica occured to me as a place which nobody else had seen, and where I should find what was to be seen nowhere else, a people actually fighting for liberty and forming themselves from a poor, inconsiderable, oppressed nation into a flourishing and independent state" (*Italy*, p. 148). It is the kind of language with which in the late 1950s a young American might, rightly or wrongly, have justified a visit to Castro in Cuba.

Although Boswell does not say so, it is apparent that he adopts the discourse of a certain eighteenth-century political theory in looking upon Corsican society as a mixture of unspoiled primitivism in Europe's own backyard and of republican Rome resuscitated, if not of Lycurgus's Sparta. Boswell is never particularly explicit on his reasons for admiring Rousseau, his "Wild Philosopher," yet it is nevertheless clear that the image he projects of Corsican society combines elements of Virgil's pastoral idyll with a more robust and politically informed, Rousseauist naturalism.

On the one hand, as he moves through the island with his Corsican guides, he encounters the bounty of primitive nature, which offers the traveler an abundance of chestnuts in its trees and of streams to drink from: "It was just being for a little while one of the '*prisca gens mortalium*,'²² who ran about in the woods eating acorns and drinking water." And, on the other hand, he finds there men who are equal to such surroundings and who are variously described as "brave, rude men" or as "a stately spirited race of people" characterized by "natural frankness and ease" (*Italy*, pp. 159–160). The twenty-five-year-old Boswell even represents himself as praising his hosts for their bravery in pursuit of liberty—"the most valuable of all possessions"—and as warning them in a distinctly Rousseauist vein not to advance too far on the path toward civilization: "But I bid them remember that they were much happier in their present state than in a state of refinement and vice, and that therefore they should be beware of luxury" (*Italy*, p. 161).

But the highpoint of Boswell's Corsican journey is, once again, the opportunity it gives him to get to know a great man. This time it is not, of course, a man of letters or a philosopher, but a man of action: Pascal Paoli, the leader of the Corsican patriots.

What Boswell discovers in Paoli is an antique Roman reborn. The vigor and the virtue of the heroic tradition that had disappeared in modern Italy have reemerged in the Corsican leader. Neither before nor after will Boswell express the same sense of living among "a circle of heroes" (*Italy*, p. 163) as he does in Corsica. The fact is, of course, that enthrallment can really take place, a powerful transference occur, only in the "presence" of the one to whom one goes in search of greatness and wisdom: "Upon my soul, I was struck. He electrified me. Every time that I looked at him, I felt a shock of the heroic" (*Italy*, p. 44). Boswell's electrical imagery here reveals that he was "star-struck" in a way that requires imaging of one kind or another. It also confirms that "love" of great men is a more important feature of his European journey than that of monuments of art and architecture.

It is, therefore, not particularly surprising if, in spite of Boswell's apparent enthusiasm for the Corsican cause, he is nowhere very explicit about his own political beliefs. He does make it clear in his *London Journal* that he was a monarchist who combined a fondness for the Stuarts with a dislike of the Hanoverians, including particularly the first two Georges. However, apart from brief affirmations to the effect that "a regular limited royal government is the best and the most conducive to the happiness of mankind" (*London*, p. 227) or that he is "a Briton born with an abhorrence of tyranny" (*Italy*, p. 184), Boswell has little to say about systems of government. It seems that his own politics begin in the paternal home, like everything else in his life. The two sentences he jotted down

²² "Primitive race of men."

while still in Germany sum up his political beliefs: "I abhor a despotic tyranny. But I revere a limited monarch" (*Germany*, p. 297). The force of the verbs suggests that the system desired is equally as valid in the family as in the state. Even Pascal Paoli is seen as a kind of limited monarch and the father of his nation, like George Washington soon afterward.

o   o   o

BOSWELL's journals of his European travels confirm the fact that the institution of the grand tour embodied a striking paradox. The tour was both a form of higher education and an instrument of social reproduction that required an extended absence from paternal surveillance and an exposure to temptation that risked subverting the institutional goals. Boswell's writings are wonderfully suggestive of the kind of tensions and contradictions to which a young male subject of his class and nationality in such a situation was exposed. A wellborn son's relationship to paternity, sexual potency, and the prospect of himself fulfilling the paternal function are all broached there in the context of the pursuit of pleasure in foreign places. And one finds similar testimony, in a very different register, in the work of Edward Gibbon. Not only was Gibbon the author of what is probably the eighteenth century's most important work of history, *The Decline and Fall of the Roman Empire*, but he also wrote a classic *Autobiography* that was edited and published posthumously by his good friend Lord Sheffield. It is of interest in the context of the present study because Gibbon lived for a substantial portion of his life on the Continent, and parts of the *Autobiography* give an account of those years, which both confirm and qualify what one learns from Boswell about the significance of foreign travel for the mid-eighteenth century. The difference between the journals of a man in his early twenties and an autobiography begun at age fifty-two by a man who had already completed the major work of his life and achieved substantial fame is, of course, considerable.

Gibbon himself emphasizes the fact with reference to the time when, in his mid-twenties, he returned to the Continent where he had spent five years as a youth: "The particular images are darkly seen through the medium of five-and-twenty years, and the narrative of my life must not degenerate into a book of travels."[23] Consequently, Gibbon substitutes the past tense of retrospective narrative summary and evaluative commentary for the anecdotes, brief evocations of scene, and repeated self-questioning of Boswell's unfolding present tense.

Yet, Gibbon's comments on the significance of travel are illuminating in spite of the denigratory tone employed in referring to the very genre

---

[23] My references are to *The Autobiography of Edward Gibbon*, ed. Dero A. Saunders (New York: Meridian Books, 1961), p. 143.

that reports on it. Although Gibbon's reputation was by far the greater in their time, he has much in common with Boswell, including in particular age—the Englishman was just three years older than the Scot—class background, education, and immersion in the classic discourse of the British Enlightenment. It is also oddly symptomatic that, at a time when there were still substantial penalties attached to professing allegiance to the church of Rome, they both converted to Catholicism at an early age without paternal consent, and subsequently abjured their conversions. It was in Gibbon's case as a consequence of this conversion that he was dispatched under duress by his father to Protestant Lausanne for five years and placed under the tutelage of a Calvinist minister.

Gibbon's first foreign journey was, in short, symptomatic of the hostile relationship between him and his father in the same way that Boswell's was. In Gibbon's case, it was a question of banishment to a safe country; in Boswell's, a flight to one perceived as morally suspect. The complex process of oedipalization and the repressed resistances to it can be read, without forcing the issue, in the respective narratives of their journeys through Europe, in the repeated crossing of frontiers, and in the powerful investments in place. Moreover, as far as the relationship to their mothers is concerned, it is the discreeter Gibbon who is for once the most explicit.[24] Finally, in their early twenties, both undertook their own grand tours of approximately two and a half years, more or less at the same time. Gibbon left England in January 1763, and Boswell in October of the same year.

As for the pleasures of life in London—pleasures to which both writers came as strangers after long residence in two Calvinist cities, Lausanne and Edinburgh, respectively—Gibbon's memoirs are remarkably similar to Boswell's journals, with the important exception of relations with women. He shared something of Boswell's scopophilia with respect to the urban scene, taking a similar pleasure in walking in order to look: "The metropolis affords many amusements which are open to all. It is itself an astonishing and perpetual spectacle to the curious eye, and each taste, each sense, may be gratified by the variety of objects which will occur in the long circuit of a morning's walk" (*Autobiography*, p. 117). And the same "curious eye" also enjoyed a vigorous London theatrical life, at the center of which stood the talent of Garrick.

Nevertheless, if the two writers have much in common, the difference

---

[24] "To preserve and to rear so frail a being, the most tender assiduity was scarcely sufficient, and my mother's attention was somewhat diverted by her frequent pregnancies, by an exclusive passion for her husband, and by the dissipation of the world in which his taste and authority obliged her to mingle. But the maternal office was supplied by my aunt, Mrs. Catherine Porten, at whose name I feel a tear of gratitude trickling down my cheek." *Autobiography*, p. 54.

of age at the time of recording the impressions of their journeys, along with differences of temperament and scholarly commitment, give rise to important contrasts in behavior. Gibbon presents himself in many ways as an anti-Boswell. He did not as a young man have the physique or the ability to please that Boswell had. Nor was he drawn in the same way to the life of a man of pleasure that so tempted Boswell: "The pleasures of a town life, the daily round from the tavern to the play, from the play to the coffee-house, from the coffee-house to the bagnio, are within the reach of every man who is regardless of his health, his money, and his company. By the contagion of example I was sometimes seduced. But the better habits which I had formed at Lausanne induced me to seek a more elegant and rational society" (*Autobiography*, p. 117).

The only love affair to which he refers was with a young Swiss woman who subsequently married the wealthy banker, minister of Louis XVI, and father of the future Madame de Staël, Baron Necker. But the brief understanding was stopped by Gibbon's father, who refused to consent to the marriage: "After a painful struggle I yielded to my fate: I sighed as a lover; I obeyed as a son" (*Autobiography*, p. 109). Some thirty years after the event, the only revenge apparently taken for submission to that paternal interdiction is in the irony of its formulation. Elsewhere in the *Autobiography* there are no references to any casual sexual encounters, and one finds just one oblique comment on a remembered surge of desire in connection with his "acquisition of a female friend" during his stay in Paris in 1763, a lady who was exquisitely named Madame Bontemps— "In the middle season of life her beauty was still an object of desire" (*Autobiography*, pp. 145–146).

From the vantage point of his early fifties, then, Gibbon shows his awareness of the risks and temptations of travel but overwhelmingly confirms its importance in his age: "The youthful habits of the language and manners of France had left in my mind an ardent desire for revisiting the Continent on a larger and more liberal plan. According to the law of custom, and perhaps of reason, foreign travel completes the education of an English gentleman" (*Autobiography*, p. 142). It is typical that, in expressing this classic view, Gibbon should implicitly equate foreign travel with travel on the European continent and, in particular, on that part of it which constituted the itinerary of the grand tour—the Low Countries, France, Germany, Switzerland, Italy and, less frequently, Spain. What was important for the completion of the education of a young man of good family seeking to make his mark in the world was to be found there—in Sterne's "politer kingdoms of the globe"—and nowhere else.

If Gibbon travels to France, it is chiefly to go to Paris and devote himself "to the visit of churches and palaces conspicuous by their architecture, to the royal manufactures, collections of books and pictures, and all the various treasures of art, of learning, and of luxury." But, beyond that, he is even more interested in the round of refined and intelligent social exchange that he associates with French aristocratic salons and with French literary and philosophic debates: "But the principal end of my journey was to enjoy the society of a polished and amiable people, in whose favor I was strongly prejudiced, and to converse with some authors whose conversation, as I fondly imagined, must be far more pleasing and instructive than their writings" (*Autobiography*, pp. 143–144). The purpose of travel is, in short, to expose oneself to different forms of civilized life that, if not always higher, are at least equal to those with which one is familiar.

It is on such grounds that Gibbon, like so many others before and after him, justifies the journey to Rome. In this case, however, it is a journey in time as well as in space that is involved. The cultural geographer has to be relayed by the cultural historian because the grandeur that was Rome has to be lovingly restored on the basis of the ruined artifacts and the literary testimony of antiquity. That is why, during his second stay in Lausanne, Gibbon prepares himself for his Italian journey by studying "the topography of old Rome, the ancient geography of Italy, and the science of medals" (*Autobiography*, pp. 149–150).

Moreover, in the *Autobiography* he dismisses the journey through Italy with a cavalier reference to his predecessors—"I shall waive the minute investigation of the scenes which have been viewed by thousands, and described by hundreds, of our modern travelers"—in order to reach the city of cities, whose singular significance for the history of civilization is expressed in its capitalization:"ROME is the great object of our pilgrimage" (*Autobiography*, p. 150). Gibbon was even more subject to the summons represented by Rome than was Boswell, to the point where he virtually trembles to be there.

It is therefore in a particularly charged site of the monumental city that the cultural pilgrim, fittingly enough, experiences one of his rare moments of quasi-religious rapture as he conjures up the great ghosts of antiquity: "After a sleepless night I trod, with a lofty step, the ruins of the Forum; each memorable spot where Romulus stood, or Tully spoke, or Caesar fell, was at once present to my eye, and several days of intoxication were lost or enjoyed before I could descend to a cool minute investigation" (*Autobiography*, p. 152). Such communing with the ghostly presences of stern and noble father figures is something of a commonplace of travel writing. Moreover, it is also apparent from his choice of words that Gibbon was in a state of rapture here that is synonymous with pleasure at its self-annihilating limit.

It was presumably in a similar mood of reverence, reinforced by the perception of the contrast between what was and what is, between the first century B.C. and the eighteenth century A.D., that Gibbon found his vocation and the subject of his famous work: "It was at Rome, on the 15th of October 1764, as I sat musing amid the ruins of the Capitol, while the barefooted friars were singing vespers in the temple of Jupiter, that the idea of writing the decline and fall of the city firsts started to my mind" (*Autobiography*, p. 154). Immediately surrounded by the noble material ruins of the most ambitious idea of civilized order recognized by eighteenth-century Europe, Gibbon, in effect, commits himself to a cause. The pilgrim to pagan antiquity finds himself in the holiest place of his cult and takes up the task not only of recovering its lost fullness, but also of perpetuating its values into the future. Finally, by explaining the causes of its collapse, he is making himself socially useful in the present. Such a catastrophe must not be allowed to overwhelm that new height of civilization, modeled on the Roman, which after such a long interval of darkness and descent into barbarism had been achieved in his own time.

In the heart of ancient Rome the grand tourist's journey in space and the historian's journey in time reach the same center or point of origin. The name of Gibbon's religion is Civilization with a capital C, Civilization of a kind that in his time refused the qualification of Western. As Raymond Williams has noted, the word in English was, in fact, an eighteenth-century coinage rejected by Dr. Johnson, and it implied process as well as a state: "It has behind it the general spirit of the Enlightenment, with its emphasis on secular and progressive human self-development. Civilization expressed this sense of historical process, but also celebrated the associated sense of modernity: an achieved condition of refinement and order."[25] Like Winckelmann, who in Rome at the same time was proclaiming the universality of classical aesthetic values,[26] along with the notion of Europe as norm and center, Gibbon was committing himself to take up the responsibilities of the heritage of European Civilization.

It is of obvious significance that it is immediately after the brief summary of his Italian journey that Gibbon in his turn devotes three para-

[25] *Keywords: A Vocabulary of Culture and Society* (New York: Oxford University Press, 1976), p. 49.

[26] In explaining that, in spite of the apparent diversity throughout the world, there is only one standard of beauty, the Greek standard, Winckelmann relies on an eighteenth-century discourse about the impact of climate on nature, including human nature. He therefore explains all deviations from the Greek norm as defects of climate at any distance from nature's "center": "But in proportion as nature grows nigher to her centre in a temperate climate, her productions are marked by more regularity of shape. . . . Consequently, our ideas and those of the Greeks relative to beauty, being derived from the most regular conformation, are more correct than those that can possibly be formed by nations which, to adopt the thought of a modern poet, have lost one half of their likeness to the creator." *The History of Ancient Art Among the Greeks* (London: John Chapman, 1850), p. 39.

graphs to describing "the benefits of foreign travel." and the qualities he deemed essential in a traveler—"a sketch of ideal perfection." He presupposes relative maturity in his traveler, freedom from prejudices, and "a competent knowledge of men and books." He also insists on physical strength, powers of endurance, a good temper, fearlessness, and "a restless curiosity." Finally, he emphasizes the need for wide-ranging literary, scientific, and practical knowledge along with various accomplishments that suggest how demanding the Enlightenment ideal of a properly educated man could be: "With a copious stock of classical and historical learning, my traveler must blend the practical knowledge of husbandry and manufactures. He should be a chemist, a botanist, and a master of mechanics. A musical ear will multiply the pleasures of his Italian tour. But a correct and exquisite eye, which commands the landscape of a country, discerns the merit of a picture, and measure the proportions of a building, is more closely connected with the finer feelings of the mind; and the fleeting image shall be fixed and realized by the dexterity of the pencil" (*Autobiography*, pp. 153–154).[27] One notes among other things that there is no question of disciplinary specialization, no division between a literary, artistic culture and a scientific, utilitarian one.

The purpose of foreign travel outlined here is summed up in another important eighteenth-century concept, that of "improvement." Applied originally to monetary operations yielding a profit, it was, in Raymond Williams's phrase, "a key word in the development of modernizing agrarian capitalism" (*Keywords*, p. 133). In the course of the eighteenth century its significance was extended to the individual as well as to society, and the word could be applied to morals, manners, taste, institutions, literature, art, science, nature, and human nature. Thus "improvement" both contains and transcends the idea of social usefulness on which Dr. Johnson insists in his characteristically moral judgment of the advantages of travel: "He only is a useful traveler who brings home something by which his country may be benefited; who procures some supply of want or some mitigation of evil which may enable his readers to compare their condition with that of others, to improve it whenever it is worse, and whenever it is better to enjoy it."[28]

If Gibbon, like so many of his contemporaries, sought to promote individual and social "improvement" in part through the practice of foreign travel, he nowhere suggests that travel outside Europe would be of any benefit. He expresses rather the extraordinary self-confidence of his

[27] There was a whole literature that in a systematic way told travelers what to observe and report on, including Bishop Tucker's *Instructions for Travellers* (1757) and Leopold Berchtold's *An Essay to Direct and Extend the Inquiries of Patriotic Travellers* (1789).

[28] Quoted by Thomas M. Curley *Samuel Johnson and the Age of Travel* (Athens: University of Georgia Press, 1976), p. 73.

time and culture in asserting the good fortune that attended his birth, the good fortune of an eighteenth-century European, who was in addition an Englishman of a certain class and income: "When I contemplate the common lot of mortality, I must acknowledge that I have drawn a high prize in the lottery of life. The far greater part of the globe is over-spread with barbarism or slavery; in the civilized world the most numerous class is condemned to ignorance and poverty; and the double fortune of my birth in a free and enlightened country, in an honourable and wealthy family, is the lucky chance of a unit against millions" (*Autobiography*, p. 204).

Yet, in spite of the good fortune and the honor of which he announces himself the beneficiary, Gibbon in the end declines a significant part of his legacy by refusing to take up the paternal function. It is difficult not to read an element of revenge for early estrangement from maternal love—"My infancy, to speak the truth, had been neglected at home" (*Autobiography*, p. 115)—in his decision to sell off his father's country estate and to refuse marriage categorically: "A matrimonial alliance has ever been the object of my terror rather than of my wishes. I was not very strongly pressed by my family or my passions to propagate the name and race of the Gibbons" (*Autobiography*, p. 157). The great British classical historian seems to have shared Stendhal's lack of enthusiasm for the paternal name.

Finally, in choosing to settle in Lausanne for the last decade of his life—"I had always cherished a secret wish that the school of my youth might become the retreat of my declining age" (*Autobiography*, p. 190)—Gibbon committed himself to the life of the expatriate and turned his back on his fatherland. One can only assume that neither Lord Auchinleck nor Dr. Johnson would have approved.

o   o   o

SMOLLETT's contribution to eighteenth-century travel literature was a broad one, for it encompassed not only the book on the grand tour that concerns us here, but also his novels in the picaresque genre—*The Adventures of Roderick Random, The Adventures of Peregrine Pickle,* and *The Expedition of Humphry Clinker*—and a collection entitled *A Compendium of Authentic and Entertaining Voyages.* There is not space in the present study to do more than indicate the way in which Smollett responded in *Travels Through France and Italy* to the issues raised in connection with the proper and improper uses of the grand tour. And by virtue of the way I have defined my corpus, I am also obliged to exclude a consideration of Laurence Sterne's famous travel novel—except to note that it was a highly influential work, which by the end of the century contributed to the breakdown, in the genre of literary travel accounts, of that balance between entertainment and enlightenment referred to above. Stendhal, among others, looked to *A Sentimental Journey Through France and Italy* as a model for his own writing in the genre.

Yet, it is worth recalling in passing that Smollett and Sterne—who also did the continental traveling on which their works are based in the 1760s—have come down in the literary tradition, partly as a consequence of Sterne's barely disguised portrait of Smollett in *A Sentimental Journey*, as two antihetical types of travelers. According to the self-categorization of the narrator of Sterne's fictionalized journey, he is a Sentimental Traveler, whereas Smelfungus/Smollett is undoubtedly a Splenetic Traveler.

The Sentimental Traveler conducts his traveling under the guidance of what Sterne calls "his heart.": "What a large volume of adventures may be grasped within this little span of life, by him who interests his heart in everything, and who having eyes to see what time and chance are perpetually holding out to him as he journeyeth on his way, misses nothing he can *fairly* lay his hands on" (*Sentimental Journey*, p. 30). As the reference to "adventures" suggests here, along with "eyes" and "hands," Sterne proved to be the kind of self-conscious theorist of the erotics of travel in his time that Roland Barthes, for example, has been in ours. But it is an erotics that, as Sterne's title suggests, is not divorced from celebration of the love object—what Freud called "overestimation"—sentiment and play. Sterne's narrator openly takes his desire on tour to what in the context of his time and place appeared to be sexual desire's promised land. As the famous opening lines inform us, "They order, said I, this matter better in France."

Perhaps the episode that best suggests the originality of Sterne's achievement is that which recounts the narrator's encounter in Paris with what he calls "the beautiful Grisset" of whom he asks his way and attempts to purchase a pair of gloves. The episode captures succinctly the ethos of tender erotic teasing between the sexes that largely accounts for the charm and power of the novel. Having first tested her pulse—"counting the throbs of it, one by one"—the narrator goes on to try on the gloves in as resonant and witty a play of double entendre as one is likely to find anywhere: "The beautiful Grisset measured them one by one across my hand—it would not alter the dimensions. She begg'd I would try a single pair, which seemed to be the least. She held it open; my hand slipped into it at once. It will not do, said I, shaking my head a little. No, said she, doing the same thing" (*Sentimental Journey*, p. 58). There follows the evocation of an exchange of looks that constitutes in its own way an incisive analysis of the ambivalent play of desire. No one previously had rendered the promise of travel quite like this.

The Splenetic Traveler, on the other hand, possesses none of this openness to what the countries he passes through so liberally put in his way. He is instead, Sterne informs us in a celebrated passage, driven by his own peculiar psychosomatic disorders: "The learned SMELFUNGUS travelled from Boulogne to Paris, from Paris to Rome, and so on, but he set out with spleen and jaundice, and every object he pass'd was discoloured or distorted. He wrote an account of them, but 'twas nothing but the account of his miserable feelings" (*Sentimental Journey*, p. 30). The implication of Sterne's typology of travelers quoted in my Introduction is precisely that the represented world is never more than the world reflected through the prism of a temperament or fixed disposition. Abroad as at home, every man remains in his humor.

Yet, what this satiric-sentimental point of view overlooks is conditionedness that is other than physiological. When Sterne and Smollett undertook their journeys through France and Italy, both were established men of letters; the former was in his late forties and early fifties, the latter in his early forties. Further, Smollett was traveling not by himself, but in a party of five, which included his wife and two other women plus his male servant. His embattled response to the inhabitants of the cities, towns, and villages through which he passes was also conditioned by the fact that he was suffering form serious respiratory disorders, had recently experienced the death of his only child, and had been dismissed by the prime minister, Lord Bute, from the editorship of the patriotic political journal *The Briton*.

Thus, the state of mind suggested by the opening letter of his *Travels* is, in the language of our time, one of depression—"traduced by malice, persecuted by faction, abandoned by false patrons, and overwhelmed by the sense of a domestic calamity which it was not in the power of fortune to repair" (*Travels*, p. 2). Nevertheless, Smollett's work is far more interesting than is implied by the contemporary comment that it should more properly be entitled *QUARRELS Through France and Italy for the Cure of a Pulmonic Disorder*.[29] Quarrels, in any case, have a symptomatic interest of their own that cannot be dismissed lightly.

If Boswell's journals are among the most representative documents of grand tour literature from the point of view of those young upper-class British males who were the most familiar tourists, Smollett's *Travels* are among the most fully documented; they fulfill abundantly the expectation that the writer be a broadly educated, well-informed, and patriotic traveler whose goal is the enlightenment of the reading public in his homeland. The increasing specialization between sentimental and/or picturesque travel writing, on the one hand, and that of natural and human scientists, on the other, is no more evident here than it is in Gibbon.

The *Travels* take the form of letters home. And letters, like a journal,

---

[29] See Frank Felsenstein's comments in his Introduction, *Travels*, p. XII.

foreground the diegetic dimension of narrative already referred to, the moving present of a writing and the mediating presence of a narrator. Yet, presumably on account of his maturity and wide range of interests, information in Smollett's work occupies far more space than the informant. Although Smollett's is hardly more of a "transparent narrator" than Boswell's, the confessional stance of the self-doubting young man on the make is altogether absent from The *Travels*. Smollett's training as a surgeon, the active role he played in the political debates of his time, and his experience as a man of letters and as a novelist had made him especially knowledgeable. As a result, he furnishes an astonishing amount of information about continental political, social, and economic life in his time.

In addition to all the things one learns about eighteenth-century religion, letters, politics, manners, art, architecture, and taste from writers like Boswell and Gibbon, Smollett's observations illuminate a wide range of other topics, including the relative power, politics, and wealth of eighteenth-century nations, the state of their commerce, the source and amount of their revenues, forms of taxation, the moral and material circumstances of life of the different classes, public health, hygiene, medical practice, diet, domestic economy, furnishings, fashions, climate, agriculture, produce, manufacturing industries, taste in landscape and gardens, fortifications, and military preparedness. Far more than with Boswell, useful descriptions and commentary suspend the foreward movement of the travel narrative or efface the instance of narration. There is also in Smollett's *Travels* a richness of evocative detail and a circumstantiality that combine the scientist's or political economist's respect for data with the novelist's power of rendering a memorable portrait or the vivacity of a scene.

One gets an idea of the pre-romantic writer's range of interest from the fact that some of the most memorable passages concern sea bathing in Boulogne, the cultivation of silkworms in Nice, evocations of the countryside of Provence or of the *campagna romana*, a fight with a hostler, a comparison between the poverty of French country life compared with the prosperity of England's, a description of the makeup and coiffures of French society ladies,[30] or graphic evocations of the lack of "delicacy," "which is the cleanliness of the mind," to be found in France: "But I know no custom more beastly than that of using water-glasses, in which polite company spit, and squirt, and spue the filthy scourings of their gums, under the eyes of each other" (*Travels*, pp. 33–34).

[30] "As to the natural hue of it [their hair], this is a matter of no consequence, for powder makes every head of hair of the same colour; and no woman appears in this country, from the moment she rises till night, without being compleatly whitened." *Travels*, p. 53.

Smollett's denunciations of various forms of behavior in France and Italy are, of course, notorious, from his descriptions of the "Yahoos" of Nice—where the artisans are "very lazy, very needy, very aukward, and void of all ingenuity (*Travels*, p. 167)—to the coach drivers and stableboys of Italy—"Of all the people I have ever seen, the hostlers, postilions, and other fellows hanging about the post-houses in Italy, are the most greedy, impertinent, and provoking" (*Travels*, p. 233)—or the inns and innkeepers of southern France—"Through the whole South of France, except in large cities, the inns are cold, damp, dark, dismal, and dirty; the landlords equally disobliging and rapacious; the servants aukward, sluttish, and slothful; and the postilions lazy, lounging, greedy, and impertinent" (*Travels*, p. 328). Such pronouncements are, in their way, examples of persistent discursive regularities of the kind Edward Said has in mind in *Orientalism*.[31] They anticipate that racist jingoism of the triumphant era of British imperialism which is summed up in the phrase "The wogs begin at Calais." Yet, the energetic hyperbole of the writing is such that Smollett transcends reportage in order to produce a caricature of the upper-class Englishman abroad. The persona of his narrator is the verbal equivalent of the apoplectic scourge of foreigners depicted by contemporary graphic artists as John Bull swathed in his Union Jack.

If one discounts the irascibility provoked in an asthmatic by any unusual exertion, the satirical energy of that picaresque tradition in the novel for which Smollett is best known, and the stout British patriotism—the Patriotic Traveler is a category that Sterne overlooks—Smollett does remind us of one important reality of eighteenth-century European travel: namely, just how difficult and unpleasant travel still was in that age. After all, his litany of complaints does begin on the road to Dover. Along with the discomfort, dirt, frequent vermin, and poor quality of food that one had to contend with in many of the post inns throughout Europe, there were the unregulated exactions of a whole "hospitality industry" which assumed that wealthy British tourists were fair game, the extreme discomfort of travel by poorly sprung coaches on badly maintained roads, and the genuine dangers represented particularly by certain mountain routes. The pleasurable smoothness of locomotion associated with travel by rail, ship, and car in the twentieth century was, of course, a phenomenon virtually unknown to the eighteenth, at least before the advent of the macadamized post roads and improved techniques of suspension late in the century in England. Yet, then as now, one of the commonest motifs of any narrative of a journey has to do with the difficulties and the risks along the way. And the heroism of travel always turns, in one way or another, on the account of dangers overcome and

[31] (New York: Vintage Books, 1978).

the resourcefulness of the voyager. From *The Odyssey* and the voyages of Sinbad to Captain Scott or the launch of the latest Apollo rocket, the greater the hardships encountered, the better the narrative.

In any case, those same inconveniences, inefficiences, and delays, which from a *remise* in Calais to a shared bedroom on the road to Lyons become in Sterne's *Sentimental Journey* the occasion and pretext for erotic play, are for the Splenetic Traveler symptoms of backwardness and social decay. Whereas the young Boswell behaves on occasion like an unregenerate rake and whereas Sterne's mature male narrator, traveling alone, presents himself as a subtle intriguer in the sport of love, happily open to such opportunities for seduction as chance puts in his way, Smollett's letter writer takes up the role of mythic father in relation to his small band. Armed with cane, sword, and pistols, the valetudinarian protector of his women, purse, and possessions declares himself ready to fight off bandits, beat up on recalcitrant hostlers, or repel the French gallants who, he assumes, are determined to seduce one or another of his females: "If a Frenchman is admitted into your family, and distinguished by repeated marks of your friendship and regard, the first return he makes for your civilities is to make love to your wife, if she is handsome; if not, to your sister, or daughter, or niece" (*Travels*, p. 59). It is not that Smollett's letter writer is always closed to the possibilities of pleasure; rather, far more than the other three travelers discussed in this section, he is preoccupied with threats to his general well-being and to his precarious health and power. Smollett's pleasures are the quieter pleasures of homeostasis under circumstances of order.

It should come as no surprise, therefore, if "convenience" emerges as a crucial concept in Smollett's book. It is for him, as for many of his contemporaries, one of the attributes of civilized life and is synonymous with the idea of material comfort and of an increased refinement in the practice of living. But, beyond that, it is related to a whole discourse of utility and order that is religious, political, social, economic, agrarian, and even hygienic as well as material. The relationships between the progressive, secular, and humanitarian thought of the Enlightenment and the emergence of what Michel Foucault has called "the disciplinary society" appear as certain discursive regularities in a variety of contexts throughout Smollett's *Travels*.

Some of the key concepts that turn out to be morphologically as well as thematically linked are clustered in a characteristic sentence of the final letter when, after an absence of two years, Smollett catches sight again of "the white cliffs of Dover"—a phrase that down through the centuries has, of course, remained a metonymic figure for Englishness, not least because of the field of signifieds that are set in motion by the signifier "whiteness." Love of one's country, Smollett suggests, should not be "a kind of fanaticism," but should depend on objective as well as subjective factors: "I am attached to my country, because it is the land of liberty, cleanliness, and convenience: but I love it more tenderly as the scene of all my interesting connexions" (*Travels*, p. 327).

The second half of this sentence evokes precisely the theme of the "motherland," not least in its reference to "interesting connexions," the very "place" where one was born and to which one is glad to return, moved by the memory of satisfactions realized. The first half of the same sentence, on the other hand, refers by contrast to those recurring concerns of Smollett's continental journey which had found expression as a series of negative evaluations over the preceding three hundred pages. Smollett's preoccupation with dirt, bad odors, offensive sights, flies and bedbugs, poor roads, squalid inns or streets, insulting behavior, indecencies of manner, and the undomesticated sexuality of young British rakes or continental society ladies—as well as his fulminations against the tyrannical exercise of power, the mismanagement of national economies, and widespread misery—all derive from an impulse to improvement and order in every sphere. On the one hand, one finds here the respect for thrift and productivity among self-regulating citizens that has traditionally been associated with the rise of capitalism in the Protestant countries. On the other, one recognizes in the letter of Smollett's pronouncements the preoccupations of an obsessional neurotic.

"There are certain mortifying views of human nature, which undoubtedly ought to be concealed as much as possible, in order to prevent giving offence," Smollett notes in a letter from Boulogne that is typical of the scatological denial that characterizes his text. And he goes on to cite as an example of such offensiveness a lady who was "handed to the house of office by her admirer, who stood at the door, and entertained her with *bons mots* all the time she was within" (*Travels*, p. 33). It is nevertheless to Smollett's credit that he is equally offended by the spectacle of poverty and human suffering in an age not noted for its tenderness. Smollett was clearly sensitive to what Robert Darnton has called "the grip of Malthusianism" in which the vast majority of France's approximately twenty million peasants were held in the closing decades of the *ancien régime*.[32]

Furthermore, it is also typical that in his account of Rome Smollett should give almost as much emphasis to the fountains, public baths, and sewers of the eternal city—the *Cloaca Maxima*—as to the Forum and the Coliseum or to Saint Peter's. Something like a cult of the cleansing power of water, along with the visible need for it, runs like a leitmotiv throughout the *Travels*, from praise for the practice of sea bathing at Boulogne or in the Mediterranean, and evocations of spas and their therapeutic

---

[32] "Peasants Tell Tales," in *The Great Cat Massacre*, p. 39.

properties, to the "prodigious quantities of cool, delicious water" in Rome itself. Smollett was also, of course, the author of a suggestively entitled *Essay on the External Use of Water*. "These works," he notes of the system of aqueducts that supplied Rome with the water for its fountains, "are the remains of the munificence and industry of the ancient Romans, who were extremely delicate in the article of water: but, however, great applause is also due to those beneficent popes who have been at the expense of restoring and repairing those noble channels of health, pleasure, and convenience" (*Travels*, p. 243).

It is finally in respect of "health, pleasure, and convenience" that Smollett is disposed to pass judgment on contemporary France and Italy as well as on ancient Rome itself. Compared with mid-eighteenth-century Britain, these are found wanting for the most part. Thus, if modern Rome has an abundance of water, its streets are nevertheless filthy, and in spite of its magnificent fountains the Piazza Navone is "almost as dirty as West Smithfield, where the cattle are sold in London" (*Travels*, p. 243). Moreover, he concludes that the ancient Romans had equally squalid habits, including the notorious practice of inducing vomiting when invited to another's house for dinner—"a beastly proof of their nastiness as well as gluttony" (*Travels*, p. 244). What Smollett chiefly praises in the civilization of ancient Rome finds physical expression in the grandeur of its public buildings, municipal gardens, baths, aqueducts, and sewers, which are, in effect, triumphs of architecture, engineering, and enlightened city planning on the grand scale. What he condemns, along with the dirt and the grossness of manners, is the cruelty of a people that took pleasure in gladitorial combats on a mass scale.

Thus, in spite of the frequent assertion of his admiration for Roman antiquity, Smollett comes out in the end on the side of the Moderns against the Ancients. And it is not simply a matter of the higher level of comfort and refinement achieved in an eighteenth-century nation such as Britain, but also a question of relative power. When compared with contemporary British maritime power, in fact, the navy that was at the disposal of Rome at the height of its empire is held to be of small consequence: "I do believe, in my conscience, that half a dozen English frigates would have been able to defeat both the contending fleets at the famous battle of Actium" (*Travels*, p. 263). If state power is found by Smollett to be so important, and if he finds Britain to be happy in possession of a great deal of it, that is in part because power is the sign that a nation is well governed, productive of wealth, and unified in its purpose.

Smollett's conception of good government and of the responsibilities of a nation's leaders is outlined indirectly in the chastisements he addresses to a boastful citizen of eighteenth-century Rome: "I asked why their cardinals and princes did not invite and encourage industrious people to settle and cultivate the Campania of Rome, which is a desert? why they did not raise a subscription to drain the marshes in the neighbour-hood of the city, and meliorate the air, which is rendered extremely un-wholesome in the summer, by putrid exhalations from those morasses? I demanded of him, why they did not contribute their wealth, and exert their political refinements, in augmenting their forces by sea and land, for the defence of their country, introducing commerce and manufac-tures, and in giving some consequence to their state, which was no more than a mite in the political scale of Europe" (*Travels*, p. 249).

Far more than in the accounts of the other grand tourists discussed, one finds in Smollett's *Travels* an incipient biopolitics of the kind analyzed by Foucault in the first volume of *The History of Sexuality*.[33] The eigh-teenth-century surgeon, political journalist, and novelist expresses the growing sense of a need for the management of populations in the gen-eral interest, which comes to be synonymous with the national interest. He argues for the putting in place of the institutions and technologies that regulate and promote a nation's health and wealth in the cause of happiness. Smollett's idea of civilized society is one in which the sociopo-litical arrangements facilitate economic production, reproduction, con-sumption, and elimination in circumstances of decency and order.

If, of the four British male travelers discussed in this chapter, Smollett explicitly associates the good life with such an ideal of social order, this seems in part to be a function of the circumstances under which he trav-eled. The persona projected by Boswell on his grand tour is that of the youthful son in revolt against a severely authoritarian father. By declin-ing country, familial estate, and his role in generational continuity, the mature Gibbon in his *Autobiography* returns a firm "Non!" to the "Nom du Père."[34] Sterne's narrator in the *Sentimental Journey* speaks with the ironically tender voice of a middle-aged philanderer. Smollett alone of the four behaves like a vigilant paterfamilias on tour, who is unsuscepti-ble to seduction and determined to defend the institution of family. It is, therefore, not surprising if he ends up as the champion of home and homeland.

In the comparisons between countries in which Smollett engages dur-ing the course of his travels, eighteenth-century Britain, therefore, emerges as coming closest to his ideal of good government. In the con-text of a discussion of the relative burden of taxes in Britain and France,

[33] Trans. Robert Hurley (New York: Pantheon, 1978).

[34] For valuable developments of these Lacanian notions, see Michel Foucault, "The Father's 'No,'" in *Language, Counter-Memory, Practice: Selected Essays and Interviews*, trans. Donald F. Bouchard and Sherry Simon (Ithaca: Cornell University Press, 1977), and Tony Tanner, *Adultery in the Novel: Contract and Transgression* (Baltimore: Johns Hopkins University Press, 1979), pp. 133–143.

he arrives at his conclusion on the basis of observations of "the face of the country" and "the appearance of the common people, who form the great bulk of every nation." But it is not so much the conclusions as the particular discursive articulation of an eighteenth-century ideal society that is significant here:

> When I, therefore, see the country of England smiling with cultivation; the grounds exhibiting all the perfection of agriculture, parcelled out into beautiful inclosures, corn-fields, hay and pasture, woodland and common; when I see her meadows well stocked with black cattle; her downs covered with sheep; when I view her teams of horses and oxen, large and strong, fat and sleek; when I see her farm-houses the habitations of plenty, cleanliness, and convenience; and her peasants well fed, well lodged, well cloathed, tall and stout, hale and jolly; I cannot help concluding that the people are well able to bear those impositions which the public necessities have rendered necessary. [*Travels*, p. 196]

This idyllic view of English country life in the age of agricultural improvement and of the enclosure movement before the Industrial Revolution suggests the possibility of a Golden Age reborn. The notions of "cultivation" and "plenty" join those of "cleanliness" and "convenience" here in a collective portrait of figures in a landscape that recalls the luminous rural imagery of Gainsborough and Stubbs. The "face" of England Smollett evokes here is that of the new agrarian capitalism, which depended in its turn on the constitutional government and the rule of law for which Britain was the envy of continental reformers in the first half of the eighteenth century. If they are to emulate the British, Smollett notes with respect to the French third estate, "They must be free in their persons, secure in their property, indulged with reasonable leases, and effectually protected by law from the insolence and oppression of their superiors" (*Travels*, p. 297). In theory, at least, it seems as if the British Tory would have sympathized with some of the goals of the French Revolution.

o   o   o

TOWARD the end of the eighteenth century Smollett and Gibbon, far from expressing the cultural self-doubt that emerges in Boswell's most Rousseauist moments, assume the superiority of Western civilization in their time. They also give no intimation that they are drawn to any extra-European alternative societies, whether those of rival civilizations or among the primitive peoples of the world. If Boswell's journey to Corsica constitutes a long detour from the classic itinerary of the grand tour, therefore, it is not just a question of distance traveled. In the same way that the critical political philosophy of Rousseau in particular challenged the doctrine of progressive enlightenment and the belief in mid-eighteenth-century Europe as the apex of civilization, so does the heroic society of Corsican patriots represented by Boswell raise doubts about life and manners in such contemporary centers of wealth and power as London, Paris, and Berlin.

The relationship between civilization and barbarism is problematized even within Europe as is the imaginary geography of center and periphery that is frequently the spatial analogue of the opposition. From such a perspective, Rome as the center of a civilizing empire comes to be evaluated as both an ideal and a falling from the ideal. And in eighteenth-century Europe, London and Paris may be regarded in a similar light. That is why there are from time to time in Boswell's travel journals intimations that Scotland, too, in its peripheral position is one of the few remaining countries in Europe where traditional heroic values are not dead, the values of the Highland Scots and the Jacobite rebellion in opposition to the venal Hanoverian court in England.

Although on the evidence of his travel journal subsequent to the journey to Corsica, Boswell rapidly descended from the level of philosophic speculation he engaged in on that island, there apparently remained an important element of Rousseauist doubt concerning the social life and institutions of the most advanced European countries to which he returned. It is something that is expressed in Boswell's journals as a quotation not from Rousseau himself, but from a certain Dr. Gregory in a book entitled *Comparative View of the State and Faculties of Man with Those of the Animal World*. The British author does no more than adopt the speculative critical discourse of his time in affirming that there occurs a moment in the development of human societies when the quality of life is at its best, a moment that is now far back in human history: "There is a certain period in the progress of society in which mankind appear to the greatest advantage. In this period, they have the bodily powers and all the animal functions remaining in full vigor. They are bold, active, steady, ardent in the love of liberty and their native country. Their manners are simple, their social affections warm" (*Italy*, pp. 171–172).

What follows is some form of decadence. There is probably not much more than an echo of the classical cyclical view of historical development here. In any case, the combination of factors that promote such peaks of human social development as those described—climactic, dietetic, and ways of life and values, according to Buffon—was the subject of widespread debate among Enlightenment thinkers. And it is a concern typically shared by a great many writers of travel books, from Boswell and Diderot at the beginning of the period here under study, to Lévi-Strauss in our own time. Such residual "Rousseauism" also appears to be endemic to an anthropological tradition that first began to detach itself from general philosophical speculation during the Enlightenment. From the beginning, it seems, the urge to take stock of the variety of the world's peoples was accompanied by an awareness of the havoc that European colonial conquests had already wrought among them.

It was also in large part because of the fusion of progressive Enlightenment thought with contemporary explorations of the globe that eighteenth-century thinkers reflected on the possibility of changing the future, frequently in order to make it more like the past. The contrasting impressions promoted in educated circles by journals of the tour of Europe, on the one hand, and of exploration of the globe, on the other, were in any case the source of significant confusion and some of the liveliest controversy in the age, not to mention the modern utopian tradition. In this connection, the often ambivalent contributions of Denis Diderot to the debate were exemplary.

Chapter II

THE PHILOSOPHE AS TRAVELER:
DIDEROT

IN HIS highly personal way Boswell gives an account of the kind of dialogic engagement that may occur in a traveler as he moves through a foreign land and is confronted by various, more or less seductive or disturbing forms of otherness. One finds in the written record of his travels through Europe a conscious effort at self-creation of a kind that Michel Foucault might have acknowledged as in conformity with his modernist ethics. The result in Boswell's text is that a culturally acquired discourse is at different moments simply reproduced or suddenly disarticulated; the pursuit of things foreign is tinged with surges of guilt; moods of self-doubt alternate with moods of self-affirmation; and the will to be his father's son encounters impulses of open rebellion. It is in any case apparent that his travel writings are the site of a struggle in which the implicitly transgressive character of travel, on the psychic as well as the sociopolitical level, is made very clear.

At the time he undertook his grand tour, Boswell was still relatively immature. He was still closer in age and experience to the youthful traveler who, the Locke of Hurd's dialogue claims, would be better off at home. Only in the Corsican period of his tour does Boswell, in effect, behave in the spirit that Locke recommends and extend his journey into a relatively unknown country. It is there that the young Boswell comes closest to being the kind of philosophic observer whose importance Locke recognized. But he does not, of course, travel outside Europe in order to enlarge in a more fundamental way eighteenth-century Europe's knowledge of the world's diverse human population.

A continental thinker who would certainly have approved of that part of the fictional Locke's attitude toward travel which pointed in the direction of a future anthroplogy was Denis Diderot, for reasons that are not hard to explain. There is, in fact, a special affinity between the new empiricism of eighteenth-century thought, which turned its attention to the variety of the human as well as the natural world, and nonfictional travel writing of all kinds. Such, for example, was the view of the first English editor of Anders Sparrman's *Voyage to the Cape of Good Hope* (Swedish

1783; English 1785): "every authentic and well-written book of voyages and travels is, in fact, a treatise of experimental philosophy."[1]

Such a view was also expressed by Rousseau when, in the notes to his Second Discourse of 1755, the *Discourse on the Origin and Foundations of Inequality among Men*, he called for a new kind of traveler, a philosophic traveler, who would report back accurately and open-mindedly on different human societies around the globe:

> It has been three to four hundred years since Europeans began to spread out across other parts of the world and endlessly publish new collections of voyages and new accounts, but I am of the opinion that the only people we know are Europeans. . . . There is no point in private citizens traveling back and forth, since Philosophy does not travel, and the Philosophy of one people is not suitable for another. As far as distant countries are concerned, the cause of this is obvious: there are only four types of travelers who set out on ocean voyages, namely, Sailors, Merchants, Soldiers and Missionaries. One cannot expect that the first three Classes furnish good observers, and as for the fourth, . . . one has to suppose that they do not voluntarily undertake inquiries that seem to be the expression of an idle curiosity, and which would distract them from the more important work to which they are devoted.[2]

Like most of the philosophes Diderot, too, had a keen interest in learning about native peoples from different regions of the globe. And his influential views on that topic will be discussed in the next chapter. At the same time, he also regarded intra-European travel as an important factor in the education of an individual and in the project of universal Enlightenment. The "Voyage" article of the *Encyclopédie* (vol. 17) is explicit on this point: "Nowadays travel to the civilized states of Europe (for it is not a question here of ocean voyages) constitutes for enlightened people one of the most important parts of their education in their youth and a part of their experience in old age. All things being equal, every nation that has a benevolent government, and in which the nobility and the wealthy travel abroad, has a great many advantages over one in which that branch of education is lacking. Travel broadens the mind, elevates it, enriches it with knowledge, and cures it from national prejudices." Moreover, the goal of travel is defined as "to observe the manners, customs, and the genius of other nations, their principal taste, their arts, sciences, manufactures, and trade." In short, the kind of travel Diderot and the *ency-*

---

[1] Quoted by Charles L. Batten, Jr., *Pleasurable Instruction: Form and Convention in Eighteenth-Century Travel Literature* (Berkeley: University of California Press, 1978), p. 7.

[2] *Œuvres complètes de Jean-Jacques Rousseau* (Paris: Pléiade, 1964), vol. 3, p. 212.

clopédistes in general had in mind, as far as Europe is concerned, took the form of what in the Introduction I called "critical travel."

As far as intra-European travel, in general, is concerned, if the grand tour was largely though not exclusively a phenomenon of British seventeenth- and eighteenth-century cultural life that derived from Britain's specific geographic, historical, and economic circumstances, the French equivalent since the sixteenth century was *le voyage en Italie*. For obvious geopolitical, historical, commercial, and even religious reasons, those inhabitants of the British Isles wealthy enough to travel to the Continent for their pleasure and instruction were disinclined to find their broader educational needs satisfied by a visit to Italy alone. Not only was there a persistent and lively interest in things French, but the British were drawn to Holland and Germany from the late seventeenth century on, in part because of the dynastic connections between royal houses and, in part, because of a common Protestant faith. Thus, such rival seventeenth- and eighteenth-century powers or commercial partners as Holland or Germany, and especially France, appeared for different reasons to be almost as interesting and in many ways more important than Italy itself.

In the wake of the political and cultural hegemony achieved in continental Europe by the France of Louis XIV, it is not surprising if the French, on the other hand, had long assumed that their only rival in terms of power and prestige was ancient Rome itself. And the only models worth emulating in the modern world, as far as arts and learning were concerned, were certain Italian city-states, including particularly Venice, Florence, and the new Rome built by the popes after their return from the Avignon exile in the early fifteenth century. Renaissance and Baroque Rome had, after all, provided French monarchs since Henri IV with the vision of an architecture of absolutism and a capital city conceived in the grand manner.

The increasing openness to North European countries—to England, Holland, Sweden, Frederick the Great's Prussia, or Catherine the Great's Russia—is, therefore, chiefly a phenomenon of the emerging critical thought associated with the Enlightenment. In a frequently marginal literature that goes back to the late seventeenth century and includes philosophic dictionaries, treatises, essays, dialogues, journals, letters, and utopian or satiric voyages, French travelers imbued with the new philosophy began to register more fully the significance of the shift of European wealth, power, and creative ideas to the north, in general, and to the North Atlantic seaboard, in particular. Either because they were in temporary exile or because they were brought in to embellish the cultural life of foreign courts and to dispense advice on philosphic, artistic, scientific, or even political and commercial matters, French thinkers and men of letters came to travel more widely in Europe. As a consequence, they looked with a renewed attentiveness to the political institutions, artistic practices, and scientific achievements of their northern neighbors.

To some extent, the choice of direction—whether to travel north or south—can be read as an indicator of ideological sympathies in the traveler, although in the eighteenth as in the twentieth century many travelers were not free to follow their sole interests. In France, far more than in Britain, for a man of letters or a cultivated amateur in the age of Enlightenment to go to Italy with the intention of visiting Rome implied a curiosity about ancient Roman civilization or about the Catholic Rome of the popes that constituted a taking of sides in the political, religious, and aesthetic debates of his homeland. It was, in some sense, either to embrace the cause of the Ancients as opposed to that of the Moderns, in the famous quarrel of the early part of the century, or to express one's allegiance to the institutions of the Catholic church. To choose to go north, on the other hand, either of one's own volition or as a preferred place of exile, was likely to be an even more emphatic ideological gesture. It was to mark a break with an inherited cultural practice and to associate oneself in one way or another with the new philosophy and its politics.

It is significant in this connection that the 1718 edition of the dictionary of the *Académie Française* defines the "philosophe" in such a way as to connect him with a marginal intellectual culture that goes back to the seventeenth-century French libertines and that had links to freethinking and a kind of scientific materialism. The "philosophe," it seems, had something disreputable about him and was associated with the idea of dissent. It is no accident, therefore, if works of travel literature such as Voltaire's *Philosophical* or *English Letters* and Diderot's *Journey to Holland* make use of their respective journeys in order to pursue their authors' campaign against the different forms of authoritarianism that characterized *ancien régime* French life at the time of their writing, almost fifty years apart. Travel writing may lend itself to the extension of power throughout the world, as Edward Said indicates in *Orientalism*[3]; it may also contribute in important ways to the subversion of power in the travel writer's homeland. And Diderot's account of his visit to Holland is one example among many of the form taken by such critical travel writing in the century of the philosophes. It is by no means the most engaging of his works, but, in spite of its representativeness, it does for its time constitute "an other way of telling." Its interest from the point of view of our present also resides in a strangeness on a number of levels that is cultural as well as an expression of Diderot's idiosyncratic authorial personality.

Even by the standards of a century that was in many ways more tolerant of textual disorder than our own, as it has come down to us Diderot's

[3] (New York: Vintage Books, 1978).

Journey to Holland is a mess of a book. What is probably eighteenth-century France's best-known account of the *voyage en Italie*, Charles De Brosses's narrative of his journey in the years 1739–1740, is dominated by the neoclassical ethos of *honnêteté* and has the shape of an epistolary novel; a series of letters home follow the itineray of a small and amiable band of friends. It is serious, but not too serious, and manages to combine anecdotes with observations on Italian life, manners, institutions, and the arts in order to satisfy the reading public's demand for pleasurable instruction.[4] Like Diderot's *Journey to Holland*, Voltaire's *English Letters* concern a North European country where he was forced into exile in the late 1720s, and the two works have a similar polemical purpose relative to the *ancien régime* French state and its institutions. Yet, unlike Diderot's travel book, the *English Letters* are composed of shapely little essays that focus in turn on British religious and political life, institutions, thought, science, and literature.

Diderot, on the other hand, left behind a manuscript that is a disorganized compendium of information in the form of notes, descriptions, and anecdotes, even though one frequently recognizes the vitality in the writing, the mixture of wit and sentimentality, seriousness and moral provocation that mark his best-known works. His *Journey to Holland*, in any case, is clearly related to those informal genres which flourished in the eighteenth century alongside the works of the neoclassical tradition, and which included the polemical and/or expository short forms of philosophical dictionaries, encyclopedias, essays, letters, brief fictions, dialogues and, of course, travelers' reports of various kinds.

Unpublished in his lifetime, the work that Diderot completed in 1780, four years before his death, from notes taken on two visits to Holland over a few months in 1773 and 1774, when he was already a man of sixty, has the form neither of a journal nor of letters nor of a guidebook. If one pole of travel writing aspires to the status of literary art and the other to provide accurate factual information, then the *Journey to Holland* is closer to the latter. It contains much of the kind of material that one would go to an encyclopedia for. Yet, it is frequently presented with a surprising randomness and is interspersed with anecdote, humor, and

[4] De Brosses is, in fact, a "good-tempered traveler," the tone of whose work is suggested in its title: *Informal Letters from Italy in Which a Young, Learned and Bon Vivant Burgundian Magistrate from the Time of Louis XV Gives a Spirited Account of His Adventures from Dijon to Venice, from the Discoveries at Herculanum to Intrigue at a Roman Conclave, from the Court of Naples to That of Turin*, ed. Pierre-André Weber (Geneva: Editions de Crémille, 1969). But even De Brosses does not quite match the philosophic equanimity displayed in the sixteenth century by Montaigne: "If it is ugly to my right, I turn to the left; if I am uncomfortable on horseback, I get off. In that way I never, in truth, see anything that isn't as comfortable and agreeable as my own home." *Œuvres complètes de Michel de Montaigne: Journal de voyage en Italie* (Paris: Conard, 1928), vol. 1, p. 132.

commentary that seem either to belie its seriousness or to introduce an energetic polemical tone. Any self-respecting modern editor would understandably want to subject the manuscript to radical revision. And that is not its only problem.

As the editor of the most recent edition, Yves Benot, points out in his introduction and notes,[5] Diderot simply lifted a great deal of his material from the works of countrymen who had made the journey to Holland earlier in the century. It is not so much that, having spent a significant portion of his life as a writer on the margins of Grub Street, he was occasionally not above behaving like a literary hack in this respect. The point is rather that the ethics of attribution were those of a very different book culture from our own, and works of compilation were far from uncommon. The amount of unacknowledged plagiarism is such, in fact, that Diderot's *Journey to Holland* might even be called a collective work; more obviously than any other travel work I have discussed so far, it suggests how all works in the genre potentially tend to a collective seeing and a recycling, with or without quotation marks, of what has already been reported or imagined. One would expect such a work to come close to embodying in its repetitions and exclusions the idea of a discourse of the kind Foucault and Said had in mind. Yet, as with Voltaire's *English Letters*, the polemical purpose of the *Journey to Holland* is to substitute an oppositional set of philosophic and political practices for those which were entrenched in the homeland. In the language of Gramsci, both writers were engaged in their different ways in a struggle for cultural hegemony. Moreover, Diderot's work typically has some of those dialogic features that cause it to speak with different voices, so that it tends to undermine the authority it elsewhere asserts. As we know from Diderot's various critical dialogues and self-scrutinizing narratives proper, he was eighteenth-century France's most celebrated theorist of the divided self and author of its most daring self-reflexive fictions. Hence the familiar difficulty that is to be found in any effort to summarize his opinions.

That we are at some remove from the values embodied in the travel writings of an *honnête homme* like De Brosses is apparent from the author's preliminary comments, "On the Means of Traveling Usefully."[6] The emphasis is placed on the "utility" of travel, on the personal and social "profit" to be derived from it. The set of precepts Diderot starts out with had become relatively commonplaces by that time. They affirm that in order to draw significant profit from his journey a traveler must have ma-

[5] *Voyage en Hollande* (Paris: Maspero, 1982); hereafter, referred to as *Journey*.

[6] Instructions on how to travel profitably were common in eighteenth-century Europe. Two of the most influential were Bishop Tucker's *Instructions for Travellers* (1757) and Leopold Berchtold's *An Essay to Direct and Extend the Inquiries of Patriotic Travellers* (1789).

turity of judgment, considerable acquaintance with an astonishing range of sciences,[7] a knowledge of his homeland, some knowledge of the language spoken in the foreign land, and an awareness of everything significant that has previously been written on that country. Further, once he has reached his destination, the traveler must exercise his faculty of observation with care, choose specialists in different fields as his informants and, above all, be suspicious of his imagination and his memory, two "faculties" that we still find problematic, though for different reasons, today: "The imagination denatures either by embellishing or by uglifying. A barren memory retains nothing; an unfaithful memory mutilates everything" (*Journey*, p. 26).

What one catches in such recommendations is an early effort to define a proper methodology for fieldwork in alien cultures. They remind us that the age that saw the birth of the "human sciences" already had highly developed ideas on how observations were to be systematized within the different branches of the tree of knowledge in the cause of truth and encyclopedic completeness. If for long stretches the *Journey to Holland* is not much fun, therefore, that is because it was not intended to be. Having committed roughly twenty years of his life to the editorship of the *Encyclopédie*, Diderot clearly conceived his Dutch travel book as a further contribution to that compendium of enlightened knowledge and counter-Bible in the campaign against dogmatic religion and absolutist practices.[8]

It is nevertheless true that, after having drawn up a list of prerequisites for useful travel of which Dr. Johnson might well have approved, he goes on frequently to ignore (much to the chagrin of many commentators) his own advice—a circumstance that has predictably led to speculation about whether or not his intention was ironic and his precepts a "mystification." Whatever else the body of his text confirms, however, it certainly does attest to the seriousness of his interest in Holland and the value of the sociopolitical example that he found there. Diderot, too, was a political pilgrim, the object of whose praise was the Dutch capitalist state. It is no exaggeration to say that eighteenth-century Holland was preeminently

[7] Diderot refers to calculus, geometry, mechanics, hydraulics, experimental physics, natural history, chemistry, drawing, geography, and "even a little astronomy." *Journey*, p. 23.

[8] The terms "encyclopedia" and "encyclopedic" have, of course, acquired two meanings, especially in French, although they do overlap. The first is relatively neutral and suggests an objective fullness of information; the second is polemical and implies ideological struggle. Thus, Johann Georg Keyssler's huge work—more than two thousand pages—*Travels Through Germany, Bohemia, Hungary, Switzerland, Italy, and Lorraine* (1740), is often cited as an example of an "encyclopedic travel book" on account of the fullness of its documentation. But it has none of that critical purpose which informs Diderot's *Journey to Holland*.

destined to be the favorite country of the *encyclopédistes* because, even before the publication of the *Encyclopédie* itself, that country embodied in its activities, values, and institutions so many of the aims the work was designed to promote. Was not the *Encyclopédie* above all intended to be, in Michèle Duchet's words, "an immense inventory of human industry in which the arts and techniques extend further the history of nature, a compendium of human knowledge achieved in opposition to the forces of prejudice and superstition, as a result of which the dignity of man is founded on the power of Enlightenment."[9] Thus, in spite of its notable formal deficiencies, the *Journey to Holland* is interesting because it articulates so forcefully, on the basis of the Dutch example, the critical philosophy and sociopolitical commitments of the philosophes.

The work touches at times, although not always in the chapters where one would normally expect it, on geography, landscape and climate, on history, politics, government, the navy and the military, the raising of money, and taxes, on state expenditures, on national wealth, trade, agriculture, manufacturing, transportation, work and leisure, on religion, ecclesiastical government, the law, the police, criminality and prisons, on towns and villages, the countryside, public health, standards of comfort, food, drink and accommodation, on manners, the two sexes and relations between them, pleasures both popular and sophisticated, and on education, learning, literature, and the arts. Inevitably, given the variety of sources from which Diderot drew his information and his relatively unsystematic presentation of the material, some of the foregoing topics are touched on only in passing—it is disappointing, for example, that although he was one of the first and most discriminating of art critics in the modern sense, Diderot says almost nothing about Dutch painting.

Nowhere perhaps does the distance between our own postromantic, post-Marxist age appear more clearly than in some of the topics he does focus on, including his comments on Dutch commercial enterprise. Probably the most interesting and certainly the most celebratory chapter in a travel book by an eighteenth-century man of letters, it turns out, is entitled "The Merchant; or, On Trade."[10] But the fact is, as Voltaire had already made clear in his *English Letters*, far from viewing the commerce of the merchant capitalist or manufacturer as an obstacle to the progress and well-being of a free humanity, the philosophes as a whole celebrated the activities of the entrepreneur.[11] In the culture of scarcity and of de-

[9] *Anthropologie et histoire au siècle des lumières: Buffon, Rousseau, Helvétius, Diderot* (Paris: Maspero, 1971), p. 437.

[10] The second section of the chapter has the suggestive title "The Citizen and the Artisan; or, On the Bourgeoisie, Corporations, Manufactures, and Workers." *Journey*, p. 85.

[11] For a recent summary of the philosophes' opinions on such matters, see John

mographic agony that *ancien régime* France had remained for the great majority of its population, the promoters of national and international trade and the producers of wealth are praised for catering to the first of all freedoms, the freedom from want.

Yet, as François Véron de Forbonnais made clear in his article called "Commerce" in the *Encyclopédie*, internal and external trade were also praised for their contribution to peace, interdependence, and communication among men in an emerging global order: "The Supreme Being forged the bonds of commerce in order to incline the peoples of the earth to keep peace with each other and to love each other, and in order to gather unto himself the tribute of their praise" (vol. 3).

Diderot, in effect, gives a gloss of materialistic philosophy to such views, when he advocates free manufacturing and free trade in the cause of the most fundamental of human rights, the right of happiness. For him, it seems, the motor of social progress is the individual's pursuit of pleasure: "The desire to take one's pleasure (*jouir*), the freedom to take one's pleasure, those are the only two stimulants to action, the only two principles of sociability among men."[12]

From the point of view of an *ancien régime* Frenchman of Diderot's sympathies, the novelty and interest of Holland were, in the first place, its peculiar and largely man-made landscape and, secondly, its republican institutions—in other words, Dutch industry and Dutch politics. The most obvious "curiosity" of Holland, then as now, was the flat perspective of polders rescued from the sea, crisscrossed with dikes, rivers, and canals, and dotted with pretty towns and villages.

If one overlooks the final damning reference to Holland's activities as an early colonial power,[13] in fact, it is clear that Diderot viewed the United Provinces of the Netherlands, as the country was then called, as a triumph of human industry, ingenuity, and rationality over a hostile nature. Moreover, he goes out of his way to note that its power as well as its wealth are, like England's, founded on trade: "It is through trade that

---

Lough, "Social and Economic Questions," in *The Philosophes and Post-Revolutionary France* (Oxford: Clarendon Press, 1982).

[12] Quoted by Michèle Duchet, *Anthropologie*, p. 437.

[13] Diderot's indictment of the mentality of Dutch colonialists is especially fierce: "What men these colonialists of Ceylon and Madagascar are! Men who have nothing, either because they were born without wealth or because they dissipated what they had; men whom greed expatriates and who, moved by the desire to see their homeland once again, are driven to all kinds of depredations. These men, who were depraved before they left, are transformed into tigers by their stay in the islands." *Journey*, p. 66. The eighteenth-century philosophe was already sensitive to the dangers that, at the end of the nineteenth, would be thematized by Joseph Conrad under the notion of "the heart of darkness." For a general discussion of the question in Diderot's thought, see Yves Benot, *Diderot: De l'athéisme à l'anticolonialisme* (Paris: Maspero, 1981).

the State first achieved strength; it is through trade that it increased that strength. If you reduce Holland and England to their local resources, you will reduce them to almost nothing" (*Journey*, p. 80). The significance of such remarks is that they indicate the extent to which Diderot, along with other philosophes, opposed the Physiocrats' fundamental tenet that the foundation of a nation's wealth and economic health was agriculture. A modern nation was unequivocally a commercial nation.

At the same time, it is characteristic of Diderot's value system that among his wide-ranging comments on Dutch commercial life and standard of living, he should find it appropriate to include warnings against the consumption of luxury items. He finds manifestations of such disturbing behavior in new country houses, flower gardens, paintings, and Asian artifacts: "The houses are stuffed full of porcelains, gold and silver jewelry, diamonds, furniture and precious materials" (*Journey*, p. 82).[14]

Arguments for and against the existence of luxury in general—its advantages or dangers for a state—were still widely rehearsed in the eighteenth century as part of the legacy from antiquity and new forms of wealth-production of the age. And, like the author of the article on "Luxury" in the *Encyclopédie* (vol. 9), Charles-François de Saint-Lambert, who distinguishes between "necessities," "comforts," and "luxuries," Diderot, on the whole, seems to steer a middle course.

In any case, comments on the display of luxury goods were a commonplace of travelers' accounts of eighteenth-century Holland, but in Diderot one finds a characteristic ambivalence based, on the one hand, on the individual's natural right to seek pleasure and, on the other, on what had come to be codified as the bourgeois or entrepreneurial values of work, abstinence, and thrift: "It is, however, inevitable that this emergent gangrene [luxury and good cheer] will through extreme self-indulgence, ambition, and a soft life of leisure extinguish all taste for commerce" (*Journey*, p. 82). Diderot's sensualist ethics apparently has its limits. When the individual pursuit of pleasure takes the form of too great a self-indulgence, it ceases to be the motor of social progress and begins to pose a threat to the stability of the social order. The object of Diderot's concern here as well as his choice of words is, of course, characteristic of that eighteenth-century philosophic discourse which held there was such a thing as too much civilization, a degree of refinement that was overrefinement.

Such comments should, in any case, be seen against the background of Diderot's pessimistic conviction that a "law of nature" governs the progress and development of all human societies, as a result of which they are

---

[14] See Simon Schama *The Embarrassment of Riches: An Interpretation of Dutch Culture in the Golden Age* (Berkeley: University of California Press, 1988).

all destined sooner or later to pass beyond the rule of law and a state of happiness into despotism. In the *Histoire des deux Indes*, he formulates the thought as follows: "That law of nature which forces all societies to move toward despotism and dissolution, all empires to rise and fall, will be suspended for none."[15] Thus, the signs of luxury he sees in Holland, like the threats to its republican form of government, suggest both the level of well-being achieved through commerce in a free society and the precariousness of it all.

Moreover, luxury in Diderot's time was also associated with the aristocratic leisure class of the absolute monarchy in his homeland. It is, therefore, in this context that Diderot's comparison of the Dutch to ants can be seen as laudatory. Merchants and traders are indefatigable searchers and gatherers who enrich their homeland as a consequence of their activities throughout the world: "The Dutch are ant-men who spread out over all the countries of the earth, collect everything rare, useful, or precious they can lay their hands on and bring it back to their stores" (*Journey*, p. 84).

If Holland was favored by its geographic position for trade with the world, it was even more favored by republican institutions that presuppose and buttress commercial prosperity. Diderot is unequivocal on this point: "The origin of [Holland's] abundant commerce is to be found in the situation of a country that stretches along the side of the sea and is crossed by two large rivers, but even more in liberty of conscience and the mildness of a government that attracts from different countries large numbers of people who settle in Holland and who bring their wealth and their industry, make their manufactures flourish, and ensure the country of that superiority it enjoys in trade and will continue to enjoy so long as she remains a republic" (*Journey*, pp. 80–81).

If in the chapter on merchants and commerce Diderot expresses most strongly his enthusiasm for a trading republic, however, it is in the following chapter, "The Inhabitant of the Country; or, On Manners," that his prose is at its most provocatively vivacious—(whether or not, as sometimes seems to be the case, certain passages are taken over from the works of other travelers). There, as elsewhere, his talent for swift satirical portraiture appears, for example, in the sketch of a large male type: "when one sees a fat Dutchman with a pipe always in his mouth, in view of his enormous size and the fact that he is fed on milk and butter, it is easy to mistake him for a living still that is distilling itself" (*Journey*, p. 39). In any case, Diderot's praise for a republican form of Dutch government finds a complement there in his appreciation of the robust, down-to-

[15] Quoted by Duchet, *Anthropologie*, p. 432.

earth qualities of the hardworking citizens of a republic whose spirit of enterprise also enables its fleets to span the globe.

Along with religion and politics, wealth and well-being, health, and beauty, Diderot, like a great many writers of travel books, also comments on sex and sexual difference. On the other hand, relatively few writers who are not economic historians have shown his precise, practical interest in domestic economy and household budgets. In the chapter noted just above, "The Inhabitant of the Country; or, On Manners," the author comments on differences of behavior between the classes, on the lack of virtue of lower-class women, and on popular forms of entertainment, including "musicos" or dances, carnivals and *kermesses*, and popular drunkenness. But most astonishing of all in this chapter is a section made up of more than seven pages that give a detailed, item-by-item account of the cost of everything ordinarily consumed by a Dutch household as well as the wages and salaries for virtually every trade, profession, or appointed official in Holland from the *stathouder* on down. In an age that saw the emergence of the modern social science of economics, such scrupulous notations are part of a self-conscious effort to provide an exhaustive account of the nation's wealth, of its production, consumption, and expenditures, its prices, wages, and taxes, with a view to further analysis and comparison with the situation in other European states.

The section also suggests how, in the eighteenth century, economic success—"the wealth of nations"—increasingly became a criterion for evaluating states and the relative value of their political systems from the point of view of human well-being. As far as Diderot's Holland is concerned, such figures are part of the general case he makes throughout concerning the superiority of Dutch life at all levels and in all spheres: "Wealth is without vanity, liberty without violence, tax collecting without vexation, and taxation without poverty" (*Journey*, p. 85). By implication, the picture drawn in this last sentence is in every particular the antithesis of what he found in contemporary France.

Another frequent preoccupation of writers of travel books is that of health and the variety of threats to it in the countries they visit or from which they depart. From Montaigne to Smollett and Fielding, there are frequent examples of prophylactic and valetudinarian travel. Moreover, Smollett in particular raised general questions of public health, notably in connection with Rome. In a similar vein, Diderot follows earlier travelers to Holland in commenting on the peculiar problems of the damp climate and the ubiquity of water in what, after all, were known as "the Lowlands": "If they do not devote to medicine an interest equal to their expenditures on dikes, the latter could end up enclosing only the sick and the convalescent, swollen, puffed and edematous people such as the inhabitants of Phase" (*Journey*, p. 39). In the philosophe's assumption that the health of a population is a matter of public policy in a prosperous, well-governed state, one recognizes the emergent discourse of biopolitics.

Such geographic and climactic circumstances are integral to the traditional concept of "Dutchness." And in the context of a natural history dominated by Buffon and his ideas on the debilitating or improving effects of climate, they also explain in part the author's less than flattering evaluations of the physical attributes of the Dutch race—among other things, they are all said to age fast and to have bad teeth—and especially of the women. With the uninhibited directness of an age that had no habit of self-censorship in cross-cultural representation, Diderot quotes a certain Dubucq to the effect that "Flemish beauties are no more than organized butter." And he adds, in his own voice, "They are beautiful if that were possible with enormous breasts and buttocks. They are exceeding plump, have bad teeth and soft flesh. As they appear in the paintings of Rubens, so they are in their houses." On the other hand, they are pronounced good and economical housewives, who rule the roost at home (*Journey*, pp. 90–91).

The disappointment expressed in the physical appearance of Dutch women reminds us of two things: first, that in the age before academic anthropology, learned analysis cohabited easily with man-of-the-world anecdotalism in commentary on foreign peoples and, second, that the association between travel and sexual adventure is age-old. One can, in fact, get no better idea of the different registers in which Diderot writes in the *Journey to Holland* than in his narration of a number of brief travelers' tales that are each centered on a curious observation. In the same way that the article called "Jouissance" which he wrote for the *Encylopédie* (vol. 8) constitutes one of the paradoxical and scandalous intertexts that occasionally shake the new tree of knowledge—it challenges the emergent doxa of Enlightenment philosophy with an unruly paradoxa[16]—so is Diderot's reference to the eighteenth-century topos of "the Hottentot Venus" an example of subversive "unofficial language" in a general context of the "official" kind.

In any case, nothing, it seems, exercises the fantasy of male travelers more than the possibility of a variation on that sexual difference with which they are familiar. An essential element in the eroticism of travel resides in the potential for exotic sexual experiences with bodies of different shades and shapes or arrestingly different in their adornments. Psychically speaking, a lot is riding on the more or less.

There is also, as Diderot's work suggests, the potential for serious dis-

[16] See Norman Bryson's brilliant analysis of the article: "Diderot and the Word," in *Word and Image: French Painting of the Ancien Régime* (Cambridge: Cambridge University Press, 1981), pp. 157–165.

appointment: the reality encountered may not live up to its representations or fantasized hopes. The sexagenarian Diderot in Holland does not express the naive greed for fresh forms of sexual gratification of the young Boswell in Italy. Nevertheless, the speculations about "the Hottentot Venus" clearly spoke to his pornographic fantasy in part because of its extra-European exoticism. Along with the pygmies and inhabitants of Tierra del Fuego in the Southern Hemisphere, and the Lapps and the Tartars in the Northern Hemisphere, the Hottentots in the emergent anthropology of the eighteenth century had the status of "limit peoples."[17] As such, from a European point of view they were subject to the uncertainties and ambivalences that are focused on the borders that divide categories. Thus, in Diderot's telling, the anecdote also suggests that something of the spirit of earlier travel legends (concerning monstrous races and fabulous creatures) persisted into the Age of Reason, on this occasion in the form of a black hermaphrodite.

Ironic, entertaining, or scabrous anecdotes were, of course, part of the stock-in-trade of the author of *Les Bijoux indiscrets* and *Jacques le fataliste*; and, in some of the most characteristic sections of the *Journey to Holland*, Diderot exercises his talents as an animated raconteur. It is significant that the anecdote I am concerned with here itself appears as a traveler's tale told the narrator by a young Briton recently returned from South Africa. In response to close questioning, the latter refutes the myth—which one might qualify as the dream of a third organ or answer to the fetishist's prayer—that Hottentot women had an apron of flesh, which extended from navel to their genital organs. The narrator learns instead that what was taken for an apron was, in fact, nothing more than "the highly extended labia which hung down like a turkey-cock's wattles and that this growth was incapable of an erection" (*Journey*, p. 134). There follows another, less lurid explanation. And it turns out that, whatever it was that was involved, it was distinctly nonphallic. It is neverthless typical of Diderot's teasing narratives that he allows some doubt to persist: "Between Mr. Gordon and the doctor, who was telling the truth?" (*Journey*, pp. 134–135).[18]

The United Provinces themselves, on the other hand, offer no such

---

[17] In a characteristically illuminating article on the topic, Stephen Jay Gould reminds us of "the racist ladder of human progress" according to which "Bushmen and Hottentots vied with Australian aborigines for the lowest rung, just above chimps and orangs." He also confirms that the "Hottentot apron," or *sinus pudoris* ("curtain of modesty"), was still a matter of lively debate in Baron Cuvier's time. The particular "Hottentot Venus" exhibited in London and Paris after 1810, however, excited male curiosity on account of the prominence of her buttocks. "The Hottentot Venus," in *The Flamingo's Smile: Reflections in Natural History* (New York: Norton, 1985).

[18] Lord Gordon was, in fact, a Scottish officer who had traveled extensively in the interior of southern Africa.

curiosities in the form of disturbing sexual mutations. And, if far from beautiful, middle-class Dutch women are at least held up as models of sobriety and domestic virtue. Like almost everything else that Diderot affirms about Holland—whether deriving from his own observations or from passages copied from the works of others with whom he presumably agreed—sexuality is found to be subject to the bourgeois morality and values of a trading republic. But those concepts have for him far less negative connotations than they were to acquire in the nineteenth century. Diderot's views on propagation and on natural morality are not addressed directly in the Dutch travel book and will, therefore, be discussed in the next chapter in connection with Bougainville's voyage. But one can discern in Diderot's scattered comments on Dutch life the outlines of a sexual economics that relates the "good" of the natural reproduction of the species to the benefits of production and exchange in general.

Nowhere more than in a brief vignette of the fishing village of Scheveling, does Diderot remind us that the ironic sensualist was also immersed in the values of the age of sensibility. In a complete change of register, the theorist of the *drame bourgeois*, author of *Le Fils naturel*, and art critic of the salons offers a moving, familial *tableau de genre* worthy of the man who was for a long time his favorite eighteenth-century painter, Jean-Baptiste Greuze—although the subject matter of the painting, in fact, concerns the topos of a storm at sea in which another contemporary specialized, Claude-Joseph Vernet. This verbal tableau possesses the qualities of "legibility, peripeteia, and hallucinatory vividness" that, according to Norman Bryson, characterize Diderot's pursuit of the transparent sign in the period of his first aesthetic (*Word and Image*, pp. 189–190). It comes closer than anything else in his strangely heterogeneous travel journal to an *exemplum virtutis* of the sentimental tradition in the novel and in drama as well as in art. Its word painting is designed to deploy the spectacle of a communitarian happiness based on the practice of virtue, a spectacle that is, therefore, capable of appealing to the spectator's heart in such a way that emulation follows.[19] Against a backdrop of sullen skies and wild waves, Diderot evokes the return of the fishing boats with the waiting wives on the shore and the joyful reunions of the fishermen with wives, children, and fathers. In this family romance of the simple life not only is there no conflict between father and son or between love and duty, but the myth of the *bon vieux temps* is represented as the lived reality in relatively remote Northern Europe.

In any case, if from the point of view of the philosophic traveler Holland was a valid model for eighteenth-century Europe, it was important to illustrate Dutch society's capacity for promoting human happiness.

[19] See "Greuze and the Pursuit of Happiness," in *Word and Image*.

Thus, although the picture of the fishing village is idyllic, the narrator clearly finds there qualities similar to those which he himself defines as bourgeois virtues, in all spheres and at all levels of Dutch society. The conduct of the nation's affairs in this respect is represented as not dissimilar from that of its domestic life. After a description of the Estates General and its meeting hall, Diderot comments: "Such is the order of the most solemn and most august assemblies in the world. It is there that the affairs of the republic and the world are aired; it is there that one sees merchants or bourgeois adopt the imposing tone and the majestic air of kings" (*Journey*, p. 48).

Diderot is describing here a bourgeois politics that has all the weight and dignity of royal politics, but without its mystique of kingship, its elaborate rituals, or its conspicuous waste.[20] In effect, in such passages Diderot is consciously seeking to extend to the political sphere proper the new hegemonic discourse and practices he had championed in the aesthetic sphere. He had argued in much the same way in his theoretical writings on theater for the creation of an ideologically appropriate bourgeois tragedy that would replace the courtly tragedy of the French classical tradition. And in his critical commentary on eigtheenth-century painting, he had elevated Greuze and Chardin over representatives of the heroic tradition.

In the end, the significance for Diderot of the republic of the United Provinces of the Netherlands is that he finds there everything he needs in order to affirm an alternative political, social, and cultural system not only to the absolutism of *ancien régime* France, but also to the constitutional monarchy of England, which Voltaire had found so much to his taste almost fifty years earlier. Eighteenth-century Holland enabled Diderot to affirm to a French public that republican government is not nec-

---

[20] With reference to what he calls "the tendentious word 'bourgeois,' " Robert Darnton comments: "It is abusive, aggravating, inexact, and unavoidable. Historians have argued over it for generations, and are arguing still." See "A Bourgeois Puts His World in Order: The City as a Text," in *The Great Cat Massacre and Other Episodes in French Cultural History* (New York: Vintage Books, 1985), p. 109. It is also a word that Diderot himself apparently found indispensable in the critical analysis of French society in his time. It was associated with an urban dwelling place, and intermediate social status, a system of values, and attitude to work, a set of behaviors, a mode of self-representation, forms of domestic life, and a style of life. As far as the latter is concerned, a contemporary dictionary confirms the kind of meaning Diderot tends to attach to the word: "A bourgeois house is a house built simply and without magnificence but in a comfortable and liveable fashion. It is opposed equally to a palace or mansion and to a cabin or cottage of the sort inhabited by peasants and artisans. . . . A bourgeois wine [is] . . . wine that has not been doctored, that one keeps in one's cellar, as opposed to cabaret wine." *Dictionnaire universel françois et latin, vulgairement appelé Dictionnaire de Trévoux* (Paris, 1771), vol. 2, pp. 11–12; quoted in *The Great Cat Massacre*, pp. 274–275.

essarily incompatible with national power, order, prosperity, or even happiness.

Diderot's knowingly polemical account of Holland as a remarkably prosperous, man-made country is, therefore, above all a story of bourgeois heroism—in the *ancien régime* sense of bourgeois—a heroism that is made to appear both more virtuous and equally as dramatic as the traditional heroism of the aristocratic and military tradition. It is a heroism not of combat, but of risk taking in trade and industry;[21] not of royal ostentation and religious pomp, but of republican dignity and enlightened calculation. Moreover, what Diderot's secular and materialist discourse implicitly affirms is that there is a moral economics at work in all spheres and at all levels of Dutch life in which a proper balance is maintained between production and consumption, income and expenditure. If Diderot expresses so much interest in the nation's domestic and sexual economies, its manners, entertainments, and public health as well as in its trade, politics, form of government, religious institutions, and military, it is because these all furnish him with further evidence of the values essential to the well-regulated state. To its great credit Holland is, in Diderot's eyes, a nation governed by bourgeois ants and not aristocratic crickets.

In sum, the example of Diderot, like that of Voltaire before him, confirms that travel writing may contribute in an important way not simply to repeating one's world, but to changing it. It would be inaccurate to say that Diderot in Holland underwent a "conversion" to a Dutch way of life, since he had already championed much of what he found there before he ever visited that country. His example, in effect, suggests that if one is to argue from the position of the Other, one has to recognize an identity of interests. In Diderot's case they might be defined, narrowly, as class interests or, broadly, as the interests of Enlightenment and human emancipation. The extent to which it is possible to achieve a similar level of sympathetic understanding for races and cultures more radically dissimilar from one's own is raised in the following chapter.

[21] Over the past couple of decades, historians of prerevolutionary France have gone a long way toward demonstrating that the bourgeois as capitalist entrepreneur and owner of the means of industrial production was a rare species indeed under the *ancien régime*. Thus, in a bourgeoisie composed almost exclusively of *rentiers*, professional men and merchants with relatively cautious business practices, Diderot would have been hard put to find in his homeland equivalents to his energetic and risk-taking Dutch.

Chapter III

CIRCUMNAVIGATION:
BOUGAINVILLE AND COOK

SINCE they first began to occur with some frequency in the second half of the eighteenth century, the voyages of circumnavigation of the globe attracted a good deal of interest with an educated European public and spawned an abundant secondary literature. This is not the place to attempt a comprehensive survey of all that one finds there. As I indicated in the Introduction, my purpose is much more modest. It is, first, to focus on the ways in which travel as represented in travel writing was invested with aspirations, hopes, and fantasies that were themselves the expression of individual or collective desire and were frequently associated with something forbidden. And it is, second, where appropriate, to take account of the writing as "a writing."

Hence the decision to concentrate here on certain aspects of the journals of two of the principal early navigators—two naval captains and two voyages that had an extraordinary impact on their age. The world tour, like the grand tour, was put to a variety of uses by those who went and those who only stayed at home to read about it—uses that were official and unofficial, political, utilitarian, and scientific or that were more clandestine, since they combined a curiosity for the exotic with the pursuit of novel pleasures.

The very word "circumnavigation," then as now, speaks to our imagination. It suggests something profoundly satisfying, something full and complete and circular like a well-told tale. "Navigation" itself is already rich in promise, since it opens onto images of a larger world, a world of waves, winds, and water, of distant shores and tropical islands. But it also implies a risk; "navigation" contains no guarantee of a return. That lack is filled precisely by the prefix, by the Latinate rotundity of a signifier in a supporting role. "Circum-" suggests that the story will end happily, the voyagers will be brought back to their point of departure from another direction as the result of the marvelous sphericity of our terrestrial globe.

Yet, if the connotations of the word "circumnavigation" seem to promise satisfactions of a kind we associate with the new and the marvelous, in certain circles the accounts of ocean voyages also generated great interest in the eighteenth century for their scientific and documentary value. The contributions of the great navigators and their trained personnel were crucial to the advancement of human knowledge about our world and its inhabitants, as the writings of the thinkers and scientists of the age attest.[1] Of course, in the journals that record the voyages of circumnavigation, "science" cohabits with "literature" in Roland Barthes's sense; as in most texts that describe an encounter with unfamiliar forms of life for a reader who has not shared the experience, the referential or cognitive function of language finds itself overlayed with the poetic function in a way that is potentially subversive of a period discourse.

It is partly as a result of this that the navigators' journals themselves could be put to a number of frequently overlapping uses, two of which have been of special importance. They were indispensable to the work of eighteenth-century natural philosophers and natural historians, and they helped lay the foundations of the universal and comparative science of man that came to be known as anthropology.[2] They also stimulated the imaginations and reinvigorated the critical thought of the philosophes and social reformers, as Diderot's response to Bougainville's account of his voyage to the South Pacific and back makes clear. In particular, the outlines drawn of simpler and happier societies living in harmony with a generous nature not only spoke to individual fantasms, they nourished a variety of utopian or revolutionary dreams on the level of the collectivity.

Thus, as Ralph-Rainer Wutherow has suggested in his general study of eighteenth-century European travel literature, the popularity of the material had more than one cause: "The hunger for 'world' must have been great at that time, certainly much greater than we can possibly imagine today; otherwise, these individual and collective publications would not have appeared in such sizes and numbers. It is likely that the thoughtful reader was looking for more than adventure and entertainment in exotic colors. He also sought instruction, enlightenment, knowledge about the world; he felt the desire to recognize himself in foreign peoples. European self-understanding developed in conjunction with information and descriptions that reached it from a foreign, unsuspected, and exotic world; it exerted itself on an unfamiliar, multiply surprising reality" (*Welt*, p. 17).

The relationship between the texts of the voyages of discovery and

[1] See Michèle Duchet's *Anthropologie et histoire au siècle des lumières: Buffon, Voltaire, Rousseau, Helvétius, Diderot* (Paris: Maspero, 1971) and Ralph-Rainer Wutherow's *Die Erfahrene Welt: Europäische Reiseliteratur im Zeitalter der Aufklärung* (Frankfurt am Main: Insel Verlag, 1980) for a detailed discussion of these connections. For recent general accounts, see also Jacques Brosse, *Les Tours du monde des explorateurs: Les Grands Voyages maritimes* (Paris: Bordas, 1983); and Lynne Withey, *Voyages of Discovery: Captain Cook and the Exploration of the Pacific* (Berkeley: University of California Press, 1989).

[2] According to Duchet, the first prominent use of the word in its modern sense is in the title of Alexandre Chavannes's *Anthropologie ou science générale de l'homme* (1788). *Anthropologie*, p. 12.

their readers is, then, a complex one, as is the process of narrativization of the material. The Russian Formalists were the first to describe systematically how narrative was modeled on the form of the journey. They were not, of course, the first to point out how, from its beginnings, the Western narrative tradition has drawn on the subject matter of travel, especially where a departure from home was fraught with a variety of risks. From Homer's *Odyssey* down through the Icelandic sagas and *Beowulf*, along with war and frequently in association with it, travel has constituted some of the most prominent matter of epic and romance literature. There is an evident continuity between the accounts produced by Western navigators of their voyages from the fifteenth through the eighteenth century and the heroic tradition in literature, even if this was not fully recognized at the time. Moreover, in spite of appearances, this is also the case with the eighteenth-century writings of such sober-minded, dedicated, and professional sailors as Louis-Antoine de Bougainville and Captain James Cook.

Thus, something occurs in their activity of verbal representation that is akin to what Bernard Smith has described in his important study as occurring among the scientific illustrators and landscape artists who accompanied the navigators.[3] One finds in these verbal accounts a heterogeneity that is perhaps most obvious with respect to narrativization. In a work whose specific focus is the semiotics of cinema, a modern heir of the Formalists, Jurij Lotman, divides the texts of the world into two categories, "plotless" and "plotted." Texts belonging to the first category are classificatory and static: "They reveal the structure of life on some level of its organization, and may be textbooks on quantum mechanics, traffic rules, train schedules, a description of the hierarchy of gods on ancient Olympus or an atlas of the heavenly bodies."[4] "Plotted" texts, on the other hand, are eventful and dynamic; they embody process, struggle, and the rupture of a system.

In spite of its usefulness for theoretic modeling, however, Lotman's dichotomy does not take account of the endless traffic between his two categories, the crossings-over and breeches of boundaries that routinely occur. And nowhere is this more obvious than in travel writing. Just as there is a continual drift from "practical" into "poetic" language, so does the process of narrativization shift the emphasis from the classificatory to the dynamic. On the one hand, a log read in sequence unfolds itself in linear time like a story; on the other, fussily discursive travelers' tales that

[3] *European Vision and the South Pacific* (New Haven: Yale University Press, 1985).

[4] *Semiotics of Cinema*, trans. Mark E. Suino (Ann Arbor: University of Michigan, 1976), p. 65. Michel Butor's account of the connections between travel and writing is to be found in "Le Voyage et l'écriture," *Romantisme* 4 (1972).

are rich in anecdote incorporate in their descriptions codified information.

Bougainville's and Cook's published journals constitute notable examples of such textual hybridization. They also focus in their different ways on a number of other questions I raised in the Introduction, including particularly the way in which travelers map and remap the world in their imaginaries or register their encounters with more or less exotic peoples for their culture of reference. The sense of entering into contact with the mythic past of the race is particularly marked, as is the question of European responsibilities and native rights. Finally, the issue of the relation between power and knowledge is raised in a new way by those travel writings which set out to represent non-European peoples. But, before proceeding any further, it is important to recall the eighteenth-century context in which the French and British navigators set out to explore the globe.

At the beginning of the Enlightenment period, scientists and philosophers were still not sure of the actual shape of the earth, even though its fixed movements in a heliocentric system were no longer a matter of doubt in scientifically informed circles. Opinion was divided in the 1730s between those who, like Gian Domenico Corsini of the Paris Observatory, believed it was shaped like a melon, elongated at the poles, and those, such as Voltaire, who followed Newton in favoring the orange as a model, namely, a sphere flattened at the poles. By the end of the century, however, these and other uncertainties would be resolved. And one of the chief instruments for the resolution of such problems was the increasingly well equipped scientific voyage of discovery.

In the view of such an historian of the Enlightenment period as Henry Steele Commager, in fact, the eighteenth century should probably be qualified preeminently as the age of exploration:

Now new worlds sprang up before the enraptured gaze of the philosophers. The fifteen and sixteenth centuries had been the Age of Reconnaissance and Discovery, yet at the dawn of the eighteenth century most of the globe was still unexplored and much of it even unknown to Europeans. The broad sweep of the Pacific was unmapped, and scores of islands, great and small, that were to be the delight and despair of Europe, were as yet undiscovered, though the vast and mysterious Terra Australis Incognita was located uneasily in the Antarctic. Of the two great American continents only the fringes had been thoroughly explored; from Hudson's Bay to Tierra del Fuego the shaggy interior was still hidden from the European gaze but did not escape its imagination.[5]

[5] *The Empire of Reason: How Europe Imagined and America Realized the Enlightenment* (New York: Oxford University Press, 1977), p. 50.

By the end of the eighteenth century, Commager goes on to point out, much of that had changed, and it was a change in which both Louis-Antoine de Bougainville and Captain James Cook figured prominently.

o   o   o

IF THE name Bougainville continues to have any currency today, it is, first, as he himself feared, because of the popular flowering shrub that he introduced into Europe and, second, because of the spirited philosophic dialogue that Diderot was moved to write after reading the journal of his countryman's ocean voyage. It is the philosophe's *Supplement to Bougainville's Voyage; or, Dialogue Between A and B* that, in a typically Derridean reversal, is far more familiar to students of literature than the original account of the voyage itself, whose resonant French title is *Voyage autour du monde par la frégate la Boudeuse et la flûte l'Etoile*.[6] The fault with the latter is in part that, like so many other travel books, it has been discursively situated outside the sphere of the literary, where its prime function over the past couple of centuries has been precisely to sustain the literariness of a dialogue that could not have existed without it.

Furthermore, as a result of recent theorizing on the topic of supplementarity itself, the prestige of Diderot's *Supplement* has, if anything, been enhanced relative to the antecedent text it claimed simply to draw out. Thus, a modern critic such as William Stowe has been able to pose the question, "Is there something about the *Voyage* and the 'manuscript' that demands or at least welcomes supplementation (interpretation), or are all texts equally susceptible to the process?"[7] Is it, in short, an accident that Diderot, before Derrida, opens up the question of the "originality of an original" in connection with a travel narrative?

A partially affirmative answer is suggested by the fact that there was already a notable precedent for such a practice: in the sixteenth century, earlier voyages of discovery had also generated supplements in the form of commentaries. It was that age which had first begun to explore the New World in the wake of Colombus's voyages and had produced narrativizations of the experience by discoverers and explorers that gave rise in turn to a flood of philosophic speculation by stay-at-home "moral phi-

---

[6] It is virtually impossible to render the various resonances of the French title in English. *Voyage Around the World of the Frigate Sullen and the Supply Ship Star* is a literal translation that fails to take into account the fact that a "boudeuse" is also a two-seater, back-to-back couch, and a "flute" a musical instrument. All references are to the La Découverte edition (Paris: Maspero, 1981), with an introduction by Louis Constant.

[7] "Diderot's *Supplement*: A Model for Reading," *Philological Quarterly* 62 (Summer 1983), p. 358. See also Christie V. McDonald, "The Reading and Writing of Utopia in Denis Diderot's *Supplément au Voyage de Bougainville*," *Science Fiction Studies* 3 (1976).

losophers" from Thomas More to Ronsard, La Boëtie, Montaigne, and Shakespeare.

As I will suggest in my chapter on Lévi-Strauss, the tradition of a narrated voyage that generates a philosophic supplement persists down to our own time in, for example, Jacques Derrida's commentary on *Tristes Tropiques* in *Of Grammatology*. On that occasion, however, it is accompanied by a theory of supplementarity. To judge from a practice that stretches from Montaigne to Diderot to Derrida, however, it does seem then that the answer to William Stowe's question is yes.[8] Narrated voyages, probably more than most categories of texts, do seem to welcome "supplementation/interpretation," including, of course, the "supplementation" of my own readings here. Common sense may with some reason privilege the "eyewitness account," but philosophic doubters or stubborn moralists in the homeland understandably find it impossible to leave well enough alone. Supplements in this sphere are, therefore, as often as not conscious or unconscious misreadings that, as Bernard Smith has shown, may be visual as well as verbal. The voyagers' own compromise formations in the aesthetic sphere frequently find themselves submitted to the secondary revision of writers and artists at home, and the outstanding example of this is the semiofficial Hawkesworth edition of Cook's first voyage.[9]

In the light of all of this, the posthumous fate of Bougainville's name and of his book is perhaps the best the man could have hoped for. This seems to be especially true since, for this modern reader as for Diderot, the greatest significance of Bougainville's *Voyage* was to invigorate the debate on the form of the ideal human society through his idyllic representations of life on a South Sea island. No flower is more emblematic of natural beauty than a bougainvillea, and no island community has been more suggestive, as Diderot immediately saw, of the idea of a lived harmony between men and a benevolent nature than Tahiti. Along with Cook and his fellow voyagers, Bougainville in his narrative of the voyage of 1766–1769 was principally responsible for launching the myth of the South Sea island that the Western imagination has lived off through Melville, Robert Louis Stevenson, Gauguin, and Margaret Mead, among oth-

[8] "The Violence of the Letter: From Lévi-Strauss to Rousseau," in *Of Grammatology*, trans. G. Spivak (Baltimore: Johns Hopkins University Press, 1976). Derek Freeman's lengthy critique of Margaret Mead's classic *Coming of Age in Samoa*, entitled *Margaret Mead and Samoa: The Making and Unmaking of an Anthropological Myth* (Cambridge: Harvard University Press, 1983), is a supplement of the aggressive kind, one that seeks to efface a predecessor text by writing over it.

[9] See Smith's discussion (*Vision*, pp. 34–42) of J. Hawkesworth, *An Account of the Voyages Undertaken by the Order of His Present Majesty for Making Discoveries in the South Hemisphere* (1773).

ers, down to the Club Med—although, from the beginning, there was also some recognition of a darker side to Tahiti.

Thus, it was Bougainville's good fortune to be taken up, a year after the publication of his *Voyage* in 1771, by a polemicist of genius who, in the relatively sober, enlightened mariner's account of the circumnavigation of the globe, found material for a characteristically energetic and satirical series of observations on contemporary French manners, morals, and institutions—observations that are also haunted by the peculiarly eighteenth-century version of nostalgia for a lost "state of nature." In Diderot's case, supplementarity takes what was for him the characteristic form of a kind of scenic reanimation. He proceeds here with Bougainville's text in a way that is similar to certain descriptions of paintings in his *Salons*; that is, he extracts from a few fragmentary tableaux scattered throughout the navigator's journal a vivid sense of their moral significance. As a result he radicalizes Bougainville's representations for critical philosophic purposes and omits almost all reference to the bulk of Bougainville's book in order to concentrate on the significance for Enlightenment Europe of human life on a single Pacific island.

Bougainville was not himself the philosopher/traveler called for by Rousseau. But he did come close to being the open-minded student of universal human nature that the Locke of Bishop Hurd's dialogue had looked for in a traveler. He was certainly aware of the kind of moral and social questions being posed by the thinkers of his age, and of the growing scientific interest taken in the human species as a whole. In any case, he was fortunate to have as commentator of his *Voyage* a leading philosophe, one who had been called in by the *abbé* Raynal to contribute a philosophic dimension to his *Histoire philosophique et politique des établissements et du commerce des européens dans les deux Indes* (*A Philosophical and Political History of the Establishments and Commerce of the Europeans in the Two Indies*), and who was as a consequence immersing himself in the history and literature of European exploration, conquest, colonization, and trade for subsequent editions. The first edition of that influential work had, in fact, appeared in 1770, a year before the account of Bougainville's voyage, and Diderot was to spend much of the following decade drawing out the philosophic and political implications of Raynal's work of historical compilation on a global scale.

As a serving officer in the French Royal Navy, Bougainville, like Cook, was a traveler by professional duty in the strictest of senses; his task was navigational, military, political, and scientific. He was therefore concerned most of the time with things other than the sex, religion, and politics that preoccupied a grand tourist like Boswell—"Before I begin, allow me to insist that my account is not intended to be a work of entertainment; it is above all for sailors that I have written it" (*Voyage*, p. 18).

Yet, Diderot's *Supplement* does not spend much time discussing these more professional features of the *Voyage* or the day-to-day events it records. The provocative subtitle of the dialogue suggests the focus of the philosophe's reading: *On the Inconvenience of Attaching Moral Ideas to Certain Physical Acts That Don't Have Any.*[10]

Whatever information Bougainville may have brought back for the enlightenment and pleasure of his compatriots or for the advancement of various sciences in his time, his voyage was undertaken in the first place as a political mission. The opening letter, in which he presents the narrative of his voyage "To the King," makes this clear. His first task on arriving in South America after having fitted out his ships was to complete a characteristic piece of eighteenth-century diplomacy by sailing to the Malouines, which were not yet the Falkland Islands, in order to transfer them officially to the Spanish crown as the Malvinas. After that, he proceeded to undertake the voyage of global circumnavigation in the king's ships as a professional naval man who was fully conscious of the novelty of the enterprise from the French point of view—"The voyage the account of which follows is the first of its kind undertaken by the French and executed in YOUR MAJESTY's ships" (*Voyage*, p. 6). And it was as an envoy of the French monarch that he went on without qualms to name and take possession of various Pacific islands, including Tahiti, on the basis of priority of discovery—a priority that in many cases was not easy to establish and in the case of Tahiti went to Samuel Wallis, if not to the early-seventeenth-century navigator, Ferdinandes de Luciros.

Both in the short letter to the king and in the opening chapter of the work itself, Bougainville is at pains to emphasize the advance achieved in voyages of exploration by the Spanish and the Portuguese, the Dutch and the English, and the need for the French, for reasons of national "glory" and national self-interest, to make up for lost time. In evoking the thirteen voyages of his predecessors,[11] Bougainville emphasizes that none of them was by a Frenchman and that only six were true voyages of exploration. Moreover, French belatedness is made to appear even more dire by the fact that, between the time of Bougainville's completion of his own voyage and his narration of it, the British had undertaken a major scientific voyage of exploration in the Pacific under the command of Captain Cook. "The anxiety of travel" in Bougainville's case, apart from anything else, also involves the recognition that he is overmatched even before the account of his voyage is completed: "Insatiable in their research, they [the British] went on to visit the Southern and Western coasts

---

[10] *Œuvres* (Paris: Gallimard, 1951).

[11] Bougainville acknowledges in a footnote that his count was wrong and that his English translator informed him of three other voyages. *Voyage*, p. 11.

of New Guinea . . . and finally anchored off the Dunes on 13th July, 1771, having enriched the world with vast knowledge in geography and interesting discoveries in the three realms of nature" (*Voyage*, p. 18).

Bougainville's consciousness of his "place" is only one of the partially submerged motifs of his text—of his place in relation to his predecessors and successors among circumnavigators of the globe, in relation to his ambiguous class position in an *ancien régime* French society that reserved top military honors for the *noblesse de cour* and, finally, in relation to his marginality as "author" in an eighteenth-century French, neoclassical literary culture with its narrowly defined norms in matters of taste. It is thus characteristic if Bougainville's apologetic tone extends to the quality of his own writing, which in a public sphere where one distinguished oneself by the brilliance of one's "style" was, in his view, incapable of compensating for the aridity of his work's content.

Given the relatively modest results obtained by the voyage, then, results that are confirmed by the editor of the most recent edition,[12] it is not surprising if the interest of the work for the broad educated public in the 1770s was more or less as Diderot defined it. Moreover, such interest was given an added piquancy in Parisian polite society because Bougainville, like other voyagers before and after him, brought back a specimen of "natural man" in the person of the Tahitian Aotourou. And Aotourou became one of the principle "curiosities" of salon society for an entire Parisian season.

Bougainville's first extensive encounter with primitive men occurs in Tierra del Fuego, and it is noteworthy that the land and its inhabitants were to become a familiar topos of Western travel literature. Bougainville had earlier registered the state of anomie that he found afflicted the natives who had been brought together in the Jesuit missions of Paraguay, but he takes no comfort from his contact with men still in a "state of nature." His reaction of shock to pristine nakedness under conditions of extreme destitution is what one might expect from a man of his age. How to look at naked bodies was an even greater problem for eighteenth-century Europeans than we like to think it is for us now. Nakedness was not easy to read; it was, so to speak, unnatural.

Thus, an encounter like Bougainville's was typically followed by a search for an explanation that included, in the thought of the times, the theory of degeneracy. And in the eighteenth century the theory of American degeneracy is associated in particular with the most celebrated natural philosopher of the age, the *comte de* Buffon, and with the philosophe responsible for writing the article on America in the supplement to Diderot's *Encyclopédie*, the *abbé* Corneille de Pauw.[13]

---

[12] See Constant's comments, *Voyage*, pp. XXII–XXVII.
[13] See Commager, *Empire*, pp. 64–65, 79–80; and Germán Arciniegas, *America in Eu-*

Bougainville refers to the natives who board the *Boudeuse* as "disgusting and incommodious guests" and goes on to note: "These savages are small, ugly, thin, and have an unbearably bad smell. They are almost naked, having as their only clothes the poor skins of seals that are too small to cover them. . . . Their women are hideous and the men show little regard for them" (*Voyage*, p. 106). What seems to disturb him even more as a sign of their brutishness is the indifference they show to the inventions of modern European civilization: "These primitive men treated the masterpieces of human industry as they treated the laws of nature and nature's phenomena" (*Voyage*, p. 105).

In effect, Bougainville seems to be defining here a zero degree of cultural achievement and moral sensitivity that is confirmed by the subsequent affirmation that "of all the savages I have seen in my life, the Pecherais are the most destitute; they are precisely in what one might call the state of nature" (*Voyage*, p. 107). Moreover, far from suggesting the advantages of such a state over that of civilized man, the encounter even leads Bougainville to reflect that the natives of Tierra del Fuego have the worst of all possible worlds. Not only are they without any of the conveniences of civilized life, he also notes that they live in one of the world's most intolerable climates.

The reference to the latter is significant because it suggests the way in which Bougainville here is reproducing the discourse of his time relative to American degeneracy—what after Edward Said one might be tempted to call eighteenth-century "Americanism," if the signified of that particular signifier had not already been fixed. American backwardness and the inferiority of its species, Buffon explained, was owing to its having emerged more recently from the Flood: "It will never produce anything but humid creatures, plants, reptiles and insects, and cold men and feeble animals are all that it will ever nurture."[14] And, indeed, what climate could be moister and more vaporous than that of Tierra del Fuego?

Buffon's comment here is to be understood in the context of a theory of the monogenesis of the human species and of the need to explain the great variety of existing human types. He found his answer in the concept of a progressive degeneration brought about by the prolonged exposure of members of the species to extreme climactic conditions. As a result, the white European race in its temperate zone was posited as the norm and center—"the most handsome, whitest, and best built in all the

---

rope: A History of the New World in Reverse (New York: Harcourt Brace Jovanovich, 1986), pp. 139–165. For a discussion of Bougainville's *Voyage* in terms of a "poetics of pathos" common to eighteenth-century voyage literature and the novel, see Jay Caplan, "A Novel World (Bougainville as Supplement)." in *Framed Narratives: Diderot's Genealogy of the Beholder* (Minneapolis: University of Minnesota Press, 1985).

[14] Quoted by Commager, *Empire*, p. 80.

earth.""¹⁵ And those peoples who lived in the least temperate climates, such as the Lapps, Hottentots, Pygmies, and Patagonians, were seen to be in sad decline from that norm.

At the same time, along with a form of primitivism that destroys the myth of the Noble Savage, the marginal bands of men in Tierra del Fuego are also found by Bougainville to share certain fundamental vices of modern civil society. The implication of his observations is that as soon as more than one family unit enters into an alliance with another, a will to power emerges. The surprise for him is in the discovery that there exists a politics in the state of nature—which is tantamount to concluding that there is no state of nature except in the negative sense of a state of deprivation.

Furthermore, it is an observation that allows him to go on to conclude unexpectedly that if the vices of civilized society are shared by those still in a state of nature, the former has virtues that are not available to the latter. In short, the Indians of South America leave Bougainville's confidence in the civilization of the European Enlightenment wholly intact. His encounter with the human society of Tahiti, on the other hand, introduces a significant element of cultural self-doubt, which Diderot consciously exploited in the ironic play of his dialogue.

Given that, in retrospect, we recognize it as one of the magic and/or fatal moments in the European voyages of global exploration—a moment that, short of an encounter with extraterrestrial beings, is in our age impossible to recapture—Bougainville's narration of his approach to Tahiti is worth quoting in full:

We were approaching the land under full sail with the wind from the bay, when we noticed a canoe which was coming from the ocean and was sailing toward the coast, using both a sail and paddles. It passed in front of us and joined an infinite number of others, which approached us from every part of the island. One of them preceded the rest; it was propelled by twelve naked men who presented us with branches of banana trees and who showed through their behavior that this was their olive branch. We responded with signs of friendship that we were able to devise. Then they came alongside and one of them, who was distinguished by an enormous head of hair that stuck up in spikes, gave us a little pig and a stem of bananas with his branch of peace. We accepted his present, which he attached to a cord that we threw him; we gave him some bonnets and handkerchiefs, and these first presents were the pledge of our alliance with this people. [*Voyage*, pp. 127–128]

¹⁵ Quoted by Duchet, *Anthropologie*, p. 255.

In Bougainville's relatively straightforward prose is focused the collective desire of an age. In any case, the idyllic simplicity of a ceremony in which two radically different cultures first communicate in a nonverbal exchange of gifts—a pig, bananas, and branches for bonnets and handkerchiefs—has a special poignancy in the light of subsequent history. Yet, it is a poignancy to which Diderot was already alert in the 1770s as both his remarks in the *Supplement* and his comments on Dutch colonialism in the *Journey to Holland* indicate. In spite of the apparent good faith on both sides, Bougainville's narrative enables us to perceive that a cultural missed encounter is involved; two alien imaginaries find themselves mirrored differently in looks that are without genuine reciprocity and in an exchange of disturbingly heterogeneous objects—the products of a stone-age agricultural community for those of preindustrial textile manufacturers in which all the advantage seems to be on the side of the Europeans. What on earth were the Tahitians supposed to do with those bonnets and handkerchiefs?

It should come as no surprise, therefore, if in the two and a half chapters devoted to the three short weeks spent on Tahiti, one finds not only a celebration of the South Sea island people but also a series of misunderstandings and confrontations, including the murder of a number of islanders. And, taken together, such incidents suggest the impossibility of any future understanding based on cultural equality or reciprocity. Bougainville's text from more than two hundred years ago reminds us of the fatal imbalance that throughout history has attended the vast majority of relations between culturally diverse peoples, an imbalance based essentially on technologically derived power, including firepower.

Perhaps the most telling of the missed encounters between the French sailors and the Tahitians occurs even before the former have disembarked. The French soon discover that the hospitality of the islanders apparently extends to offering their women for the pleasure of their guests, women who in their nakedness are found by the narrator to be fully in conformity with eighteenth-century European ideals of female beauty: "The canoes were filled with women who as far as the attractiveness of their face is concerned are in no way inferior to the great majority of European women and who for the beauty of their bodies are superior to them all. Most of these nymphs were naked, for the men and the old women with them had removed the loin cloth with which they normally cover themselves."[16]

---

[16] Bougainville's naturalist, Philibert Commerson, was even more dithyrambic in his journal: "Born beneath the most beautiful of climes, fed by the fruits of an earth that is bountiful and requires no cultivation, governed by loving fathers rather than by kings, the only god they know is the god of Love. Every day is devoted to his worship,

Then, in a series of observations that make it clear why Bougainville found it appropriate to draw on the neoclassical topoi of his age and call the island the New Cythera, he notes: "They first made from their canoes provocative gestures in which, in spite of their innocence, one could detect a certain embarrassment, either because nature has everywhere embellished their sex with a naive timidity or because, even in lands where the freedom of the Golden Age still reigns, women appear not to want what they desire the most" (*Voyage*, p. 131). Thus does an eighteenth-century European male "look," fix, and interpret the behavior of alien women of color.

That, in order to represent the peculiar intensity of this encounter, Bougainville was reaching for an imagery and a stylistic register that find their models in literature is clear in such and similar passages. The classical idea of the Golden Age is invoked in the context of references to a sexual freedom wholly unknown to contemporary European society. Further, Bougainville discovers, sexual favors are not only granted liberally as a rite of hospitality, they are also on such occasions conducted in public on the floor of a hut: "the earth is strewn with leaves and flowers, and musicians sing accompanied by a flute a hymn to carnal pleasure. Venus is the goddess of hospitality here, her worship sanctions no mysteries, and every act of love consummated is a festival for the nation" (*Voyage*, p. 138). When coupled with the mildness of the climate, the beauty and natural abundance of the island itself, and the evident state of well-being of its population—"everywhere we saw the reign of hospitality, repose, sweet joy, and all the appearances of happiness" (*Voyage*, p. 139)—such observations naturally lead Bougainville to supplement his comparisons to classical myth with a reference to the biblical paradise: "I thought I had been transported to the Garden of Eden" (*Voyage*, p. 138).

Nevertheless, Bougainville was by no means so totally under the spell of his discovery of a form of prelapsarian life to neglect his duties as the political envoy of an absolutist monarch, as a navigator, and as a philosophically educated student of human behavior. Thus, in a chapter following his narration of their arrival, contacts, and departure—a departure accompanied by the shedding of tears by the islanders, which was a fitting proof of their "humanity" in the age of sensibility—Bougainville furnishes a variety of useful information on the coastline, reefs, bays, anchorages, elevations, soil, climate, animal life, vegetation, and produce.

Like other European travelers of his time who realized the significance for the thought of the age of the study of primitive man and exotic societies, Bougainville turns himself into an amateur ethnographer by offer-

---

the whole island is his temple, all the women are his altar, all the men his sacrificial priests." Quoted by Constant, *Voyage*, p. XVII.

ing a brief account of the Tahitians' physical appearance, dress, and forms of adornment, including tatooing—"The fashion of painting oneself is thus fashionable as it is in Paris" (*Voyage*, p. 154)—crafts, such as canoe building and the making of tapa, manners, politics, religion, and family structure, in which he notes that polygamy is the norm—"Since their only passion is love, a great number of wives is the great luxury of the rich" (*Voyage*, p. 157). He also comments with some wonder on the apparent absence of private property, the openness of their households, the apparent lack of crime, the nonviolent behavior, and the mildness of most forms of punishment, but he does note that they are frequently at war with neighboring islands and revises his first impression of the egalitarian nature of Tahitian political life.

At the same time, it is with something like an air of relief that he is able to conclude that there is one negative consequence of such a life of pleasure and indolence—"Here a sweet idleness is the lot of women, and the task of pleasing their most serious occupation" (*Voyage*, p. 158)—namely, a superficiality of character, a reluctance to make any significant effort, and the briefest of attention spans. However, such a rare caveat does little to dispel the overwhelming impression that never before in the modern world have Europeans come closer to rediscovering the Golden Age of classical myth or the biblical Eden.

Yet, in the end, as the chiefs among the islanders seem to fear at certain moments, even as mediated through Bougainville's narrative, the Tahiti he leaves after a stay of barely three weeks is no longer the island he first discovered. And this is so for at least two important reasons. First, there is the political act of a formal, if disguised, taking of possession in the name of the French monarchy; second, there is the question of venereal disease.

The Tahitians first express their disquiet concerning the activities of the French sailors when the latter set up camp on land without, apparently, requesting the islanders' permission. But the latter's fears are quieted when they are assured that the French will be leaving in eighteen days. Yet, it is precisely on the site of this camp that Bougainville hides the document affirming France's claim to the island: "I buried near the shed an act of taking possession inscribed on an oak board along with a sealed bottle containing the names of the officers of the two ships. I followed the same method for all the territories that I discovered in the course of the voyage" (*Voyage*, p. 144). By such a devious act, in any case, New Cythera ceased to be mythic in order eventually to become French; Bougainville's gesture effectively politicized paradise and forced Tahiti to enter European historical time and geopolitical space.

It is noteworthy that Bougainville solemnizes the political act of taking possession in most cases with an act of naming—what speech-act theorists call a "performative." The assumption involved is that to possess is also to take discursive possession. But as Bougainville does not acknowledge, such naming—even in the eighteenth century—is almost always a re-naming; it is a symbolic substitution that is also a writing over of a previously given name in a language other than one's own and, therefore, an erasure of a past. That is why, with our historical hindsight, we can read something like an allegory of European colonialism into the brief anecdote wherein one of Bougainville's sailors finds half-buried in the sand a broken plaque bearing the remnants of English words: HOR'D HERE/ICK MAJESTY'S. "The savages had obviously torn the plaque down and broken it in pieces," notes Bougainville, without, of course, being in a position to see that the future course of European colonization and decolonization is foreshadowed in this enigmatic fragment of a political text.

With the discovery that venereal disease was also widespread on the island comes a further sign that paradise was no sooner found than lost, and in both cases the implication is that the Europeans were to blame. The loss of political innocence is in any case accompanied by the disease best qualified, before the emergence of AIDS, to be interpreted as a punishment for the sin of sexual promiscuity. Bougainville's narrative assumes that it was the Europeans who brought the plague, although there is some possibility that it was already endemic in Tahiti. In any case, a second British expedition of 1769 accused Bougainville's crew of having infected the islanders, and Bougainville suggested that it was probably Wallis's sailors who were guilty, since they had spent a month on the island eight months before his own visit.

Neither before nor after the visit to Tahiti does Bougainville encounter any native peoples who seem to him nearly so attractive as those of that fortunate island. Frequently, in fact, he reports on the suspicion and hostility met with as the French ships approach different islands in the hope of replenishing their supply of water or supplementing their diet. After Tahiti, in fact, much of Bougainville's narrative concentrates on a more traditional form of the heroism of travel than the one that Freud will be concerned with. Bougainville is, for understandable reasons, preoccupied with the dangers of navigating in relatively uncharted waters, with assaults from natives, and with the very serious deficiencies in the crews' diet and the spread throughout the two ships of venereal disease and scurvy. From the point of view of a contemporary reader, however, probably the most interesting sections of the *Voyage* after Tahiti are Bougainville's eyewitness accounts of eighteenth-century Dutch colonialism on the ground at a time when visits by outsiders to the Dutch East Indies or the "Spice Islands" were systematically discouraged. He shows the other face of Holland, the one that is referred to but not explored in Diderot's celebratory book on that trading nation, but that was central to his philosophic meditations in the *Histoire des deux Indes*, and that would be taken up a century later with reference to European colonialism, in general, in Conrad's tales as well as, in our own time, in Lévi-Strauss's autobiographical work.

◦   ◦   ◦

IN THE light of Bougainville's comments on the exploitative commercial politics of eighteenth-century colonialism, it is no wonder if Diderot in his *Journey to Holland* exclaims: "These men who were depraved before they left are transformed into tigers by their stay in the islands."[17] Nor is it surprising that in the *Supplement* he anticipates Lévi-Strauss by some two hundred years and interprets Bougainville's discovery of Tahiti as a disaster for that tropical island. Diderot's dialogue is, in short, exemplary of its genre, and it is for once worth looking briefly at the philosophic and political meaning attached to a work of travel by a contemporary. Just as Bougainville's efforts to understand Tahiti find themselves mediated by eighteenth-century thought and neoclassical taste, so Diderot's secondary misprisions are animated by the tasks of his present.

The *Supplement* as a whole is a meditation on the state of contemporary European society and an elegy for a paradise lost at the precise moment of its emergence into the European consciousness and political sphere of influence. Bougainville's account of the Jesuit colonization of Paraguay and the Dutch colonization of the East Indies, in particular, can be seen in retrospect to confirm for Diderot something that he was learning from other sources: namely, that the sadness of the tropics was already a phenomenon of the eighteenth century. In many ways, that age's equivalent of Lévi-Strauss's lament on the state of the globe in the wake of modern European colonialism was the *Histoire des deux Indes*, in spite of the fact that Diderot was, on the whole, no Rousseau and, as in his Dutch travel book, affirmed his belief in the potentially universal benefits of world trade. Yet, his conviction that the "revolution" brought about by European commerical interests would in the long run promote new forms of pleasure for the individual did not blind him to the consequences of conquest, subjugation, and exploitation of native peoples, including the horror of slavery. In her authoritative account of Diderot's contributions to the *abbé* Raynal's new global history, Michèle Duchet writes: "The History of the Europeans in the *Deux Indes* turns into a long indictment of violence, lust for gold, fanaticism, superstition, and despotism, that also serves to show the evils the people of the old world also suffer from as victims of the same tyranny."[18]

[17] *Voyage en Hollande* (Paris: Maspéro, 1982), p. 66.
[18] *Diderot et l'Histoire des deux Indes ou l'écriture fragmentaire* (Paris: Nizet, 1978), p. 170.

Duchet summarizes as follows the melancholy conclusions to which Diderot came in his contributions to the *Histoire des deux Indes*: "The dominant impression is that the savage world will not be able to escape destruction. Condemned to die by the ferocity of the wars of conquest, ravaged by diseases and by vices that the Europeans transmitted to them, divided by internal dissension, driven to rebellion or despair, it increasingly withdraws from a history to which it will never belong" (*Anthropologie*, pp. 225–226). The combination of guilt and compassion, regret, anger, and sadness that one finds in *Tristes Tropiques* had in many ways already been expressed by Diderot two hundred years earlier. And similar feelings emerge in the *Supplement to Bougainville's Voyage*

In effect, the scenes of Bougainville's encounters with the Tahitians are read by Diderot as if they were artistic representations of what Norman Bryson has called "a core narrative." That is to say, as in Jean-Baptiste Greuze's dramas of domestic life, they concern peripeteia that are susceptible to subsequent narrativization; they fix for our contemplation a climactic moment "of threshold or transformation."[19] Moreover, no such peripeteia painted by Greuze, or imagined by Diderot for that matter, would ever equal that of the world-historical encounter between the heroic primitives the Tahitians were taken to be and the worldly European voyagers caught up in the various alienating structures of European civilization.

In the section of his dialogue entitled "The Old Man's Farewell," Diderot's theme is, in fact, the barbarism of a European civilization that fails in its representatives to respect the innocence of a people and a way of life that have remained simpler and closer to nature and the origins of humanity than is the case in Europe. That cultural self-doubt which shadows the Enlightenment's faith in the progress of human understanding and morality is expressed in an harangue that Diderot imagines the Old Man addressing to Bougainville himself: "And thou, chief of those brigands who obey thee, remove thy vessel from our shores immediately. We are innocent, we are happy, and thou canst only spoil our happiness. We follow nature's purest instinct, and thou hast tried to erase it from our souls. Here everything belongs to everyone and thou hast preached some kind of distinction between *thine* and *mine*. . . . We are free. And we find thou hast buried in our earth the deed of our future enslavement" (*Œuvres*, p. 1000). Adapting a famous title from Greuze, Diderot might equally as well have entitled the section concerned "The Patriarch's Curse." There is in the scene he evokes a similar, highly legible moral outrage and fierce gestural potency of the kind one finds among Greuze's offended fathers.

[19] *Word and Image: French Painting of the Ancien Régime* (Cambridge: Cambridge University Press, 1981), p. 190.

Such extrapolations from Bougainville's *Voyage* by the militant philosophe find some justification in the text, although the royal sailor dutifully avoids Diderot's polemical tone throughout. There is, however, a sphere in which it is no exaggeration to say that Diderot misreads his countryman in a way that is curiously symptomatic, given that it is in the crucial sphere of Tahitian sexual relations and the characteristics of Tahitian female beauty. In spite of the fact that Bougainville, in the passage quoted above, affirms that Tahitian women are the equal of European women as far as their faces are concerned and superior as to their bodies, one of Diderot's dialoguists concludes without contradiction that female beauty in Tahiti is submitted to the rule of reproductive utility: "The woman who attracts the eye and who arouses desire is the one who promises a lot of children . . . and who promises that they will be active, intelligent, brave, healthy, and strong. There is almost nothing in common between the Athenian Venus and the Tahitian one; the first is an amorous Venus, and the second a fertile Venus" (*Œuvres*, p. 1015).

Moreover, it is in this connection that one must understand Diderot's sexual politics, his praise of the sexual freedom of Tahiti; such freedom is interpreted, above all, as a freedom to procreate. An openness to the pleasures of sex—a kind of *morale de la volupté*—is, therefore, not mere licentiousness but the expression of a higher collective wisdom. Like the beauty of women on the island, such pleasures are posited as in the service of the general welfare. In the article on "Jouissance" Diderot had written for the *Encyclopédie* (vol. 8), he had already defined the word as "the physical pleasure (*volupté*) that perpetuates the chain of living beings." And he goes on to imply that such pleasure is a ruse of nature; the body, so to speak, has its reasons, or at least nature acting through the body. Thus, in his *Supplement* he confirms once again that the function of sexual freedom before the age of scientific contraception is to ensure the production of an abundant and vigorous population.

One recognizes here the reasoning on which Diderot was soon afterward to found his praise of the United Provinces of the Netherlands in his *Journey to Holland*. The sexual morality of the Tahitians, it turns out in Diderot's surprising reading, has a great deal in common with the bourgeois values of the North European trading nation, since it promotes a large and active population that increases the productive capacity of a people, its wealth, and general well-being. Diderot apparently shared with many of his contemporaries a belief that the ultimate source of the wealth of a nation is in part its population and, with the emergent human sciences of the eighteenth century, a belief in the need to regulate human sexual behavior in the cause of procreation.[20]

[20] In his discussion of the dialogue, Arthur Wilson notes that "Diderot was con-

Finally, if Diderot, along with other philosophes, denounces priests in the *Supplement,* it is because they are celibate and non-procreative and therefore, from a socioeconomic point of view, useless. That moral sense of the Tahitians which tells them to do what comes naturally in sexual relations—the *liberté de jouir*—turns out to be good racial and socioeconomic sense; it is, in fact, a *liberté de reproduire.* In adopting the large view of the nation and not the narrow one of the family in the sphere of procreation, they also show how the European tradition of patrilinear descent is linked to an ideology of private property frequently at odds with the interests of society at large.

Nevertheless, in posing the alternative between civilization and a state of nature as a radical opposition, Diderot's dialoguists equivocate rather than come down firmly on one side or the other. Thus, although "B" affirms that to his knowledge only in Tahiti can man be said to be happy, it is also implied that there is no obvious way back to that modified state of nature for modern Europeans. And this is so in spite of the discontents that are the consequence of contemporary eighteenth-century life, discontents that in Diderot's discourse have peculiarly Freudian associations—"a civil war within the cave": "You want to know the short history of almost all our misfortune? It is as follows. There once existed a natural man; an artificial man was admitted inside that man; and there occurred a civil war within the cave which lasts a lifetime. Sometimes natural man is stronger; sometimes he is overcome by moral and artificial man. But in both cases the miserable monster is divided, tugged, tormented, stretched on the wheel" (*Œuvres,* p. 1028).

Only under "extreme circumstances," it is affirmed, may he return to original simplicity. What those "extreme circumstances" are which enable man to reverse the course of human history and overcome the tensions of Diderot's version of the split subject are not made explicit—although, on the basis of the references in the *Supplement* to the need for the reform of France's laws, codes, and institutions, a modern reader with historical hindsight is likely to supply the word "revolution." In any case, it is a latent desire for a return to the presumed originary wholeness of a lost state of nature that haunts Diderot's dialogue and, as a result, helped launch Bougainville's Tahiti as the this-worldly locus of a two-hundred-year European dream.

Neither Bougainville nor Diderot invented the myth of the tropical island as paradise on earth. If any single author can be said to be responsible for that in post-Renaissance Europe, it was Daniel Defoe. And he was inspired by the tale of an earlier traveler: namely, Woode Rogers's

---

cerned with eugenics and he was a populationist." *Diderot* (New York: Oxford University Press, 1972), p. 591.

story of Alexander Selkirk. With Robinson Crusoe, Defoe was the first to invest the image of a tropical island with the idea of fruitfulness and multiple satisfactions through richly detailed descriptions of climactic conditions, fauna, and flora. Moreover, under the guise of representing the goodness of a God-given creation before the advent of men, as seen through the eyes of a celibate Englishman struggling with his faith, Defoe succeeds marvelously in appealing directly to a profoundly sexualized, Western imaginary. In his fictionalized detailing, a tropical island comes to be figured as the original Good Place, the place of a mother's body.

The lure of Tahiti for eighteenth-century Europeans had much in common with the appeal of Defoe's island paradise. The big difference is, of course, that Tahiti had its own indigenous population, which seemed to have invented the art of living in fully sexualized harmony with their benevolent environment on a social and not simply on a solitary level. Under the circumstances, one can read into Bougainville's will to political possession and Diderot's ironic denunciation of it the ambivalence of a European culture that recognized in its achievements both an opportunity and a threat for rival cultures everywhere. European concupiscence is shadowed by European guilt.

Yet, a certain critical distance from the nostalgia for a prior state—implied in Bougainville's *Voyage* and made explicit in Diderot's *Supplement*—should prevent us from embracing wholeheartedly a catastrophe theory in the cultural sphere, equivalent to that which accounts for the disappearance of species in the natural world. It is too simplistic to substitute Europeans for comets or asteroids in a tale of cultural extermination. As we know from the radical changes wrought in Western societies over the past couple of centuries, the transformation of a culture is not the same as the disappearance of a species. The past—even a long-standing, culturally homogeneous past—is not always superior to the heterogeneity of the present. Moreover, we should not forget that without the extinction of the dinosaurs we might well have remained small, nocturnal rodents.

o   o   o

IN THE record he left behind of the voyage of the *Endeavour*, Captain Cook frequently goes over the same ground as Bougainville. And he does so in such a way as to confirm many of his French predecessor's findings and to cast doubt on others. Cook's work is of special interest in this context because it illuminates both at the discursive and the thematic level, as well as at the level of language, the conflicting imperatives out of which travel writings are typically composed.

On the one hand, the account of Cook's first voyage is a wonderfully suggestive document on the way in which British political hegemony was extended into a new area of the globe; it pinpoints the mixed motives of the voyage and the different, ideologically conditioned representations of the same events by those on board. On the other hand, it confirms the impossible purity of Lotman's two categories by the manner in which the classificatory descriptions of "plotless" texts are interrupted again and again by the task of telling the story of a voyage and vice versa. Here, too, there are crossings-over; the imperative of the referent and of the demands of the anecdote require more or less equal time. At the same time, a similar slippage of register occurs at the level of language itself; the "practical language" of the sea captain becomes "poetic" in a variety of unexpected ways. In short, Cook's journal is illuminating in this context because it shows both how a voyage of discovery is "politicized" and how scientific observation is "poeticized."

As noted above, Bougainville paid tribute to Captain Cook's first voyage of circumnavigation of the globe, the voyage of the *Endeavour*,[21] in the introduction to his own narrative. Although the British navigator's expedition ended in July 1771, more than two years after Bougainville's return to France, a version of his journal had already appeared, and the Frenchman praised the quality of the work accomplished by the British ship: "this voyage seems to me to belong to the modern variety of its kind in which the most discoveries have been made in all fields" (*Voyage*, p. 16). And, in effect, the three-year voyage of the *Endeavour* was immediately acknowledged as establishing new professional and scientific standards for the conduct of such voyages of exploration.

Perhaps the most striking difference between the two expeditions was that Cook was accompanied by Joseph Banks's party. Banks was only twenty-three when the voyage began, but he had already established himself as an antiquary, was a member of the Society of Dilettanti, and was what was known at the time as a "virtuoso"; that is, a wealthy and well-connected gentleman who was enthusiastic about the arts, scientific inquiry, and world travel. In any case, he shared with some of the most advanced minds of his age the conviction that well-trained botanical and zoological illustrators and landscape artists should be part of all voyages of exploration. As a result, Cook's first expedition, like the subsequent ones, brought back an unprecedented graphic record of his discoveries.

Yet, even if one restricts oneself to the sphere of verbal representation, simply to compare a few pages of Cook's journal of his first voyage with Bougainville's is to understand the new professionalism Cook introduced. Cook, so to speak, never misses an entry. He systematically records his ship's position in its progress around the globe, its latitude and

---

[21] All references are to the magisterial J. C. Beaglehole edition, *The Journals of Captain James Cook*, vol. 1: *The Voyage of the Endeavour, 1768–1771* (Cambridge: Cambridge University Press, 1955).

longitude on a given day, the weather, force and direction of the winds, the currents and tides. And whenever he approaches a coast, he reports his soundings and charts the location of harbors, reefs, and shoals. Cook's personal responsibility on the mission was that of navigator as well as captain, a task that committed him to an incremental mapping of the portions of the globe he sailed through. His goal was useful knowledge of a kind that was readily translatable into geopolitical power.

The voyage had a specific scientific purpose as well as a more general, exploratory one. It was undertaken in mid-1768 at the behest of the Royal Society, which wanted to send an astronomer to the South Seas to observe Venus's transit across the sun in June 1769. But there were other specialists apart from the astronomer Charles Green on Cook's ship. Other forms of scientific and artistic expertise were represented by Joseph Banks himself, the naturalist Daniel Solander, the professional scientific illustrator Sydney Parkinson, and the landscape artist Alexander Buchan—and when, much to Banks's chagrin, the last-mentioned died shortly after reaching Tahiti, the assistant naturalist Herman Spöring took over Buchan's role. It would, of course, be anachronistic to expect the presence of an anthropologist on board in an age in which the "human sciences" were only beginning to detach themselves from general philosophic and moral commentary on human behavior. But this turns out to be a lack that several of the voyagers, including Cook himself, set out to fill; and, along with brief descriptions of the climate, topography, vegetation, and animal and sea life of the lands visited, Cook gives us descriptions of native populations. Like Bougainville, Cook made it part of his duty as a reporter to play the role of amateur ethnographer. It is, he notes, "my duty as well as inclination to insert in this Journal every and the least knowledge I may obtain of a people who for many centuries have been shut up from almost every other part of the world" (*Endeavour*, p. 134). In its relative systematicity and precision, the amount of information he records goes a long way beyond the casual impressions of the vast majority of previous travel writings.

At another level of knowledge production, Cook reveals himself to be an outstanding naval officer who records in detail all those factors which contributed to the success of his voyage, from the design of the ship and its fitting-out to the diet and the health of the crew. He reports on the maintenance and repair work carried out during the course of the voyage and on the difficulties of navigating a sailing ship through uncharted waters, difficulties that almost ended in disaster in the area of the Great Barrier Reef.

In the context of the ship's company and passengers, Cook was not only the commander, who was ultimately responsible for the success of the voyage and who himself prepared the expedition with the greatest of care for all aspects of the ship's performance, he was also the chief military officer and political representative of his king and country. And in this capacity he proved himself to be fully conscious of the interests of his maritime and trading nation. The success of the expedition demanded a tradition of professionalism and disciplined service. It is no accident, therefore, that it was carried out in a Royal Navy ship under the command of a Royal Navy officer.

Given the difficulty, time, and expense of such expeditions, it is also not surprising if both the government and the scientific community of the day sought to achieve maximum benefit and obtain knowledge of manifold aspects of the physical world, its plants and creatures, as well as of unknown and potentially exploitable territories and their human inhabitants. Further, in 1768 the question of whether or not a southern continent existed, as opposed to islands and more or less isolated land masses, had still not been resolved, and another goal of the the voyage was to shed light on that matter. Was there a *terra australis nondum incognita* that balanced in the Southern Hemisphere the *terra septemprionalis incognita* which stretched across the northern part of the globe? Once India and the East Indies had to a large extent yielded to European penetration, even the remote prospect of being the first to discover a new New World gave some urgency among European nations to all such voyages of exploration in the South Pacific.

With Cook as with Bougainville, then, we encounter complexly motivated, collective travel of a peculiarly arduous and prolonged kind. The story the British captain tells is of a voyage of almost three years under very difficult conditions in a surprisingly small, highly efficient, lightly armed, and heavily laden ship—the *Endeavour* was fewer than one hundred feet long, had a crew of ninety-four men (including twelve marines), and carried eleven civilians. The world of Cook's ship in that age of sail was a complex, hierarchical, and largely self-supporting community characterized by a marked division of labor. Cook and his ship's company constituted, in fact, a complex recording apparatus and knowledge-producing machine, whose explorations were supported by a military code of discipline and, when necessary, by firepower. Yet, that does not mean that the response of the individuals themselves to their various encounters was uniform.

Something of the complexity of the sailing machine itself is suggested by journal entries that report on shipboard life. Although mostly outward-looking, the focus of Cook's observation is occasionally inward, on the time and the circumstances within which the instance of narration was itself situated. Entries report, as a matter of record, on the routines and incidents of shipboard life and thereby constitute brief vignettes of eighteenth-century British attitudes and practices in a number of

spheres. One finds, for example, comments on food and disease, flog-
gings, burials at sea, and even a singular episode in which a drunken
sailor has his clothes and part of his ears cut off by his mates as a practical
joke. The latter is one of those cultural anecdotes passed down to us from
the dead of the kind Robert Darnton has focused on in the title essay of
The Great Cat Massacre. It reminds us through its oddness of how different our ancestors were from us.[22]

Like Bougainville, however, Cook is nowhere more informative of
mid-eighteenth-century cultural practices and beliefs than when he records his impressions of native populations and the British expedition's
dealings with them,[23] in his references to the climactic and cultural environment of native life in the South Seas, and in his overt political acts
and comments on economic activity. It is in this sphere in particular that
the ambiguity of Cook's mission from its inception appears most obviously. Even though he took his orders from the Admiralty in London,
his expedition was also under the sponsorship of the Royal Society. And
it was from both these august bodies, from the principal instrument of
Britain's imperial power and from the preeminent scientific society of the
age, that he received instructions on how to approach natives. The Admiralty is brief and straightforward in instructing him to observe their
"Genius, Temper, Disposition and Number" and to "endeavour by all
proper means to cultivate a Friendship and Alliance with them, making
them presents of such Trifles as they may Value, inviting them to Traf-
fick, and Shewing them every kind of Civility and Regard" (*Art*, p. 2).
Viewed from the perspective of the late twentieth century, such a discourse appears transparently duplicitous: a generalized humanitarianism
and a civilized correctness do not exclude the intention of taking advantage of native gullibility in order to prepare future useful alliances.

On the other hand, the "Hints" on the same subject drawn up by James
Douglas, the president of the Royal Society, for the benefit of Captain
Cook and his colleagues, constitute a nobler and more forthright document of Enlightenment humanism in that it acknowledges a common humanity under God. Douglas, in effect, emphasizes the fundamental inequality of the power relations between Europeans and natives. He
underlines the responsibility of the former in preventing bloodshed and

[22] See "Workers Revolt: The Great Cat Massacre of the Rue Saint-Severin," in *The
Great Cat Massacre and Other Episodes in French Cultural History* (New York: Vintage
Books, 1985).
[23] Rudiger Joppien and Bernard Smith note that "drawings and paintings, . . . illus-
trating encounters between Cook's men and the indigenous peoples of the Pacific,
came to constitute one of the significant categories that occupied Cook's artists." *The
Art of Captain Cook's Voyages*, vol. 1: *The Voyage of the Endeavour, 1768–1771* (New Haven: Yale University Press, 1985), p. 10.

recognizes the natives' political right to their homelands. Thus, he urges the officers and gentlemen of the *Endeavour*:

> To exercise the utmost patience and forbearance with respect to the Natives of the several Lands where the Ship may touch.
>
> To check the petulance of the Sailors, and restrain the wanton use of Fire Arms.
>
> To have it still in view that sheding the blood of those people is a crime of the highest nature:—They are human creatures, the work of the same omnipotent Author, equally under his care with the most polished European; perhaps being less offensive, more entitled to his favor.
>
> They are the natural, and in the strictest sense of the word, the legal possessors of the several Regions they inhabit.
>
> No European Nation has a right to occupy any part of their country, or settle among them without their voluntary consent.
>
> Conquest over such people can give no just title; because they could never be the Aggressors. [*Endeavour*, p. 514]

Cook clearly remained mindful of the responsibilities laid upon him by these two, potentially contradictory sets of directives in his subsequent relations with native populations. And on those occasions when, for one reason or another, firearms were used and lives taken, he takes care to justify the action as some form of self-defense or even on occasion to condemn it.[24]

In this connection, the tone of Cook's journal becomes apparent in his first description of a native people: namely, those same Indians of Tierra del Fuego whom Bougainville had found so unprepossessing. It is characteristic that Cook gives a more objective account of their physique and way of life: "They are something above the Middle size of a dark copper Colour with long black hair, they paint their bodies in Streakes mostly Red and Black, their cloathing consists wholly of Guanacoes skin or that of a Seal, in the same form as it came from the Animals back, the Women wear a piece of skin over their privey parts but the men Observe no such decency" (*Endeavour*, pp. 44–45).

When one compares this brief and sober description not only with Bougainville's account of the miserable condition of the inhabitants of Tierra del Fuego but also with Alexander Buchan's gouache painting, the contrast is striking. The painting in particular emphasizes the sheer

---

[24] Cook is, however, much less upset than the Quaker Sydney Parkinson by the first shooting incident on Tahiti: "A boy, a midshipman, was the commanding officer, and, giving orders to fire, they obeyed with the greatest glee imaginable, as if they had been shooting at wild ducks, killed one stout man, and wounded many others." *Endeavour*, p. 80, n. 2.

brutishness and state of deprivation of a group of people draped in skins
and crouched around a wood fire in a rudimentary hut, one of whom
seems to find no immodesty in virtually exposing his genitalia. Moreover,
the transformation to which Buchan's work was subjected by the history
painter G. B. Cipriani for the engraving of Hawkesworth's *Voyages* is one
of the most notorious examples of the impact of taste and ideology on
representation. As Smith indicates, the addition of two figures in particular "transformed the state of miserable wretchedness depicted by
Buchan into the state of primitive elegance imagined by Hawkesworth.
The transformation is helped greatly by the introduction of a landscape
setting—a Claudean tree in the foreground, Salvator Rosa's rocks and
knotty branches, and the mountainous background together represent
the state of untamed nature as Rousseau and Fénelon conceived it."[25]

Cook offers nothing comparable to Bougainville's evocative description of his arrival in Tahiti, but in the course of the journal entries that
cover his three-month' stay on that island, there emerges a portrait of the
people which corroborates and extends many of the findings Bougainville reported after his stay of three weeks. Cook describes them as
friendly and easygoing and for the most part willing to trade island produce, especially for the more useful products of European civilization.
However, like Bougainville, he finds their habit of systematically picking
pockets and pilfering not only trying but, in the end, damaging to good
relations between the two peoples—when the quadrant is stolen with
which the British intended to observe the transit of Venus, Cook takes a
chief hostage until it is returned.

Cook also comments on the behavior and apparent attitudes of the Tahitians in matters of sexual relations without, however, giving them as
much prominence as his French predecessor or in any way mythifying
the island. Such comments appear, like almost everything else that is interesting in the journal, under the order of the notable, coming under
such titles as "Remarkable Occurrences" or "Description of." Thus, in
what is virtually his first reference to sexual customs, Cook reports with
wonderful understatement on the arrival of a man and two women,
"whose manner of introduceing themselves was a little uncommon" (*Endeavour*, p. 92). One of the two women ceremoniously disrobes before the
eyes of the astonished British sailors: "with as much Innocency as one
could possibly conceve, [she] expose'd herself intirely naked from the
waist downwards" (*Endeavour*, p. 93).

Perhaps the most remarkable thing about the entry, however, is Cook's

[25] See *Vision*, p. 40. For a comprehensive account of illustrations in eighteenth-cen-
tury travel writing, see Barbara Maria Stafford's important book *Voyage into Substance:
Art, Science, Nature, and the Illustrated Travel Account, 1760–1840* (Cambridge: MIT
Press, 1984).

absence of comment. For whatever reason, he did not feel called upon to condemn or even explain such behavior, nor does he try to recuperate it through reference to European myth. On another occasion, Cook follows a reference to the conduct of their own Sunday service with the evocation of a scene "where a young fellow about 6 feet high lay with a little Girl of about 10 or 12 years of age publickly before several of our people and a number of the Natives." This time he adds soberly that "it appear'd to be done more from Custom than Lewdness" (*Endeavour*, pp. 93–94). On the other hand, Cook does feel called upon to condemn both a dance performed by prepubescent girls—"a very indecent dance which they call *Timorodee* [copulation] singing most indecent songs and useing most indecent actions"—and what he perceives as a form of free love that is followed by infanticide whenever a birth occurs—"a Custom so inhuman and contrary to the first principals of human nature" (*Endeavour*, pp. 127–128).

Although, for the most part, Cook avoids mythic imagery in his representations, in one important respect Cook's Tahiti does, in fact, recall "the soft primitives" of classical mythology—as opposed to "the hard primitives" Hawkesworth was determined to find in Tierra del Fuego. The island's climate, soil, and vegetation are such that it supplies virtually all fundamental human needs in abundance and at very little cost in human labor: "in the article of food these people may be said to be exempt from the curse of our fore fathers: scarcely can it be said that they earn their bread with the sweet of their brow, benevolent nature hath not only supply'd them with necessarys but with abundance of superfluities."

On this occasion, as on others, Cook's description becomes a purple passage in spite of itself; the catalogue of the island's produce manages to suggest the sensuous ripeness it represents—and not simply because the exoticisms of Cook's eighteenth-century syntax, spelling, and capitalization and his use of foreign words foreground his language poetically: "The produce of this Island is Bread fruit, cocoa-nuts, Bananoes, Plaintains, a fruit like an apple, sweet Potatoes, yams, a fruit known by the name Eag Melloa and reckoned most delicious, Sugar cane which the inhabitants eat raw, a root of the Salop kind call'd by the inhabitants Pea, the root also of a plant call'd Ethee and a fruit in a Pod like a Kidney bean which when roasted eats like a chestnut and is call'd Ahee" (*Endeavour*, pp. 120–121). Given the limited diet of contemporary North Europeans in the eighteenth century, such exotic fruitfulness must have seemed even more paradisical.

Diderot's *Supplement* bore witness to the impact on a philosophe of Bougainville's evocation of apparent prelapsarian life. And Cook's representations are just as provocative in this respect. He even goes on to conclude that the inhabitants of the island largely live up to the standards set by their benevolent environment. The physique, attitudes, manners, and personal hygiene of Tahitians of both sexes are found admirable: "They have all fine white teeth and for the most part short flat noses and thick lips, yet their features are agreeable and their gate gracefull, and their behaviour to each other is open affable and courtious" (*Endeavour*, p. 124). At the same time, he discovers much that is impressive in their arts and crafts or the rituals of their social life, describing in turn the construction of their houses, canoes, tools, weapons, and cloth and the different techniques they employ in all these spheres.

Finally, Cook pays some attention to Tahitian political and religious life and to their funerary rites. The *marae*, or sacred sites, turn out to be of special significance because Cook finds there skulls and jawbones as well as corpses and skeletons. But it is here that he is led to raise questions about such darker aspects of Tahitian life as their conduct of warfare, the treatment of prisoners, and the possibility that they committed human sacrifice and even ritual cannibalism. Cook, in fact, has to be regarded as one of those who have given an "eyewitness account" of a practice that remains controversial among anthropologists, even though he did not apparently see the butchering or actual ingestion of human flesh: "Soon after we landed we met with two or three of the Natives who not long before must have been regailing themselves upon human flesh, for I got from one of them the bone of the fore arm of a Man or a Woman which was quite fresh and the flesh had been but lately pick'd off which they told us they had eat" (*Endeavour*, p. 236). The effect of such a description was, in any case, even more disturbing than that of the classical topos *Et in Arcadia Ego*, since it seemed to confirm the existence of barbaric practices and thereby reinforced the contemporary European tendency to collapse the original neutral sense of "native" into "savage and heathen"—an attitude that would subsequently justify Christianizing interventions in the South Seas. Tahiti, it seemed, was after all no more than a "tainted paradise."[26]

Nothing seems to have fascinated Cook more, however, than the Polynesian custom of body painting or tattooing. And he takes up some space describing the technique used, the quality of the designs (he shows himself particularly impressed with the art of the New Zealand natives) and their placement—there is great diversity on Tahiti, except that "all agree in having their buttocks cover'd with a deep black, over this most have arches drawn one over a[n]other as high as their short ribs which are near a quarter of an Inch broad; these arches seem to be their great pride

[26] See *Vision*, p. 49. According to Smith and Joppien, it was precisely Parkinson's "marae drawings, with the associated funerary practices, that came to exercise, of all his work, perhaps the most telling effect on the European imagination." *Art*, p. 32.

as both men and women show them with great pleasure" (*Endeavour*, p. 125). The precision of his observations suggests that Cook himself looked with some pleasure at this body art. In any case, the fetishistic value for the Tahitians of these tattooed "arches" rising above the buttocks seems to be confirmed by the eagerness with which they put this painted area of their anatomy on display.

This is corroborated in an interesting way by what is perhaps the most celebrated of all the pictorial representations to be brought back from Cook's various voyages: namely, William Hodges's *Oaitepeha Bay*, also called *Tahiti Revisited*, which was painted during the voyage of the *Resolution* (see Frontispiece). As Smith points out in his detailed analysis of it, the painting manages to combine neoclassical elements of composition with a more original capacity to render effects of atmosphere and light. It resolves in its own way the contradiction between the connoisseur's taste for the classical picturesque and documentary faithfulness to the difference of tropical landscape.[27]

It is particularly suggestive in the context of the present study, however, because it manages to encapsulate in a single, memorable image the idea of a "tainted paradise" referred to above. It combines the qualities of what in the landscape design of the period was known as "an expressive garden"—i.e., one that suggests a mood—with the emblematic devices that constituted points of interest. Along with the grandeur of the natural scenery, the elegant lushness of the vegetation, and the golden light, Hodges also locates in the bottom right-hand corner of his painting the silhouette of a pagan idol and the Tahitian equivalent of classical nymphs. A generalized exotic sublime contains an unexpected but fantasmatic point of interest. What for the eighteenth century was the negative face of Tahiti is made graphic in the threat of dark divinities and a pair of female buttocks that are not neoclassically smooth and bare, but are partly splayed and presented to the spectator's gaze in order to emphasize the prominent tatoo. Against that paradisical background this composition within a composition becomes, as it were, an objective correlative for wanton desire. In any case, the fetishistic charge communicated by the tattooing of certain body parts could hardly be rendered more directly than by the painting of a prominent pattern in the place of lack and setting it against an erect and darkly knotted phallic idol.

Moreover, no images that were brought back from the voyage of the

[27] In discussing the development of Sydney Parkinson from an illustrator of natural history into a landscape painter, Joppien and Smith also comment on his mixed results in the sphere of visual representation: "Most of his work in the Society Islands is of a hybrid character: it adopts a picturesque mode of composition, which is used to enframe new information gathered about the terrain and vegetation of the islands and the manners and customs of the inhabitants." *Art*, p. 26.

Endeavour are more arresting or have been reproduced more frequently than Sydney Parkinson's tattooed heads of Maori warriors. Cook's prose does not attempt to render the impression of weird symmetry and mysterious power that Parkinson's engravings communicate. It is difficult to imagine anything more alien to eighteenth-century European culture and aesthetic values, in fact, than the strange geometry and indecipherable hieroglyphs of these blackened faces, which are further adorned with long pendants, earrings, plumes, and combs. And those Europeans raised in a Protestant tradition were likely to be particularly troubled by what amounted to a defilement of faces and bodies held to be made in God's own image and by a startling propensity toward personal adornment. Tattooing, in short, had all the characteristics that one was likely to associate with a demonic art. Under the circumstances, the recorded reactions of Cook and his companions, like those of Bougainville, were surprisingly mild.

Furthermore, by the end of his prolonged contact with the natives of Australia ("New Holland"), Cook permits himself a rare comparative judgment in which he associates himself for once with the European champions of "primitivism": "From what I have said of the Natives of New-Holland they may appear to some to be the most wretched people upon Earth, but in reality they are far more happier than we Europeans; being wholy unacquainted not only with the superfluous but the necessary Conveniences so much sought after in Europe, they are happy in not knowing the use of them. They live in a Tranquillity which is not disturb'd by the Inequality of Condition" (*Endeavour*, p. 399).

If at such moments Cook reminds us that he was a man of the Enlightenment able to maintain a certain critical distance from that European civilization which made his voyage and his observations possible, he was also the armed emissary of a mercantile power that was becoming accustomed to its imperial role in the world. The British philosophe in him has no trouble cohabiting with the naval officer whose mission involves not only charting unexplored areas of the southern seas but also searching out opportunities for trade, taking possession of previously undiscovered territories, and prospecting for the sites of future British colonies.

The east coast of Australia, for example, leaves him heady with a kind of collective desire at the thought of what might be produced if it were to be colonized by an industrious people with a knowledge of agriculture: "We are to Consider that we see this Country in the pure state of Nature, the Industry of Man has had nothing to do with any part of it and yet we find all such things as nature hath bestow'd upon it in a flourishing state" (*Endeavour*, p. 397).

Given the promise contained in such passages of the good life under gentler climes, it is no wonder that the impulse to establish colonies took hold in Northern Europe and that, after the loss of their North American colonies, the British were drawn to the Southern Hemisphere. Before opposition to the whole concept of empire and colonization began to be formulated, at around the time of the American Revolution, there was, as Cook's words suggest, little trace of embarrassment in advocating the establishment of settlements overseas that remained in many ways dependent on the motherland. Whether they were absolutist or constitutional monarchies, *ancien régime* European societies were more flattered than disturbed in looking to the *imperium romanum* as their model.

It was in such a frame of mind that Cook, like other European voyagers, including Bougainville, frequently made it his practice to lay claim to various territories on behalf of the British crown, whether they were inhabited or uninhabited. In the most important instances, the claim was solemnized by a formal act of taking possession of which the ceremony performed at Queen Charlotte's Sound is typical: "After I had prepared the way for setting up the post we took it up to the highest part of the Island and after fixing it fast in the ground hoisted thereon the Union flag and I dignified this Inlet with the name of *Queen Charlottes Sound* and took formal possession of it and the adjacent lands in the name and for the use of his Majesty, we then drank Her Majestys hilth in a Bottle of wine and gave the empty bottle to the old man (who had attended us up the hill) with which he was highly pleased" (*Endeavour*, p. 243).

One does not have to be a very sophisticated modern reader to read into this episode a cynical parody of exchange in which vast virgin territory in New Zealand was acquired at less cost by Europeans than the legendary purchase of Manhattan by the Dutch. Yet, in an age that antedated modern colonialism, if not colonies, not all the innocence is on the side of the elderly Maori with the empty wine bottle. In spite of some equivocation, there is evidence here and throughout Cook's journal of a kind of naive and paternalistic good faith that relations between Europeans and native peoples might be equitable and mutually beneficial in spite of the imbalance of power.

The other characteristic element in the ritual taking possession quoted above is in the act of naming. If there is something of the seductive magic of biblical beginnings and of quasi-divine omnipotence in Captain Cook's imposition of names on tracts of earth that still had for Europeans, if not necessarily for their inhabitants, an edenic freshness, it is impossible in our time to ignore the fact that nomination is a form of action and that, in this case, it is a specifically political form of action. Thus, there is a heady sense of power of the kind we associate with *conquistadores* in the way in which Cook on occasion sails along a coastline, more or less randomly fixing topographic features with a name that calls them into discursive existence in the English language under British hegemony.

o   o   o

The Voyage of the Endeavour is without doubt an important form of travel writing, but it is not the kind literary intellectuals usually have in mind when they think about the subject, the kind that became increasingly popular from the romantic period on and achieved the status of a minor literary genre. Cook's journals belong rather to the category of historical documents of great interest to various kinds of historians or to those social scientists whose professional work relates to some of the areas that he reported on. And he himself clearly had no literary ambitions of a traditional kind.

Yet, even from the point of view of its content, although there is an enormous amount that is now of an arid kind of documentary interest— I am thinking particularly of Cook's nautical observations—his journals are also peculiarly rich in the kind of material that heroic narratives of sea voyages and visits to remote places have been made of, from *The Odyssey* to *Moby Dick, Treasure Island, Lord Jim* and, as I will suggest below, *Argonauts of the Western Pacific.* Moreover, Cook himself, with the help of his "martyr's death" in Hawaii, was to be celebrated as one of the heroic adventurers of the British imperial tradition.

At the same time, there are a great many passages of his journals in which a modern reader is likely to encounter some of those multiple textual excitements or pleasures of the text that we have come to associate with the category of "the literary," as defined above. At times consciously and at others apparently not, the professional sailor and amateur observer's text escapes the constraints of the logbook and the catalogue and displays its richly hybrid character.

Something of this is already suggested in the journal's subtitle, *Remarkable Occurences on Board His Majestys Bark Endeavour.* If a modern reader is responsive to this line, it is because he is sensitive to the feature of language Roman Jakobson first called "the message" and associated with "the poetic function."[28] The formal, archaic English attracts attention to itself as language and connotes a voyage into eighteenth-century Europe that is almost as exotic as the ocean voyage itself. The two hundred years between Cook's writing of his journal and our reading it have, in fact, made his language resonant with associations not available to a reader of his own time.

Nowhere does this appear more clearly than in the variety of Cook's eighteenth-century spelling and in the frequent capitalization of his nouns. Words and phrases such as "opposission," "Munkey," "weapons of Warr," "enterr the Body," "these people not only beleive in a Supream

---

[28] See "Closing Statement: Linguistics and Poetics," in *Style in Language,* ed. T. Sebeok (Cambridge: MIT Press, 1971).

being but in a futerue state also," "Shade" for "Shed" in a context of funerary rites, "more Custom than Lewdness," "Antiscorbutick," and the memorable "Sour Krout" oblige us to attend to their materiality as signifiers; the written word loses its apparent transparency and becomes palpable, the cognitive or referential function yields to the poetic—which is also a way of saying that it destabilizes itself as discourse in Edward Said's sense.[29] A reader raised in the modernist tradition in literature discovers in Cook's "misspellings" and capitalizations the pleasures of solecism of a kind that Joyce in particular taught us to enjoy, and Freud to interrogate; such distortions subvert the production of meaning and engage the punning play of semiosis. At such moments, not only does a professional sailor's journal become "a text," but one also understands the risk that, according to Robert Darnton, historians are subject to in their explorations of the past: namely, that of being "won over by the otherness of others."[30]

In another important way, too, *The Voyage of the Endeavour* turns out to subvert its own authority as objective reportage. As noted above, a journey inevitably becomes a narrative in its telling, no matter how much it seeks to classify and render its material static, because it involves movement through space in chronological time, one thing after the other. And in the case of Cook's work there are a great many passages that not only have the episodic character of narrative in general, but that clearly find their models in the literature of heroic adventure. Captain Cook is what Gérard Genette has called an "autodiegetic narrator." That is to say, he is a narrator who participates in the action of the story he tells as its principal protagonist. And numerous passages are calculated to record the steadfastness of himself and his men when faced with hostile natives or the great dangers of the voyage. Such passages from Cook and from other heroes of the British imperial tradition were to furnish models for conduct in the face of danger that, in many circles, even managed to survive the First World War.

Cook's taste for narrative appears most clearly, however, in his account of the *Endeavour* running aground off the northeast coast of Australia and the subsequent attempts to extricate it from the extremely dangerous area of the Great Barrier Reef—something that was achieved only by dint of extraordinary qualities of seamanship. For the great majority of the time, Cook's descriptions of land and sea, flora and fauna, native populations, their customs and artifacts, are wonderfully functional and precise; they are also mostly nonpicturesque and nonheroic. On such occasions as the episode off the Great Barrier Reef, however, it is as if the tension of their struggle for survival with the forces of the wind, sea, and

[29] *Orientalism* (New York: Vintage Books, 1978).
[30] See Introduction, n. 20, above.

rocks off northeastern Australia moved Cook for once to reach for a stylistic level that, in the light of the action involved, one might even call
"Homeric":

> We had at this time not an air of wind and the depth of the water
> was unfathomable so that there was not a possibility of Anchoring,
> in this distressed situation we had nothing but Providence and the
> small Assistance our boats could give us to trust in. . . . the same Sea
> that washed the sides of the Ship rose in a breaker prodigiously high
> the very next time it did rise so that between us and distruction was
> only a dismal Vally the breadth of one wave and even now no
> ground could be felt with 120 fathoms. . . . A Reef such is here spoke
> of is scarcely known in Europe, it is a wall of Coral Rock rising all
> most perpendicular out of the unfathomable Ocean, always over-
> flown at high-water generally 7 or 8 feet and dry in places at low-
> water; the large waves of the vast Ocean meeting with so sudden a
> resistance make a most terrible surf breaking mountains high. [*En-
> deavour*, pp. 377–378]

Both Bougainville's and Cook's accounts make very explicit the strong
contrast between the kind of risk and high adventure faced by the eighteenth-century circumnavigators of the globe and the mere discomforts
and inconveniences of intra-European travel. Yet, even though an enlightened eighteenth-century European might as a consequence be more
inclined to celebrate the advantages of European civilization, the well-
documented testimony of the voyagers obliged once again a reconsider-
ation of the material and human dimensions of the globe and Europe's
place in it. In the eighteenth as in the sixteenth century, the reports of
world travelers on previously unexplored regions had something of the
effect of shaking a global kaleidoscope. If, in the decades following the
discovery of the New World at the end of the fifteenth century, there
occurred a major displacement of Europe's idea of itself, something similar took place on a smaller scale with the opening up of the Pacific to the
more or less informed gaze of a new breed of explorers.

Whether or not the intra-European travelers still regarded Rome as
the historical center of something called European civilization, as the sacred site of an origin, they also sometimes looked for alternatives within
the European tradition of social and political thought. Yet, neither England nor Holland, for example, had the capacity to reactivate age-old
myths in the same way as the South Pacific. After a visit to Tahiti, Rome
or such eighteenth-century imperial surrogates as Paris or London would
never seem the same again. Tahiti proved to be the most disturbing of
Others, the one most calculated to challenge the self-confidence of a cultural tradition. Less ambiguously than the various Indian peoples of the

Paul Gauguin, *Where Do We Come From? What Are We? Where Are We Going?*
Courtesy of the Museum of Fine Arts, Boston.

American continent, Tahiti promoted the dream of alternative modes of existence that were freer and happier, and that were supported by more natural social arrangements. One island, at least, had been found that stirred racial memories of a lost mythic paradise and confirmed the powerful thought that perhaps humanity had, after all, taken a wrong turn.

The questions that go unformulated as such by the circumnavigators who made the earliest European contacts with Tahiti and its inhabitants were expressed at the very end of the nineteenth century by another European traveler in search of a lost paradise. The title of one of the most monumental and most mysterious paintings that Gauguin brought back from his visits to the South Sea islands is precisely *D'où venons-nous? Que sommes-nous? Où allons-nous? (Where Do We Come From? What Are We? Where Are We Going?)* Such questions are the kind that come to be raised "in the field" through the surprise of an encounter with radical otherness. As Karl Mannheim once put it in a discussion of the emergence of the critical intellectual, "The question, 'Who are we?,' has always been asked, but it is always through the medium of different objects that such questions are faced. Man hardly ever wonders about himself unless he is confronted with things or situations. . . . We understand ourselves primarily through the views of others."[31] And I take that last phrase in the original German to be a subjective as well as an objective genitive; that is, through the viewing as well as the being viewed.

[31] "The Problem of the Intelligentsia," in *Essays in the Sociology of Culture* (London: Routledge, 1956), p. 92.

PART TWO

Romantic Transgressions

Chapter IV

TRAVEL FOR TRAVEL'S SAKE:
STENDHAL

As Charles L. Batten, Jr., shows in connection with English travel writing, by the end of the eighteenth century the compromise implied by the notion of "pleasurable instruction" had begun to break down.[1] The quest for novelty and the emergence of a new interest in nature led in particular to self-consciously literary forms of writing in which the kind of useful information associated with guidebooks, encyclopedias, or the wide-ranging observations of travelers like Smollett, Diderot, and Arthur Young assumes a smaller and smaller place. From the turn of the century, the focus of some of the most memorable works in the field is on the evocative verbal representation of scenes and the intensity of the traveler's experience. Pleasure, albeit of a supposedly higher form, overwhelms the demand for instruction.

Nowhere is this more apparent than in the emergence of the concept of the picturesque and of picturesque travel. In a work first published in 1792, *Three Essays: On Picturesque Beauty; on Picturesque Travel; and on Sketching Landscape: with a Poem on Landscape Painting,*[2] William Gilpin explains how "picturesque beauty" is to be "pursued" throughout nature: "We seek it among all the ingredients of landscape—trees—rocks—broken-grounds—woods—rivers—lakes—plains-vallies—mountains—and—distances" (*Three Essays*, p. 42). And in a self-consciously eroticized imagery he goes on to explain the sharpness of the pleasures of scopophilia in the eye, "the picturesque eye," that has been taught how to focus its look. There are references to "agreeable suspense," to "the love of novelty," to the "gratification," after the pursuit, of "the attainment of the object" (*Three Essays*, p. 48). The purpose of picturesque travel, Gilpin makes clear, is in a form of "high delight" that overwhelms the autonomous ego: "some grand scene strikes us beyond the power of thought. . . . In this pause of intellect; this *deliquium* of the soul; an enthusiastic sensation of pleasure overspreads it, previous to any examination by the rules of art" (*Three Essays*, pp. 49–50). Looking here has become an end in itself: no further satisfaction is desired, no gain in

[1] *Pleasurable Instruction: Form and Convention in Eighteenth-Century Travel Literature* (Berkeley: University of California Press, 1978).

[2] (London: Cadell and Davis, 1808).

knowledge claimed. The goal of picturesque travel is to come upon "pictures" in nature that induce a sensation of rapture or ravishment. The theorists of "art for art's sake" in the nineteenth century were to do little more than substitute "artistic" for "natural beauty" as the object of the gaze in their own artistic credo.

The focus at such moments is, in any case, on the encounter between the aroused individual psyche and those features of the natural world that speak to it in mysterious ways. In Gilpin's reflections on travel one recognizes elements of the discourse associated with European romanticism, the discourse that informed the poetry and fiction of writers from Rousseau and Goethe through Byron, Wordsworth, Shelley, Chateaubriand, Lamartine, and Victor Hugo. Shelley and others in the Alps, Wordsworth and others in the Lake District, were inspired in their poetry to celebrate grandiose natural scenes in many ways similar to contemporary travel writers.

The poet who was for many one of the most influential of his time and who, in effect, invented a new form of "travel poetry" was, however, Byron. This is in part because he, too, cultivated the picturesque, and thereby demonstrated that poetry was capable of representing passionate encounters with both natural and artistic beauty in ways beyond the reach of prose:

> We gaze and turn away, and know not where,
> Dazzled and drunk with beauty, till the heart
> Reels with its fulness . . .[3]

At least as important is the fact that in *Childe Harold's Pilgrimage* a recognizably new attitude to travel is given narrative form, and a new kind of traveler is delineated in the form of the romantic rebel. What Jurij Lotman takes to be the transgressive character of plotted narratives in general—"The structure of the world faces the hero as a system of prohibitions, a hierarchy of boundaries which it is forbidden to cross"[4]— emerges with a new obviousness in romantic travel writing. The "dynamic hero" does cross the forbidden frontier.

It is, in fact, with Byron that my book catches up with my first epigraph: "The only true travelers are those who leave / For leaving's sake." For Baudelaire's midcentury narrative poem, "Le Voyage," clearly owed an important debt to the author of *Childe Harold*. Not least because both poets celebrate the separation from home and homeland, thematizing the pursuit of intense and novel forms of experience at or beyond the

[3] References are to *The Poetical Works of Lord Byron* (London: Oxford University Press, 1930).

[4] *Semiotics of Cinema*, trans. Mark E. Suino (Ann Arbor: University of Michigan Press, 1976), p. 65.

pleasure principle and culturally prescribed limits, often at great risk to the self-conserving ego.[5]

In this context, the case of Stendhal as travel writer is a complex and illuminating one. On the one hand, only exceptionally does he follow Byron's example in practicing the art of the picturesque as such. On the other hand, the pursuit of intensely pleasurable experiences—*la chasse au bonheur*—is just as important a motif of his travel writings as it is of his fiction. Also, from the beginning, they are premised on a form of rebellion; and, as with the English poet, overt references to a resistance to oedipalization are woven into a commentary on the European political situation in post-Napoleonic Europe.

In certain respects, the models for Stendhal's works in the genre are to be found in the eighteenth century, in Sterne's *Sentimental Journey* and De Brosses's *Italian Journey*: Sterne because he "interested his heart in everything"[6] and openly associated continental travel with sexual pleasure, and De Brosses because of his spontaneity, wit, general stance of tolerant openness, and fondness for piquant anecdotes. Yet, the way Stendhal transcends such models—especially that of his countryman De Brosses, who was in many ways closer to him—is important for an understanding of the transgressive character that travel writing frequently came to assume in the romantic age.[7] The egotism decried by eighteenth-century critics of contemporary travel literature finds its unembarrassed celebrant in Stendhal.

In one of the many brilliant passages of a work that in other ways now appears stranded by history, *Ou'est-ce que la littérature?* (*What is Literature?*), Sartre characterizes the French nineteenth-century writer as *déclassé* upward in relation to the bourgeoisie of his time. He is, as a result, "a stranger to his century, displaced, *maudit*," and he comes in his own eyes to constitute a new kind of aristocracy. Sartre adds: "Beyond art itself, he finds nobility in only three kinds of occupations. First, in love because it is a useless passion and because women are, as Nietzsche said, the most dangerous of games. In travel, too, because the traveler is a

---

[5] As the imagery of the following lines confirm, *Childe Harold*'s narrator is explicit on the subject: "Apart he stalk'd in joyless reveries, / And from his native land resolved to go, / And visit scorching climes beyond the sea; / With pleasure drugg'd, he almost longed for woe, / And e'en for change of scene would seek the shades below" (Canto I, IV).

[6] (London: J. M. Dent, 1967), p. 30.

[7] Some of the material in this section appeared in "Politics, Happiness, and the Arts: A Commentary on Stendhal's *Rome, Naples et Florence en 1817*," *French Studies* 24 (July 1970) and "Reinventing Travel," *Genre* 16 (Winter 1983). My colleague William M. Johnston has adopted the interesting tactic of focusing on the responses of travel writers to specific sites: *In Search of Italy: Foreign Writers in Northern Italy since 1800* (University Park: Pennsylvania State University Press, 1987).

perpetual witness, who moves from one society to another without ever staying in any, and because, as a foreign consumer in a collectivity at work, he is the very image of parasitism. Sometimes, finally, in war, because war involves a huge consumption of men and goods."[8] In many ways, it seems that Sartre might have had Stendhal in mind, were it not for the fact that so many other writers in the course of the nineteenth century might have fitted such a description even more closely. Nevertheless, the passage is a highly suggestive opening for a consideration of the role travel was to play in Stendhal's life and writings.

o   o   o

STENDHAL'S first travel book, *Rome, Naples et Florence en 1817*,[9] appeared between the publication of the first two cantos of *Childe Harold* and the last two, at a time when its author had already paid several visits to Italy, beginning with his triumphal crossing of the Alps in the wake of Napoleon's army in 1800. The idea of writing yet another book on Italy based on a journal kept during his two-and-a-half-month stay in 1811 seems to have first occurred to the author on his return from Russia in 1813. Yet, he did not complete the work until shortly before its publication in 1817.

If I draw attention to dates again, it is because, as in the case of *Childe Harold's Pilgrimage*, the years involved were of particular historical moment. The European political context, with the dominant figure of Napoleon at its center, overshadows Stendhal's narrative of his Italian journey. Between the time of his visit of 1811 and the final composition of the edition of 1817, there had occurred the watershed event of Waterloo. As a result, *Rome, Naples et Florence en 1817* offers an account of Italy that is based on the contrast *before* Waterloo and *after*, a contrast that gives as explicit a political character to his first travel book as is to be found in *Childe Harold*.

Stendhal's second exercise in the genre, *Promenades dans Rome*, did not appear until 1829, after Stendhal had been resident in Italy for many years. The contrast between the works of 1817 and 1829 is particularly instructive because, although Stendhal's political loyalties appear relatively unmodified in the latter volume, one finds there an attitude, if not of resignation, then at least of accommodation to life under political systems of an authoritarian, *ancien régime* style. Whereas the earlier work is written directly under the impact of historical events that had put an abrupt end to Stendhal's political hopes for the immediate future, *Promenades dans Rome* is a travel book that teaches the lessons of moral survival

[8] (Paris: Gallimard, 1948), pp. 158–159.
[9] References are to Henri Martineau's critical edition (Paris: Le Divan, 1956). I am not concerned here with the very different edition of the work published in 1826.

and of the pleasures of exile in times that were politically hard on someone of Stendhal's liberal convictions. It is thus, in its way, an early distil-
lation of that mixture of passion and of tough-minded, unreconcilable
wisdom to be found in the extraordinary *Charterhouse of Parma* of a decade later.

Byron was perhaps fortunate in the time and manner of his death. To
die heroically in 1824 as a recognized champion of Greek independence
was to live the revolutionary dream of universal emancipation to the end.
It was to avoid Stendhal's fate of having to learn accommodation to the
decades of reaction.

Stendhal's two Italian travel books are of special interest for a number
of reasons. In the first place, at a critical moment in the emergence of a
modern form of consciousness, they make both explicit and implicit connections between the development of an individual's pscyhic life and his
political commitments. The autobiographical *Life of Henry Brulard* would
date the emergence of the young Henri Beyle's sympathy for the revolutionary cause in the 1790s to an association between paternal tyranny
at home and the absolutist monarchy in the French state. Second, in one
of the most explicit evocations of the oedipal triangle by a pre-Freudian
writer, Stendhal was also to suggest there how a combination of hostility
to his father and passionate love for his mother, who died when he was
six, proved to be a powerful impetus to his departure from home at an
early age and to his pursuit of lost plenitude first in France and then
outside it.[10]

Finally, although Stendhal affirmed his belief in the libertarian cause
and in part sought satisfaction for his individual demands through the
collective solutions of politics, in his travel books as in his other writings
he resists the various dogmatisms of his age. Consequently, the idea of
the homogeneity of a period discourse has rarely been put to a sterner
test than in these texts, which are traversed not only by the author's desires and hates, but also by his resistances, doubts, and second thoughts.
Stendhal, as we know, aspired to an art of composition that was antithetical to art as traditionally conceived, to a "natural art," in fact. As a result,
he comes closer than any other writer discussed in this book, in his autobiographical and travel writings at least, to a form of barely edited free

[10] A celebrated passage from *The Life of Henry Brulard* expresses the oedipal moment
with characteristic decisiveness: "I wanted to cover my mother with kisses and didn't
want any clothes in the way. She loved me passionately and often kissed me; I returned
her kisses with such fire that she was often obliged to leave. I always wanted to kiss her
on the breast. Be good enough to remember that I lost her in childbirth when I was
barely seven years old." He goes on to note how her death initiated a new and painful
phase in his life: "It was then that my moral life began." *Œuvres intimes de Stendhal*
(Paris: Gallimard, 1955), pp. 26–27.

association that is both driven by desire and subject to the scrutiny of a skeptical intelligence after the fact. To read him is to encounter a writer who continually reopens a space of play both in the passions and ironies of his self-interrogating texts and in the making and remaking of a so-called identity in the world.

A decade before the appearance of his first novel, *Rome, Naples et Florence en 1817* proclaims its interest in a combination of issues that were to become the hallmark of Stendhal's fiction from its title page and its preface on. Politics, manners, the pursuit of happiness, and the role of the arts were what chiefly excited his attention in the Italy of the early Restoration period, and they would continue to do so until the end of his life. The fictitious name on the title page, "By M. de Stendhal, Cavalry Officer," is Henri Beyle's first public use of the famous Germanic pseudonym with which he was to be known in the world.

The motivation for the erasure of his French patronym has been discussed at length in Stendhal scholarship and is certainly not simple. Among its components, one has to include the refusal to be his father's son, the desire to cut a more worldly and cosmopolitan figure than is suggested by that plaintive, bourgeois Beyle (*bêler* = to bleat), and, finally, the need to mask an identity that in both France and Italy was politically suspect. The last-mentioned reason probably explains why, in the case of his 1817 travel book, he also gave himself a title and a military rank. The nationality and social position implied by "M. de Stendhal, Cavalry Officer" were calculated to reassure the police of all those authoritarian regimes with which the author was likely to come into contact in the course of his peregrinations north and south of the Alps.

Yet, any potentially censoring gaze that ventured beyond the title page to the brief preface would have been immediately discomfited. It is there that the author announces in a characteristically forthright and truculent way the direction given his book, largely in spite of himself, by the suspicious temper of the age. In affirming that music is the only art that is still alive in Italy, he, in effect, attributes its continuing vitality to the survival in that sphere alone of the benefits of a lost liberty that had once animated all forms of artistic creativity south of the Alps: "This divine fire was once upon a time ignited by liberty and the grand manners of the republics of the Middle Ages" (*1817*, p. 3).[11]

Stendhal then goes on to emphasize a progression that will be observable in his text, ostensibly in spite of himself; he moves from observations

[11] The most comprehensive general account of Stendhal's complex and passionate relationship with Italy is Michel Crouzet's *Stendhal et l'italianité: Essai de mythologie romantique* (Paris: Corti, 1982). Crouzet notes in his opening chapter that "there is, as the well-known but imperfect formula has it, a 'myth' of Italy in Stendhal, a set of desires of which Italy is the mirror and the support" (p. 2).

on music to comments on manners, evokes the relationship between manners and the forms of government responsible for producing them and, finally, comes to "the influence of one man on Italy." As an apparent concession to the censoring apparatus of the immediate post-Napoleonic reaction, the fallen emperor goes unnamed; but the theme of his crucial, revolutionary role in the Italian peninsula will prove to be one of the major themes of Stendhal's work.

The preface concludes with a sentence that encapsulates his insight into the way in which the revolutionary period and the empire marked a profound break in French historical continuity, a break that was visible by the time of the Restoration in a new form of politicized consciousness: "The melancholy star of our century is such that an author who merely wanted to enjoy himself, ends up darkening his picture with the gloomy tones of politics" (*1817*, p. 3). In spite of Stendhal's well-documented libertarian sympathies and his lifelong commitment to liberal political values, he implies here something like a nostalgia for the innocence of a prerevolutionary and apolitical mode of consciousness. "The sadness" widely associated with the nineteenth century from its early years is attributed by Stendhal to the loss as well as the gain embodied in the thoroughgoing politicization of social life.

His 1817 work proper opens with an entry whose date and place— "Berlin, 4 October, 1816"—are fictitious, like the itinerary throughout, but whose sentiments are expressive of the author's beliefs and establish his filiation with the Byronic model: "I open the letter which grants me four months' leave—I am transported with joy, my heart beats faster! How wild I still am at thirty! I shall see beautiful Italy, then. But I carefully hide my feelings from the Minister; eunuchs are in a permanent state of anger against libertines. I expect two months of hostility on my return. But this journey gives me too much pleasure; and who knows if the world will last another three weeks" (*1817*, p. 5). Along with the expressions of joy at sudden liberation and the provocative insouciance of this exclamatory prose, in the reference to castration one also finds the rebellious son's explcit challenge to paternal interdiction.

The contrast with Goethe's account of his departure from Germany in *The Italian Journey* is instructive. Although the thirty-seven-year-old German writer does leave without the Duke of Weimar's permission—"I slipped out of Carlbad at three in the morning, otherwise I would not have been allowed to leave"[12]—his flight is accompanied by powerful guilt feelings to friends, family and, above all, his duke. Moreover, he goes out of his way throughout the Italian tour to make sure he spends

[12] References are to the translation by W. H. Auden and Elizabeth Mayer, *The Italian Journey: 1786–1788* (San Francisco: North Point Press, 1982).

his time profitably. He even ends up reinterpreting his clandestine journey as a mission undertaken with the duke's belated blessing in the service of knowledge and *Bildung*—his own, his country's, and humanity's at
large.

If Goethe's Italian journey is repeatedly affirmed to be conducted under the sign of work and duty, Stendhal's, like Byron's, is conducted
openly in the cause of pleasure. The note of *libertinage* struck in the opening entry of *Rome, Naples et Florence en 1817* was first sounded in *Childe
Harold* a few years earlier. That travel narrative in verse is set in motion
with a rebellion against a father's name, an ancestral home, and the role
of dutiful son, and it goes on to recount the flight to southern Europe in
pursuit of pleasure: "His house, his home, his heritage, his lands, /. . . /
Without a sigh he left to cross the brine" (Canto I, xi).

Whereas in the age of the grand tour the journey south could be ideally figured as an apprenticeship undertaken in order to perpetuate civilized social order and patrilinear descent in the homeland, romantic
travel in the post-Byronic mode takes the form of flight from repressive
authority with no intent of return. Thus, like the English poet, although
Stendhal was occasionally to return to France for relatively brief periods
after the publication of his first travel book, he was to live the greater
part of his life in exile from his native land. The contrast with the career
and attitudes of De Brosses or Goethe in this respect could hardly be
more marked.

From the opening pages of his first travel book, then, Stendhal establishes in a highly self-conscious way the connection between private and
public life, the individual psyche and politics. Moreover, the opening reference to *libertinage* should not be allowed to mask the work's serious concerns. The journey of the still young but well-traveled Frenchman to Restoration Italy gives him the opportunity to reflect, in particular, on the
relationship between politics and pleasure, systems of government and
happiness. At the heart of the fundamental Stendhalian concept of "egotism" is, of course, the famous *chasse au bonheur*. It is this which, at the
collective as well as the individual level, is at the center of his concerns in
contemporary Italy and explains his ambivalence.

The 1817 travel journal projects the persona of a young man, who is
an enthusiastic connoisseur of art and of beauty in all its forms, and who
is receptively open to the variety of experiences furnished by Italian life,
including its landscapes, cities, art, architecture, monuments, social life,
manners, and women. He is, above all, a passionate music-lover whose
first act on arriving in a new city is to rush to the opera house. Yet, almost
from the beginning, it is apparent that the great pleasure he takes in
things Italian is often spoiled by the conditions of modern Italian life.
His enjoyment of the peculiar *douceur de vivre* he encounters in Milan or

for the naturalness, gaiety, and *bonhomie* of the Italian character in general is marred by more somber observations. It becomes clear in the course of the narrative that the art-loving dilettante is also a student of the philosophes and of the revolutionary cause in his time. Consequently, he finds that, although one's appetite for music and for affairs of the heart are abundantly satisfied in Italy, "one dies poisoned by melancholy if one is a citizen" (*1817*, p. 9). Such observations suggest that his journey south often has the character of a negative political pilgrimage: it reveals all that is wrong about the application of state power.

A major concern of the work is, in fact, the state of Italy, as the fuller title of an English edition, published in France and in the same year as the first French edition, makes clear. *Rome, Naples, and Florence in 1817; or, Sketches of the Actual State of Society, Manners, the Arts, Literature, etc. in These Three Famous Towns* is a title that sums up the underlying and more serious preoccupations of the breathless tourist. Stendhal's observations express again and again that eighteenth-century sense of the interconnectedness between systems of government, social well-being, creativity, and the state of the arts. It is out of a fascinating mixture of enthusiasm and concern for Italy at a dark moment of its history that the narrator is led to explore the "Italie morale," which he claims has escaped the attention of most travelers.

In short, the work itself spends a great deal of time elaborating on the summary judgments of its preface and exploring the political causes of the state of decadence observed. And Stendhal's partisanship is evident throughout. His first venture into the genre is thus declared by his best-known modern editor, V. Del Litto, to be "in spite of appearances a political pamphlet,"[13] a political pamphlet in which an acute and well-traveled comparatist in European societies, north and south of the Alps, hands down his diagnosis of Italy's sickness to the infatuated dilettante. The work takes its focus from a crucial question: "Chance having interrupted the forward march of this young people in 1814, what will happen to the sacred fire of genius and liberty? Will it be extinguished?" (*1817*, p. 174).

Yet, in spite of his obvious partisanship—Maurice Bardèche once described the work as "a tour of Italy by a young liberal"[14]—*Rome, Naples et Florence en 1817* is a complex and ideologically unstable work, full of the ironies and paradoxes that make for the richness of texture of the novels of Stendhal's maturity. What Italy offers the young liberal and champion of Napoleon is, in effect, a marvelously concrete test case for his libertar-

[13] See *La Vie intellectuelle de Stendhal: Genèse et évolution de ses idées* (Paris: Université de Grenoble, 1959), p. 544.

[14] *Stendhal romancier* (Paris: La Table Ronde, 1947), p. 84.

ian cause. All those factors required for human happiness and for artistic creativity are present on the peninsula except the right form of government.

The evidence of decadence is overwhelming and the young traveler's judgments are harsh, especially on the Italy south of Florence: "civilization ends in Florence. . . . Rome and Naples are barbarian countries dressed up in a European fashion" (*1817*, p. 85). As far as Rome itself is concerned, "All is decadence here, all is mere memory, all is dead. Active life is in London or Paris. . . . a stay here tends to weaken the soul, to plunge it into a stupor" (*1817*, p. 21). And the reason is that the passionate and creative Italian character, though fundamentally unchanged, has been forced to lead a subterranean existence for two and a half centuries because of political absolutism and religious intolerance: "The Italian character like the fire of a volcano has only been visible in the spheres of music and sensuous life. From 1550 to 1796 it was crushed beneath the enormous mass of the most suspicious, feeblest and most implacable of tyrannies. And religion, coming to the aid of authoritarianism, finally smothered it" (*1817*, p. 169).

Thus, Stendhal's hatred of absolutism and his lifelong anticlericalism are confirmed by the state of Italy. And his prescription for national regeneration is a liberal one—constitutional government with two legislative bodies and a free press. In the notes gathered together for a revised edition of the work, under the title *Italy in 1818*, the lesson of Italian history is reduced to an aphorism italicized for emphasis in the text: "*Nothing without liberty, everything with liberty*" (*1817*, p. 262). Such is Stendhal's law concerning not only the progress of civilization, but also social well-being in general.

Yet, and here we come to one of those sharp paradoxes that make Stendhal an uncomfortable writer for dogmatists of all factions, politically guaranteed liberties are not by themselves enough to ensure happiness and the amenities of civilized life. If southern Europe in Stendhal's analysis merely needs to adopt the political institutions of the north to alleviate its problems, the north has shortcomings of its own which are not amenable to the simple solution of political revolution. The art-loving libertine finds the example of life in the homelands of contemporary liberalism, England and the United States, disturbing, the first because of its preoccupation with politics and the second on account of its single-minded pursuit of wealth.

As a result, he comments on the one hand—in an aside that suggests the distance traveled since Diderot—"Those things needed for the arts to prosper are often antithetical to those nations need to be happy" (*1817*, p. 259). And on the other, he points to an even graver incompatibility between a politicized consciousness and that romantic cult of the individual sensibility associated with the experience of the various arts. The thoroughgoing politicization of social life to be found in the politically most advanced countries proves inimicable to the finer feelings. "In the 20th century," Stendhal writes with some prescience, "all peoples will discuss politics and read the *Morning Chronicle* instead of going to applaud Marianne Corti" (*1817*, p. 51).[15] In Stendhal's analysis, political activity is an essential stage on the road to freedom and happiness, a stage to be transcended as soon as possible. There are, in short, sharper sensations and higher pleasures that are far more important than politics because, for a postreligious sensibility, they alone stir the whole being. That is why, in spite of all those things that shock the young tourist, he remains determinedly open to the novelties and pleasures of travel: "What variety and what vivacity in our activities and sensations today! That's what traveling is all about."[16]

In his three major novels Stendhal demonstrates that there has never been a novelist who was a more astute analyst of those who exercise power; yet, it is no accident if most of the heroic protagonists of his fiction end up renouncing power and withdraw from public life for the sake of some private passion. *Rome, Naples et Florence en 1817*, then, in its modest way does no more than anticipate the future novels; like them, it is a "political pamphlet" that ironically asserts the limits as well as the necessity of politics in the nineteenth century.

o   o   o

THE difference in the attitude to Rome expressed in the 1817 travel book and the *Promenades dans Rome* of 1829 is striking. Whereas the politically self-conscious narrator of the earlier work remarked on the decadence of the city of the popes, the predominant tone of the *Promenades* is celebratory. The author of the latter work was a man in his mid- to late forties who had spent a great deal of time in Italy in the intervening years and who had come to terms with living the life of an expatriate man of letters in an age of reaction, even if he remained until the end of his life unreconciled to that fate. The guarded references in the foreword to the changing political circumstances in Rome at the time of the author's various visits serve to alert the reader to the fact that politics will not be ignored.

Thus, one does not have to read many pages of the *Promenades* in order to discover that the significance of Rome for its author has been substan-

[15] Stendhal is more explicit in *Racine et Shakespeare* (Paris: 1928), where he identifies three weaknesses in constitutional monarchy. "The Charter," he notes, "1. destroys leisure; 2. separates through hatred; 3. kills l'esprit de finesse" (pp. 133–136).

[16] Quoted by V. Del Litto in his Pléiade edition of Stendhal's *Voyages en Italie* (Paris: Gallimard, 1973), p. XXXVI.

tially revised. That is not to say Stendhal returns in his maturity to a neoclassical or even Goethean view of that city. In becoming the apologist of Rome in his time, Stendhal contributes in important ways to its reinvention for the European imagination. Consequently, though the site of the many-layered city cannot help but remain that of the capital of the classical world and of the Western image of empire, Renaissance creativity, and Baroque religious power, the meanings it is made to embody for the Stendhalian traveler are radically renewed. Compared with earlier representations of the city, including even Byron's, Stendhal's text effects what might be called a "deromanization" of Rome. The signs of this process are manifold.

In this respect, the contrast with Goethe is again suggestive. In the denouement to *The Italian Journey* the narrator finds himself confronted with the monumental urban architecture of patriarchal power—the heroic statues, triumphal arches, the Capitol and the Coliseum—that arouses deep buried fears. To the extent that it encapsulates the kind of interpellation to which male travelers to Rome seem to have been traditionally subject, it is worth quoting the passage in full:

> After having wandered along the Corso—perhaps for the last time— I walked up to the Capitol, which rose like an enchanted palace in a desert. The statue of Marcus Aurelius reminded me of the Commendatore in Don Giovanni, for it seemed to be intimating to the wanderer that he was venturing upon something unusual. Nevertheless, I walked down the steps at the back. There I was suddenly confronted by the dark triumphal arch of Septimius Severus, which cast a still darker shadow. In the solitude of the Via Sacra the well-known objects seemed alien and ghost-like. But when I approached the grand ruins of the Colisseum and looked through the gate into the interior, I must frankly confess that a shudder ran through me, and I quickly returned home. [*Italian Journey*, p. 497].

Ancient Rome here becomes the site of a psychodrama in which it is both a sacred space (Via Sacra) and a grand opera set—the reference to Don Giovanni's transgressions and the Commendatore's revenge are particularly suggestive. Moreover, the effect of the ghostly encounter is powerful enough to cause the traveler to submit to patriarchal power and scurry home again.

Such scenes of atavistic dread are not respresented as such in Stendhal's Roman travel book. On the contrary, the whole work is in its way a celebration of the possibilities opened up when paternal interdictions and threats of revenge are removed. Its unstated purpose is precisely to exorcise Goethe's vengeful ghosts.

The difference is immediately apparent on the level of the formal characteristics of the *Promenades* that are most likely to strike the modern reader, along with its apparent artlessness—like *Rome, Naples et Florence en 1817*, it is a "natural work"—namely, its heterogeneity, a heterogeneity that is even more striking here than in other works in a genre rarely noted for homogeneity or coherence.[17] There are occasions when it has the air of the guidebook the title suggests, but it is apparent from the beginning that the guidebook form is to be disrupted by the author's improvisational strategies and by the incorporation of material alien to that authoritative, documentary genre. The fact that the work is an *œuvre de circonstance* of the kind designed to earn some money for an author without a stable source of income is perhaps responsible in part for its discontinuities and apparent carelessness of execution. Yet, Stendhal was convinced of the virtues of "spontaneity" in a writer even in his most committed fictions; that calculated negligence, or *sprezzatura*, which Castiglione prized in the courtier was an important principle in Stendhal's art of living and writing.

The result in the *Promenades*, in any case, is apparent throughout. At one moment the "guidebook" neglects altogether to describe certain major sites, at another it piles up information on eighty-six churches in the space of seventeen pages or gives a detailed description of Saint Peter's over forty-four pages. The history of Rome itself is summarized in a few passages that might well have come from a contemporary *dictionnaire des idées reçues* and that were, in fact, constituted from memories of school history lessons or plagiarized directly from the guidebooks and histories of more learned predecessors. Like some of those predecessors, Stendhal also gives a detailed account of the politicking involved in the course of the conclave for the election of a pope.

At the same time, unlike the impersonal narrator of a guidebook who asserts authoritatively what the reader should visit and what he should expect to find there, Stendhal's narrator foregrounds the problematic nature of his task. Not surprisingly, given the author's values and attitudes, the pedagogue's role is one he is reluctant to assume. We are a long way from those precepts, entitled "On the Means of Traveling Usefully," with which Diderot prefaced his *Journey to Holland*. Instead of informing the traveler where to go and why, therefore, in the name of a tradition that he relays but does not acknowledge, Stendhal subverts the narrator's authority and the tradition along with it.

He does this, first, by suggesting that the best preparation for visiting Rome is to read no guidebook at all: "When you arrive in Rome, do not

[17] See Wendelin A. Guenther's discussion of the reading problems posed by Stendhal's *Promenades*: "Reading the Romantic Journal: Meaning Formation in the Discontinuous Text," *Romanic Review* 78, no. 3 (May 1987).

allow yourself to be poisoned by any opinion, do not buy any book; the time of curiosity and of science will too soon replace that of the emotions."[18] The opposition implied between heart and intellect, pleasure and knowledge, and the narrator's unambiguous championship of the former is characteristic. At worst, he goes on, the traveler should consult the book and then immediately efface it: "I advise the reader to cross out each page with the stroke of a pencil as soon as he has seen the monument in question" (*Promenades*, p. 3).[19] Second, Stendhal undermines the impersonal authority of his work by intermittently fictionalizing his material. On this occasion, however, it is not just a matter of the Germanic pseudonym and the invented itinerary of *Rome, Naples et Florence en 1817* or the projection of an idiosyncratic narratorial personality. For his Roman travel book, he also produces a small group of figures, including a thoughtful German, "Frederic," and a witty, French Voltairean called "Paul," along with shadowy women characters—presumably in order to promote the pleasurable idea of an amicable band of travelers of both sexes.

There are also moments when the *Promenades* resembles a memoir or fragment of autobiography, which, as in the works of Boswell or Goethe, is really a journal that narrates the personal encounter with Italy of a traveling man of letters. There are, finally, long passages that appear to belong to a novel of manners as well as certain suggestive episodes that have the flavor of embryonic *chroniques italiennes*. The faith Stendhal places in the anecdote or story and even in what might be called significant gossip, both in the *Promenades* and elsewhere, is a sign of his distrust of the abstract discourse of that Enlightenment philosophy which he also respected as the sole voice of truth. It is a sign of his sense of the superiority of the art of the novel over the treatise in its power to illuminate the conditions of life in his time.

The narrator also goes out of his way to assure the reader of the authenticity of his representations in the *Promenades*. And he does so on the basis of the immediacy of his transcription of lived experience. The claim is made that the work is composed of notes taken, if not during the course of excursions themselves, then at the latest in the evening after the narrator's return home. Yet, by the very fact that he foregrounds his presence as an engaging *original*, instead of effacing personality in the interest of the material, he announces an important characteristic of romantic travel writing. As the example of both Boswell and Sterne makes clear, the pleasures of an engaging narrator, especially when combined

[18] *Promenades dans Rome*, ed. Armand Carracio (Paris: Champion, 1938), p. 3.
[19] "I do not pretend to dictate a plan of activities for travelers; to each his own in this sphere; I am merely narrating my way." Quoted by Del Litto, *Voyages*, p. xxxviii.

with moral earnestness and rakishness or with sensibility and eccentricity, were not unfamiliar in eighteenth-century travel literature. But the opening pages of the *Promenades* reveal something more. Stendhal's narrator appeals without apology to the the traveler's interest in the cult of his self. Stendhal's 1829 travel book is a *bréviaire d'égotisme* in which Roman historical sites, monuments, and works of art no longer serve the traditional functions of education and connoisseurship. Like the art of music, which furnishes the author with his touchstone for ecstatic moments, they serve instead to procure in the traveler a series of exquisitely beautiful sensations.

The narrator lets his reader know from the beginning that his main focus will be on Roman manners, with particular reference to the pursuit of happiness, and on the elaboration of an art of travel that will offer discriminating travelers a maximum yield of pleasure. On the one hand, he notes, "We hope to discover Italian manners. . . . We want to understand those social habits of Rome and Naples in the pursuit of everyday happiness" (*Promenades*, p. 6). On the other, he advises his readers not to visit Rome systematically, district by district, but "each morning to run after the kind of beauty one feels drawn to on getting up. . . . Like true philosophers, every day we will do what seems most enjoyable on that particular day" (*Promenades*, p. 12). It is noteworthy that "philosophers" here retains some of that older, disrespectful meaning that in early eighteenth-century France, at least, connected it to the tradition of the libertines.

In fact, not the least paradox of the *Promenades* is the complaint that because a traditional guidebook has a didactic function and makes a duty of sightseeing, it renders unmediated perception impossible and constitutes an obstacle to pleasure: "We ended up wandering about almost at random. We enjoyed the happiness of being in Rome in total liberty, *without thinking about our duty* to see [italics in the text]" (*Promenades*, p. 14). Such un-Goethean thoughts express the nostalgia for an impossible immediacy of experience in which no cultural text of any kind interposes itself between the desiring self and its objects in the world. Insofar as Stendhal elaborates an aesthetics of travel in his anti-guidebook, like Sterne's before him, it is not goal-oriented and avoids the straight line; it is an aesthetics not of the tour but of the detour.

In short, the implication of the *Promenades* is that the most important reason for visiting Rome has nothing to do with knowledge, social utility, and the reproduction of a given hegemonic order, or even with taste and self-improvement of an eighteenth-century kind, but with the philosophic egotism of the pursuit of individual happiness. In his 1829 work, Stendhal refines further the Byronic notion of travel for travel's sake in order to promote the idea of travel as a fine art: "Travel, which is a great source of pleasure for me, has the effect of fine music through the enjoyment (*jouissance*) I find in the beautiful prospects of nature" (Del Litto, *Voyages*, p. xxxv).[20]

This also explains his choice of Italy in the first place. In an important respect, Stendhal shows he is a champion of traditional Eurocentric cultural values. If he journeys south of the Alps, it is above all in search of the various refinements and pleasures of peculiarly European civilization; the exotic novelties of extra-European travel among primitive peoples that had seemed so important to the eighteenth-century thinkers discussed previously in this book are of no interest to him: "we travel to see new things; not barbarous tribes like the intrepid adventurer who seeks out the mountains of Thibet or who disembarks on a South Sea island. We look for more delicate shades; we want to see ways of life that are close to the perfections of our own civilization" (*Promenades*, p. 6).[21] In this respect, Byron (along with a great many romantic writers and artists from the opening decades of the nineteenth century) was bolder, for he pursued his journey into the Middle East.

Nevertheless, to the question Why travel to Rome? Stendhal gives an answer that would have seemed intolerable to many in the age of the grand tour. If his *Promenades* are an anti-guidebook, it is because he does not go to Rome as an inheritor, but as an aesthete and lover. He does not visit the famous sites so as to be interpellated by the monumental patriarchal order that Goethe encountered, an order of which a man of Stendhal's nationality, class, and education might recognize in himself a living representative. He goes instead to be ravished by the spectacle of beauty in the land where, more than in any other—in its women and landscapes, classical monuments, architecture, painting, and music—it makes itself available to the traveler.

Given Stendhal's famous definition of beauty as the promise of happiness, it follows that the hunt for the latter is best carried out on Italian soil. The force of his erotic transference onto a country becomes apparent in an early impression at a Milanese ball in 1816, and it persists more or less throughout the rest of his life: "I have never in my life seen such a company of such beautiful women; their beauty obliges one to turn one's eyes away. For a Frenchman it has a noble and grave character which makes one think of that happiness of the passions more than of the ephemeral pleasures of lively and gay flirtation. It seems to me that

[20] "These remains of walls blackened by time have on the soul the effect of Cimarosa's music." *Promenades*, p. 24.

[21] See also remarks that confirm the early-nineteenth-century European insensitivity to unfamiliar aesthetic values when Stendhal compares the effect of Roman ruins with the effect of those which are visible in the Middle East: "these temples astonish but they do not delight." *Promenades*, p. 33.

beauty is nothing more than the promise of happiness."[22] If such was the promise, it is no wonder that Stendhal remained for so long on Italian soil in order to pursue its realization. As was the case with the author of *Childe Harold*, the narrator of the *Promenades* recognized, in effect, that the journey to Italy is not simply an intermediary term between a departure from home and a return to it. It is instead an end in itself. It is not the final stage in one's preparation for life and for the assumption of a socially prescribed role in one's homeland, but the place to be.

If at the time of writing the *Promenades*, Stendhal's only finished novel was *Armance*, the tentative fictionalizing of his Roman travel book already suggests a few of the qualities his future Italian novel would possess. In the small band of amiable travelers one finds the theme of a collective egotism that was to be consecrated more than once under the rubric of "the happy few." Probably the boldest embodiment of that dream in Stendhal's works is precisely the utopian moment of the opening chapters of *The Charterhouse of Parma*, where, as I have suggested elsewhere,[23] the mature novelist transforms his own memory of the arrival of Napoleon's youthful army in Lombardy into the fantasm of "a land without fathers." Since, in the novel, the patriarchs had retreated with the Austrian Imperial Army, it was the Italian women and the rebellious sons who remained behind to welcome their French liberators. In the *Promenades*, as in *Rome, Naples et Florence en 1817*, some of the most suggestive passages are those which echo the nostalgia of that moment and anticipate its fuller elaboration in the *Charterhouse*.

Within the suprisingly guiltless space of Stendhalian egotism, then, the Italian journey occupies a crucial place because, for the time of his absence at least, the traveler escapes from paternal surveillance, both at the private level of his bourgeois Grenoblois family and at the public level of the restored French monarchy. In Italy, Stendhal encounters the possibility of a way of life more in conformity with an hypothesized inner self, that recently discovered country of romantic soulfulness. Consequently, travel writing comes to be reinvented more self-consciously than it had been before, as a privileged genre for the expression of the libertarian dream—which from Rousseau to Marcuse and contemporary feminism has identified repressive patriarchal authority as the obstacle to individ-

[22] *Rome, Naples et Florence* (1826), in *Voyages en Italie*, ed. V. Del Litto (Paris: Gallimard, 1973), pp. 310–311.

[23] See "Stendhal: Histoire et mythe personnel," *Stendhal Club* 82 (January 1979). Crouzet comments: "Aren't we warned that Italy will be the land without prohibitions, where all forms of unrestrained natural behavior will be at home, where one can say what one likes and do what one likes, as if the 'superego' did not exist, and where one might perhaps be anything, as if there were no longer even an ego." *Italianité*, pp. 80–81.

ual happiness and self-fulfillment. Stendhal's travel works are an important part of a broad psycho-political project that embodies a revolt
against a socially and biologically reproductive role.

In the fantasmatic geography of egotism, in fact, a substitution occurs
that is also a hierarchical reversal. Post-Napoleonic France as a center of
autocratic power and giver of the Law in the modern world changes its
gender and occupies the place of the "fatherland" in a sense that could
only be ominous to the son of Cherubin Beyle. Italy, on the other hand,
including patriarchal Rome, takes over the function of the "motherland"
and of pre-oedipal plenitude. Given the traditional image of classical
Rome—in the iconography of the French revolutionary and Napoleonic
periods even more than in the age of the grand tour—there is an apparent paradox here. But the paradox is dissolved if one is attentive to the
"deromanizing" rearticulation of neoclassical discourse that is effected in
the *Promenades*. One might even call the process the "maternalization" of
Rome.[24]

As noted above, in the eighteenth century the grand tour was an ideological cultural practice that was calculated to give a North European *fils
de famille* a sociopolitical as well as a worldly and aesthetic education. And
the place of Rome as originary source and center of a continuous European civilizing tradition was crucial. In the discourse of our time, Rome
was the mystified ground of a European phallocentric order and of its
hegemonic power. The model of the Roman imperial system, its normative Latin language and literature as well as its legal code, found a concrete embodiment for the tourist in such monumental civil-engineering
projects and artworks as Roman roads and aqueducts, radial city planning, coliseums, triumphal arches, and equestrian statues. And insofar as
the Italian Renaissance adapted classical models, it produced an urban
architecture of equal authority which culminated in the grandiose edi-
fices for princes of the Baroque church.

The discourse of Stendhalian egotism in the text of the *Promenades* subverts such monumentality, however. And it does so by scrambling history,
by peopling Rome differently, and by fragmenting the celebrated sites
and cityscapes into so many occasions for the contemplation of *la beauté
sublime* and so many pretexts for the bittersweet reverie that *la beauté sublime* promotes. Stendhal accomplishes this in part by updating the neoclassical vogue for the picturesque in which it is not classical artifacts as

---

[24] Byron's narrator had already practiced a traditional form of transference in which
his attachment to place takes the form of "mother love." This is true in relation to
nature, to the country of Italy—"Mother of the Arts"—and to Rome itself—"Oh Rome!
my country! city of the soul! / The orphans of the heart must turn to thee, / Lone
mother of dead empires!" (Canto IV, LXVIII).

such but their ruins which communicate the aesthetic charge, especially where such ruins have been reclaimed by a resurgent nature.

The beauty that touches the soul turns out to derive from the spectacle of a grandeur overthrown or suffused by those painterly effects of light, associated with sunset or moonlight, that soften sheer monumentality and the artifacts of power. Involved here is an aestheticizing vision that grasps every opportunity to transform what it sees into the equivalent of a work of art. It is no accident that, before he ever considered writing fiction, Stendhal first published three works devoted to music, painting, and travel, in that order: namely, the *Letters on Haydn, Mozart, and Metastasio*, the *History of Painting in Italy*, and *Rome, Naples et Florence en 1817*.

Further, Stendhal also affirms in his Roman travel book that the most memorable moments for the traveler will be produced not only by Italian music, poetry, fine arts, architecture, and painterly landscapes, but also by the spectacle of Italy's contemporary life, including the life of the people of Rome and of a salon society animated by the presence of spirited women. Finally, in the *Promenades*, as elsewhere in Stendhal's work, there are suggestions that it is through the experience of love *à l'italienne* that the promise of happiness comes closest to being realized. He was, after all, the author of a treatise on love, *De l'Amour*, which included comparative studies on European women. In sum, the narrator advises his readers that they should travel to Rome for its present as much as for its past, and not in spite of modern Romans but because of them.

Although there are important differences of tone and attitude between the two Italian travel books discussed here, it is important to note that the passage of a dozen difficult years for their author does not give rise to a recantation. If the 1817 book is more programmatically political, the later work does not so much renounce the earlier beliefs as put them in the context of the new political times. There is more distance; in 1829, the author allows himself to reflect on the art of living appropriate to an unreformed society.

The paradox in the end is that in Stendhal's elaborate psycho-political fantasm, Paris, London, and Vienna are made to change places with Rome as signifiers of patriarchal potency. The capital of the classical world and of autocratic Western Christendom is rearticulated in such a way that it ceases to signify power, the Law, and duty and is transformed instead, like the Milan of the earlier travel book, into the maternal place of powerlessness and pleasure.

Readers of *The Life of Henry Brulard* do not need to be reminded of that "dissatisfaction with home and family" which is expressed there and which Freud held to be such an important motive of travel (see Chapter VII, below). Nor are they likely to forget that, in the secondary revisions of his autobiographical text at least, Stendhal's "early wishes" focus on the recovery of a lost "good mother." Given the familial as well as the historical circumstances of his life and longings, it should come as no surprise if, under the spell of Italy, Stendhal reverses the directionality of the grand tour. In the textual substitutions of the *Promenades*, it is paternal Paris that is experienced as an exile and maternal Rome as a return home.

Chapter V

DARWIN'S PASSIONATE VOYAGE

THE NAME OF Charles Darwin is not nowadays usually associated with the idea of transgression except in those circles where "creationism" still remains a dogmatic faith. Nor on the whole does the epithet "romantic" seem to be appropriate in view of the fact that it is usually reserved for period taste and values in the aesthetic sphere, and Darwin has survived in legend, if not in fact, as the great scientist whose preoccupation with fact and theory cut him off from feeling or the inner life, at least in the practice of his science. Yet, to read *The Voyage of the Beagle* is to encounter a work that is a classic of travel as well as of scientific "literature." In spite of its generally measured tone, it is traversed by many of the drives, tensions, dissatisfactions, and more or less intense pleasures that are to be found in European travel narratives from the mid-eighteenth century on, particularly in romantic travel writing.

Moreover, an air of transgression hung over the departure of the young Charles Darwin's voyage around the world. And no journey has been so massively transgressive as in the long-cogitated consequences that emerged in 1859 with the publication of *On the Origin of Species by Means of Natural Selection; or, The Preservation of Favored Races in the Struggle for Life.* Between these two poles, moreover, the account of Darwin's voyage, which from 1831 to 1836 spanned almost five years of the author's life, is peculiarly rich in its record of novelties encountered and of intense passions aroused. It turns out that Darwin the naturalist is in many ways the equal of Byron the poet, even frequently on the level of verbal representation. It is, in any case, on these aspects of Darwin's account of his voyage that I shall concentrate here. I do not pretend to be making a contribution to the history of science, nor am I directly concerned with the impact of the theory of evolution on the science, thought, literature, or common sense of his age or ours.

The interest immediately aroused by the publication of *The Voyage of the Beagle* in 1839 confirms in its own way the centrality of travel writing in the development of European thought and science from the eighteenth-century on. In his introduction to the National History Library edition, Leonard Engel even claims that "in its influence on modern man's outlook upon the world, no voyage since Columbus matches the

voyage described in this book."[1] Engel presumably means that had a series of obstacles not been overcome and had Darwin not been appointed
as the naturalist on H.M.S. *Beagle*, the theory of the origin of species by
natural selection would not have occurred to Darwin, and some form of
"creationism" or Lamarckism would for a long time have continued to
dominate humanity's conception of the creation and its place in it.

Yet, as Stephen Jay Gould among others has warned us, we must avoid
taking the ideology of "scientism" and of the "heroic" scientific pioneer
for the realities of scientific practice. The myth of the *Beagle* is, in his
words, "that Darwin became an evolutionist by simple, unbiased observation of an entire world laid out before him during a five-year voyage
around the world."[2] Darwin did not, in fact, become an evolutionist until
several months following his return to London, after he had been able to
consult with other scientists on his specimens and data and realize the
full significance of that material. The point is important for Gould because it enables him to demonstrate how the collective practice of science
works, in his view, and to reflect on science's necessarily "impure" nature:
"The vision of such pure and unsullied brilliance has nurtured most legends in the history of science and purveys false views about the process
of scientific thought. Human beings cannot escape their presuppositions
and see 'purely'; Darwin functioned as an active creationist all through
the *Beagle* voyage" ("Sea," pp. 358–359).

Perhaps the most important recurring theme of Gould's brilliant little
essays over the years has, in fact, concerned the need to rehistoricize science, to free science from the ideology that has attached itself to it and
that has reduced the history of science itself to a purely anecdotal interest—"for it can only chronicle past errors and credit the bricklayers for
discerning glimpses of final truth." And, he goes on to comment in the
same essay, "Changes in theory are not simply the derivative results of
new discoveries but the work of creative imagination influenced by contemporary social and political forces."[3]

The point of view Gould expresses here is in some ways close to Michel
Foucault's. The late French thinker's discourse theory derived, in effect,

[1] (New York: Anchor, 1962), p. ix.

[2] "Darwin at Sea—and the Virtues of Port," in *The Flamingo's Smile: Reflections in Natural History* (New York: Norton, 1985), p. 347.

[3] "On Heroes and Fools in Science," in *Ever since Darwin: Reflections in Natural History*
(New York: Norton, 1979), p. 201. See also Robert M. Young's tightly argued essays
on nature and natural philosophy in nineteenth-century England, in *Darwin's Metaphor: Nature's Place in Victorian Culture* (Cambridge: Cambridge University Press, 1985).
The title of his book and of the essay from which it derives is intended "to convey that
at the heart of its science we find a culture's values. Both are irreducibly anthropomor-
phic and social" (p. 125). Young's substantial bibliography suggests the range of Darwin studies.

from his efforts in works like *The Order of Things* to write a counterhistory of science. But whereas Gould explains the determinants and constraints that inhibit the emergence of radically new ideas in terms of ideology as traditionally conceived, Foucault substitutes the theory of interdisciplinary period paradigms that are inscribed in discourses and material practices; and the latter are not self-evidently determined by factors outside themselves, such as the forces and relations of production. Yet Foucault's histories of science, like Gould's, illuminate the role of the collectivity and problematize the whole notion of "epistemological breaks," although neither denies that such breaks occur. Both are concerned with invisible boundaries and impurities in a discipline often dominated by an ideology of romantic progressivism which projected the image of solitary and persecuted genius as the source of scientific development.[4]

Boundaries and impurities are, of course, of particular importance in this study of travel writing on a number of levels. But I am concerned here to explore the role they play at the level of the text, rather than at the level of scientific practice (in Gould's sense) or of discourse (in Foucault's). The sources and sites of resistance to an inherited collective seeing are as interesting as what is uncritically retransmitted; different forms of defamiliarization produce kaleidoscopic effects that shatter familiar patterns.

What this means, first, is that *The Voyage of the Beagle* invites an approach that relocates representation and the practice of science itself in the matrix of an individual as well as of a collective history. To read Darwin's travel book alongside his *Autobiography* is, for example, to realize that the motivation of his voyage of circumnavigation had a lot more in common with that of the travels of Boswell, Byron, and Stendhal than is usually assumed. It means, in addition, that although the *Voyage* is of unique scientific interest, it is by no means limited to such an interest. Its richness, in fact, is such and is manifested in such a variety of ways that it obliges the reader to focus on its "literariness." Its author was clearly conscious of the need to deploy the tropes of literary discourse in the narration of a story in which he was both narrator and heroic protagonist.

Given Darwin's education and historical moment, this should not necessarily surprise. In her study of the impact of the theory of evolution on British culture in general, and on the development of the British novel in particular, Gillian Beer makes the point that works of science in the nineteenth century could for the most part still be read without difficulty by lay readers. At the same time, scientists themselves were far more

---

[4] The classic modern work on this subject is, of course, Thomas Kuhn's *The Structure of Scientific Revolutions* (Chicago: University of Chicago Press, 1962).

likely to be familiar with the literary tradition; and she cites the range of Darwin's readings to prove it.[5]

If *The Voyage of the Beagle* has remained a consistently popular work since its first publication in 1839, it is, in fact, partly because of its young narrator's engaging openness to a wide variety of experiences. The journal form allows the informant who registers his experiences to become almost as much the focus of the reader's interest as is the information he purveys. The attention of the young Cambridge graduate was excited by a range of phenomena that go far beyond natural history, and he managed to transmit the complexity of his response through a prose which articulates that complexity. In the evocations of marvels and monsters, of the beauty and sinister in life, it is no exaggeration to say that, in spite of its measured and often neutral tone, *The Voyage of the Beagle*, even more than the voyages of his eighteenth-century predecessors, communicates some of the pleasures of Homer's *Odyssey*, including the narrative of dangers overcome and the stirring evocation of natural scenes. Unlike the eighteenth-century naval captains, Darwin also regards his voyage as largely the affair of a private citizen with a duty to truth and to science; he exploited fully the far greater freedom of commentary that was allowed him.

The enthusiasm and endlessly renewed interest its author expressed for almost all aspects of the created universe, organic and inorganic, was probably matched in his time only by Alexander von Humboldt in *Personal Narrative of Travels to the Equinoctial Regions of the New Continent*. Moreover, like Humboldt, Darwin by no means neglects his own species. The scientifically trained observer of rocks, plants, and animals also frequently records his encounters with the different races of mankind. The professional naturalist turns out to be, among other things, a perceptive amateur ethnographer, who comments on racial or cultural difference as well as on diverse forms of collective behavior or social organization. And he even occasionally pronounces judgment on the political vices and virtues of the different countries through which he passes.

Further, if Darwin's *Voyage* is more successful as a continuous narrative than Bougainville's or Cook's, it is because the intradiegetic narrator succeeds in transmitting a sense of his own involvement in scenes and events, as well as his varying moods of enthusiasm, disgust, or self-doubt. Scientific observations are also entangled in the more mundane concerns of a young man exposed to alien ways of life and forced to share a cramped cabin for almost five years with the stubbornly orthodox Anglican and authoritarian commander of the *Beagle*, Captain Robert Fitzroy. The

[5] *Darwin's Plots: Evolutionary Narrative in Darwin, George Eliot, and Nineteenth Century Fiction* (London: Routledge and Kegan Paul, 1983), p. 30.

theme of travel as flight from a repressive paternal power that is implicit in *The Voyage of the Beagle* is similar to what may be found in the works of other male travelers before and since, although not even Gibbon or Goethe can claim to have transformed their journeys into such triumphal returns as Darwin. Given the years spent away from home and his father's apparent misgivings that they would be misspent, not the least motive for writing the journal of his voyage was that of an accounting and a self-justification similar in many ways to Boswell's. It is no accident, in fact, if in retrospect the *Voyage* may be read as a tale of moral rebirth. Its remote narrative model is to be found in such New Testament parables of the conversion of misguided sons as the story of Paul on the road to Damascus or that of the prodigal son himself.

Some forty-five years after the event, Darwin himself suggests in his *Autobiography* the air of the random and the marvelous that seems to have hovered over the whole adventure: "The voyage of the *Beagle* has been by far the most important event in my life and has determined my whole career; yet it depended on so small a circumstance as my Uncle offering to drive me 30 miles to Shrewsbury, which few uncles would have done, and on such a trifle as the shape of my nose."[6] It was, of course, Darwin's uncle who persuaded his father to change his mind and allow the young naturalist to embark on the *Beagle*; not surprisingly, Robert Darwin did not see the profit for his son in such a protracted jaunt. The autobiographer's reference to his nose concerns Captain Fitzroy's distrust of that feature on Darwin's face as a result of his readings in the Swiss theologian Johann Lavater.

The serious interest the young Darwin had come to take in the phenomena of the natural world halfway through his undergraduate career is not in doubt. Yet, it is also true that a world tour must have seemed even more promising than a grand tour to an apprentice naturalist still living under the shadow of a powerful father—a man who was apparently 6 feet, 2 inches tall and weighed some 336 pounds. Although he is less forthcoming on the subject than Boswell, Darwin's relationship to his physician father seems to have been as fraught as the young Scot's with Lord Auchinleck. The *Autobiography* is particularly suggestive in this respect, less though in what it affirms than in the portrait it draws.

In retrospect, Darwin even attributes quasi-divine powers of divination to his father: "But the most remarkable power which my father possessed was that of reading the characters, and even the thoughts of those whom he saw even for a short time. We had many instances of this power, some of which seemed almost supernatural" (*Autobiography*, p. 15). The convic-

[6] Charles Darwin and T. H. Huxley, *Autobiographies*, ed. Gavin de Beer (Oxford: Oxford University Press, 1983), p. 44; hereafter, referred to as *Autobiography*.

tion transmitted here by the narrator's language suggests that the young Darwin, too, must have experienced a sense of his own transparency in the face of such clairvoyance. Even in the absence of a developing passion for natural history, there is motivation enough for a long journey in an escape from that demanding look—especially when squeamishness at the sight of blood and the lack of a vocation had led him to abandon the thought of two respectable middle-class careers, medicine and the church respectively.

It is also significant that the word "power" returns with symptomatic frequency with reference to Robert Darwin in passages that emphasize the man's capacity to see into people's minds and to win their confidence. Charles Darwin even manages to intimate that his father is somewhere between a priest and a psychoanalyst on account of his practice of listening to his patients and of recognizing that not all illnesses are somatic in origin: "Owing to my father's power of winning confidence, many patients, especially ladies, consulted him when suffering from any misery, as a sort of Father-Confessor. He told me that they always began by complaining in a vague manner about their health, and by practice he soon guessed what was really the matter. He then suggested that they had been suffering in their minds, and now they would pour out their troubles, and he heard nothing more about the body" (*Autobiography*, p. 14).

On one level, such commentary by an autobiographer in his late sixties may seem remote from the narrative of a voyage undertaken in his early twenties. Yet, on another, it is impossible to ignore the impact of such a powerful father on a son barely beyond adolescence who was very conscious of the demand that he make some kind of mark in the world.

That the voyage and the theory of evolution to which it gave rise were associated in Darwin's mind with a sense of guilt and moral misgivings is confirmed by what has been called "Darwin's delay."[7] Although he started to speculate seriously on a theory of evolution several months after returning to England in 1836 and later recalled that the reading of Malthus's *On Population* suggested to him the mechanism that explained the process of speciation, the *Origin of Species* was not published, of course, until 1859. And it is clear that Darwin was under a heavy moral and psychological burden over the significance of evolutionary theory for a social order founded on Christian faith. Gould, in fact, attributes the delay to the "fear" Darwin experienced at the profoundly heretical character of his ideas—in a man, one might add, who was not born with a heretic's temperament. A variety of symptoms suggest he did suffer from a peculiar psychic burden as well as from physical pain. Even if the mysterious illness with which Darwin was afflicted after his return to England

[7] See prologue, *Ever since Darwin*, pp. 12–14.

was purely organic—recent speculation has focused on Chagas' disease—
he was obliged to live like a virtual recluse at Down in Kent for most of
the rest of his life with what Beer calls his "affective powers" (*Plots*, p. 30)
dimmed and without that interest in art, literature, and music which had
excited him as a young man. He did, after all, play the major role in
substituting an immensely bleaker view of the universe and of humanity's
privileged place in it for the biblical tale of divine creation, the fixity of
the species, and providential unfolding. "Evolution," Stephen Jay Gould
reminds us, "is purposeless, nonprogressive, and materialistic."[8]

o   o   o

As FOR the young Darwin on his voyage, it is clear that he by no means
felt obliged to limit his observations solely to the objects of his scientific
curiosity. He is a "scientist," in fact, only with part of himself part of the
time. At other moments, he allows himself to be solicited by all the sights
and experiences that a well-educated young man of his nationality, age,
class, beliefs, and inherited values was likely to be susceptible to. The
table of contents of the *Voyage*'s twenty-one chapters suggests, with a
characteristic nineteenth-century fullness, the incomparably wide range
of material touched on or evoked at some length in the body of the text.
The table alone suggests the virtually limitless curiosity of its author for
all manifestations of life and for the history of the earth that supports
them. At the same time, a modern reader at least is likely to find there a
specifically verbal pleasure that complements encyclopedic range with
sheer heterogeneity and incongruous juxtapositions or with the inventive
imagery of scientific nomenclature. That frequent slide from the referential to the poetic function of language which characterizes the body of
the work begins with the chapter titles.

Thus, apart from the more or less exotic names of places visited, from
Cape Verde, Brazil, and Tierra del Fuego to Valparaiso, the Galapagos
archipelago, Tahiti, and Saint Helena, there are references to subjects
that include agreeable or menacing natural phenomena, geological formations, plant life, birds, insects, mammals, human societies, sociopolitical institutions, wars, genocide, and slavery. In a rare display of verbal
transgressions, Darwin manages to invent the kind of arbitrary colloca-
tion of categories of which Jorge Luis Borges was the modern master.
Among the more fascinating, apparently whimsical or deeply disturbing
topics specifically mentioned are "Habits of a Sea-slug and Cuttle-fish,"
"Singular Incrustations," "Causes of Discoloured Sea," "Slavery," "Musi-

---

[8] See "Darwin's Delay," in *Ever since Darwin*, pp. 12–24. See also F. J. Sulloway, "Darwin's Conversion: The *Beagle* Voyage and Its Aftermath," *Journal of the History of Biology*
15 (1982).

cal Frogs," "Phosphorescent Insects," "Spider with an unsymmetrical Web," "Estancias attacked by Indians," "Negro Lieutenant," "Numerous gigantic extinct Quadrupeds," "Habits of Oven-bird," "Indian Wars and Massacres," "Causes of Extinction," "Miserable Condition of the Savages," "Cannibals," "State of Miners," "Great Earthquake," "Sagacity of Mules," "Proofs of the gradual Elevation of the Cordillera," "Great Subsidence," "Antiquity of the Indian Race," "Ornithology, curious finches," "Great Tortoises, habits of," "Gradual Extinction of the Aborigines," and "Splendour of Tropical Scenery."

If this is science, then most of the world's population does not know what it is missing. It is not often that a table of contents promises to reward a reader's curiosity at so many different levels with such a various and demanding fare. Not the least notable feature of this table is that it reinforces our sense that Darwin had a peculiarly sharp eye for the odd or anomalous, for whatever breaks the pattern or does not fit the paradigm. And the lesson of twentieth-century theory in both science (Thomas Kuhn) and literature (the Russian Formalists' concept of "defamiliarization") is that such an eye is the sine qua non of genuinely creative thinking in both spheres. In the light of the table of contents, it is not surprising if, in the terminology of Jurij Lotman, the narrator of Darwin's *Voyage* turns out to be a "dynamic hero" who ends up crossing some of the most forbidden boundaries in his culture and shattering the sacredness of an inherited natural world order.

The first paragraph of the *Voyage* sustains the excitement of the table of contents on a different level, by opening directly onto the prospect of heroic adventure with its evocation of a mission and a difficult departure: "After having been twice driven back by heavy south-western gales, Her Majesty's ship *Beagle*, a ten-gun brig, under the command of Captain Fitz Roy, R.N., sailed from Devonport on the 27th of December, 1831. The object of the expedition was to complete the survey of Patagonia and Tierra del Fuego, commenced under Captain King in 1826 to 1830—to survey the shores of Chile, Peru, and of some islands in the Pacific—and to carry a chain of chronometrical measurements round the World" (*Voyage*, p. 1).

It is difficult to imagine a more splendid or, in its way, a more illuminating opening paragraph for a work of scientific travel literature. On the one hand, through its references to gales, to the institution of the Royal Navy, to an armed ship of war—"a ten-gun brig"—and to relatively remote and exotic lands, Darwin's deceptively plain prose immediately suggests the risks of the undertaking and the adventures likely to be encountered. On the other hand, through his explanation of the ship's mission, he also by implication makes the connection between power and knowledge in his time. The "scientific" expedition is to be carried out in one of "Her Majesty's" ships, and it assumes without question the right exercised by a great power to "survey" the shores of independent countries a continent away.

It is, moreover, a further manifestation of Britain's status as the premier naval power of the age if the "chain of chronometrical measurements round the World" signifies the taking of longitudinal readings that, by international convention, were all relative to the zero of the Royal Observatory at Greenwich. In taking the British capital as its center for purposes of global measurement, science was acknowledging its complicity with power.

The excitement of that opening paragraph recurs in a variety of forms in diverse situations in the body of the text. The narrator's interest in the natural world will frequently prove to be of the passionate kind associated with the romantic movement in literature, art, and music. And the more or less intense experiences he records run the gamut from religious awe to astonishment at novel encounters, or a simple delight in physical movement. The dominant tone of Darwin's *Voyage*, like Byron's *Childe Harold*, is, in fact, celebratory. But the young naturalist was exposed to a vaster and more marvelous world than the poet; and he proves to be unusually open to the vividness of his sense impressions, to the unexpected vibrancy of color or the splendors of scale. His descriptions of certain scenes recall William Gilpin's observations on "picturesque travel" and the pleasures of the pursuit,[9] but the scenes Darwin encounters frequently shatter the canons of the European picturesque. What, in her discussion of the *Origin of Species*, Beer has called Darwin's "romantic materialism" (*Plots*, p. 42) emerges in the *Voyage of the Beagle* as a celebration of turbulent and boundless creative energies in a kind of symphonic nature that is beyond the power of words to express.[10]

The narrator's evocation of his first encounter with the Brazilian rain forest goes a long way toward confirming the definition of "naturalist" that Bruce Chatwin quotes in his own pursuit of human origins in the Australian desert, *The Songlines*: namely, "a man who is in love with the world."[11] The passage from Darwin's *Voyage* is in many ways typical of the sense of wonder that pervades long stretches of the work: "The day

[9] *Three Essays: On Picturesque Beauty; on Picturesque Travel; and on Sketching Landscape: with a Poem on Landscape Painting* (London: Cadell and Davis, 1808).

[10] "When quietly walking along the shady pathways, and admiring each successive view, I wished to find language to express my ideas. Epithet after epithet was found too weak to convey to those who have not visited the intertropical regions, the sensation of delight which the mind experiences." Quoted by Beer, from the *Journal of Researches*, in *Plots*, p. 34.

[11] (New York: Viking Penguin, 1987), p. 241. See Keith Thomas's richly informative *Man and the Natural World: A History of the Modern Sensibility* (New York: Pantheon Books, 1983) for the emergence of such an attitude to nature between 1500 and 1800.

has passed delightfully. Delight itself, however, is a weak term to express the feelings of a naturalist who, for the first time, has wandered by himself in a Brazilian forest. The elegance of the grasses, the novelty of the parasitical plants, the beauty of the flowers, the glossy green of the foliage, but above all the general luxuriance of the vegetation filled me with admiration" (*Voyage*, pp. 11–12). And, a few pages later, he sums up even more emphatically the strength of his feelings for this new Brazilian world: "It is easy to specify the individual objects of admiration in these grand scenes; but it is not possible to give an adequate idea of the higher feelings of wonder, astonishment, and devotion, which fill and elevate the mind" (*Voyage*, p. 25).

Darwin's writing in such passages alternates between that of aesthetic appreciation—"the elegance of the grasses . . . the beauty of the flowers"—and religious reverence—"higher feelings of wonder, astonishment, and devotion." He is in one sense hardly behaving as a scientifically trained naturalist here at all. But it is important to note how looking itself is by implication doubly legitimated: first, for religious reasons and, second, for scientific ones. Evidence of the divine in nature is in itself justification enough for observing with scientific exactitude. In Darwin's time, "naturalists" were not yet biologists but were still associated with that eighteenth-century tradition of "natural philosophy." And in Britain, at least, a lot of them were passionate amateurs, who were clergymen by vocation.

The sense of religious awe Darwin evokes in this passage and others recalls, of course, the praise of the divine in nature associated with the romantic tradition in literature from Rousseau and Goethe to Wordsworth and Lamartine. It also anticipates Freud's discusssion of "the oceanic feeling" in *The Future of an Illusion*, with the important difference that in Darwin's case it would be more appropriate to speak of a "forest feeling," a feeling for the lush abundance of an enclosed vegetable world and its multitudinous life. Yet, in retrospect he, too, found himself haunted by the spectacle of the empty plains of Patagonia: "Why then, and the case is not peculiar to myself, have these arid wastes taken so firm a hold on my memory?" (*Voyage*, p. 500). Writing after the fact, Darwin notes here the mysteriousness of a foreign place and the haunting persistence of its vast spaces in memory.

The experiences of Tierra del Fuego and Patagonia combine, in fact, to induce a powerful feeling of doubt about the ultimate benevolence of the Creation. "An ill-defined but strong sense of pleasure" may be excited by the great Patagonian plains; but one's faith is also put to a stern test, as a quotation from Shelley's "Lines on M. Blanc" suggests: "The wilderness has a mysterious tongue, / Which teaches awful doubt" (*Voyage*, p. 169). The quotation confirms, if confirmation were needed, the affinities between Darwin's attitudes and values and those of the English romantic poets. Moreover, the choice of Shelley is of particular significance, given his reputation as, along with Byron, the great rebel and expatriate among them.

One finds throughout the *Voyage* passages that express both reverence for the natural world and shock at the consequences of some of its awesome powers—the experience of an earthquake in Chile is an especially notable example of the latter. But it is something of a surprise to discover that the purpose of travel for the narrator of the *Voyage*, equally as much as it was for the protagonist of *Childe Harold*, often seems to be the pursuit of powerful sensations, albeit ostensibly elevated ones. Moreover, they occasionally occur in negative as well as positive forms.

In his closing remarks, Darwin also manages to anticipate some of the ideas of his great admirer, Sigmund Freud—the Freud of *Civilization and Its Discontents*—as well as such twentieth-century champions of a new primitivism as André Gide and the two Lawrences. It is true that Darwin does affirm the moral and cognitive seriousness of travel in the advice he gives a would-be world traveler, advice of which Dr. Johnson, Hurd's Locke, and Goethe presumably would have approved. One should undertake such a world tour, he concludes, only if one is drawn to make some contribution to the advancement of human knowledge: "It is necessary to look forward to a harvest, however distant that may be, when some fruit will be reaped, some good effected" (*Voyage*, p. 498).

On the other hand, Darwin also acknowledges the extraordinary and various pleasures he found at so many moments of his journey in spite of all the hardships and suffering—a word of rather high frequency in the *Voyage* is "delight," whether in its verbal, adjectival, or substantive form. Like Lévi-Strauss after him, the narrator of the *Voyage* notes, for example, the incomparable rush of pleasure at being "first" in the field: "I do not doubt that every traveller must remember the glowing sense of happiness which he experienced, when he first breathed in a foreign clime, where the civilized man had seldom or never trod" (*Voyage*, p. 502). In retrospect, in fact, no "delight" appears greater to him than that encountered on finding oneself virtually alone, surrounded by pristine nature.

What is interesting here, however, is the explanation he gives for the force of the feelings involved: "It has been said, that the love of the chase is an inherent delight in man—a relic of instinctive passion. If so, I am sure the pleasure of living in the open air, with the sky for a roof and the ground for a table, is part of the same feeling; it is the savage returning to his wild and native habits" (*Voyage*, p. 502). Darwin here is as alert as any poet or novelist to feeling. His theme is, in fact, the return of the repressed on the philogenetic level or the persistence in civilized, modern man of primitive instincts and of the pleasure of instinctual satisfaction. And he reminds us that one of the potent consequences of travel is self-discovery as much as discovery, a recognition of the disturbingly familiar within. In this case, it turns out that what he finds in himself is as old as the race. Darwin's suggestive explanation for the appeal of the wilderness already points to the idea of that split human subject which has become part of the currency of twentieth-century thought.

The "glowing sense of happiness" referred to is a phrase that, probably more than anything else in the *Voyage*, suggests the troubling intensity of the pleasure Darwin took—and it occurs, paradoxically, in the work of the world's most famous "naturalist"—with reference to the reemergence in civilized man of the powerful feelings of the hunter—"a relic of instinctive passion." Darwin's biographers tend to interpret his transition while at Cambridge, from horseman and hunter to naturalist, as a kind of conversion associated with the discovery of a vocation. The implication of the above passage is, however, that a form of sublimation is involved in which the scientific pursuit of new species derives from the same impulses as (and turns out to be hardly less intense than) the pleasures of the kill. Darwin's position is not, in fact, far from the psychoanalytic theory of sublimation, according to which the aims of the sex drive and its component instincts, including sadism and masochism, are held to be susceptible to being directed into artistic and intellectual activities.

Darwin knowingly makes the connection in his *Autobiography* between primitive instincts and elevated callings in an ironic choice of words: "In the latter part of my school life I became passionately fond of shooting, and I do not believe that any one could have shown more zeal for the most holy cause than I did for shooting birds. How well I remember killing my first snipe, and my excitement was so great that I had much difficulty in reloading my gun from the trembling of my hands" (*Autobiography*, p. 23). The emotion evoked is that of sadism, in the psychoanalytic sense of the word, a sense that, it will be clear, has a frequent application in Flaubert's oriental journey. In any case, the autobiographer reveals here how passionate an individual was the scientist responsible for one of the most revolutionary of paradigm changes in the history of science.

At the time of writing the *Autobiography*, Darwin himself interprets his gradual abandonment, in the course of the voyage, of the satisfactions of the hunt for those of science as a transition to a morally higher sphere of activity without any necessary loss in pleasure: "I discovered, though unconsciously and insensibly, that the pleasure of observing and reasoning was a much higher one than that of skill and sport. The primeval instincts of the barbarian slowly yielded to the acquired tastes of civilized man" (*Autobiograhpy*, p. 45). The passage is interesting to the extent that it speaks to the potential *contents* of civilization and not its *discontents*—a change of aim and object is not necessarily accompanied by a decrease in instinctual gratification.

Right to the end of the *Voyage*, Darwin affirms both the pleasures and the educational value of travel for the traveler: "In conclusion, it appears that nothing can be more improving to a young naturalist than a journey in distant countries. It both sharpens, and partly allays that want and craving, which, as Sir J. Herschel remarks, a man experiences although every corporeal sense be fully satisfied" (*Voyage*, pp. 502–503). The two sentences stand in odd contrast to one another; the theme of self-improvement in a young man with a vocation stands in opposition to the notation on the insatiability of human desire, its excess in relation to any possible object. The remark, in effect, gives a brief theoretic formulation of that "want and craving," which from Boswell to Byron to Stendhal and down to our own time traverses the most interesting travel writing. It seems that, in Darwin's case, even a five-year voyage around the globe could only "partly allay" the longing that it also excited.

○   ○   ○

THE MOST famous chapter of the *Voyage* is, of course, the one entitled "Galapagos Archipelago," since it was there that Darwin was able to observe in the field that differentiation of related species in isolated environments which furnished much of the data for the *Origin of Species*. Part of the pleasure of reading the chapter now is the pleasure of hindsight in which, with the edition of 1845 at least, the first tentative approaches to the theory of evolution by means of natural selection appear between the lines of the scenes evoked. Even more pleasure is located in Darwin's wonderfully sharp descriptions of those scenes for their own sake.

The relationship between narrative and description is, of course, a complex one, as was noted above.[12] Although description can exist without narrative and does in a variety of discourses, literary and nonliterary, whenever a story is told description is subordinated to it. Narrative, on the other hand, is never entirely pure of description. In works of travel writing that place a particular emphasis on documentary value, however, description comes to be the *raison d'être* and the narration of events its support. And this is especially true where the writer is a scientist like Darwin. Many of his descriptions have a taxonomic exactitude because he is concerned to identify and report on the variety of familiar and unfamiliar natural phenomena for the scientific community in his homeland. Yet, often enough even here, where the referential function of language is primary, the attentive looking and the precise descriptions that

[12] See Philippe Hamon, "What Is a Description?" in *French Literary Theory Today: A Reader*, ed. Tzvetan Todorov (Cambridge: Cambridge University Press, 1982).

result carry a strong emotional charge. The effort to efface the observer and to desubjectivize language in the interest of the object is only exceptionally brought off. The impression given is often that the desire to capture with a look has replaced the desire to hunt. In short, the vocation of the naturalist is made to seem both less pure and more interesting on account of the libidinal investments it supports.

Darwin's mastery of the rhetoric of narrative emerges clearly in the passages on the Galapagos. The chapter begins by noting the location of the islands and describing their geological formation before giving some concreteness to the narrative through personal impressions and suggestive anecdotes. It also incorporates the famous detailed, scientifically precise descriptions of the mammals, reptiles, and birds, many of which are unique to the Galapagos Islands.

"Nothing could be less promising than the first appearance," Darwin notes on landing on the first of the islands he was to visit and finding himself surrounded with black basaltic lava. Yet, he almost immediately comes upon two of the monstrous creatures from which the archipelago takes its name, and he finds himself transported to the realm of prehistory and legend: "The day was glowing hot, and the scrambling over the rough surface and through the intricate thickets, was very fatiguing; but I was well repaid by the strange Cyclopean scene. As I was walking along I met two large tortoises, each of which must have weighed at least two hundred pounds: one was eating a piece of cactus, and as I approached, it stared at me and slowly stalked away; the other gave a deep hiss, and drew in its head. These huge reptiles, surrounded by the black lava, the leafless shrubs, and large cacti, seemed to my fancy like some antediluvian animals" (*Voyage*, pp. 375–376). This, as the imagery suggests, is as close as the protagonist of the *Voyage* ever comes to Ulysses in his encounters with mythic monsters. The excitement of the encounter is in the destabilizing thrill of the return to the prehistory of the Creation.

The force of Darwin's response here to an encounter with a wild and wholly astonishing creature has recently been finely rendered by Barry Lopez: "Few things provoke like the presence of wild animals. They pull at us like tidal currents with questions of volition, of ethical involvement, of ancestry."[13] The whole scene in the *Voyage* is, in any case, evoked with novelistic precision in order to communicate the impact of a confrontation in which the science of natural history yields to its romance. The author has recourse to the rhetoric of fictional representation in order to express the astonishment of coming face to face with what is, in effect, a "wonder" for science. Moreover, the effect of the surprise is to engage

---

[13] *Arctic Dreams: Imagination and Desire in a Northern Landscape* (Toronto: Bantam Books, 1987), p. 33.

his imagination and not his reason, although the narrator of the *Voyage* at least soon recovers in order to resume with an appropriate scientific discourse. It is, in any case, characteristic of Darwin's narrative technique that he should dramatize the scene with himself as intradiegetic narrator and heroic protagonist. In accordance with the post-Jamesian orthodoxy of Anglo-American literary criticism, in fact, Darwin prefers "scene" to "narrative summary" for its greater power of mimetic illusion. "Scene," after all, implies an unmediated looking that caters to reader pleasure by setting events before the mind's eye.

Darwin's following twenty pages are devoted to relatively detailed descriptions of the mammals, reptiles, and birds of the Galapagos that begin with a wonderfully understated comment: "The natural history of these islands is eminently curious, and well deserves attention" (*Voyage*, p. 378). And Darwin makes no attempt to conceal his sense of wonder at the uniqueness of such a range of creatures inhabiting a limited and geologically recent territory: "Hence, both in space and time, we seem to be brought somewhat near to that great fact—that mystery of mysteries— the first appearance of new beings on this earth" (*Voyage*, p. 379). Darwin confirms here, if confirmation were needed, that like so many world travelers before and after him, at the heart of his search is a quest for origins. The questions Darwin touches on are those which were to be formulated by Gauguin, at the end of Darwin's century, in one of his most haunting and most symbolist of paintings, referred to above in Chapter III, *Where Do We Come From? What Are We? Where Are We Going?*

If, therefore, Darwin's language here expresses a quality of religious awe, this is hardly surprising. After all, the traditional explanation in the West of that "mystery of mysteries" to which he refers is to be found in the biblical story of the Creation, along with all that it implied concerning both a single creative moment and the fixity of God-given species.

The immense appeal of the voyage for the man who was also a naturalist is made even clearer in the rest of the chapter. Darwin goes on to exclaim at the novelties of the natural world in which he finds himself and at the extraordinariness of its points of similarity with what he had previously encountered: "It was most striking to be surrounded by new birds, new reptiles, new shells, new insects, new plants, and yet by innumerable trifling details of structure, and even by the tones of voice and plumage of the birds, to have the temperate plains of Patagonia, or the hot deserts of Northern Chile, vividly brought before my eyes" (*Voyage*, p. 393). "Newness" was, of course, the feature that also attracted jaded romantic sensibilities to travel, from Byron's Childe Harold to the narrator of Baudelaire's "Le Voyage" and Huysmans's decadent hero par excellence, Des Esseintes.

But the rhetorical insistence on "newness" is coupled in Darwin's narrative with a significant element of suspense. He does not produce in these pages the legendary "Eureka" that announces a major scientific breakthrough, but he does suggest the excitement of an informed mind's sudden perception that something extraordinary for science is implied by a previously unacknowledged pattern in the data: "My attention was first thoroughly aroused, by comparing together the numerous specimens, shot by myself and several other parties on board, of the mocking-thrushes, when, to my astonishment, I discovered that all those from Charles Island belonged to one species (Mimus trifasciatus)" (*Voyage*, p. 395).

The consequences of *The Voyage of the Beagle* for science are well known. If no single voyage since that of Columbus has had a greater impact on humanity's view of the world than Darwin's, that is above all owing to the encounter between a man educated to understand the outstanding scientific questions of his age—the anomalous data that do not fit the paradigm in a given field—and an apparently virgin continent that could shed new light on them. It appears likely that Darwin was gradually weaned away from the Creationism of orthodox Christians of his time to a form of Uniformitarianism by the mounting evidence before, during, and after the voyage.

As has been often noted, Charles Lyell's *Principles of Geology* was the crucial text that in the early 1830s had made the case for the gradual and continuous change of the earth in opposition to the periodic catastrophism of a certain natural theology. And it was Lyell's work that Darwin took with him on the *Beagle*. It is not surprising, therefore, if some of the most thrilling moments of the *Voyage* for its author turn out to be those when he comes upon physical confirmation of the truths of the new geology, notably in the fossil remains in the mountains of Chile.

At such moments, Darwin the naturalist is frequently overwhelmed by the significance of what he has seen from the point of view of the Creation and produces brief odes in prose. The scientific theorist's delight in finding fossil shells in the rare air of the Andes is matched by the man's joy in a view that he renders with a studiedly evocative prose that aims for effects similar to those of the verses of *Childe Harold*: "Neither plant nor bird, excepting a few condors wheeling around the higher pinnacles, distracted my attention from the inanimate mass. I felt glad that I was alone: it was like watching a thunderstorm, or hearing in full orchestra a chorus of the Messiah" (*Voyage*, p. 324). The passage as a whole could be cited as an example of the picturesque as romantic sublime. Its intensity is reinforced by two self-conscious images connoting powerful emotions.

If Darwin traveled officially as a "naturalist," who took the whole of nature and its history for his domain, he was also frequently its opposite, or what might be called a "culturalist." In the story of his voyage around the world, he shows almost as much interest in his own species, its social and political organization and uneven development, as he does in forms of natural life or in geological formations. Darwin's concerns are, in fact, probably more global than those of any other writer I have discussed in this work, with the possible exception of Claude Lévi-Strauss.

The differential development of the human race and the unequal relations between its various subgroups is, for example, one of Darwin's major preoccupations, as it was for certain eighteenth-century predecessors. After Humboldt's account of his American travels and his own experience, Darwin is naturally disinclined to accept Buffon's theologically inspired explanation of American backwardness. Like other world travelers before him, Darwin comments on the native populations of such *loci classici* of the literature of circumnavigation as Brazil, Argentina proper, Tierra del Fuego, Tahiti, New Zealand, and Australia. His impressions sometimes confirm and sometimes contradict the findings of those who went before. He is, for example, mostly struck by the beauty of the South American Indians of General Juan Manuel Rosas's "banditti-like army," and he praises the Tahitians both for their physical beauty, including their skin color,[14] and their gentleness: "There is a mildness in the expression of their countenances which at once banishes the idea of a savage." The Fuegians, however, provide him, too, with an example of *Homo sapiens* at the lowest rung of the developmental ladder. The first sight of even the taller Eastern Fuegians almost gives rise to a category confusion: "I could not have believed how great was the distance between savage and civilized man: it is greater than between a wild and domesticated animal, inasmuch as in man there is a greater power of improvement" (*Voyage*, p. 205). With these Fuegians, it is apparent, Darwin's capacity for intraspecies fellow feeling reaches its limit; there is, so to speak, a shock of nonrecognition: "Viewing such men, one can hardly make oneself believe that they are fellow-creatures, and inhabitants of the same world" (*Voyage*, p. 213).

Throughout the *Voyage*, the politics of colonial societies and relations between racial groups are often at the forefront of the concerns of this young man with a Whig family background and a commitment to the progress of civilization in the spirit of the Enlightenment. He comments both in sadness and in anger at certain examples of the dominance of Europeans or their descendants over peoples of other races, although he by no means impugns the colonial system as such—of white over black in Brazil, where its most objectionable form is to be found in the institution

[14] "A white man bathing by the side of a Tahitian, was like a plant bleached by the gardener's art compared with a fine green one growing vigorously in the open fields" (*Voyage*, p. 404).

of slavery; of white over red in Argentina, where he encounters firsthand the campaigns of extermination commanded by General Rosas against the pampas Indians; of white over brown and black in the South Seas, New Zealand, and Australia, where he encounters British settlers exercising different forms of subjugation.

It is in Australia particularly that he reflects on the devastating impact of the arrival of the more powerful and culturally advanced outsiders on native populations. Once again, a traveler from a much earlier period anticipates Lévi-Strauss's theme of the melancholy of the tropics. Apart from anything else, anyone who has read Bougainville's and Cook's descriptions of their visits to Tahiti is likely to experience shock at the references in Darwin's *Voyage* to Christian missionaries, churchgoing natives, and Presbyterian-style sabbaths on New Cythera. Finally, Darwin takes little comfort from his observations of the new Latin American republics in the decades shortly after their independence from Spain. In Argentina he finds that "sensuality, mockery of all religion, and the grossest corruption, are far from uncommon. Nearly every public officer can be bribed" (*Voyage*, p. 157).

o   o   o

THERE ARE at least two occasions in *The Voyage of the Beagle* when Darwin anticipates Freud's comments on travel which are the subject of a later chapter. They are no more than asides casually thrown out before the British naturalist moves on to other things, but in both cases Darwin's incisive reflections illuminate attitudes that Freud was to explore more deliberately. On the first occasion, Darwin discusses his feelings at standing on a mountain peak in Chile; on the second, sailing toward New Zealand, he is reminded of childhood experiences of doubt and wonder.

The first experience touches on the peculiar narcissism of travel: "Every one must know the feeling of triumph and pride," he comments in Chile, "which a grand view from a height communicates to the mind. In these little frequented countries there is also joined to it some vanity, that you are perhaps the first man who ever stood on this pinnacle or admired this view" (*Voyage*, p. 283). Unlike Freud, Darwin does not specifically associate such an experience with the mingled sense of triumph and guilt at the idea of having gone beyond his father. Nevertheless, the self-regarding heroism invoked here is that of the explorer or pioneer, who manages to go farther or higher than all predecessors, including his own progenitor.

In the second case, as Darwin first approaches the coast of New Zealand, he notes that he has crossed "the meridian of the Antipodes" and is now on his return journey to England. It is an experience that leaves him strangely disillusioned: "These Antipodes call to one's mind old recollections of childish doubt and wonder. Only the other day I looked forward to this airy barrier as a definite point in our voyage homewards; but now I find it, and all such resting-places for the imagination, are like shadows, which a man moving onwards cannot catch" (*Voyage*, p. 416). It is not often that one finds a more moving evocation of the kind of early denial Freud was to dub "derealization," of the persistence of early memory, and of the restlessness of a desire that circles the globe and still fails to discover anticipated satisfactions. Darwin, the scientist, formulates a similar sense of loss to Baudelaire, the poet:

> To the child in love with maps and prints,
> The universe is the equal of his vast appetite.
> Oh! how big the world seems by the light of a lamp.
> How small it appears to an eye that looks back.
>
> ["Le Voyage"]

Nevertheless, all in all, Darwin's experience of circumnavigation of the globe in the 1830s is such that it leaves him a chastened observer of his fellow humans and an awed celebrant of the natural world, although it is significant that he makes virtually no reference to the Creator. In the *Autobiography*, Darwin speculates that it was the images of distant lands encountered in a schoolbook on the Wonders of the World that excited in him the desire to travel. And that desire results many years later in the extraordinary book of his own voyage, a book in which the wonders are natural phenomena of a complexity and magnitude that once virtually defied belief. An order of things is registered that dwarfs even the most astonishing human achievements.

The point is made succinctly in connection with the formation of coral reefs, in one of Darwin's boldest early scientific hypotheses: "We feel surprise when travellers tell us of the vast dimensions of the Pyramids and other great ruins, but how utterly insignificant are the greatest of these, when compared with these mountains of stone accumulated by the agency of various minute and tender animals! This is a wonder that does not at first strike the eye of the body, but, after reflection, the eye of reason" (*Voyage*, p. 464). The reason the final metaphor here is especially suggestive of Darwin's stance as traveler is that it places the emphasis on the relationship between an exceptional emotional experience stimulated by a look, "wonder," and intellectual inquiry. The scopic drive itself is subject to the mechanism of sublimation and is made to serve the end of knowledge. The naturalist, it turns out, is a traveler who trains the passionate intensity of his gaze. Darwin's natural history is a science of looking twice.

Chapter VI

THE PERVERSE TRAVELER: FLAUBERT IN THE ORIENT

IN HIS travel writings, from *Rome, Naples et Florence en 1817* to *Promenades dans Rome*, Stendhal made it very clear that he had no interest in traveling outside Europe. If the Italian peninsula was the source and center of Western civilization since the Renaissance, then he saw no necessity to emulate Byron's Childe Harold in this respect, at least, by pursuing his travels into the Eastern Mediterranean and the Near East. The purpose of travel for Stendhal, as for the grand tourists in general, was to move up on the scale of civilization, not down, to go from a land where artistic creativity and the arts of social living were less developed to one where they were more so. To travel in the opposite direction would certainly have struck him as perverse.[1]

Yet, by the late 1820s Stendhal appears to have been something of an exception in his homeland, since it was precisely that kind of travel which a great many travelers with literary and artistic ambitions began to seek out. It was non-Europe that interested them, mostly for reasons that were very different from those of the emergent anthropology of the eighteenth century; they were drawn to otherness for its own sake, the otherness of "the uncivilized" or of lands at least uncontaminated by the Christian religion, Enlightenment humanism, democratic politics, or industrial progress. Nowhere is this more apparent than in the vogue of the so-called Orient, a vogue that largely overlaps with the romantic movement in French art, literature, and music, and whose most familiar icons are Victor Hugo's collection of poems, *Les Orientales* (1829), the sketches and paintings of Delacroix that were inspired by his official visit to Algeria in 1832, and Gustave Flaubert's own *Salammbô* (1862).

At least since Napoleon's incursions into Egypt, the French state under various regimes down through the nineteenth century sought to assert political hegemony of one kind or another over a number countries in North Africa and the Middle East, often in competition with Britain. The subjugation of Algeria began in earnest in 1827, as a response to a perceived provocation, but was not completed until 1847; and in 1836 the erection of the obelisk of Sesostris on the Place de la Concorde was in

[1] A shorter version of this chapter appeared in *L'Esprit Createur* 29, no. 1 (Spring 1989).

itself a grand hegemonic gesture, designed to affirm the kind of homage the French imperial state expected from tributary nations.

Furthermore, French artists, writers, and scholars were not loath to follow the flag, especially in exploring North African and Middle Eastern countries and their cultures, for purposes that were frequently in conformity with the discourse of French public life but often were not.[2] In fact, as far as writers were concerned, from Chateaubriand—whose *Itinéraire de Paris à Jerusalem* of 1811 became something of a model—to Lamartine, Théophile Gautier, Gérard de Nerval, Pierre Loti, and Maurice Barrès, the *voyage en Orient* came to assume the character of an obligatory journey, a challenge to one's imagination and a test of one's powers as a writer—although, as notably with Lamartine, that did not necessarily prevent such writers from asserting French geopolitical rights and civilizing duties.

By the time Flaubert set out on his journey south on 29 October 1849, in the company of his friend Maxime du Camp, the literary and artistic avant-garde already associated the Orient with the emancipation of all the senses that Rimbaud was to pursue barely two decades later and that found its most memorable formulation in his poetic narrative of an hallucinatory voyage, "The Drunken Boat." Flaubert as traveler is situated somewhere between the early-nineteenth-century Bohemian and the *poète maudit* of its closing decades. The account of his journey is, in fact, such that it calls for the addition of yet another type to Laurence Sterne's catalogue of travelers: namely, the Perverse Traveler, a type that emerges in its fullness only with the late romantic moment.

The Stendhal of *Promenades dans Rome* still belongs to the eighteenth-century, sentimental tradition in travel writing that Sterne inaugurated; he shares his predecessor's propensity "to overestimate" a feminine love object, and the sites and cities associated with it. The Perverse Traveler of Flaubert's *Voyage en Orient*, on the other hand, indulges in no such fantasies. He expresses none of the celebratory Enlightenment attitude of the grand tourist toward Western civilization. Nor does he show the combination of tenderness and sensuality for a partner of the opposite sex that the Freud of *Three Essays on Sexuality* (1905) associated with the sex drive of the normal adult and the traditional idea of "love"—a combination that has a prominent place in Nerval's *Voyage en Orient*, for example. In Flaubert's oriental journey one finds instead a symptomatic fondness for forms of sexual deviance, including scenarios of voyeurism and sadism.

---

[2] The role played by such scholars and thinkers as Silvestre de Sacy, Edgar Quinet, and Ernest Renan in the formation of the discourse of "Orientalism" is, of course, at the center of Edward Said's concern in *Orientalism* (New York: Vintage Books, 1978).

The importance of Freud's *Essays* for the understanding of perversity was, of course, that they insisted on the extraordinarily polymorphous character of human sexuality and on the fact that the sexual drive of the mature adult is not a simple given. On the contrary, it is constructed out of a number of component drives that are precariously integrated in the course of the complex process of physiological maturation and the assumption of human subjecthood under the aegis of a genital sexuality that identifies a partner of the opposite sex as its object and genital satisfaction as its aim. Freud concludes the *Three Essays on Sexuality* with the summarizing comment that "a disposition to perversions is an original and universal disposition of the human sexual instinct," and "normal sexual behavior is developed out of it as a result of organic changes and psychical inhibitions occuring in the course of maturation."[3]

Given that the various drives are born separately and develop relatively independently, the potential for deviation from the object and aim that Freud defines as the norm is great—for the dissociation of the component instincts, regression, and fixation on pregenital modes of satisfaction. Further, Freud interprets perversion as a pathological structure of the adult human being that results from the unsatisfactory overcoming of the Oedipus complex under the threat of castration. Preliminary acts are preferred to the normal sexual act, and the choice of object is sometimes a person of the same sex (homosexuality) or a detached part of the partner's body (fetishism).

Finally, for the purpose of my argument, it is important to remember two more points in Freud's discussion of the perversions. First, the drive as such—looking or offering oneself to the other's look, sexual aggression or passivity—is not in itself a perversion. It becomes so only if it turns out to be the principal source of sexual satisfaction for the adult libido and if it has the kind of psychic fixity for which psychoanalysis invented the categories of voyeurism and exhibitionism, sadism and masochism. Thus, the scopophilia that is the drive classically associated with travel assumes a perverse form only exceptionally, and it does so increasingly in travel writings from the romantic age on. Second, as Freud notes in the "Summary" of the *Essays*, "neurosis is, as it were, the negative of perversion" (*S.E.*, vol. 7, p. 231). The opposition between the two pathological structures consists in whether perverse fantasms are consciously acknowledged or are repressed by the subject, are directly narratable or emerge only as symptoms. In a carefully argued discussion of the issue, Patrick Valas summarizes the distinction as follows: "the *unconscious* fantasms of the neuroses (witnesses of the original perverse im-

---

[3] In *The Standard Edition of the Complete Psychological Works* (London: Hogarth, 1955), vol. 7, p. 231; hereafter, referred to as *S.E.*

pulses) are identical in the their smallest details to the conscious fantasms of perversion."[4] Just how "conscious" such fantasms may become in the self-conscious elaborations of a travel narrative is apparent in Flaubert's *Voyage en Orient*.

For Freud, then, looking was a perversion if it ceased to be a component instinct of genital sexuality and became an end in itself; it was present wherever the eroticized curiosity found all the satisfaction it required in the intensity of a look. Moreover, an extra charge is attached when it is not just a matter of looking, but of "over-looking"; voyeurism is an eavesdropping of the eyes. The voyeur is mostly, but not invariably, an unseen seer. Thus, it is no accident if that phrase calls up Michel Foucault's discussion of the panopticon. The pleasures of voyeurism are commonly related to the exercise of power in one form or another. That is why, in Flaubert's *Voyage* as elswehere, it is frequently associated with sadism. The powerful curiosity to see the body of a potential sexual partner is joined to the desire to overpower and to despoil it. In the end, this whole complex of more or less potent impulses are written into the text of Flaubert's journey to the Middle East as an orientation toward destruction and death.

Studies of Flaubert's adolescent literary taste, his letters, and his posthumously published *œuvres de jeunesse* have amply demonstrated his enthusiasm for the clamorous and flamboyantly iconoclastic writings of the so-called *petits romantiques*, for the imperial decadence of ancient Rome, or for the extravagant lives of saints and sinners in general.[5] The other face of Flaubert's famous withdrawal from active life in the solitary cult of his craft was, in fact, his occasional excursions into the Bohemian world of Parisian artistic circles. Long periods of denial of the senses in Normandy were interupted by more or less brief interludes of sensual indulgence in the capital.

Moreover, from early on the young Flaubert contrived to *épater le bourgeois* in his own way. He took, in particular, a special pleasure in inventing ways to shock his putative readers. Thus, there is an obvious continuity between the enthusiastic overwriting of the early, more or less gothic tales, with their grotesque twists and macabre detailing, and the Middle Eastern travel book itself. On one level, the *Voyage en Orient* reminds us how single-minded its author was from the beginning to the end of his career. "If ever I play an active role in the world," Flaubert wrote when he was still an adolescent, "it will be as a thinker and demoralizer. I will

---

[4] "Freud et la perversion," *Ornicar: Revue du Champ Freudien* 45 (1988), p. 35.

[5] See, for example, Jean Bruneau, *Les Débuts littéraires de Gustave Flaubert* (Paris: Colin, 1962); and Dennis Porter, "Mythic Imagery in Flaubert's *Œuvres de jeunesse*," *Australian Journal of French Studies* 9, no. 2 (1972).

simply tell the truth, but it will be horrible, cruel, and naked."[6] Not surprisingly, therefore, the truth he discovers in the lands bordering the Mediterranean is his kind of "truth," one associated precisely with a laying bare that shocks and unsettles beliefs.

That Flaubert was single-minded throughout the course of his artistic life does not, of course, imply that his works are monotonously repetitive or even unified. The *Voyage* is no exception to this general rule. Although there are a great many passages in which Flaubert turns himself into a kind of underground guide to forbidden, disturbing, and even horrifying spectacles or activities, at other times he evokes episodes that belong to the register of heroic adventure or describes sites and natural scenes with the painterly precision of the picturesque tradition.

Nevertheless, if, as I noted in the previous chapter, Sartre was accurate in enumerating the major themes of the nineteenth-century *déclassé* writer as, after art itself, love, travel, and war, Flaubert's career in letters can be seen to have marked a decisively new and more disturbing stage in the way such themes are developed compared with Stendhal's. Art, of course, had become preeminent. Love comes to be sacrilegiously reconnected to a scandalously corrupt body. Travel is embraced as a form of *voyage maudit*. War, finally, is uncoupled from the heroics of *la grande armée* and survives in the *Voyage* in the frenzies of the hunt. Sartre glossed the situation of the nineteenth-century French writer in general as a form of destructive parasitism: "That discredit with which military, aristocratic societies regarded the professions is taken over by the writer. But it is not enough for him to be useless, like the *ancien régime* courtiers; he seeks to trample underfoot utilitarian work, to smash, burn, and destroy things, thus imitating the carelessness of feudal lords who led their hunt across fields of ripe grain."[7]

o   o   o

THE JOURNEY south that began in October 1849 in a mood of depression was completed some eighteen months later when, in June 1851, Flaubert returned to his home at Croisset. The journal that gives an account of Flaubert's journey was first published in something like its entirety under the title *Notes de Voyage en Orient* in the Conard edition of 1910.[8] Like the subsequent editions, this one retains the disparate and fragmentary character of a work that the author himself never recast for the purpose of publication.

In spite of frequent *longueurs* and whole pages where the author

---

[6] *Correspondance* (Paris: Conard, 1926–1933), vol. 1, p. 41.

[7] *Qu'est-ce que la Littérature?* (Paris: Gallimard, 1948), pp. 159–160.

[8] See Antoine-Youssef Naaman, *Les Lettres d'Egypte de Gustave Flaubert* (Paris: Nizet, 1965), for an account of much of this same material in Flaubert's correspondence.

merely reproduces the kind of shorthand catalog of artifacts or perfunctory guidebook descriptions that are of little interest to a modern reader,
Flaubert's *Voyage en Orient* is a disturbing and symptomatic text on a number of levels. On the one hand, like the systematic apologists for empire
whose writings were analyzed in Said's *Orientalism*, Flaubert underwrites
throughout the inherited binary opposition between an Occident associated with European civilization and an Orient that begins in Alexandria
or Beirut. On the other hand, he more often than not reverses the traditional Eurocentric hierarchy in order to contrast Oriental wisdom with
Western cultural smugness. For him, the East frequently reveals the very
"truths" of existence that Western sentimentality and Western hypocrisy
have made it their task to conceal in the bourgeois century. Thus, the
writing of Flaubert's travel book—like that of the version of *The Temptation of Saint Anthony* he completed just before setting out on his journey
or that of the subsequent *Salammbô*—belongs at least as much to what
Mario Praz first called "the romantic agony"[9] as to what Said calls "Orientalism." It speaks to the discontents of a repressive civilization whose
values it goes out of its way to subvert.

The Flaubertian self is no more homogeneous or consistently self-pres-
ent than any other. There are, therefore, a great many passages in the
text that express indirectly the peculiarly overdetermined character of
any encounter with foreign places and peoples.[10] The themes raised in
the opening pages of the *Voyage* as well as the odd chronology of the
presentation make this immediately apparent. Right after the leave-tak-
ing of October 1849, there follows a section written on a boat on the Nile
in February 1850; and that section itself begins with the recall of the author's first voyage to Corsica ten years previously, when he was eighteen
years old. Further, interspersed with a few references to the Nile and a
description of the scene, are longer passages that call up memories of
other journeys, including the one south to Marseilles from which he had
embarked for Egypt just three months before but which, to the writer on

[9] *The Romantic Agony* (Oxford: Oxford University Press, 1933).
[10] The concept of overdetermination is useful in suggesting why my reading of the
Voyage is so different from Richard Terdiman's in "Ideological Voyages: On a Flaubertian Dis-Orient-ation." He affirms that his object is "to detect in Flaubert's writing
concerning the trip the structures by which the discourse which he would so fervently
have wanted to expunge from his own persisted within it." *Discourse/Counter-Discourse:
The Theory and Practice of Symbolic Resistance in Nineteenth-Century France* (Ithaca: Cornell
University Press, 1985), p. 234. While not denying the force of that "dominant discourse" from which Terdiman sees Flaubert struggling in vain to escape, I focus on
the multiple, contradictory, individual psychic investments that are written into Flaubert's disturbing text. They are often ironically of such a kind, in fact, that they manage
to make the "dominant discourse" look not so bad by comparison.

the Nile, now seems so long ago—"My God, how distant it all is."[11] In short, not too far into his Eastern journey, Flaubert scrambles memories of the immediate and remoter past along with more generalized cultural reminiscences of the significance of travel as psychic loss and recovery.

The point to note is that, in Flaubert's novels as in the *Voyage*, when travel is at issue the present opens effortlessly onto the past or fantasizes a future somewhere else, memory becomes reverie and vice versa. As a result, it is sometimes difficult to disentangle real events from their representation *après coup*. The *déjà vu* of travel is "located" in the sense that the countries one is passing through for the first time are part of a complex transferential network; they belong to one's own intimate geography as lands already desired or feared.

In this connection, a stretch of Flaubert's journey from Paris by that older mode of locomotion beloved of the German romantics, the stagecoach, inspires a suggestive question: "In the corner of your memory doesn't there exist the still vivid reminiscence of some hill dominating a desired land?" (*Voyage*, p. 553). That reference to "a desired land" remembered—"in the corner of your memory"—may serve as a reminder that human psychic activity is such that no approach to a foreign country is ever wholly unprepared. On his Oriental journey, Nerval, like Baudelaire after him, even speculated about the persistence of memories from *une vie antérieure*.

It is no accident, then, that Flaubert's travel book begins where, at their deepest level, all travel books begin, whether or not that fact is acknowledged in the text: at home. Yet, among such books not written under external duress, few give a greater emphasis to the pain of departure. It is a pain that is associated chiefly with separation from the author's mother but, in part, also with the phobia of travel—our late-twentieth-century fear of flying had a nineteenth-century counterpart, most notably in the traumas associated with journeys by rail.[12]

The narrator opens his story by describing the day he took leave of his mother as "an atrocious day, the worst I have ever lived through." And he goes on to evoke the scene in his mother's little garden and house at Nogent with a sharpness that recalls the peculiarly wrenching emotions of significant departures. After having mentioned the kisses and caresses he gave her seated in her armchair, he concludes the episode with a reference to the memorable last sound he heard her make: "What a cry she uttered when I closed the living room door! It reminded me of the one I heard her emit at the death of my father, when she took his hand"

[11] *Œuvres complètes* (Paris: Le Seuil, 1964), p. 555.

[12] See "The Pathology of the Railroad Journey," "The Accident," and "Railway Accident," in Wolfgang Schivelbusch, *The Railway Journey: The Industrialization of Time and Space in the 19th Century* (Berkeley: University of California Press, 1986).

(*Voyage*, p. 551). It is a cry that suggests at least two important and incompatible ideas. On the one hand, Flaubert hears in it a recognition of the fact that he now occupies the place of his dead father; on the other, there is also the implication that his decision to leave signifies his own death as far as his mother is concerned. The narrator's reaction is characteristically ambivalent. The guilt he apparently felt at the demand for love spurned cohabits with a sense of power. There is pleasure as well as displeasure in his mother's pain.

It is thus characteristic that, like such celebrated travelers as Byron and Stendhal before him, Flaubert rejects the path of familial duty. In a symptomatic sentence that follows immediately the one just quoted, the devoted son refers to his other life in the capital, a life in which the apparent overestimation of a mother gives way to the systematic underestimation of women of another kind: "The next two days I lived in the grand style, feasting, drinking, and whoring; the senses are not far from tenderness, and my poor nerves had been so cruelly twisted, they needed to relax" (*Voyage*, p. 551). This nineteenth-century neurasthenic recognized his depressive symptoms and prescribed his own treatment through a form of emancipation in which the perversions of voyeurism and sadism were frequently engaged in. Flaubert's text demonstrates the validity of Valas's comment that "perversion is a subjective position (and not a manifestation of instinct) that is sustained by a conscious fantasm, a fantasm that the subject may be led to realize in modes of behavior which are organized in terms of this fantasm" ("Perversion," p. 37).

In any case, as Freud makes clear in the *Three Essays on Sexuality* and elsewhere, psychoanalysis relates perverse behavior in an adult to an early sexual history in which a strong fear of castration plays a prominent role. As a result, love for the mother is repressed but, for a variety of reasons, does not reemerge as love for a substitute female love object. In Flaubert's case, one finds instead a form of homoeroticism that narcissistically celebrates maleness by repeatedly exposing and calling attention to the signs of imperfection on female bodies. His apparent mother-love disguises a depreciation of the mother that is nevertheless displaced onto other women in his fantasms.

The fact that Flaubert celebrates travel as transgression more systematically than any of his predecessors is confirmed, in part, by the fact that throughout the whole *Voyage* he only once mentions the possibility that a traveler might have responsibilities to home and country that transcend the pursuit of individual pleasure or self-cultivation. He mentions the possibility precisely in order to reject it mockingly, when he suddenly realizes how bored he is by Egyptian temples: "Doing what one is supposed to do! Being always, as circumstances require (however repugnant you happen to find it), like a proper young man, a traveler, an artist, a son, a citizen, etc. is supposed to be" (*Voyage*, p. 581). Flaubert's Orient exists for the traveler's personal use or, in other words, his pleasure.

Even before leaving France, Flaubert's narrator makes clear two of the major motifs of the travel book as a whole; they have nothing to do with the notion of dutifulness. The first concerns the different degrees of pleasure associated with travel and registered in the body as one moves at different speeds through space. A little later in the text, with the description of the traveler's first sight of Marseilles, the pleasures of the journey become sharper. He wakes up and suddenly finds himself looking down on the Mediterannean city in the early morning light. The pleasure here is in the look itself: "I had a sensation of virile pleasure (*volupté virile*) such as I have never felt since. I fell immediately in love with this ancient sea that I had so often dreamed about!" (*Voyage*, p. 555). One recognizes in the discourse of the passage that *romantisme flamboyant* which associated the south with sensuality and vibrancy of local color. The narrator finds himself stirred by the warm air to an anticipatory "Oriental indolence (*mollesses orientales*)," and he concludes the paragraph with a future conditional that was to be the characteristic tense of Emma Bovary's reveries: "the large paving stones of the Canebière, which warmed the soles of my pumps, made my calves stiffen at the idea of the burning beaches on which I would have liked to walk" (*Voyage*, p. 555). One hardly needs the adjective "virile" at the beginning of the passage to be alerted to the erotic metonymic displacements down to the passionate surrender of self implied by the "burning beaches" of the end.

The second major motif of this early section is connected to the first, because it involves an active kind of looking animated by a more obvious, sexually charged curiosity. Curiosity may, of course, be associated with a sublimated form of looking, the kind associated with cognition and socially useful discovery in Darwin's *Voyage*. But in Flaubert's journal it is conflated with a scopic drive that associates knowing with a laying bare. Thus, an illuminating passage connects the narcissistic satisfaction in the rise of virility contingent on a proffered sight to a form of looking that is a progressive unveiling or, in the context, undisguised sexual aggression. The object in this case is not a city but a woman, a fellow passenger on a boat on the Saône.

The circumstances of the meeting, along with elements of the portrait Flaubert presents, anticipate the celebrated opening chapter of *Sentimental Education*. In both cases, the narrator begins with a characteristically precise description of a woman's clothes and the outlines of a body they simultaneously hide and reveal. The fetishistic circumstantiality displayed is, of course, an expression of that preoccupation with "fashion" which is a typical feature of nineteenth-century French literature. It is also, in Flaubert's fiction at least, the preliminary tableau that fixes a certain image of woman as the fullness of an ideal, before that image is progressively "disrobed" in the course of the narrative.

The difference between Flaubert's novel and his travel book is that whereas in the former he distances himself from his material in order to allow his narrative to unfold, in the latter he theorizes the curiosity he feels as a writer. The inquisitiveness he expresses about the woman is at the same time the curiosity of a man and of a novelist; the desire to know here is, on the one hand, a desire to see and possess and, on the other, a desire to expose what has been seen and possessed through the act of writing: "For I have that mania of constructing books on the people that I meet. In spite of myself, an ungovernable curiosity makes me wonder what kind of life a passerby might lead. I would like to know his profession, his country, his name. . . . And if a woman is involved, especially a middle-aged woman, then the itch becomes unbearable. Admit how you would like straightaway to see her naked, naked to her very heart" (*Voyage*, p. 554).

Such a passage connects the activity of the novelist with an aggressive male voyeurism—"naked to her very heart"—that finds in travel a wonderful variety of exciting new objects for its look. The violence done involves a form of forbidden seeing that is exercised on an unwitting victim. And such a visual pursuit of nakedness of and beyond the unclothed body is a recurrent motif in the *Voyage*. The perverse scenario of this and other passages anticipates in a more explicit way Frédéric Moreau's experience of women. It even suggests that that wayward hero's famous "N'est-ce que ça?" (Is that all there is to it?) is less the lament of a disabused idealist than that of an embittered fetishist who compulsively repeats in disgust and anger his encounter with nonphallic woman.

Furthermore, the force of the scopic drive that is here directed at the female body focuses with a symptomatic repetitiveness at other moments in the text on precise evocations of eroticism and death that embody the grotesque and the macabre. In the same way that clothes hide that nakedness which is the "reality" of the flesh, so the flesh in its turn hides the profounder nakedness of what lies beneath. In the *Voyage*, as throughout Flaubert's work, to go to the end of a significant experience is to experience the *néant* in a beyond of pleasure. One is reminded that in his fiction Flaubert is an especially acute observer of decay. His narrators typically find satisfaction in recording scenarios of loss and even of dismemberment.

Yet, before exploring these themes further, it is worth recalling that all is not "romantic agony" in Flaubert's *Voyage*. The nineteenth-century Bohemian-cum-*poète maudit* is different from the eighteenth-century rake, in part because his rebellion against society's moral codes and values is informed by the cult of art. And throughout his travel book Flaubert attempts to do justice to the sights and scenes in a self-consciously literary prose that, like Byron's verse, takes up the challenge of its object and of the sensations inspired. There are, therefore, numerous more or less short descriptive passages that would not be out of place in a contemporary novel. There are set-piece descriptions of landscapes, village or urban scenes, evocations of architectural monuments, palaces, temples, ruins, celebrated sites, and pictures of crowds or memorable individuals. There is also the more than usual number of those incidents and strange encounters which are the stock in trade of travel writing.

At the same time, anyone who is habituated to the idea of Flaubert as a prototypical nineteenth-century aesthete is likely to be surprised by the elements of heroic adventure in the *Voyage*. In his late twenties at least, Flaubert often appears very different from the aesthete or *fin-de-siècle* decadent with which he is sometimes associated.[13] Much of the time in Egypt and the Near East, making full use of France's network of colonial relations, he and his companions traveled on horseback or occasionally by ass. They passed through the desert and were exposed to the risks and hardships—from fleas and bedbugs to extreme cold— of travel in that region at the time. Not only do they often camp out and enjoy the traditional male camaraderie of campfire scenes by night, they also go armed and carry swords, frequently hunt with the characteristic wantonness of nineteenth-century European hunters, and on at least one occasion are pursued by brigands, who shoot at them from their horses.

The sentiments expressed on such occasions are consistent with the homoerotic excitement that the narrator reveals from time to time for the fierce primitivism of the desert Arabs. In the swift sketches he draws of one of contemporary European man's most radical Others, the narrator is clearly attracted not by languor but by instinctive directness and male pride. "Fierceness of manner and laughter"—he notes of an Arab and a Negro passing by together, beating their camels as they go—"Accents guttural and harsh, and with large gestures of their arms" (*Voyage*, p. 560). Moreover, such and similar praise of male attributes and beauty is not subsequently undermined, as it is in the case of women, by means of a scenario of disrobing.[14]

[13] Decadent travel, as Julia Przybos has pointed out, is an oxymoron. It implies a "voyage immobile." See her "Voyage du pessimisme et pessimisme du voyage." *Romantisme* 61 (1988).

[14] The remarks Flaubert makes, in a letter of January 1850, to his friend Louis Bouilhet concerning the practice of homosexuality in Egypt and his own failed encounter with a boy in a public bathhouse are not themselves celebratory. The tone he adopts is, rather, that of ribald irony. Homosexual adventure is rendered here as a spirited, nineteenth-century French male traveler's patriotic duty: "Traveling in order

If all is not "romantic agony" in the text of Flaubert's Oriental journey, its most memorable moments nevertheless concern perversely charged, erotic encounters—not "heroic" but "sexual adventures" that are pornographic in kind—and experiences at the limit in confrontations with death, ecstatic religion, or hallucination. At its extreme, adventure of such an order is less an assertion of the self-regarding, self-preserving ego than the kind of swooning annihilation of ego for which Jacques Lacan reinvented the word *jouissance.* Flaubert's Near Eastern journey afforded him opportunities not available in the same way in Europe to push beyond the limits of the pleasure principle. The writer who was preoccupied both before and after he left France with the appropriate means to represent the temptations of Saint Anthony in the desert, was peculiarly open to the traditional expressions of the anguish and transcendence of the flesh.

There are, then, a number of moments in the *Voyage* where the narrator finds himself deeply stirred in ways that are incompatible with the functioning of the pleasure priniciple. One such concerns the approach to Thebes along the Nile, and another, also near the Nile, the encounter of Flaubert's party with a passing caravan in a sandstorm. In the former case, the whole spectacle inspires in him an unusual, if not unprecedented, response of quasi-religious awe, an "oceanic feeling": "It was while I was enjoying (*jouissais*) these things . . . that I felt rise within me a sense of solemn happiness which went forward to meet the spectacle, and I thanked God in my heart for having made me capable of taking pleasure (*jouir*) in such a way. . . . I experienced an inner joy (*volupté*) of my whole being" (*Voyage*, p. 573).

The second occasion concerns one of the moments where adventure in the heroic sense is transformed into something that is both more exciting and more disturbing. The camels with their hooded drivers and veiled women emerge out of the swirling, reddish-brown sand like spirits immersed up to their bellies in clouds. The image strikes the narrator with all the power of an hallucination that leaves him beside himself: "I felt something like a sensation of terror and of furious admiration run along my spine; I sneered nervously; I must have been very pale, and I felt a rush of pleasure (*jouissais*) that was extraordinary" (*Voyage*, p. 595).

The motivation for Flaubert's journey to the Middle East is to be found in the pursuit of such experiences.[15] The continuity with Byronic roman-

---

to further our education and charged with a mission by our government, we considered it our duty to try out that mode of ejaculation." *Œuvres complètes de Gustave Flaubert* (Paris: Club de l'Honnête Homme, 1974), vol. 12, p. 674.

[15] Rather than in the fully conscious, programmatic "need" that Terdiman attributes to him, "the need to utilize the trip to the Orient to liberate a counter-discourse which

ticism resides in a similar flight from the *ennui* of the well-regulated, bourgeois Europe of the emergent Industrial Revolution into a world that offered powerful, novel sensations. It is, therefore, no surprise if the young traveler was especially drawn to what the Middle East offered in the way of exotic sexual experiences, for it is in that sphere above all that the lure of Europe's Orient and of Oriental difference has proved the most potent. And it is in this connection that his text gives a special emphasis to the scopic drive.

Probably no writer more than Flaubert has managed to suggest so well throughout his works the way in which the look is drawn by the play of highlights against a muted background or through a veil; it is the intermittence of light that attracts, in a titillating game of revelation and concealment, of now you see it, now you don't. Thus, women seen in Constantinople fix his attention precisely because their dress reveals a brilliance that it simultaneously conceals: "Women in golden carriages, a natural palor beneath their veil or created by the veil itself; through their veils, the rings of their fingers, the diamonds of their foreheads. How brilliant their eyes are! When you look at them for a long time, it doesn't excite so much as impress; they end up looking like spirits stretched out on divans. The divan follows the Oriental everywhere" (*Voyage*, p. 647). The brief notation is typical, not least for the way in which desire is arrested by the spectacle itself; not only is seeing enough here, it also disincarnates the women involved and leads into a characteristic Orientalist generalization, concerning the celebrated signifier of Oriental indolence and sensuality, the divan.

The most famous sexual adventure of the *Voyage* concerns Flaubert's visit to the celebrated courtesan Kuchak Hanem. And what is most apparent in the episode is the power of the look that fixes the images in that act of recall which is narration. In this case, however, seeing does not stop desire but stimulates the protagonist to seek genital satisfaction. But it turns out that such satisfaction is characteristically located between two looks.

The narrator dramatizes the scene with great care, from the first impression of Kuchak Hanem standing on the stairs of her apartment—with pink trousers and a violet gauze wrap covering her otherwise-naked upper body, smelling of sweet-scented turpentine—to the moment when, the act of sex complete, he watches her sleeping next to him and recalls the sensations he had felt. The voyeur's pleasure resides in observing with detached attention a sleeping woman unaware that she is observed.

As with the woman seen on the boat on the Saône, the narrator records details of clothing and body with a fetishistic precision that is even more

---

might annihilate the dominant discourse he felt was so painfully blocking him." *Discourse*, p. 251.

marked here, apparently because of the fascination exercised by a Middle Eastern woman in her difference and by the fashion that helps constitute that difference. The way every detail of her hair is recorded in a verbless, pedantically punctuated sentence is typical—"Her black hair, curly, resistant to the brush, separated in two bands by a part on the forehead, small tresses caught up at the nape of the neck." Even more characteristic is the decisive notation of the smallest sign of physical decline: "The upper incisor on the right is beginning to decay" (*Voyage*, p. 573). That decayed tooth is, in the context, another of those signifiers of female imperfection which are scattered throughout Flaubert's writings, the mark of a mutilation that recalls the constitutive mutilation of femininity: castration.

Perhaps the most fully developed of Flaubert's perverse scenarios in the *Voyage* is, however, that which concerns Kuchak Hanem's "dance of the bee." It is a dance that is also a striptease and, in order to heighten the voyeuristic charge, it was performed for "the eyes" of the two visiting European males only—her musicians are blindfolded. The climactic moment of the performance is precisely the point at which the play of show and hide is brought to an end by the throwing aside of the scarf that is the dancer's last garment and that apparently gave the dance its name. Once the bee has flown away, for the pleasure of the voyeur and the pain of the fetishist, sexual difference can no longer be disavowed.

Flaubert goes on to savor narcissistically the satisfaction of his own genital potency in the crude language he characteristically has recourse to in his more or less private papers: "After the most brutal of f—s, she falls asleep with her folded hand in mine, and snores. . . Her little dog slept on my silk jacket on the divan . . . I gave myself up to the nervous intensity of feelings rich in reminiscences. The sensations produced by her belly on my —s, her —, even hotter than her belly warmed me like a hot iron" (*Voyage*, pp. 574–575; I reproduce the dots of the French edition).

That the narrator reports on the sensations experienced after the fact is also characteristic. In the kind of striptease Flaubert practiced as both male traveler and author, the relative passivity of voyeurism sooner or later gives way to action; the looking turns into an unveiling and an exposure. If there are references to Kuchak Hanem's decaying tooth, to her snores, or to the heat of her sexual organs, and if a traditional male slang is used to describe sexual activity, it is because to see and to know all there is to know about a woman is to see the "reality" of mutilation and future decay beneath the lure of the flesh. The ironist's "N'est-ce que ça?"—the "N'est-ce que ça" of Frédéric Moreau in the *Sentimental Education*—masks behind its melancholy the satisfaction of the sadistic as well as the scopic drive.[16]

---

[16] It is of no surprise that Flaubert in Jerusalem itself should make a similar refer-

It is, therefore, consistent with such an attitude if throughout the *Voyage* the narrator seems to take a particular pleasure in noting both the fascination of women's bodies clothed in novel and richly various, regional, or ethnic fashions and the frequent grotesqueness or ugliness of those same bodies once exposed. That most visible icon of femininity as mother or as desired sexual other, the breast, is a particular focus of the desecrating look. Misshapen breasts draw an eye that enjoys lingering with cruel relish over the female grotesque: "A Negress's tit—it certainly hung down at least as far as her navel, and it was so flaccid that there was scarcely more than the thickness of the two skins; when she goes on all fours, it must certainly touch the ground" (*Voyage*, p. 596).

Given the importance accorded the scopic drive in Flaubert's text as well as a more generalized openness to exotic sexual experiences, it would be surprising indeed if the topos of the harem did not figure there.[17] The harem had long been a peculiarly charged signifier to the extent that, for the Western fantasy at least, it signified an inaccessible space in which the omnipotence of a master male over compliant women is juxtaposed both with the powerlessness of the excluded males and with the physical impotence of those mutilated males who serve the master's women, the eunuchs. The harem is thus the site of a threat as well as of a promise; the despotic power of the sultan comes closer than anything in modern Western man's experience to the mythic concept of the primal father. And to a traveler such as Flaubert, it is the threat embodied in that power which is the most visible.

Thus, like others before and after him, Flaubert is both fascinated and disturbed in the Old Seraglio of Constantinople at the sight of the eunuchs, not least because they are white. After having evoked their wrinkled, old women's faces, and their elaborate costumes, he goes on: "The sight of a white eunuch makes a disagreeable impression, as far as one's nerves are concerned; it's a strange product, one difficult to take one's eyes off; the sight of black eunuchs never caused a similar reaction in me" (*Voyage*, p. 648). In effect, Flaubert is acknowledging here the shock—"one's nerves"—of the spectacle of castration in a male with whom he can identify: namely, a white male.

The closest the narrator comes in this section to evoking the promise of the harem is in a brief reference to "the stolen odalisque (*l'odalisque ravie*)": "It is in such a place that one could live with a stolen odalisque.

---

ence to the lost illusions of travel: "But who knows what were the disappointments of the patient Middle Ages, the bitterness of the medieval pilgrims, when upon their return to their native land, they were asked with looks of envy: 'Tell me about it! Tell me about it!' " (*Voyage*, p. 609).

[17] See, for example, Alain Grosrichard, *Structure du sérail: La Fiction du sérail dans l'Occident classique* (Paris: Le Seuil, 1979).

This crowd of veiled women with their large eyes that look straight at you, this whole unknown world . . . arouses a dreamy sadness that seizes hold of you" (*Voyage*, p. 647). It is characteristic that the narrator should fantasize possession of a sexual object not from the point of view of the master of the harem, but from that of the oedipal son as the theft of a woman. Flaubert's Oriental journey is lived as the flight of two young bachelors and aesthetes from the paternal Law, from duty and responsibility. Thus, along with the displaced aggression that the *Voyage* expresses relative to the mother figure, one finds throughout an implied refusal to identify with the father. The passage that concerns the motif of "the stolen odalisque" seems, in fact, to embody the regressive desire for a return to the original duality of the imaginary register. The smoking of a narghile and the drinking of raki are conducive to the pursuit of formerly forbidden pleasures in the forever-closed space of one's private harem. In any case, it is apparent that, far from being associated with the reproductive function of genital sex, the properly paternal function, Middle Eastern eroticism is associated in Flaubert, as in the discourse of his European contemporaries, with a voluptuous retreat from life.

The reference to "a dreamy sadness that seizes hold of you" points to another aspect of the Middle East that appealed to Flaubert's late-romantic sensibility. His particular *mal du siècle* enjoyed evoking all the evidence of death and decay in the midst of life and discovering true Oriental wisdom in a kind of languorous embrace of death. On the one hand, this gives rise to his fondness for that form of grotesque associated with death: namely, the macabre. And, on the other, it leads to reflections on the extinction of self achieved either through quietistic reverie or ecstatic experience.

Representations of the macabre abound throughout the *Voyage*. The traveler visits pyramids, tombs, charnel houses, leper colonies, and hospitals. Everywhere he discovers the openness with which the distressing facts of physical existence are displayed in the Middle East. The narrator comments frequently on the ubiquity of human and animal remains, on the piles of bones and detritus, or on the bloody and mutilated carcasses around which circle such predators as vultures, wild dogs, and jackals. The same precision he gave to the description of women's fashions is, in fact, expended on the effects of disease upon a human body.

The portrait of a leper next to a fountain is typical—"His lips, all eaten away, reveal the bottom of his throat; he is hideous with purulence and sores; in place of his fingers green rags hang, it's his skin; before I put my lorgnette on, I thought it was cloth" (*Voyage*, p. 621). Equally typical is the exhibition the narrator witnessed at a hospital near the Nile: "At a sign from the doctor, they all stood up on their beds, unbuttoned the belt of their trousers (it was like a military exercise) and opened their anuses with their fingers to show us their cankers" (*Voyage*, p. 565). The reference to the lorgnette is, of course, calculated. It draws attention to the self-conscious voyeurism of the pose and to the provocative coolness the aesthete is able to bring to the horrors of the flesh, "paring his fingernails."

In the end, the scene that presents in its most concentrated form the combination of voyeurism and sadism that invests the *Voyage* concerns a hunting expedition alongside an aqueduct near Cairo. Having finished hunting eagles and kites, the narrator and du Camp start shooting with reckless indifference at the wild dogs that swarm around a kind of open-air slaughterhouse: "The hot sun makes the carcasses stink, the dogs doze as they digest or peacefully rip up the remains." But there is more to this particular day's sport than the simple sadism of hunting.

Beneath the aqueduct, soldiers' whores are plying their trade and Flaubert decides to indulge the hired help: "I treated to Venus our three donkey-drivers for the small sum of 60 paras (one and a half piasters, about six sous)." And the expense was apparently worth it, since it afforded Flaubert a particularly memorable, voyeuristic shock: "I shall never forget the brutal movement of my old donkey-driver as he seized the whore, taking her with his right hand, stroking her breasts with his left, and dragging her away in a single gesture, laughing through his big white teeth, with his little black wooden chibouk slung over his shoulders, and his rags wrapped around the bottom of his diseased legs" (*Voyage*, p. 568). This long sentence reads like a peculiarly harsh allegory, a kind of sadistic parody of "Death and the Maiden" that was to recur with the leitmotiv of the blind beggar in *Madame Bovary*; it captures the oppositions of youth and age, female and male, aggression and passivity, sex and death in a single complex image. The observer typically takes his pleasure in witnessing the peculiar ferocity of the sexual assault. In the precision and energy of his writing in such passages, in any case, Flaubert outdoes that literary hero of his youth, Sade himself.

It is, then, no accident if one of the great masters of fictional prose ends his vignette with a resonant reference to poverty and disease. Played out against the particularly sinister Egyptian background referred to, the passage contains in its way the demoralizer's last debunking word on romantic love and the virtues of femininity implied by the tradition of chivalry. This consciously elaborated fantasm of a *Liebestod* is not designed to satisfy the genital drive for heterosexual union that classical psychoanalysis posited as the adult norm; it speaks instead to those component drives which, once they become fixated as perversions, we know as voyeurism and sadism.

There are other episodes in the *Voyage* in which the narrator evokes the startling proximity of eros and death that attracted the Perverse

Traveler, episodes in which sex in a cemetery is substituted for sex near
a slaughterhouse. At other times still, however, Flaubert's peculiar "nec-
rophilia" has a less lurid, though equally destructive, aspect. It frequently
takes the more common form of a desire for extinction of self, or death
wish. Thus, the narrator describes enthusiastically on more than one occasion the ecstatic dances of the whirling dervishes. What he finds there
is a "volupté mystique," which in the context is also synonymous with
jouissance.

Finally, the narrator reveals that he, too, was open to that enchantment
which European travelers have traditionally associated with the Orient
since the pre-romantic period: namely, the enchantment of slow-paced,
ritualized movement, of mythic landscapes as old as Homer or the bible,
and of the spaciousness and silence of the desert: "that's the true Orient,
a melancholy effect that makes you feel sleepy; you sense right away
something immense and implacable in the midst of which you are lost"
(*Voyage*, p. 559). The pleasure for this particular Western traveler is in
that loss, in the tranquil submission of self to a force more powerful than
that which animates the self-assertive ego. In short, the Middle East caters wonderfully to that *hantise du néant*, or seduction of the void, first
celebrated by the romantics. And Flaubert in his travel book showed himself to be peculiarly receptive to such seduction.

o   o   o

WHATEVER their quarrels with their fatherlands, both Byron and Stendhal remain firm in their commitment to "Western civilization" as embodied in the tradition of Greece, Rome, and Renaissance Italy. Moreover, they both sympathized with the cause of liberal reform and national
emancipation in their time. It is characteristic of the attitudes embodied
in Flaubert's *Voyage*, on the other hand, that the part which concerns his
return journey through Italy is the most perfunctory. The section is limited almost entirely to enumeration and the driest of descriptions of museum artifacts.

In effect, it turns out that Flaubert is the first of the travel writers in
this book to express that central motif of the early-twentieth-century, European avant-garde from *fauvisme* to Futurism and Dada: *delenda est
Roma*. In an important sense, Flaubert never outlived the fiercely iconoclastic fantasy of his youth to storm Rome as a barbarian. In the *Voyage*,
as elsewhere, the demoralizer's destructive energies take the form of the
death wish not simply on the individual level but also on that of Western
civilization. Flaubert expresses neither reverence for the past nor faith in
the future, which is also a way of saying that he was as contemptuous of
traditional Western religion as he was of its substitute in the postrevolu-
tionary, secular age: the politics of emancipation. The brief notation on

his first entry into Jerusalem is typical of a generalized apostasy vis-à-vis all that the West has held sacred: "We enter by the gate of Jaffa and I emit a fart beneath it as I cross the threshold, but not on purpose; I was even, in fact, a little angry at the Voltaireanism of my anus" (*Voyage*, p. 607).[18] The denial is, of course, undermined by the fact that he chooses to narrate the incident nevertheless.

On the level of belief, the testimony of the *Voyage* is that the only thing left following the death of faith is the pursuit of experience for its own sake and the consequent transformation of life into spectacle. From such a perspective, travel becomes a particularly privileged activity. On foreign territory one is apparently without any responsibilities whatsoever except to the savoring of fresh encounters with the new and, if one is a writer, to the precision of its representation. Where all has become spectacle, one's only commitment is to one's art; the only morality, a morality of composition, perspective and color combinations. The goal of the romantic colorist, in prose as in painting, was to promote powerful, dissonant sensations. And Flaubert found the Middle East peculiarly rich in the raw materials of such a colorist's art. The extraordinary contrasts the region offered between great power and powerlessness, luxury and squalor, refined pleasure and deprivation were central to its appeal for him. That is why poverty, leprosy, prostitution, and death are grist to Flaubert's aesthetic mill, equally as much as landscapes, pyramids, mosques, and ruins. The only thing that shocks the aesthete on his travels is bad taste, and in the Middle East of the nineteenth century that tended to be supplied by fellow tourists from Europe.

On another level, what Flaubert also touches on is the melancholy of travel made manifest in particular in the phenomenon of tourism. That there never was a golden age of travel is confirmed, if confirmation were needed, in Flaubert's comments on the evidence left by his predecessors at certain hallowed sites. The name "Thompson of Sunderland," written in letters three feet high on the base of Pompey's column, is only the most glaring example of the futile gestures made by countless travelers from numerous countries over the centuries to record that they came, saw and, in the eyes of their own narcissistic egos at least, conquered. The effort "to make one's mark" by defacing a monument with one's name is a kind of poor man's claim to fame and immortality. It is also, in a sense, a pastiche of the gesture of those more sophisticated travelers who prefer to record their journey by means of a narrative.

[18] It is also symptomatic and characteristically ironic that the narrator finds the holiest place of patriarchal religion to be suffering from the father's curse: "Ruins everywhere, it smells of the grave and of desolation; the malediction of God seems to hover over the city, the holy city of three religions that is dying of boredom, stench, and neglect" (*Voyage*, p. 608).

The peculiar form of the anxiety of influence to which the latter are subject is touched on by Flaubert as he surveys the writings on the colossi of Memnon: "Stones that have interested so many, that so many men have come to see, are a pleasure to look at. How many bourgeois eyes have looked up there! Everyone had his little word to say and then left" (*Voyage*, p. 590). The pleasure, it seems, is mitigated for the traveling aesthete by the very fact that he risks repeating the absurd gestures of those bourgeois for whom he professed the utmost contempt. The simultaneous fascination and horror Flaubert felt for the cliché and the *idée reçue* make him peculiarly sensitive to the risks of falling into similar traps on his own Oriental journey.

It is finally at Baalbek that he succumbs fully, less to that eighteenth-century melancholy of ruins than to the melancholy of tourism of the kind that has become virtually ubiquitous in the late twentieth century.[19] The sight of ancient inscriptions on the gutted temples at Baalbek written over with endless graffiti in English, French, Turkish, and Arabic, leaves Flaubert profoundly chastened: "This testimony to so many unknown lives, read in silence while the wind blows and all is quiet, has a more chilling effect than the names of the dead on the tombs of a cemetery" (*Voyage*, p. 624). The lesson of the world's tourist monuments is not, in the end, one's heroic self-importance at having come so far, but one's insignificance.

In short, whereas the religious pilgrim prostrates himself at a hallowed shrine and happily acknowledges his nothingness in the presence of the divine principle, and whereas the cultural pilgrim is uplifted at the spectacle of artistic greatness, this particular nineteenth-century aesthete on his travels is conscious of nothing so much as his belatedness. Moreover, like the layered graffiti, the travel narrative that will be the final test of his sensibility on tour is also, in its way, a form of "writing over," a redefacing of already defaced monuments in the futile endeavor "to make one's mark." In the resonant silence of Baalbek, Flaubert acknowledges the ultimate nakedness of the void against which no writing is proof.

[19] Among recent approaches to modern tourism, the following are particularly helpful: Dean MacCannell, *The Tourist* (New York: Schocken, 1976); Georges Van Den Abbeele, "Sightseers: The Tourist as Theorist," *Diacritics* 10 (1980); Jonathan Culler, "The Semiotics of Tourism," *American Journal of Semiotics* 1 (1981).

PART THREE

Europe and Its Discontents

Chapter VII

FREUD AND TRAVEL

IN AN EFFORT to explain the fascination an old photo of the Alhambra exercises over him, Roland Barthes brings together Baudelaire's reflections on the promise of place in "Invitation au voyage" and "Vie antérieure" with Freud's concept of the *unheimlich*, or uncanny. And in doing so, Barthes, in effect, reanimates the notion of "homeness" in the root of the German word that is lost in the English translation, of *Heim, heimlich,* and *Heimat* or "home," "homey," and "homeland." Something in the faraway house represented in the image makes it *heimlich,* "homey," makes Barthes want to live there. And, as a result, he discovers within himself a "desire to inhabit (*désir d'habitation*)" that is characterized as neither dreamlike nor empirical, but "fantasmatic"—it "has to do with a kind of visionary sense that leads me forward toward a utopian future or draws me backward to somewhere unknown within." He goes on to comment that when faced with his "favorite landscapes it is as if *I were certain* I had been there before or was to go there sometime." Then, having quoted Freud to the effect that there is no place one is so certain of having been as in one's mother's body, he encounters his own desire in the powerful attraction of the maternal "home": "Such then is the essence of a landscape chosen by desire: *heimlich,* it awakens the Mother within me (and is by no means disturbing)."[1]

Barthes, in other words, draws on Baudelaire's poetry and Freud's theory of the uncanny in an effort to understand the obscure forces that draw or repel him in his relations to different places. And it is for similar reasons that, in a work devoted to the travel writing of a wide range of writers, it is appropriate to take account of Freud's contribution. If this study of European travel writings can itself be said to have a "center," in fact, it is probably here. As I indicated in the Introduction, it was psychoanalysis that first prompted me to think in terms of "haunted journeys"; and in previous chapters I have occasionally drawn on fundamental psychoanalytic concepts, or referred forward to Freud's scattered comments on the subject of travel, in an effort to clarify some of the motivations at work in the writings of his predecessors.

Yet, the idea of "a Freudian theory of travel writing," like any other

---

[1] *Camera Lucida,* trans. Richard Howard (New York: Farrar, Straus, and Giroux, 1981), p. 40.

theory, needs qualification. It is not simply a matter of a metalanguage that distances itself from its textual objects in order to master them in some way. As will be clear from the following discussion, Freud's own reflections on the topic derive largely from self-observation in connection with his own experience as traveler or potential traveler; as with other matters that came under his scrutiny, Freud is both subject and object of the inquiry. It is in Freud the traveler at least as much as in Freud the scientist that I am interested here.

In this sphere as in others, it is apparent from the works of travel writing already discussed that Freud was once again anticipated in a number of important ways by the insights of poets and writers. In a sense, Freud is only following their example when he reveals how he was both excited and troubled by travel. Moreover, from Boswell, Byron, and Stendhal on, their narratives are entangled in the themes of "the family romance," foreground the questions of desire and transgression, point to the conflict between the pursuit of pleasure and the path of duty, or waver between sentiments of triumph and guilt. By the time of Flaubert, moreover, the death drive is narrativized in a number of contexts, even if it is not named.

It turns out that Freud, in his real and dreamed journeys, is caught up in a dialogic engagement that furthers his self-reflexive practice and that, in his own case, allows him to shed light on motives that had previously been mysterious to him. Thus he, too, forms part of that rich tradition in European travel writing on which he also comments—a tradition that, virtually from the beginning, has made its contribution to the theory of its own practice. And that is why it is important to locate him, like the other writers I discuss, in his own historical moment.

My debt to Freud is both general and specific. I am indebted to the general theory of psychoanalysis and, as is apparent from the foregoing chapters, to a number of its fundamental concepts, in particular, including the unconscious, the drive, perversion, scopophilia, transference, the uncanny, the return of the repressed, and overdetermination. The notion of the pleasure principle has also been important to me along with that countervailing force which, in the final formulation, was called the death drive. Finally, psychoanalysis also demonstrates how we are not free, in ways that are different, but no less constraining, than those affirmed by Edward Said and by Foucauldian discourse theory. The burden of a subjective as well as of a collective, culturally transmitted past determines in complex and unpredictable ways our relations to foreign places and peoples. And this, too, is written into the literature of travel, often in opposition to a given hegemonic culture. In our excursions into previously unknown lands, we discover much that is strangely familiar;

and such troubling encounters may destabilize inherited categories as well as confirm them.

My more specific debt concerns those passages in Freud's works that, over a span of almost forty years, focus on questions of place and the meaning of travel in his own life. And because the contribution of general psychoanalytic theory to this study is diffused throughout my readings of individual works (as well as in the Introduction), it is on my specific debt that I shall concentrate in this chapter. In the fragmentary auto-analyses of dreams and experiences from *The Interpretation of Dreams* (1900) through *Civilization and Its Discontents* (1930) and "A Disturbance of Memory on the Acropolis" (1936), Freud furnishes an outline for a psychoanalytic theory of travel. These writings give sharper relief to the motifs of dutifulness and pleasure, interdiction and transgression that recur in European travel writing at least from the eighteenth century on. In some ways Freud, like Darwin, can also be said to associate travel with a search for origins, albeit of a different kind. In any case, as Freud's most recent biographer, Peter Gay, confirms, Freud experienced powerful cathexes, positive and negative, on a number of places, including his Moravian birthplace, Vienna, Rome, Paris, and England.[2] But it is to Freud's own textual handling of some of these themes that I shall limit myself here.

In his own more sustained reflections on the topic of place and travel, what Freud in general finds are the vicissitudes of unconscious desire in the face of various unconscious resistances. Yet, given psychoanalysis's reputation as an ahistorical and apolitical body of theory, probably the greatest surprise of Freud's comments on travel is in his insights into the way in which the personal and familial are so often collapsed into the political. In the light of the significance that Rome has had for so many European writers of travel books, it is of obvious interest that central to Freud's early preoccupation with travel is the avoidance of that city. Thus, although only "A Disturbance of Memory on the Acropolis" can be said to resemble the other travel writings I analyze in this book, the relevance of the Freudian material is such that it fully deserves to be looked at with some care in the present context.

In his seminal work of 1900 especially, Freud briefly explores the kinds of meanings that attach themselves to signifiers of place in dreams. And the fact that almost all the dreams concerned are the author's own turns out to be particularly revealing. The autobiographical nature of the material enables Freud to trace his personal investments in place back to experiences in adolescence and infancy at the same time that he exposes

[2] *Freud: A Life for Our Time* (New York: Norton, 1988). See especially "Foundations: 1858–1905."

the mechanisms of transference and displacement involved. The most notable example of Freud's handling of the topic is, in fact, to be found in *The Interpretation of Dreams*, specifically in part V, "Material and Sources of Dreams," subsection B: "Infantile Material."[3] They are what might be called "dreams of travel," and perhaps the most remarkable feature in Freud's narration of them is that he manages, within the space of four or five pages, to touch on the psycho-sexual, political, and racial meanings that are typically attached to places on the map of the world.[4]

In Freud's early masterpiece, one or two such places in particular are associated with the fulfillment of early wishes. The chief example cited of this is to be found in the series of dreams on Rome that, taken together, reveal what might be called a "Hannibal complex" in the dreamer. Freud begins the discussion of this material with a brief reference to a central concept in his theory of dreams that might also be read as the point of departure for any psychoanalytic theory of travel: "In another instance it became apparent that, though the wish which instigated the dream was a present-day one, it had received a powerful reinforcement from memories that stretched far back into childhood. What I have in mind is a series of dreams which are based upon a longing to visit Rome" (*S.E.*, vol. 4, p.193).

Freud then goes on to narrate four dreams of varying complexity and interest in which that city figures prominently. The first two concern views that the protagonist of the dream has of the city from some distance, and Freud interprets them as embodying "the theme of the promised land seen from afar" (*S.E.*, vol. 4, p. 194). They are, in effect, expressions of a desire for the ideal city that, for reasons which are subsequently divulged, is found to encounter a powerful resistance. Moreover, that the obstacle to satisfaction is wholly psychic is apparent immediately in the contradiction between the body of the text and a footnote of 1909, which was further reinforced by a phrase added in 1925.

After the two sentences quoted above, Freud adds: "For a long time to come, no doubt, I shall have to continue to satisfy that longing [to visit Rome] in my dreams: for at the season of the year when it is possible for me to travel, residence in Rome must be avoided for reasons of health."

---

[3] In *The Standard Edition of the Complete Psychological Works* (London: Hogarth, 1955), vol. 4; hereafter, referred to as *S.E.*

[4] Carl Schorske has, of course, focused on this material from *The Interpretation of Dreams* in order to demonstrate the manner in which political, professional, and personal elements are combined in Freud's "mid-life crisis" of the 1890s. See the subtly argued "Politics and Patricide in Freud's *Interpretation of Dreams*," in *Fin de Siècle Vienna: Politics and Culture* (New York: Alfred A. Knopf, 1980). See also William J. McGrath, *Freud's Discovery of Psychoanalysis: The Politics of Hysteria* (Ithaca: Cornell University Press, 1986).

Even if it were not for the footnote of 1909, it would be difficult to avoid reading a certain unconscious irony in that final phrase. In the subsequent footnote, he dismisses his earlier reasoning with a peremptoriness that is surprising from the inventor of psychoanalyis: "I discovered long since that it only needs a little courage to fulfil wishes which till then have been regarded as unattainable; [added 1925] and thereafter became a constant pilgrim to Rome" (*S.E.*, vol. 4, pp. 193–194). In the light of the interpretation of the Roman dreams furnished by the text and Freud's lifelong hostility to religion, however, the word "pilgrim" in the second revision to the original text also resonates ironically.

In the third dream, Freud actually reaches Rome—only to be disappointed by the strangely rural scenery, whose character he traces back to personal associations with Ravenna and Karlsbad. The next move in his interpretation is significant because it leads him to invoke dream material from two "facetious Jewish anecdotes" of a kind that he defines as characteristic and worthy of the highest praise for what might be called their outsider's ethnopolitical intelligence. He notes that these Jewish jokes contain "so much profound and often bitterly worldly wisdom and which we so greatly enjoy quoting in our talk and letters." In the first of these celebrated anecdotes, the joke concerns the increasingly painful efforts of an impecunious Jew to reach the spa town of Karlsbad without the benefit of a railway ticket. The punch line is in the Jew's response to an acquaintance who asks him where he is going: "To Karlsbad . . . if my constitution can stand it" (*S.E.*, vol. 4, p. 195).

The second anecdote also concerns the idea of the unattainability, for a Jew, of a famous place. On this occasion, Paris is involved—for a long time another goal of the author's "longings," as he points out. The obstacle in this anecdote is the Jew's inability to ask his way because he does not speak French. Nevertheless, Freud concludes that the dredging up of this unconscious material satisfies the impulse to wish-fulfillment: first, because Paris reminds him that some of his deepest wishes are, in fact, susceptible of being gratified; second, because the very formulation of the dream, "asking the way," promises that his desire to reach Rome will also eventually be satisfied, since "all roads lead there" (*S.E.*, vol. 4, p. 195).

If the third Roman dream draws on material that foregrounds the anxieties and aspirations of the Jew as an outsider in the European political and cultural sphere, the fourth dream involves the confusion of Rome with Prague and the political tensions between German- and Czech-speaking Czechs. The fact that in his dream Freud is surprised to find posters in German on a Roman street is, in effect, read as another example of the overcoming of a threat felt by someone who is a member of a linguistic and ethnic minority.

In the light of the auto-analysis concerning the significance of Rome that follows the narration of the four dreams, however, the presence of German on the street walls of the Eternal City suggests an interpretation that Freud himself does not offer. Since German was his native language and the native language of psychoanalysis as well as of Austria, its use in Rome implies the hegemonization, by a Jewish migrant to the north, of the city of the Romans and of the universal Catholic church itself. The rest of the section goes a long way toward confirming the validity of such a reading.

Freud begins his explanation of the mechanisms operating in his four dreams by describing the moment when he first understood that his powerful cathexis on Rome could be traced back to crucial youthful experiences: "It was on my last journey to Italy, which, among other places, took me past Lake Trasimene, that finally—after having seen the Tiber and sadly turned back when I was only fifty miles from Rome—I discovered the way in which my longing for the eternal city had been reinforced by impressions from my youth" (*S.E.*, vol. 4, p. 196). In the act of planning once again "to by-pass Rome," he remembers a sentence from a classical German author that triggers two pages of reflections on a youthful identification, which was ethnic and political in origin: " 'Which of the two, it may be debated, walked up and down his study with the greater impatience after he had formed his plan of going to Rome—Winckelmann, the Vice-Principal, or Hannibal, the Commander-in-Chief?' I had actually been following in Hannibal's footsteps. Like him, I had been fated not to see Rome" (*S.E.*, vol. 4, p. 196).

In short, Freud realizes that he had been unconsciously modeling himself on Hannibal—"the favourite hero of my later school days"—in simultaneously longing to visit Rome and resisting such a visit. Moreover, he himself attaches the ethnic and political meaning to the identification by affirming his preference for the Carthaginians over the Romans: "And when in the higher classes I began to understand for the first time what it meant to belong to an alien race, and anti-semitic feelings among the other boys warned me that I must take up a definite position, the figure of the semitic general rose high in my esteem. To my youthful mind Hannibal and Rome symbolized the conflict between the tenacity of Jewry and the organization of the Catholic church" (*S.E.*, vol. 4, p. 196). One finds in such a passage an expression of the notion of *delenda est Roma* that I attributed to Flaubert. In Freud's case, however, it is accompanied by an at least equally powerful cult of classical antiquity.

In the retrospective construction of the author of *The Interpretation of Dreams*, in any case, Rome is associated with a political awakening in late adolescence, an awakening in which he is made conscious of his own ethnic identity in opposition to the surrounding Christian culture. For

Freud (as for many of the other European travelers discussed in this book), Rome is the center, then, but it is the center of an overlapping religious, political, and cultural empire that is inimical to his very existence as a Jew. Under the circumstances, Freud's unconscious avoidance of Rome is understandable, in spite of both a classical German education—in which the teachings of a Winckelmann and a Goethe could not have failed to figure prominently—and the spectacle of the newly romanized Vienna that had been constructed around him in his own lifetime. Freud's deep ambivalence concerning Rome derived from his dual cultural identity as a German-speaking, Austrian-educated Jew, who was himself faced with the choice between following in the footsteps of Winckelmann, the original theorist of German classical culture and a converted Roman Catholic priest, or of Hannibal, the North African Semite and anti-Roman. Freud's ambivalence emerges in the peculiar way in which he struggled throughout his life to follow both paths.

That a great many powerful emotions were for Freud concentrated in the signifier "Rome" is confirmed a little later in the same section. "Thus the wish to go to Rome," the analyst notes, "had become in my dream-life a cloak and symbol for a number of other passionate wishes. Their realization was to be pursued with all the perseverance and single-mindedness of the Carthaginian, though their fulfillment seemed at the moment just as little favoured by destiny as was Hannibal's lifelong wish to enter Rome" (S.E., vol. 4, pp. 196–197). "Passionate wishes," "perseverance," and "single-mindedness" in relation to places on the map suggest a level of commitment that one associates with conversion to a religion or a political cause. And the familiar incident Freud narrates in the following paragraph, concerning his father's humiliation in the street, at the hands of an anti-Semitic Christian, confirms that a conversion to an ethnopolitical cause was precisely what was involved. It is this passage that brings into sharpest focus Freud's "Hannibal complex."

Through the story told him by his father when he was about ten years old, Freud explains the persistent reemergence in his life of the Roman phobia—at least up to the moment when his auto-analysis focused on the Roman dreams. The youthful Freud contrasts his father's "unheroic" response to the provocation with the legendary heroism of another Semitic father and his admired son: "the scene in which Hannibal's father, Hamilcar Barca, made his boy swear before the household altar to take vengeance on the Romans. Ever since that time Hannibal had had a place in my phantasies" (S.E., vol. 4, p. 197). The reference is unequivocal in what it displaces onto the inventor of psychoanalysis in modern Christian Europe: Hannibal's role as avenger of the humiliations suffered by a Semitic father at the hands of pagan Rome. Such an interpretation appears even more convincing when one remembers the imperial role to which Vienna aspired in Freud's time.

As noted above, probably the greatest surprise of Freud's analysis of the Roman dreams is the important political component he uncovers there.[5] The "passionate wishes" that were "cloaked" by Freud's longing to go to Rome prove to be an expression of ethnic solidarity that is also subversive of the majority culture. Moreover, the exercise in auto-analysis involved here does not stop with ten-year-old Sigmund's assumption of Hannibal's anti-Roman oath, but is pursued two stages further back into childhood, "so that once more it would only have been a question of a transference of an already formed emotional relation to a new object" (*S.E.*, vol. 4, p. 197). Freud first recognizes in his early enthusiasm for Napoleon and for one of his supposedly Jewish marshals the anti-Roman motif: "Napoleon lines up with Hannibal owing to their both having crossed the Alps" (*S.E.*, vol. 4, p. 198). The triumph here is in the transgressive force of that "crossing." Freud finally stops pushing back the boundaries of his preoccupation with "the martial ideal" in a reference to the intimidation from which he suffered, at age three, from a slightly older friend. At the traceable origin of Freud's desire for, and resistance to, Rome is the wish to overcome an inherited weakness.

In this connection, it is also notable that in his first published analysis of a work of literature, Wilhelm Jensen's *Gradiva*, Freud chose a novella at the center of which was a place that had long exercised a great fascination over him and that was part of his own imaginary geography: namely, Pompeii. He was obviously drawn to *Gradiva* because it seemed to furnish independent verification of some of the central concepts of psychoanalytic theory, including the proper interpretation of dreams, the mechanisms of delusion and repression, and the practice of the cure. But the fact that it connects the way a woman steps (*gradi* = to step) and "transstepping" male desire with Pompeii—its author calls it "a Pompeiian fantasy"—clearly also contributed powerfully to Freud's interest. Pompeii, of course, was for Freud a superb metaphor for repression—"There is, in fact, no better analogy for repression, by which the mind is at once made inaccessible and preserved than burial of a sort to which Pompeii fell a victim and from which it could emerge once more through the work of spades."[6]

---

[5] Schorske first demonstrates this and then goes on to conclude that "in *The Interpretation of Dreams* Freud gave this struggle [with Austrian sociopolitical reality], both outer and inner, its fullest, most personal statement—and at the same time overcame it by devising an epoch-making interpretation of human experience in which politics could be reduced to an epiphenomenal manifestation of psychic forces." *Vienna*, p. 183.

[6] "Delusions and Dreams in Jensen's *Gradiva*," in *S.E.*, vol. 9, p. 40.

Yet, insofar as *Gradiva* is the story of a young German archaeologist who returns to Pompeii for unconscious reasons of which he becomes aware retroactively only as the result of his "cure," the tale provides another illustration of the powerful cathexes on place that Freud had acknowledged in himself: "The journey was undertaken for reasons which its subject did not recognise at first and only admitted to himself later on, reasons which the author describes in so many words as 'unconscious' " (*S.E.*, vol. 9, p. 66). Moreover, central to the experience of the hero in the place of all places that may be said to be an archaeologist's dream is the encounter with the ghosts of noon time—"which the ancients regarded as the hour of ghosts" (*S.E.*, vol. 9, p. 16).

o   o   o

THAT THE wish to travel was in Freud's own case both singularly powerful and strongly resisted is confirmed by the 1936 paper entitled "A Disturbance of Memory on the Acropolis." Equally as much as the journeys of other travelers, Freud's erratic itineraries were in their way compromise formations dictated by the conflict between a "passionate desire" and the demands of filial duty. "When I recall the passionate desire to travel and see the world by which I was dominated at school and later," the author comments, "and how long it was before that desire began to find its fulfilment, I am not surprised at its after-effect on the Acropolis."[7]

The "after-effect" referred to concerns once again the ambivalence experienced at the prospect of visiting a famous, culturally charged site. And the continuity between Freud's auto-analysis here and the observations of nearly forty years before is particularly fascinating; in both cases, his relation to his father and their different life circumstances figures prominently. It is also of obvious significance that the paper takes the form of an open letter to Romain Rolland on his seventieth birthday, when its author was himself a man of eighty in exile from Nazi persecution in London. Rolland was in his time an internationalist, humanist, and tireless champion of the cause of justice and peace who had assumed on the European stage something of the legacy of Tolstoy. In other words, the French writer combined a commitment to enlightened causes and a militant energy that made him worthy, like Hannibal, Oliver Cromwell, Napoleon, Copernicus, Charles Darwin, and Emile Zola, of Freud's personal pantheon of great men—a pantheon to which the elderly exile in London clearly aspired to belong.[8]

[7] *S.E.* vol. 22, p. 243.

[8] Schorske summarizes Freud's political values as "partisanship for Napoleon as conqueror of backward Central Europe; contempt for royalty and the aristocracy . . . ; undying admiration for England, particularly for the great Puritan, Oliver Cromwell,

The ostensible subject of the 1936 paper is the phenomenon of "derealization (*Entfremdungsgefühl*)," which Freud defines as a sudden and apparently unmotivated sensation of disbelief in the face of a given reality. His example of the phenomenon is a personal anecdote in which he is overcome with surprise, when first standing on the Acropolis with his brother, that it all really existed as his schoolbooks had described it. His own unawareness that he had doubted the reality leads Freud to speculate on the hidden causes of his incredulity. And he comes up with two general characteristics of derealization that are of particular interest in the context of a discussion of travel writing. First, according to Freud, derealization serves the purpose of defense and involves a denial. Second, it depends on the continuing vitality of repressed memories of earlier, painful experiences.

In the event, the analyst discovers that there was a psychic resistance at the prospect of visiting Athens similar to that in the case of Rome. Yet, the unconscious motivation is not the same. In spite of his longing to go to Rome as the ancient capital of Western civilization, Freud's behavior had focused on the obstacles of getting there and the difficulty of the journey. In the essay on the Acropolis, however, the repressed motivation is less obviously ethnopolitical. In its undistorted form he explains his moment of incredulity as a displacement and expression of the idea, "I could really not have imagined it possible that I should ever be granted the sight of Athens with my own eyes—as is now indubitably the case" (*S.E.*, vol. 22, p. 243). Thus, the important element of disbelief concerns not the reality itself but his own right ever to enjoy the sight of it. The "disturbance of memory" that is referred to in the title concerns the unconscious misrepresentation of the past, a misrepresentation that masks his sense of guilt in relation to his father:

> It is not true that in my school-days I ever doubted the real existence of Athens. I only doubted whether I should ever see Athens. It seemed to me beyond the realms of possibility that I should ever travel so far—that I should 'go such a long way.' This was linked up with the limitations and poverty of our conditions of life. My longing to travel was no doubt also the expression of a wish to escape from that pressure, like the force which drives so many adolescent children to run away from home. I had long seen clearly that a great part of the pleasure of travel lies in the fulfillment of these early wishes, that it is rooted, that is, in dissatisfaction with home and family. [*S.E.*, vol. 22, pp. 246–247]

---

for whom Freud, the sexual liberator, named his second son; and above all, hostility to religion, especially to Rome." *Vienna*, p. 189.

This last sentence is as close as Freud ever comes to pointing to a theory of the general motivation of travel, and it is clearly centered on the persistence of conflicts deriving from an imperfect resolution of the Oedipus complex.

Freud goes on immediately to connect once again the overcoming of the constraints of early life, socioeconomic as well as interpersonal, to the legendary heroism previously associated with Hannibal and Napoleon. He even makes the claim that the traveler who reaches an apparently remote goal, a goal that had previously been the object only of his fantasy, feels himself to be in his own way a hero: "When first one catches sight of the sea, crosses the ocean and experiences as realities cities and lands which for so long had been distant, unattainable things of desire— one feels like a hero who has performed deeds of improbable greatness" (*S.E.*, vol. 22, p. 247).

What emerges in such a passage is, among other things, the narcissism of heroism. And it is a narcissism from which Freud himself was not immune, even though he was at the same time its theorist. In this case, even ordinary bourgeois travel is shown to have its heroic dimension and is associated with "the martial ideal" referred to in *The Interpretation of Dreams*. In the earlier work, that ideal had been excited in the young Freud by the revelation of his father's weakness; in the 1936 paper it reappears in connection with an affirmation of the sons' strength—his own and his brother's—through a comparison with the modern Hannibal, Napoleon. Freud on the Acropolis finds himself moved to echo a legendary remark Napoleon is supposed to have made during his coronation as emperor to his brother: "What would *Monsieur notre Père* have said to this, if he could have been here today?" (*S.E.*, vol. 22, p. 247).

Probably nowhere more than here, in this identification with Napoleon, does Freud reveal his own susceptibility to the traditional masculine cult of heroic self-affirmation, although the passage is not without irony. To stand on the Acropolis next to his brother was to know a singularly self-regarding, self-congratulatory moment. Moreover, he is able to recognize the fact that he is standing on a pinnacle of achievement in large part through imagining himself seen by that once all-powerful father of his infantile fantasy. He recognizes his own power in the mirror of that imagined look. And it is this anecdote which provides the clue to the discomfort the two brothers experienced in Trieste when they first realized that a visit to Athens was actually possible. The pleasure at the thought of satisfying their desire was mitigated by the sense of guilt at having gone so far; the impulse to repudiation follows immediately on the promise of satisfaction: "there was something about it that was wrong, that was from earliest times forbidden. . . . It seems as though the essence of success were to have got further than one's father, and as though to exceed one's father were still something forbidden." Thus, the Acropolis calls up for the brothers the ghost of their relatively uneducated, small-businessman father, to the point where they experience something of the awe Goethe himself had expressed in *The Italian Journey* in the face of demanding fathers on the Capitol: "Thus what interfered with our enjoyment of the journey to Athens was a feeling of *piety*" (*S.E.*, vol. 22, pp. 247–248). The passage also makes clear that the "Hannibal complex" implies both the desire to fulfill a task inherited from a dead father and the desire to go beyond him in a way that promotes guilt.

In this connection, finally, Freud's paper can be seen not only to provide a psychoanalytic interpretation of the closing scenes of Goethe's visit to Rome, which I discuss in my Stendhal chapter. The paper also focuses briefly on some of the central themes of one of Europe's founding epics, Virgil's *Aeneid*—a work with which both Goethe and Freud were more than familiar. The Latin author's masterwork was considered by ancient critics to have combined the *Odyssey* with the *Iliad*, an epic of heroic voyaging with an epic of war. Moreover, the chief virtue of the heroic protagonist himself is piety, piety to father, family, and the gods. Aeneas, it will be remembered, proves the most loyal of sons by carrying his blind father on his shoulders from the ruins of Troy, and by taking Anchises with him on his dangerous journey.

In any case, Freud's psychoanalytic interpretation of the heroism of travel and of a concomitant sense of guilt relate in an interesting but not wholly unexpected way to that modern narrative theory referred to above, and updated by Jurij Lotman in his discussion of "plotless" and "plotted" texts—the latter are narratives that are centered on heroic protagonists who disturb a given order, defy interdictions, cross boundaries.[9] If this is true for narratives in general, it is even more obviously true of travel narratives, where the opening move always involves a departure from home and the crossing of the boundaries constituted by more or less forbidden frontiers in the course of the traveler's progress through the world. Lotman does not take account of the model afforded by Aeneas of taking one's father with one, but it seems to persist in Freud's relationship to travel as the focus of his guilt.

Rome is also invoked in *Civilization and Its Discontents*, but it appears there, like Pompeii in *Gradiva*, chiefly as a metaphor for the human psyche. Those different layers of civilization which are uncovered as the result of the archaeological excavation of classical sites are claimed by Freud to resemble the memory traces of different ages within the psyche. Everything is preserved, although in most cases it is buried beneath the

9 *Semiotics of Cinema*, trans. Mark E. Suino (Ann Arbor: University of Michigan Press, 1976), pp. 65–66.

successive structures that have risen on the same spot. The choice of metaphor also has its own ethnopolitical interest because it implies that a
pagan Rome, which was the apparent object of Freud's admiration, still
survived beneath the city of the popes.

A more significant aspect of *Civilization and Its Discontents* from the
point of view of the present study is that it raises, in a new and disturbing
way, the eighteenth-century question of the benefits and disadvantages
of civilization as such. And although it is not stated in so many words, the
specific focus of Freud's doubt is European civilization. To that extent,
the 1930 work is thematically linked to certain eighteenth-century travel
works discussed above, to the writings of Freud's nineteenth-century predecessors from the romantic period on, as well as to those twentieth-century texts that are the subject of the following chapters.

The problem of civilization for which Rome stood as a metaphor for
so long was one that in Freud's time had already exceeded Europe and
that in our own has become thoroughly global. Evidence for the malaise
that Freud uncovers at the heart of modern civilized life was abundantly
at hand not only in individual and collective behaviors of his time, but
also in the body of texts we usually associate with the "romantic agony."
And in a certain sense the writings of Freud's contemporaries that antedated *Civilization and Its Discontents*—among them works by D. H. Lawrence, André Gide, and T. E. Lawrence—are expressions of the impulse
to overcome the perceived decadence of European culture through the
embracing of different forms of "primitivism." It was a problem that was
also addressed, in a different way, by anthropologists from Bronislaw
Malinowski to Claude Lévi-Strauss.

Civilization and Its Discontents is Freud's most ambitious work of culture
criticism, and this is not the place to explore the full range of its meanings. But because of the relevance of its theme to the travel writings I am
concerned with, I would simply like to connect it to the passage from *The
Interpretation of Dreams*, quoted above, concerning the youthful Freud's
commitment to a pious cause. The mature author refers to the existence
in his Roman dreams of certain "passionate wishes" that were to be pursued "with all the perseverance and single-mindedness of the Carthaginian."

Nevertheless, Carl Schorske concludes his essay on Freud in *Fin de Siècle Vienna: Politics and Culture* by finding in the implied opposition between Hannibal and Winckelmann the older Freud's preference of the
latter as his model, the preference of what Schorske calls "the scientist"
over "the conqueror." This is in line with the general case he makes for
reading Freud's narration and analysis of his own dreams in *The Interpretation of Dreams* as the story of the overcoming of politics by the new science of psychoanalysis. By the time of Jakob Freud's death in 1896,

changing historical circumstances led to the working through of political questions in the dream book. As a result, in Schorske's ingenious reading, not only was Freud liberated from his Roman "neurosis," visiting Rome for the first time in 1901, but his political commitments were also neutralized through his scientific ones. Schorske concludes that the central principle of Freud's "mature political philosophy" is that "all politics is reducible to the primal conflict between father and son" (*Vienna*, p. 197).

Yet, it seems to me that a more pyschoanalytically informed reading would have to acknowledge that the unconscious is not susceptible to maturation and that although our neuroses may sometimes be liquidated through the work of analysis, the persistence in memory of the kinds of painful experiences evoked in the Roman dreams never makes possible the erasure of the psychic past. The concept of "the cure" in psychoanalytic theory, as Freud indicated on more than one occasion, remains a problematic one. The whole force of the archaeological imagery in *Civilization and Its Discontents* serves to remind the reader that the various layers of history and prehistory are not reducible in the psyche any more than they are in the Eternal City.

The fact is that Winckelmann was not only a "scientist"; he was also preeminently, in the German tradition, the great eighteenth-century theorist of a Western civilization whose norms and values were held to be universal and established once and for all in classical antiquity. And it is this civilization more than any other that is submitted to Freud's peculiarly ambivalent critique in *Civilization and Its Discontents*. The reference to "discontents" (a rather weak equivalent for the *Unbehagen* of the German title) echoes the widespread diagnosis of Western decadence that reached far back into the nineteenth century. The term also implies the need for a theorist of Western civilization who would at bottom be an anti-Winckelmann.

Nevertheless, *Civilization and Its Discontents*, in effect, attempts to have it both ways. It is a work that seeks to combine the projects of both Winckelmann and Hannibal. Unlike Flaubert, say, who in his way championed the cause of "barbarism" in his time, Freud retained a lifelong attachment to classical culture. Yet, nowhere more than in his 1930 work, with its theoretic questioning of European culture itself, does Freud come closer to assuming the role of "Semitic general" at the gates of Rome. A broader view of politics than the one Schorske adopts, one that is attentive to cultural questions and to those practices subsumed under the notion of "hegemony" in Antonio Gramsci's sense, would thus find in psychoanalytic theory itself politics by another means.

In brief, a work such as *Civilization and Its Discontents* can be read not as a "counterpolitical" dissolution of Hannibal's oath, but as its realization. It is, in its way, an expression of "the tenacity of Jewry" to which

Freud referred. His exposure of the negative face of "Western" civilization through psychoanalysis amounts to a project of hegemonization of the symbolic center and its consequent decentering. The "Jewish science" is also a "Jewish politics." There is, in the end, a culminating irony in the fact that, as in the condensed material of his fourth Roman dream, the language which comes to invade the streets of this symbolic Rome, the language of psychoanalysis itself, is also the German of Winckelmann and Goethe.

All in all, Freud's probing of the significance of travel in his own life, over a span of some forty years, does not occupy much space in his collected works. Yet, the force of his insights is such that it enables a reader of Western travel literature to understand more fully the reason for the persistence of certain themes or the motivations that impel individuals to leave their home and homeland. On the one hand, Freud's comments on the topic affirm that the attractions and phobias of travel derive from unconscious desire and its repudiation. On the other, his narration of certain anecdotes confirms how private humiliations and transferential relations to place, as well as to people, may be rearticulated as pious political commitments.[10] From Boswell and Diderot to Barthes and Naipaul, the issues of desire, transgression, and guilt are rarely far below the surface of the writings of Europe's male travelers. Moreover, from the beginning those writings bring into focus the tensions and conflicts within the culture that in 1930, at a particularly ominous moment in European history, Freud was to call its "discontents."

[10] Further confirmation of transferential relations to a country is to be found in the most recent work of the British travel writer Jonathan Raban. The intimate connection between the two words *pater* and *patria* was one of the few things he claims to have understood in Latin. And he goes on to write: "For England was really my father's country. It was the country where the uniformed warrior-priest, returned hero and man of God, was at home. Blue-chinned, six-foot-two, robed in antique black and puffing smoke like a storybook dragon, my father was a true Englishman—and I knew that I was always going to be far too puny, too weak-spirited, ever to wear his clothes except in make-believe." *Coasting: A Private Journey* (New York: Viking Penguin, 1987), p. 22. As my second epigraph suggests, Barry Lopez, in his well-informed and wonderfully alert *Arctic Dreams: Imagination and Desire in a Northern Landscape* (Toronto: Bantam Books, 1987) is also especially attentive to the promptings that drive individuals into remote regions of the planet.

Chapter VIII

THE OTHER ITALY:
D. H. LAWRENCE

AMONG modern British writers, no one has expressed more forcefully his discontent with the state of twentieth-century European civilization than D. H. Lawrence. In works in a variety of genres, Lawrence took issue with the founding values of that civilization going back to the Renaissance and beyond. The fierceness of his rebellion against home and homeland is comparable to that of Byron's a century earlier, at least in the way he felt driven to leave England. And his passionate search for alternative ways of living in the world led him into a restless exile in Italy, Mexico, and Australia up to his death in 1930, when Freud's celebrated essay on our discontents was published.

Lawrence's various contributions to the literature of travel constitute a moving and often anguished record of different moments in that search. And this is especially true of the Italian travel books on which I will concentrate here. The complexity of the encounters Lawrence evokes there reminds us once again that "literature" in Roland Barthes's sense is the site where, under pressure from various drives, discourse may be subverted in unpredictable ways—although Lawrence would probably have seen no more than Gallic soullessness in Barthes's reference to "that salutary trickery, that art of evasion, that magnificent deception."[1]

Lawrence's fourth and final work in the genre and his third on Italy, *Etruscan Places*, begins with a characteristically iconoclastic denunciation of Rome that suggests immediately the distance between what Italy meant to him and what it had meant to writers in the European cultural mainstream, to John Ruskin, Henry James, and Norman Douglas, for example: "The Etruscans, as everyone knows, were the people who occupied the middle of Italy in early Roman days, and whom the Romans, in their usual neighbourly fashion, wiped out entirely in order to make way for Rome with a very big R."[2] In place of Freud's ambivalence toward

---

[1] *Leçon inaugurale de la chaire de sémiologie littéraire du Collège de France* (Paris: Le Seuil, 1978), p. 16.

[2] *D. H. Lawrence and Italy* (New York: Viking Penguin, 1985), p. 1; hereafter, referred to as *Places*. For a valuable account of Lawrence in relation to Victorian and Edwardian travelers and of his extensive readings in connection with travel, see Billy T. Tracy, Jr., *D. H. Lawrence and the Literature of Travel* (Ann Arbor: UMI Research Press, 1983). See also Del Ivan Janik, *The Curve of Return*, ELS Monograph Series (Victoria, B.C.: University of Victoria, 1981); and Jeffrey Meyers, *D. H. Lawrence and the Experience of Italy* (Philadelphia: University of Pennsylvania Press, 1982).

the imperial city and its classical culture, there is categorical rejection. And in the body of the work that was published posthumously in book form, Lawrence goes on to invent a land that has little in common with, say, the Italy of Henry James's *Italian Hours*. Lawrence travels there to satisfy demands that are very different from those of a cultural pilgrim such as James. The latter's Italy, like modern European civilization in general, was for Lawrence, as for much of the European avant-garde from the turn of the century on, less a triumph than a calamity.

Moreover, Lawrence's hostility extends not only to Rome and the imperial ideal but also to power in general, to politics in all its forms, to industrial capitalism, and even to the classical tradition in architecture, museums[3] and works of art—"One wearies of the aesthetic quality." (*Places*, p. 107). He is also no respecter of history. Since history was in his time virtually synonymous with a Western history that located its origins in classical Greece and Rome, he focuses on what is still often characterized with the hegemonically charged term "prehistory." Lawrence's last Italian journey, one that was undertaken when he was already a dying man, is certainly a journey in time as well as in space, but the time that interests him is preserved only in the excavated sites of Etruscan burial places.

As frequently with Freud, travel is associated with archaeology, the journey in geographic space with a voyage back in historical time in search of more archaic forms of consciousness. Lawrence is not drawn by the monuments of classical or even Renaissance Italian civilization—which in his aggressively apolitical way he also equates with monuments of barbarism—but in manifestations of a lost and more vital art of living that the Romans were the first to erase. From Lawrence's point of view, the point of origin of that Western civilization which had attracted the grand tourists to Rome was the site of a genocide and a mythic Fall.

As a result, where James appears in retrospect as the most reverent of pilgrims in the church of European Culture with a capital C, in his travel writings as well as elsewhere, Lawrence reveals himself to be the celebrant of Life with a capital L, Life of a kind that had retreated to the margins of continental Europe or persisted, if at all, in those "uncultivated" classes that lived close to nature. What this gives rise to in practice—and once again the contrast with James is illuminating—is an explicit and programmatic resexualization not only of relations between human beings, but also between human beings and the created world. Lawrence is not only aggressively apolitical, he also goes out of his way to

---

[3] "Museums, museums, museums, object-lessons rigged out to illustrate the unsound theories of archaeologists, crazy attempts to co-ordinate and get into a fixed order that which has no fixed order and will not be co-ordinated!" *Places*, p. 114.

dehistoricize experience by substituting a mythopoeic discourse for that of history.

Finally, apart from Freud himself he is the first of the writers I am concerned with to have had a significant knowledge of psychoanalysis. In fact, the earlier version of Lawrence's *Fantasia of the Unconscious*, entitled *Psychoanalysis and the Unconscious*, came out in the same year as his *Sea and Sardinia*, in 1921. If his second and third Italian travel books, therefore, appear to be especially "haunted," the richest in references to strange stirrings of the blood and to ghostly apparitions on the phylogenetic as well as on the ontogenetic level,[4] this is in part a reflection of Lawrence's interest in—and determination to distance himself from—psychoanalytic theory. The fact that the words "queer" and "queerness," in their traditional sense, recur with a symptomatic frequency in *Etruscan Places* is a sign that Lawrence was peculiarly attentive to the strangely familiar, Freud's "uncanny"—although, from a theoretic point of view, Lawrence was, in fact, closer to the Carl Jung of *Man and his Symbols*, a work with which he was familiar. Lawrence, in any case, was alert to a whole range of images (including particularly those of places and people) that excited unexpected movements of sympathy and antipathy—as well as to disturbing reminiscences he did not control: "that which half emerges from the dim background of time is strangely stirring" (*Places*, p. 20).

Those Etruscan tombs and their fragmentary artifacts spoke to him, therefore, at atavistic levels that recall Freud's archaeological metaphors in connection with many-layered Rome in *Civilization and Its Discontents* or Pompeii in Wihelm Jensen's *Gradiva*. More systematically than Freud, in fact, Lawrence develops an implicit analogy between human history and the development of the individual psyche, an analogy that equates the conscious mind with history and civilization, the unconscious with prehistory and primitive, instinctive life.

The issue had already been formulated in a particularly suggestive passage of *Sea and Sardinia* where Lawrence laments the age-old occupation of the Italian peninsula, but he also finds there an opportunity that is central to his quest, or what he calls "a process of rediscovering backwards": "One begins to realise how old the real Italy is, how man-gripped and how withered. . . . The land has been humanised through and through: and we in our own tissued consciousness bear the results of this humanisation. So that for us to go to Italy and to *penetrate* into Italy is like a most fascinating act of self-discovery—back, back down the old

---

[4] "There is a haunting quality in the Etruscan representations. Those leopards with their long tongues hanging out: those flowing hippocampi; those cringing spotted deer, struck in flank and neck; they get into the imagination, and will not go out." *Places*, p. 48.

ways of time. Strange and wonderful chords awake in us, and vibrate again after many hundreds of years of complete forgetfulness."[5]

There is, in fact, a kind of progression in Lawrence's travel works in the search for a more unified and natural mode of consciousness among primitive men, from the Italians of northern Italy, the peasants of Sardinia, and the Indians of New Mexico to the prehistoric Etruscans. It is thus that in *Etruscan Places* he penetrates to the deepest and most forgotten layer of human life on the Italian peninsula and discovers in the vestiges of Etruscan culture an embodiment of that "phallic consciousness" he sought to affirm in his own life and works.

It is on the beach at Ladisfoli that he speculates most movingly on the prehistory of the Mediterranean world and on the peoples who had migrated to the Italian peninsula before the foundation of Rome or even "before Ulysses." His prose knowingly communicates an existential shiver along with a fond compassion as he tries to delineate the lost cultures whose disappearance was to signal the emergence of Western history, including the very idea of "the West": "They were, we must feel, of an old, primitive Mediterranean and Asiatic or Aegean stock. The twilight of the beginning of our history was the nightfall of some previous history, which will never be written. Pelasgian is but a shadow-word. But Hittite and Minoan, Lydian, Carian, Etruscan, these emerge from shadow, and perhaps from one and the same great shadow come the peoples to whom the names belong" (*Places*, p. 19).

The key word in the passage is, of course, "shadow," from which there escapes into the light of historical consciousness only the resonant signifiers themselves. As such, they bear witness to previous existences that, though largely suppressed in a history written by descendants of the conquerors, return like the Freudian repressed at unguarded moments to trouble certain representatives of the cultures that conquered and survived.

In his last travel book, then, the importance of Italy was for Lawrence almost exclusively a matter of its Etruscan tombs and artifacts. They constituted a series of revelations concerning the vitality of a lost world and a lost art of living. In his own way, Lawrence was the most passionate and single-minded of pilgrims who was searching for a primordial, natural religion that had been destroyed with the emergence of what we in the West recognize as civilization. The goal he had pursued since adolescence, a goal that explains in large part his deep disaffection with contemporary England and his choice of exile, is suggested in two characteristically lambent sentences: "The active religious idea was that man, by vivid attention and subtlety and exerting all his strength, could draw

[5] (New York: Viking Press, 1963), p. 122.

more life into himself, more life, more and more glistening vitality, till he became shining like the morning, blazing like a god. When he was all himself he painted himself blazing like the throat of dawn, and was god's body, visibly, red and utterly vivid" (*Places*, p. 50). In such passages, one recognizes that a form of heroic self-affirmation is involved that has nothing to do with Flaubert's romantic agony, in spite of the brazenness of the colors. Lawrence here embraces Eros not Thanatos, although at other moments the pull of the latter is occasionally manifest.

o   o   o

IF SUCH an active religious idea was explicitly pursued largely in the mode of elegiac meditation in *Etruscan Places*, it also animates his two earlier Italian travel books and explains in part their concentrated power. *Twilight in Italy*[6] is composed of a series of essays deriving chiefly from Lawrence's extended stay in that country, from September 1912 to April 1913, in the months following his flight from England with his French professor's wife, who would be Lawrence's companion for the next eighteen years of his life, the former Frieda von Richthofen. *Sea and Sardinia* focuses on a journey of less than two weeks from Sicily to Sardinia and back that occurred in February 1921. *Twilight in Italy* is a travel book unlike any other, and although *Sea and Sardinia* has from a formal point of view more in common with traditional works in the genre, it, too, is characterized by passages of visionary intensity and explosive insights of a kind that we recognize as peculiarly Lawrentian. In both works the rage and vituperation, the passion, the celebration and tenderness that are also so much part of the texture of Lawrence's fiction remind the reader that the stimulus and provocation of travel can lead to writing of a sustained seriousness equal to that of any other kind of prose.

In many ways Lawrence is as splenetic and resolutely English a traveler as Smollett and, like the latter, also in pursuit of good health. But Lawrence would have abhorred Smollett's British patriotism and would have had no patience with the Enlightenment writer's improving purposes. Lawrence is preeminently a visionary traveler and celebrant of the life of the senses who sought what he took to be truths obscured by the Enlightenment tradition to which Smollett belonged.

From its resonant opening lines, *Twilight in Italy* wastes no time in engaging the reader with issues of vast magnitude, issues that concern the cultural memory of a people and the destiny of nations over hundreds of years: "The imperial road to Italy goes from Munich across the Tyrol, through Innsbruck and Bozen to Verona, over the mountains. Here the great processions passed as the emperors went South, or came home

---

[6] (New York: Viking Press, 1962).

again from rosy Italy to their own Germany" (*Twilight*, p. 3). Then, without referring specifically to his personal circumstances or to the historical moment of his writing shortly before the outbreak of the First World War, Lawrence goes on immediately to speculate on the impact that its long-standing position as the heartland of the Holy Roman Empire had on the German national soul and on what he calls Germany's *Grössewahn*. Something of that earlier history and of the papal ceremonial that was part of it still seem to him to pervade the Bavarian highlands in the very crucifixes that line the route south and to account in part for the sense of strangeness and remoteness he feels there.

It is characteristic that in an opening essay which evokes the approach to Italy from north of the Alps, Lawrence makes no effort to introduce himself as narrator or to explain the motives of his journey. The opening voice is oracular. Further, in this first Italian travel book there will at first be no references to such trivia as personal motivation, modes of travel, or the difficulties and pleasures of a journey. Nor will there be any mention of visits to famous cities, classical ruins, or museums. Although by the end there are a significant number of vignettes of Italians and others, and reports in direct or indirect speech of a great many conversations, Lawrence never lets his reader forget that his concern is with the state of the Italian national soul and, beyond that, with the soul of humanity itself.

Twilight in Italy already turns out to be both a celebration and an elegiac lament. In spite of Richard Aldington's demurral on the jacket blurb of the Viking Press edition of the book, its title is suggestive of the author's findings. The beauty and the bounty of the Italian countryside notwithstanding, the struggle in Italy between, on the one hand, the pagan openness to life of a past that goes back to the Renaissance and, on the other, the attraction of the new industrial future raises disturbing questions. At the work's center is the mind/body dualism that for Lawrence had already been resolved in the wrong way in Northern Europe.

The essential questions are broached in the opening essay of the volume, "The Crucifix Across the Mountains," and resurface throughout, down to the concluding chapter, "The Return Journey," which describes the narrator's impressions on his return on foot to Italy across the Alps from Switzerland. In the first essay, Lawrence evokes the mode of being of the Bavarian highland peasant in terms of a lived opposition between intense sensuous life and an apprehension of the nonbeing that is figured by the snow and ice of the Alpine peaks.

In a resonant set piece of descriptive writing in which Lawrence demonstrates his mastery of the poetic function of language, the narrator does not merely evoke what a traveler passing through might see, he pushes the notion of dialogic engagement with otherness to the point of entering the body of his subject. And in thus representing the sensations of "the peasant," he aggrandizes him to the dimension of myth: "The body bent forward towards the earth, closing round on itself; the arms clasped full of hay, clasped round the hay that presses soft and close to the breast and the body, that pricks into the arms and the skin of the breast, and fills the lungs with the sleepy scent of dried herbs: the rain that falls heavily and wets the shoulders, so that the shirt clings to the hot, firm skin and the rain comes with heavy, pleasant coldness on the active flesh, running in a trickle down toward the loins, secretly; this is the peasant, this hot welter of physical sensation. And it is all intoxicating." Over against all this "clasping" and "pricking" and "clinging" and "trickling," all this "soft, moist fire of the blood" that so excites the narrator, transcending all, stands the realm of ice and snow in its "timeless immunity from the flux and warmth of life." It is a situation that, in Lawrence's reading, forces a man to live "under the radiance of his own negation." Yet, it also explains the strength and beauty and completeness of the Bavarian peasant, "the only race with the souls of artists" (*Twilight*, pp. 5–7). Even before Lawrence's text turns to Italy, it discovers a way of being in the world that manifestly represents for its author a kind of ideal, a living out of a kind of Nietzschean opposition between a full-bodied affirmation of life and a recognition of the icy supremacy of nonbeing that surrounds it.

The themes, along with the concreteness and sudden intensities of the prose, of the opening essay in *Twilight in Italy* suggest very well the high seriousness with which Lawrence invested his travel writing and its continuity with both his fiction and his poetry. What is different here is the greater directness of assertions and judgments.

"The Crucifix Across the Mountains" functions, in fact, as a prologue in order to raise the question of the choice open to Western man at the beginning of the twentieth century. And it does so in typically Lawrentian fashion, not in political or social terms, but in terms that are simultaneously psychic and mythopoeic. It is no accident if the narrator does not identify himself here, since the text presents itself in the guise of an exalted meditation that is far removed from the accidents of personality; it recalls, if anything, the urgency of the voice of Nietzsche's *Thus Spake Zarathustra*. The "I" that speaks is no circumscribed ego but an "I" that implicitly claims the faculty to enter into the souls of other living beings, plants, animals, and men, and to speak for them as well as for itself.

The reflective, troubled discourse of *Twilight in Italy* is frequently characterized by bold and often startling generalizations, a use of anecdotes drawn from encounters and observations with ordinary Italians of both sexes and various occupations, and an imagistic prose style that probes the mythic unconscious of modern civilized life. In a series of more or less rambling and often confusing assertions, which occasionally appear to contradict what is said in other parts of the book, national differences are defined—frequently in terms of a north/south, or industrialized/preindustrialized, split—and European history is broken down into blocks of several centuries in which a given spirit is claimed to have prevailed over another. He equates, for example, that of contemporary Italy with the way of the senses and the subjugation of mind, the way of the tiger and the soldier: "He, too, walks with his consciousness concentrated at the base of his spine, his mind subjugated, submerged. The will of the soldier is the will of the great cats, the will to ecstacy in destruction, in absorbing life into his own life" (*Twilight*, p. 45).

All of this is in sharp contrast to the development of the self-denying, outward-looking "Northern races", who turned to scientific control and mechanized force. The choice is finally posed as one between a pagan "selfishness" and the "selflessness" of the industrial age, between the sun and machines, between Italy and England. Yet, in spite of the harmonious beauty of the northern Italian lake—"all the peace of the ancient world still covered in sunshine"—and the squalor of the new industrial England—"the great mass of London, and the black, fuming, laborious Midlands and north country"—there is a surprising ambivalence in Lawrence's response: "It is better to go forward into error than to stay fixed inextricably in the past" (*Twilight*, p. 68). The apocalyptic vision with which the second section of "On the Lago di Garda" concludes is of a world overcome by the English malady of conquest of the outer world and of desiccation of the soul. The only hope is that a recognition of the horror that has been wrought will cause England to change direction before it is too late.

What finally is most significant in Lawrence's groping for an explanation of the malaise of modern Western civilization, and in his effort to prescribe a cure, is that he parts company both with Christianity and with the Enlightenment tradition in Western thought. Unlike most intellectual historians, in fact, with a sweeping Nietzschean reversal he even establishes a continuity between them insofar as he finds that Christian charity and self-denial laid the groundwork for those outward-looking, scientific, and reformist attitudes which we associate with the late seventeenth and eighteenth centuries.

The importance of Italy for an Englishman of Lawrence's generation was that, against the background of a spreading malaise in the soul of modern Western man, he encountered a country whose spiritual and cultural development had been significantly different from that of his homeland, and one that seemed on the surface at least to offer greater cause for hope. Yet, it is soon made apparent that Italy, too, was going through a period of change in which the assumptions of the national

cultural past were being challenged in ways that Lawrence found deeply
disturbing. The modern malaise had invaded Italy and, if anything, the
Italians were even less prepared to deal with it than the English had been
before them.

This is something that becomes particularly clear in Lawrence's representations of Italian men. The traditional question raised, explicitly or
implicitly, by male travelers is, as Sir Richard Burton pointed out in
his *Personal Narrative of a Pilgrimage to Al-Madinah and Meccah*, "What are
the women like?"[7] Lawrence is one of the relatively rare European male
writers into the early decades of the twentieth century to ask the same
question about men. The notion of an essential maleness was, of course,
an abiding obsession throughout his creative life. In any case, the attraction of male beauty is experienced here as more potent than that of female beauty.

As a result, among the dozen or so important characters evoked in
Twilight in Italy, the great majority of them are male. What on the evidence of this book Lawrence found so attractive in Italy, apart from its
natural beauty, its climate, landscapes, trees, and abundance of fruits and
flowers, was the way of being of certain Italian men. He draws celebratory portraits of several male types, which are invested with a quality of
vital sensuousness and instinctive animal quickness that is nonetheless
combined with the signs of a lack or a disturbing restlessness. Such, for
example, is the case with *il Duro*, in whom Lawrence recognizes a
strangely attractive yet ultimately unknowable Other that excites his desire and is apparently excited by him.

In an hallucinatory passage that transfigures a grafter of vines into a
pagan divinity, Lawrence makes clear that what he seeks in Italy is remote from the interests of the average cultural tourist. His richly allusive
prose confirms that his goal is a form of libidinal satisfaction of an elemental kind—namely, that connectedness with the natural world or
"Pan-consciousness" which obliterates ego:

> All the morning and afternoon he was among the vines, crouching
> before them, cutting them back with his sharp, bright knife, amaz-
> ingly swift and sure, like a god. It filled me with a sort of panic to
> see him crouched flexibly, like some strange god, doubled on his
> haunches, before the young vines, and swiftly, vividly, without
> thought, cut, cut, cut at the young budding shoots, which fell un-
> heeded on to the earth. Then again he strode with his curious half-
> goatlike movement across the garden, to prepare the lime. . . . He
> was not a worker. He was a creature in intimate communion with the

[7] (New York: Dover, 1964), vol. 2, p. 85.

sensible world, knowing purely by touch the limey mess he mixed. [*Twilight*, pp. 139–140]

The "panic" referred to at the spectacle of this half-human, half-animal earth god has its full etymological meaning restored to it; it is compounded of desire and of fear at a prohibition transgressed. In a typically imagistic way, Lawrence opens up the questions of unconscious desire and prohibition. On the one hand, one recognizes the Lawrentian cult of instinctive, unself-conscious maleness and, on the other, the acknowledgment of a threat. The insistences in the imagery, the repetitions, and the rhythmic energies of Lawrence's prose—"cut, cut, cut"—reinforce the perception that this beautiful male is created in the image of a castrating god. *Il Duro* is a vital but inwardly divided modern version of what "Panconsciousness" had once been.

Throughout the various sections of "On the Lago di Garda" as well as in the two final chapters, entitled "Italians in Exile" and "The Return Journey," respectively, Lawrence describes local scenes and local characters in order to extend and rework his reflections on the discontents of contemporary Western civilization and the mounting tensions to which European men and women are exposed. In the owner of an hotel and his wife, in Paulo and Maria, the peasant proprietor of an inn and his wife at San Gaudenzio, in a local theatrical production of Ibsen's *Ghosts*, in the rehearsal of a play among Italian exiles in Switzerland, in a dance at an inn, in *il Duro*, in Giovanni, in the returned emigrant and his parents, or in Giuseppino in his Swiss exile, Lawrence finds himself solicited again and again to describe and redefine the difference that is Italy and the malaise that grips it in spite of its magnificently tangible strengths.

In effect, all the figures that are evoked at any length, along with the landscapes which are the background of their lives, are greatly magnified so as to become characters in a new kind of libidinally charged morality play. Against the backdrop of two millennia of West European history, the struggle for possession of modern man's soul is being acted out within and without. As the discussion shifts back and forth between such oppositions as the spirit and the senses, the mind and the body, male and female, past and present, north and south, the old and the new, rootedness and emigration, Lawrence's writing largely obliterates superficial differences of personality and social class in favor of a mythopsychic simplicity. Yet, every now and then a reference to socioeconomic or even political realities recalls the fact of Lawrence's awareness of the contemporary historical conjuncture and betrays his sense of urgency.

Lawrence's alertness to the socioeconomic change that was taking place in contemporary Italy as a consequence of the emergence of modern bourgeois capitalism in its industrial phase is suggested in a passage whose prose nevertheless possesses an elegiac, almost biblical solemnity: "The old order, the order of Paolo and of Pietro di Paoli, the aristocratic order of the supreme God, God the Father, the Lord, was passing away from the beautiful little territory. The household no longer receives its food, oil and wine and maize, from out of the earth in the motion of fate. The earth is annulled, and money takes its place" (*Twilight*, pp. 121–122).

One recognizes here Lawrence's preoccupation with the alienating power of a cash nexus in the modern world that replaces lived relationships between men, and between men and the earth. There is, however, a significant mystification in the association of a twentieth-century landowner with a biblical patriarch, as well as in the implication that there is no continuity at all between preindustrial wealth and industrial wealth. Nor is it made very clear why we should lament the end of such an age-old and authoritarian patriarchal order as is implied by Lawrence's roll call of divine father figures. Unless, of course, one acknowledges with awe the Law of the Father and celebrates patrilinear descent.

It is by contrast with the emergent new world that, in Lawrence's reading, the evanescent pastoral world of patriarchy suggests some of its attraction. Lawrence refers only in passing to Italian nationalism in the age of colonialism, in an episode that has a wounded colonel returned from Tripoli wave from his balcony to a band playing jingoistic songs—"They all seemed so sordidly, hopelessly shabby" (*Twilight*, p. 146). In a much more significant passage of the closing pages of the book, it is the socio-economic change that impresses the narrator so negatively. As he walks back down the mountains of northern Italy, he is stricken with terror at the industrial sprawl along the new Italian roads, "where these great blind cubes of dwellings rise stark from the destroyed earth, swarming with a sort of verminous life, really verminous, purely destructive" (*Twilight*, p. 210). The peasant has become a workman, life there is "slave-work," and the only bond between human beings is the cash nexus; money has taken over.

The restlessness and uncertain future of Italy is, in fact, encapsulated with a particular poignancy in the experience of the returned Italian emigrants and exiles whose portraits Lawrence sketches. This is nowhere more apparent than in the characterization of the Italian exiles in Switzerland, who in spite of all the promptings of their flesh would never return, unlike Paolo or *il Duro* in whom the dominance of the old pagan spirit of Italy was too strong.

Lawrence finds among the former a determination to forge a new spirit, even at the cost of "a death in the flesh." Yet, in one of those rarefied dialogues with a certain Giuseppino, the moral and intellectual leader of the group, in which soul speaks to soul, the narrator finds himself totally out of sympathy with the naive anarchism of these people for whom he simultaneously feels so much love: "my soul was somewhere in tears, crying helplessly like an infant in the night. . . . I knew the purity and new struggling towards birth of a true star-like spirit. . . . my soul could not respond. I did not believe in the perfectibility of man. I did not believe in infinite harmony among men. And this was his star, his belief" (*Twilight*, pp. 174–178). Politics and political culture for Lawrence were a symptom of the modern malaise and not part of its solution. *Twilight in Italy*, indeed, when the noblest of her sons are forced into exile and are portrayed as seduced by the false gods of anarcho-syndicalism.

o   o   o

ONE OF THE MOST notable aspects of Lawrence's first Italian travel book is how much it leaves out. As noted above, the traditional tourist's Italy to which Henry James as cultural pilgrim paid such splendid and loving tribute in *Italian Hours* is virtually absent from Lawrence's representations of Italian life in and around Lake Garda. If anything, moreover, his postwar *Sea and Sardinia* pays even less attention to the traditional centers of Italian high culture. "Horrible Messina" is where he and Frieda start from, after leaving the Sicilian village that was their temporary home; Rome is mentioned because it is there the Lawrences change trains; Naples is where he has to fight with thirty other men for a steamer ticket and avoid being robbed in the process.

The point is important because it demonstrates once again that Lawrence was in Italy for reasons that were radically different from those of the great majority of travelers who, since the eighteenth century, had made the pilgrimage south because Italy was the locus of the birth and rebirth of classical civilization. That immense challenge to a faith in the continuity of the civilized European tradition which was the First World War served to confirm in Lawrence attitudes that were already firmly entrenched before the war, as the most cursory reading of *Twilight in Italy* reveals.

Lawrence's journey to Sardinia might be more properly called antitourism, if tourism is understood in its original association with the grand tour. It has more in common with late-nineteenth-century anti-decadentism and the cult of primitivism, with Gauguin and the *douanier* Rousseau, the young Gide, and the cultural speculations of Freud, than with the reverential tour through Europe's past. Down to their mode of travel with rucksack and "kitchenino" for snacks and tea, third-class compartments, cramped ships' cabins, and *tables d'hôte* in primitive country inns, the Lawrences belonged to a new Bohemian age of travel that avoided the main routes of cultural pilgrimage and had no entrée into the salons or country houses of the powerful and the wealthy. Lawrence is much more interested in a peasant at his work than in a society lady or the portraits on the walls of her elegant villa: "I am sick of gaping *things*, even Peruginos. I have had my thrills from Carpaccio and Botticelli. But now I've had enough. But I can always look at an old, grey-bearded peasant in his earthy white drawer and his black waist-frill, wearing no coat or over-garment, but just crooking along beside his little ox-wagon. I am sick of 'things', even Perugino" (*Sea*, p. 150).

The reason why *Sea and Sardinia* is both a more traditional and more exciting work than *Twilight in Italy* is, first, that Lawrence foregrounds the instance of narration and the tormented psyche of his narrator, and, second, that he pays attention there to a greater range of sights, places, events and people; to the sea and the sky, to the stars and the mountains, to plants, flowers, animals, to fellow passengers from all walks of life and to Sicilians, mainland Italians, and Sardinians who bore him or outrage him, excite him, or elicit his deepest admiration. And, much more frequently than in the earlier work, the passionate and quicksilver personality of the narrator is put on display in encounters that inspire his wonder, regret, irascibility, and even despair, but that do not lead, as in *Twilight in Italy*, to such lengthy speculative musings or spiritual exhortation.

In his recent study of Lawrence, Anthony Burgess states unequivocally: "The outstanding travel book is *Sea and Sardinia*, the most charming work he ever wrote and by far the best introduction to his oeuvre."[8] Moreover, in a 1921 review in the *New Republic*, Francis Hackett gave right off a perceptive appraisal of the work's originality: "For D. H. Lawrence is so susceptible, so saturable, that what one receives (outside his *agacement* and his human judgments) is as keen a sense of actual experience as any traveller ever gave."[9] Among the earlier important commentators on Lawrence's work, on the other hand, his friend and companion of Katherine Mansfield, John Middleton Murry, with some justice partly demurred: "*Sea and Sardinia* is a lively and lovely book, but it seethes with weak and childish contradictions. Lawrence's right hand does not know, or seems not to know, what his left hand is doing."[10]

The reason Lawrence gives in the opening lines for the journey to Sardinia in the unpromising month of February 1921 is characteristically a powerful desire: "Comes over one an absolute necessity to move. And what is more, to move in some particular direction. A double necessity then: to get on the move, and to know whither" (*Sea*, p. 1). The urgency

[8] *Flame into Being: The Life and Work of D. H. Lawrence* (New York: Arbor House, 1985), p. 143
[9] *D. H. Lawrence: The Critical Heritage*, ed. R. P. Draper (New York: Barnes and Noble, 1970), p. 175
[10] *Son of Woman: The Story of D. H. Lawrence* (New York: Jonathan Cape and Harrison Smith, 1931), p. 145.

of the prompting is all the more mysterious, as Lawrence makes clear, because the Sicily in which he finds himself seems so agreeable. For more than two pages he waxes rhapsodic over the beauty of Sicily and especially over Mount Etna, which he looks at through the eyes of Greek mythology and personifies as a woman, a seductive Circe. But the point in the end is that the demand is for some kind of European Other, a land that has remained untouched by Greek mythologizing and Greek culture, or by any of the dominant national cultures that constitute the continuum of civilizations: "They say neither Romans, nor Phoenicians, Greeks nor Arabs ever subdued Sardinia. It lies outside; outside the circuit of civilisation" (*Sea*, p. 3). The call Lawrence is responding to is the call of the primitive and the unknown, "outside the circuit of civilisation."

It is for this reason that he responds with so much excitement to Mount Eryx on the western end of Sicily. For not only does that peak have pre-Greek associations with the mythical goddess Astarte—"Venus of the aborigines, older than Greek Aphrodite"—it also looks out across the Mediterannean to the great and mysterious Other that was for millennia, and in the European imagination of his generation still remained, Africa: "To men it must have had a magic almost greater than Etna's. Watching Africa! Africa, showing her coast on clear days. Africa the dreaded." Yet as the prose here makes very clear, Lawrence recognizes in the fantasized continent a promise as well as a threat. The excitement aroused in him by the prehistoric site is, in effect, one he attributes to the memory in his blood of the Other within or to what, after Freud, he might have figured as the unconscious desire of a "prehistoric" self. That low mountain was in its day also a center, a center of an ancient lost world: "It seems to me from the darkest recesses of my blood comes a terrible echo at the name of Mount Eryx: something quite unaccountable. The name of Athens hardly moves me" (*Sea*, p. 34). It would be hard to express more succinctly than in these two sentences the return of the culturally repressed from beyond the remote origins of Western civilization.

Lawrence, in fact, finds in the polarity between the eastern and western ends of the island of Sicily a refiguring of the classic binary opposition between civilization and barbarism in which the traditional hierarchy is, however, reversed. Whereas the eastern end opens onto the Ionian Sea and to Greece, the western end faces the world beyond Europe in Africa and America. And it is to the strange, disturbing beauty of these other continents that Lawrence is drawn: "this great red, trumpet-flaring sunset had something African, half-sinister, upon the sea: and it seemed so far off, in an unknown land. Whereas our Ionian dawn seems near and familiar and happy" (*Sea*, p. 42). The difference expressed here in Lawrence's resonantly figurative language is one that in our time has been rearticulated as an opposition between the categories of pleasure and *jouissance*, between a cultivated delight at the level of the ego and of civilized continuity and a turbulence that shatters the very idea of self in a drive beyond the pleasure principle. That is why, in a sense, Murry's complaints about the "inward division and uncertainty" (*Son*, p. 142) in the work are misplaced. Lawrence, in effect, cultivates spontaneity precisely in order to give expression to his contradictory drives.

Throughout the rest of *Sea and Sardinia* there will be echoes of the themes evoked here, references to sites in Sardinia or Spain or on the Celtic fringes of European civilization that still possess some of the primitive wildness that has disappeared from most of modern Europe, including Italy. Thus, even the Abruzzi does not satisfy Lawrence's longing for the primitive and prehuman: "Life is so primitive, so pagan, so strangely heathen and half-savage. And yet it is human life. And the wildest country is half-humanised. . . . Wherever one is [in Italy], the place has its conscious genus. Man has lived there and brought forth his consciousness, given it its expression, and, really, finished it" (*Sea*, p. 122).

In different ways, both the frequent references to ancient myth and the luminous, celebratory descriptions of the sea, sky, and stars constitute efforts to reassert contact with whatever in the past remains beyond the reach of historicizing capture or in the present is outside the reach of human consciousness. But it is above all the sea itself that arouses a sense of awe in Lawrence's "wild innermost soul," a sensation of freedom unlike any other: "Ah, God, liberty, elemental liberty. I wished in my soul the voyage might last for ever, that the sea had no end, that one might float in this wavering, tremulous, yet long and surging pulsation while ever time lasted" (*Sea*, p. 27).

One recognizes here Baudelaire's "true traveler" and the great, nineteenth-century poetic theme of embarcation for the new and the unknown that embodies fantasies of an "easeful death." Once again Lawrence manages to suggest that willing psychic abandonment to a state beyond pleasure, associated with the satisfaction of primordial drives that are indifferent to the fate of the self-preserving ego, drives that seek instead a return to a previous, preanimate mode of existence. No other writer discussed in this book, in any case, comes as close as Lawrence does in the imagery of the above passage to suggesting that the mythical "good place" resembles the preconscious existence within the mother's body.

In a subsequent passage, Lawrence relates this drive to the dream of the romantic voyager for freedom from the social constraints associated with the land: "Land has no answer to the soul any more. It has gone inert. Give me a little ship, kind gods, and three world-lost comrades. Hear me! And let me wander aimless across this vivid oyster world, the world empty of man, where space flies happily" (*Sea*, p. 46). Lawrence's theme and his language here are remarkably close both to Baudelaire's poem "Le Voyage" and to the response aroused in *Etruscan Places* by the fascinating scenes of departure represented on the walls of a tomb, scenes that he assumes picture "the journey of the soul" (*Places*, p. 110).

What one also recognizes—as in a later passage that refers to the magic of the first and most thrilling journeys of Western literature, *The Odyssey*—"All the lovely morning-wonder of this world, in Homer's day!" (*Sea*, p. 196)—is the world-weariness of the latecomer, the romantic nostalgia for the freshness of origins and of a time before time. If Lawrence is no tourist, therefore, it is because travel for him is in modern times a demand of the soul. Moreover, he locates its golden age not prior to the Second World War, as Paul Fussell has suggested,[11] but before recorded history.

The journey through Sardinia confirms for Lawrence that the best the land has to offer is occasionally its topography, landscapes, trees, plants, animals, and those humans who are closest to nature and the least corrupted by modern civilization: the peasantry. There is here something like a descending order that starts with what men are least responsible for and moves through those spheres in which human intervention is increasingly visible. Thus, the sight of some of the island's wild vegetation stirs him deeply: "This Sunday morning, seeing the frost among the tangled, still savage bushes of Sardinia, my soul thrilled again. This was not all known. This was not all worked out" (*Sea*, p. 122). And although almond trees in bloom may have been cultivated by men, in their "weird valley" they nevertheless constitute for Lawrence a momentary revelation, a sudden sense of being in the presence of the divine: "How beautiful they were, their pure, silvery pink gleaming so nobly, like a transfiguration, tall and perfect in that strange cradled river-bed parallel with the sea" (*Sea*, p. 157).

On other occasions, it is the "glow" of something as banal as eggs in a market that draws the gaze—"eggs in piles, in mounds, in heaps, a Sierra Nevada of eggs, glowing warm white." Or ordinary vegetables are defamiliarized before the reader's eyes: "The intense deep green of spinach seemed to predominate, and out of that came the monuments of curd-white and black-purple cauliflower: but marvellous cauliflowers, like a purple flower show, the purple ones intense as great bunches of violets" (*Sea*, pp. 63–65). Finally, it is the surprise in the splendor of a team of oxen plowing or the beauty and mythic strangeness of goats seen from a moving bus that moves him: "They fly like white shadows along the road from us, then dart down-hill. I see one standing on the bough of an oak

[11] See "From Exploration to Travel to Tourism," in *Abroad* (New York: Oxford University Press, 1980).

tree, right in the tree, an enormous white tree-creature, complacently munching up aloft" (*Sea*, p. 129). It is presumably writing of this order that Anthony Burgess is referring to when he says that the work's "magic lies in what the power of poetic observation can do with the ordinary" (*Flame*, p. 144).

In any case, the eggs, the vegetables, the oxen, and the goats are, of course, all related to the world of men; they are, in part at least, the product of human labor, yet for one visionary moment they are, as it were, restored to their startling and original strangeness. In all such passages, what Lawrence manages to communicate is the intensity of a look that not only seeks out the unfamiliar and the lovely, but also makes the familiar strangely beautiful. They are instances of what in classical rhetoric was known as "hypotyposis"; that is to say, a form of description that has all the intensity and vividness of a picture. The look here defamiliarizes the ordinary with a vengeance. In any case, for Lawrence the importance of travel to a place such as Sardinia is obvious. That island at its best furnishes a variety of occasions for renewing contact with whatever is beyond civilization, whatever remains wild and unspoiled and astonishing to the senses.

Among human beings, it is the peasant and all those who have retained some link to the natural world and its creatures that interest and occasionally excite him. In this respect, no one could be closer to the natural order than the group of men in sheepskin tunics and stockingcaps who get into the third-class carriage in which Lawrence is seated: "And how they smell! of sheep's-wool and of men and goat. A rank scent fills the carriage. They talk and are very lively. And they have medieval faces, ruse, never really abandoning their defences for a moment, as a badger or a polecat never abandons its defences. There is none of the brotherliness or civilised simplicity" (*Sea*, p. 89). Elsewhere, it is the shapes and colors of traditional costumes that draw his attention—and the play of sexual differences on which the costumes insist—the ritual procession of a feast day, the provocative histrionics and elaborate costumes of the maskers, and the popular female impersonation of carnival.

Finally, other occasions allow him to elaborate on his particular kind of susceptibility to male beauty and to a kind of fierce male pride, for he finds in Sardinia a quality of maleness that has disappeared from the Italian peninsula and from most other parts of Europe as well: "One realises, with horror, that the race of men is almost extinct in Europe. Only Christ-like heroes and woman-worshipping Don Juans, and rabid equality-mongrels. The old, hardy, indomitable male is gone. His fierce singleness is quenched. The last sparks are dying out in Sardinia and Spain" (*Sea*, p. 62).

Given the urgency and the passion that transforms Lawrence's trip to

Sardinia into a passionate pilgrimage of a very un-Jamesian kind, it is not surprising if he reacts with exasperation and even rage at the frequent reminders of the disturbing political and socioeconomic realities of the postwar world. He has, for example, little patience with the pettiness and conversational banalities of ordinary people. In this respect, he is particularly hard on various elements of the lower middle classes, including especially the despised figure of the commercial traveler, and on any sign of the emergent, utopian universalism of the proletariat—"save us from proletarian homogeneity and khaki all-alikeness" (*Sea*, p. 92). What makes him angriest, however, is the popular xenophobia of which he is occasionally the target—"Underneath, they hate us, and as human beings we are objects of envy and malice" (*Sea*, p. 192)—or the consumer of the press who stuffs "wads of chewed newspaper into [Lawrence's] ear" (*Sea*, p. 49).

It is in the end significant, however, that unlike *Twilight in Italy*, *Sea and Sardinia* concludes on a peculiarly Lawrentian upbeat note that also reverberates disturbingly. Francis Hackett was presumably responding to such and similar passages in the text when he wrote in 1921: "There you have Mr. Lawrence's present note. Manliness, by God, manliness. Kick your wife in the stomach. No damn nonsense about tenderness and sympathy, sweetness and light" (*Heritage*, p. 173).

The episode in question describes a marionette theater in Palermo that the Lawrences visit on their way home. Lawrence himself discovers a world that is not only without women—there are none in the audience besides Frieda Lawrence—but that defines itself, through the very themes of its spectacle, as being in opposition to them. In the traditional epic tales of medieval paladins that are reenacted there, it is the men who are the heroes, and the only woman mentioned is the witch who locks them up. In what Lawrence himself calls "a very psycho-analytic performance," he finds that the male voice of the narrator speaks to buried layers of his self: "Again the old male Adam began to stir at the roots of my soul." The witch, on the other hand, awakens atavistic feelings that are equally deep, but full of hate: "I felt my heart getting as hot against her as the hearts of the lads in the audience were. Red, deep hate I felt of that symbolic old ghoul-female" (*Sea*, p. 203).

The whole performance is, in effect, an auto-da-fé or a ritualistic reenactment, for males only, of a matricide. The episode seems to be once again an expression of Lawrence's ambivalence toward women, going back to his relationship with his own mother; the powerful attraction certain women exercised over him was countered with an equally determined resistance against being absorbed by too smothering a love. The result frequently was the celebrated cult of maleness, the will to an identification with the phallus and with phallic consciousness. What charac-

terizes the primal horde of male spectators in the Sicilian marionette theater is, therefore, not hatred of the father and competition for access to
women, but solidarity among males in the consummation of revenge
against a castrating mother and all that is controlling in women.

Given this final hallucinatory episode, it is impossible not to attribute a
peculiarly hostile significance to the fact that Lawrence refers throughout
to his wife, Frieda, as "the queen bee," or "q.b." for short. Long before
the new feminism, Hackett had noted Lawrence's deliberate effacement
of his traveling companion: "Also we have a silhouette of his accompanying wife, a mere outlander who prices vegetables and shops for saddle-
bags and wants to go to the marionette show and is rather annoyingly
interested in the native" (*Heritage*, p. 174). Yet, along with the teasing
hostility, part of the explanation for this effacement of Frieda is surely to
be found in the fact that the acknowledgment of a companion of any
kind would have been felt as an obstacle to immediacy of contact and of
vision. The intense communion Lawrence sought with a certain nature
and with the natural in men was not susceptible to being shared.[12]

Although the marionette episode may be the end of the book, it is
clearly not the last word on the movements of Lawrence's desire. A truer
gauge of that occurs much earlier in a section that is once again best
understood in terms of the "uncanny." It is another potent example of
the *déjà vu* of travel. The sight of a handsome Sardinian peasant in a
traditional black-and-white costume comes back to haunt him, since it
reminds him of something he has dreamed of, or lived through, before:
"the uneasy sense of blood-familiarity haunts me. I know I have known
it before. It is something of the same uneasiness I feel before Mount
Eryx: but without the awe this time."

It is an insight that occurs to him in the context of reflections on the
disappearance of male pride from Europe and on "the foul lavishness of
the war-masters" who had despoiled Italy. And the context gives a peculiar urgency to his uncanny moment. What Lawrence seems to be reaching deep into himself for is an original lost object of desire, the repressed
memory of a satisfaction of the time before separation and the assumption of a sexualized identity: "Two peasants in black and white costumes
are strolling in the sun, flashing. And my dream of last night was not a
dream. And my nostalgia for something I know not what was not an illusion. I feel it again at once at the sight of the men in frieze and linen,
a heart yearning for something I have known, and which I want back
again" (*Sea*, pp. 62–63).

[12] See Martin Green, *The von Richthofen Sisters: The Triumphant and the Tragic Modes of
Love* (New York: Basic Books, 1974), for an account of the relationship between the
Lawrences.

The moment is peculiarly poignant. It is by means of the detour of the journey to Sardinia that this Englishman from Sicily achieves a moment of insight into the nature of his desire, only to lose it again. Like the "flashing" costumes of the peasants, there is in this sexual signaling an insistence that he will never quite master and that will never be satisfied.

o   o   o

NEVERTHELESS, in the years down to his death in 1930 Lawrence pursued his search for satisfaction on other continents, returning to Italy only shortly before the end. The importance of *Etruscan Places* is that it makes explicit in a consciously sexualized, mythic discourse his sense of the fundamental dichotomy that explains the dynamism of all life as well as the continuity between life and death. In his choice of imagery, moreover, Lawrence is curiously close to *Beyond the Pleasure Principle* with its formulation of the third and final stage of Freud's theory of the instincts as an opposition between a drive to preserve life and a drive to end it, and with its startling affirmation that "the aim of life is death."[13]

In two different passages, Lawrence develops the recurrent theme of the complementarity and separateness of the phallus and the womb. In the first of the two passages, he makes the metaphoric substitution of an ark for a small Etruscan stone house, in order to suggest that the place of the emergence of life is also the tomb to which all life returns: "And that is what it is, the Ark, the arx, the womb. The womb of all the world, that brought forth all the creatures. The womb, the arx, where life retreats in the last refuge" (*Places*, p. 14). And close by that same stone house he also identifies the phallic stones that participate equally in the mystery of procreation.

In the second passage, Lawrence returns to one of the favorite objects of his meditations, the sea: "The sea is that vast primordial creature that has a soul also, whose inwardness is womb of all things, out of which all things emerged, and into which they are devoured back." The phallus in this case is figured as a dolphin: "He is so much alive, he is like the phallus carrying the fiery spark of procreation down into the wet darkness of the womb" (*Places*, p. 53). But at the beginning, as at the end, is the creative and devouring womb. No wonder Lawrence took such pleasure in the matricide reenacted in the Sicilian marionette theater. He may have recognized the inevitability of the final return to the inanimate state of prenatality, but all the energy of the phallus in his personal mythology was focused on the life-affirming injunction "Not yet!"

Through a curious chiasma, the Freudian discourse of *Beyond the Plea-*

[13] In *The Standard Edition of the Complete Psychological Works* (London: Hogarth, 1955), vol. 18, p. 38.

sure Principle and the Lawrentian imagery of *Etruscan Places* relay each other at a crucial moment. Freud's theory employs the metaphor of a journey to suggest the passage through life of a human subject inhabited by the contradictory drives of the life and death instincts. And Lawrence on his journey associates the Etruscan objects he encounters with the psychoanalytic categories of phallic life and womb death. In the narrative of his encounters in Italy, it is as if the English novelist were evoking what Freud called "the ever more complicated detours" and "the circuitous paths" (*S.E.*, vol. 18, pp. 38–39) we take through life on the way back to that time before birth.

Chapter IX

POLITICAL WITNESS:
T. E. LAWRENCE AND GIDE

D. H. LAWRENCE's contemporaries, T. E. Lawrence and André Gide, shared in different ways his dissatisfactions with the European civilization of their time. At a number of moments in their lives, therefore, they both went out of their way to expose themselves to alternative forms of existence through foreign travel outside Europe. Gide traveled extensively in North Africa during the 1890s and the opening decade of the twentieth century, and was later to travel in west-central Africa and the Soviet Union. T. E. Lawrence began his solitary exploration of life abroad when still an undergraduate at Oxford. He was profoundly marked by his years in the Middle East, first as an archaeologist and then as a leading participant in the Arab revolt against Turkish occupation. Moreover, both men left a substantial written record of their various journeys.

Yet, unlike D. H. Lawrence's travel books for the most part, at least some of the works they wrote as a result of their experience abroad address directly the political questions of their age. This is clearly not unexpected in the case of T. E. Lawrence, insofar as the book of his that most interests me, *Seven Pillars of Wisdom*,[1] is a chronicle of war and a history of the Arab revolt against the Turks (at the time of the First World War) as well as an extraordinary work of travel literature that focuses on Arabia and its peoples. The political dimension is, at first sight, more surprising in Gide's case because of his reputation as the novelist of a pagan openness to life and of individual rebellion against the constraints of religious and social law, as the man who once summed up the fierce energy of his rebellion in the provocative phrase, "Families, I hate you." Gide was clearly drawn to the emancipatory promise of travel from quite early in his life, and it was non-Europe that held out the greatest promise. Yet, the work of his that concerns me here, *Back from the USSR; followed by, Afterthoughts to My Back from the USSR*,[2] turns out to be, for

---

[1] (Harmondsworth: Penguin, 1962). A few of this chapter's pages devoted to T. E. Lawrence were published in 1982 as part of a conference proceedings, *The Politics of Theory* (University of Essex). Among some thirty biographies, see Malcolm Brown and Julia Cave, *A Touch of Genius: The Life of T. E. Lawrence* (London: J. M. Dent, 1988), for a recent, "balanced" account of Lawrence's life and his role in the Arab revolt.

[2] *Retour de l'U.R.S.S. suivi de Retouches à mon Retour de l'U.R.S.S.* (Paris: Gallimard, 1978), pp. 145–146; hereafter, referred to as *Back* or *Afterthoughts*, as appropriate.

reasons that will become clear, much less a record of the desires and re-sistances of the narrator's private self, and less self-consciously "literary," than *Seven Pillars of Wisdom*. In his polemical works for the public arena, Gide even adopts the discourse of politics more consistently than Colonel Lawrence does in his troubled war memoirs. Both writers, though, took equally seriously the mission of political witness.

Given that political witness is one of the poles to which European travel writing has tended since the eighteenth century, that will be my focus here, although (as Lawrence's work, in particular, illustrates) it is in the end impossible to disentangle personal motivations from political ones. Lawrence is not being disingenuous when, on the final page of *Seven Pillars of Wisdom*, he himself claims that "the strongest motive throughout had been a personal one" (p. 684), to which he adds the motives of "pug-naciousness," "curiosity," and "historical ambition."

Boswell's tour of Corsica and Diderot's *Journey to Holland* are reason-ably typical examples of Enlightenment writing in a genre that has com-monly merged reflections on comparative government or sociological studies of institutions and manners with impressions of landscapes, cities, people, and behavior. Frequently such writing has taken the form of a self-conscious political intervention in the debate in the homeland. The works by both the twentieth-century writers under discussion here are of this type, if not exclusively so. Like Freud's commentary on travel, they also confirm the extent to which private fantasms inform public aspira-tions and political purposes. One way of responding to unsatisfied de-mands is to travel to lands where they are apparently realizable; another is to participate in a collective remaking of one's own society, partly as a consequence of observations in foreign lands. One can attempt to con-struct an abroad at home, or one can give more or less passionate support to those in other countries who are engaged in an heroic or utopian ef-fort of reconstruction.

o   o   o

THERE IS no doubt that T. E. Lawrence's heroic narrative of Arabia and the Arab revolt is a limit case that pushes beyond the boundaries of travel writing as traditionally defined. But its significance in this context resides in the fact that it gives a peculiarly intense form to the topoi and psychic investments that characterize such writing. If for so many travelers a cru-cial element in the motivation of travel has been the pursuit of adventure that puts the self at risk, then rarely outside the pages of heroic literature proper does one find "adventures" that surpass those narrated in *Seven Pillars of Wisdom*. Stanley and Rodelle Weintraub summarize Lawrence's most extreme experiences as follows: "He had been wounded numerous times; been captured, tortured, and homosexually abused; endured endless privations of hunger and weather and disease; been driven by military necessity to commit atrocities upon the enemy and murder his own wounded to prevent the Turks from doing worse; and witnessed in Damascus the defeat of his aspirations for the Arabs in the very moment of their triumph"[3]

Thus, the motifs of desire and transgression are woven into the texture of this long and complex work, and not only in the more notorious scenes of sex and carnage in which peculiar homage is paid to Eros and Thanatos. One can expose oneself to no greater risk on foreign soil than that of battle; one can encounter no more shattering a sexual experience than that of a brutal rape. What a critical reading of Lawrence's astonishing book also reveals is how close he was to those nineteenth-century French writers discussed above whose major preoccupations, after art, were love, travel, and war. It is difficult to think of a work of modern literature in which they are combined with quite the same intensity as *Seven Pillars of Wisdom*. The revelation for this reader was in the discovery of how in a single psyche a military hero may cohabit with a *poète maudit*.

At the same time, a particular interest attaches itself to Lawrence's work in this context because one would expect to find there, probably more than anywhere else, evidence of that hegemonic discourse Edward Said has called "Orientalism." Yet, from the opening pages, it is apparent that Lawrence's work is in many ways a self-interrogating, fissured text that subverts many of the ideological presuppositions that it also asserts. Unlike Louis Althusser's Marxist theory, say, Foucauldian discourse theory in its pure form does not envisage the possibility of the relative autonomy of aesthetic production or of the specificity of "the literary." As a result, it has no theoretic ground for making a qualitative distinction between those works which offer no internal resistance to the ideologies they reproduce and those such as *Seven Pillars of Wisdom* which, at least sometimes, display a self-questioning density of verbal texture.[4]

[3] *Lawrence of Arabia: The Literary Impulse* (Baton Rouge: Louisiana State University Press, 1975), p. 6. See also, in this connection, Paul Fussell's comment in his introduction to *The Norton Book of Travel* (New York: Norton, 1987): "[Byron,] who held that 'the great object of life is . . . to feel that we exist,' discovered that feeling in three things: gambling, battle, and travel, all of them 'intemperate but keenly felt pursuits . . . whose principal attraction is the agitation inseparable from their accomplishment' " (pp. 14–15).

[4] As a distinguished literary scholar and critic, Said is, of course, aware of the qualitative differences and relative textual complexity among the various works he touches on: "One remembers that Lane's *Manners and Customs of the Ancient Egyptians* is a classic of historical and anthropological observation because of its style, its enormously intelligent and brilliant detail, not because of its simple reflection of racist superiority." *Orientalism* (New York: Vintage Books, 1978), p. 15. Yet, he does not draw out the fuller implications of such notations.

Given that Lawrence's book is an account of human experience at the limit of the endurable, it is not surprising that the personal intersects with the political on a number of levels. T. E. Lawrence's investments in the men among whom he lived for so long on terms of intimacy turn out in the end to be more powerful than his commitment to the relative abstractions of country and duty. If there is any lesson to be gained from the oft-told tale of Britain's upper-class spies—of Guy Burgess, Donald Maclean, Kim Philby, and Anthony Blunt—in fact, it is precisely that all of our engagements have an overdetermined character. Moreover, both E. M. Forster and Graham Greene in their different ways have indicated that if forced to choose between loyalty to friend and loyalty to country, their respect goes to those who choose the former.

Lawrence's work of close to seven hundred pages is, then, a complexly determined product of the early twentieth century, characterized by heterogeneity and fragmentation in spite of the generic pressures that seek to unify it. It may take the form of a journey that begins with a departure and ends with a return, but such symbolic closure fails to reduce the contradictory energies that traverse it, especially when its own prologue problematizes the narrative even before it begins. Lawrence's story of the Arab revolt and his part in it contains innumerable anecdotes and events, descriptions of place and people, evocations of mood and of attitude. His text is crosshatched with historical, political, socioeconomic, and psychic references and determinations that occasionally make the concept of Orientalism itself appear like a countermystification.

The reason why *Seven Pillars of Wisdom* is likely to be resented not only by Arabs but by all those whose sensibilities have been heightened to racial doctrines by twentieth-century history is obvious enough. Because it tells the story of the Arab nationalist cause from the point of view of a British army officer, it suggests that the prime mover in the cause of Arab unity and its leading military strategist was an Englishman. It promotes the myth that a white European male in a position of leadership is an essential ingredient if people of color are to pursue a national goal and be an effective fighting force.[5] In other words, Lawrence's book lends itself to a reading that relates it directly to the discourse of Western power/knowledge. And there are, indeed, many passages that would support such a reading.

The opening chapters in particular may serve to remind us that, before he was commissioned as a liaison officer to Arabia, Lawrence had some experience as an "Arabist" and had worked for two years as an archae-

---

[5] Lawrence himself does affirm in his introduction that "it was an Arab war waged and led by Arabs for an Arab aim in Arabia" (*Pillars*, p. 21). For an Arab perspective on Lawrence's role, see Suleiman Mousa, *T. E. Lawrence: An Arab View* (Oxford: Oxford University Press, 1966).

ologist in Syria and Mesopotamia. It is no accident, therefore, if the authoritative voice that sketches in the history of the Middle East up to the
outbreak of the First World War and that comments on the racial and
cultural characteristics of the peoples involved is the voice of Orientalist
discourse as described by Said.

It is such a tradition that allows Lawrence to refer unequivocally to "the
Semitic consciousness" and to assert the existence of an essence possessed
in common by all Semites. In Lawrence's lexicon, it should be noted that
Semite is virtually synonymous with Arab, although it also includes Jews.
Typically, Lawrence's assertions take the form of a proper noun or third-
person pronoun linked by the usually plural copula "are" to an adjective
or adjectival phrase. Sentences such as the following are not untypical:
"Semites had no half-tones in their register of vision. They were a people
of primary colours, or rather of black and white, who saw the world always in contour. They were a dogmatic people, despising doubt, our
modern crown of thorns. They did not understand our metaphysical difficulties, our introspective questionings" (*Pillars*, p. 36).

At such moments, Lawrence shows no critical awareness of that nineteenth-century European discourse on race in general that he reproduces, a discourse that transmitted the doctrine of national characteristics, fixed ethnic identities, and transported essences that were enabling
or disabling for individual members of a given group. It is such a received "wisdom" that allows him to dismiss the Syrians as "an ape-like
people having much of the Japanese quickness but shallow" (*Pillars*, p.
45).

Seven Pillars of Wisdom, then, is an extreme case, a work apparently
written from a position of power and privilege—the power and privilege
of race, nation, class, and gender—within the Western imperial system.
Yet, it is soon evident that Lawrence's book is also the site of a struggle
in which other, counterhegemonic voices struggle to be heard for a complex set of psychological and social reasons. Whether or not one attributes such resistances in the text to factors such as Lawrence's illegitimacy
or homophilia, his own sense of his marginality to mainstream English
culture and his determined pursuit of alternative forms of existence
among alien peoples are evident. Consequently, not only does he allow
his own consciousness of contradiction to surface, he also becomes absorbed by the problems of verbal representation and the play of words
on the page, such that unanticipated possibilities often emerge unbidden
from their combinations. Desire finds a way to speak through an inherited cultural discourse.

Stanley and Rodelle Weintraub open their book with the unequivocal
assertion that "T. E. Lawrence's highest ambition was literary" (*Impulse*,
p. xi). Thus, much of their effort goes to marshaling the evidence to

support their thesis, including identifying Lawrence's literary models and quoting him on his concerns to get the writing right. What emerges is confirmation of how self-conscious Lawrence was in the intertextual weavings that constitute his major work: "As a great reader of books, my own language has been made up choosing from the black heap of words those which much-loved men have stooped to, and charged with rich meanings and made our living possession" (*Impulse*, p. 29).

It turns out that *Seven Pillars of Wisdom*, even more than most travel writing, is characterized by great heterogeneity. With the account of a geographic region and its peoples, it combines elements of a campaign diary, an autobiographical memoir, a history, a romance, and a modern epic in prose of men at war with all its horror and heroism. Yet, the book's heterogeneity is also its strength. Because it follows no single literary model, but often shifts within a single chapter from history and politics to landscape description, autobiography, and epic, discursive dissonances emerge at the very moment when the narrator was himself a serving officer in the state apparatus that contributed most to the maintenance of the imperial system, the British army. Such a circumstance is perhaps best explained as the result of a double overdetermination, that of an author and of a text.

To begin with, it is obvious that Lawrence himself was no political innocent, no Beau Geste. The politics of the Arab revolt in their international context are right up front in the work's introduction and opening chapters. Lawrence makes it very clear that the Arab war against occupation by the Ottoman Empire was treated by the Western allies and by Germany as an extension of the European war into the Middle East. The Anglo-French goal was to defeat Germany's allies, the Turks, in order to maintain their influence over the area and to keep open their strategic links with the Far East through the Suez Canal. To this end, as Lawrence shows, elements in the British government and military establishment saw the usefulness of making common cause with the Arabs in a campaign against Turkey. At the same time, unknown to some of the principal players, there was a secret understanding between Britain and France and Czarist Russia, the Sykes-Picot agreement, on how to divide up the former provinces of the Ottoman Empire into spheres of influence.

Inserted into such a military and geopolitical conjuncture by historical forces beyond his control, Lawrence asserts how from early on his loyalties were divided. Insofar as a war between imperialist powers was in this case also an anticolonialist struggle of liberation, the war itself was fought on behalf of a contradiction that Lawrence himself was forced to live. As an officer in the British army, he was committed to pursuing the war aims and colonial policies of the government he served. As a companion in arms to the bedouin Arabs, he believed himself morally committed to the cause of Arab national independence. The guilt he frequently confesses to in *Seven Pillars of Wisdom* is in this case related to those companions. One may doubt the sincerity of a commitment narrated some time after the event; yet, it is difficult to overlook the fact that the work's opening dedication takes the form of a love poem apparently addressed to the young Arab who was his assistant during the prewar archaeological expedition to the ancient Hittite city of Carchemish.

Moreover, the introduction itself—suppressed in the first edition on the advice of George Bernard Shaw—makes clear how Lawrence interpreted the conflict less as one between nations and races than as one between generations; the fathers won back at the conference table what the young men had won on the field of battle. Like that liberating French army in northern Italy which Stendhal celebrates at the beginning of *The Charterhouse of Parma*, Lawrence fantasizes his Arab war as a briefly realized dream of youthful male solidarity in a land without fathers: "We were fond together, because of the sweep of the open places, the taste of wide winds, the sunlight, and the hopes in which we worked. The morning freshness of the world-to-be intoxicated us. We were wrought up with ideas inexpressible and vaporous, but to be fought for. We lived many lives in those whirling campaigns, never sparing ourselves: yet when we achieved and the new world dawned, the old men came out again and took our victory to re-make in the likeness of the former world they knew" (*Pillars*, p. 22). The postwar settlement constituted, therefore, a return to patriarchal authority that had for the narrator a kind of mythic inevitability.

The difference between Lawrence's Arabia and that equally fresh and youthful world evoked in Stendhal's novel, however, is in the sex of the love objects pursued in the absence of the fathers. Where the French novelist dreams of satisfied heterosexual desire, Lawrence's passion goes to his more or less youthful male companions. Since his youth, he had prepared himself mentally and physically for the kind of chivalric service that made the ascetic life of the desert Arabs and their cause peculiarly sympathetic for him. Thus, Lawrence's introduction, whose discursive present situates the narrator in the postwar peace conference at Versailles, is also his bitter epilogue; it tells of the betrayal of Arab hopes to which he himself was a reluctant party—"the only thing remaining was to refuse rewards for being a successful trickster" (*Pillars*, p. 24). And it is, of course, true that in conformity with the self-chastising behavior that characterized his life as a whole, Lawrence refused the Order of Bath and the Distinguished Service Order as well as offers of high office. As the Weintraubs note, "A colonel at thirty, Lawrence was a private at thirty-four" (*Impulse*, p. 7).

The complexity of the narrator's persona, his aspirations and self-doubt, his sense of estrangement from his own culture, the sympathy for and distance from the Arab culture he was immersed in for roughly two years, all are part of the story Lawrence tells. What he does not tell us in so many words is the contradictions he was forced to live at other levels.

In common with a great many other men of his generation and upper-middle-class background, Lawrence was subjected to the peculiarly British ideological apparatuses of the public school, the Church of England, an Oxford college, an academic mentor who was both an Arabist and a recruiter for the British Intelligence Service, a British archaeological expedition to the Near East, and the British army itself. On the basis of his biography, it is possible to go even further in reconstructing the kind of ideologically saturated discourses to which he would have been exposed in a late-Victorian and Edwardian school, society drawing rooms and college common rooms, as well as in the canonical texts of history, thought, and literature that were the prescribed readings for the worthier aspirants to higher functions within the British imperial order of his time. Yet, resistance to his constitution as an imperial subject is apparent both in the biographical data and in Lawrence's text itself.

He was himself sensitive to the contradiction embodied in the notion of the "amateur soldier." To put on a uniform against one's will is to see oneself as a divided person, to reserve part of oneself from the commitment to soldiering, and to establish a distance between one's role and a private self. In Lawrence's case, the complexity of the situation was further heightened when he gave up British khaki for the costume of an alien culture—"the efforts for these years to live in the dress of Arabs, and to imitate their mental foundation, quitted me of my English self, and let me look at the West and its conventions with new eyes: they destroyed it all for me. At the same time I could not sincerely take on the Arab skin: it was an affectation only. . . . Sometimes these selves would converse in the void; and then madness was very near" (*Pillars*, p. 30). As with Sir Richard Burton's earlier travels to Arabia, a form of cultural transvestism was involved that enhanced the ambiguities of a self already subject to doubt in the sexual sphere.

In Lawrence's case, the cross-dressing he ostensibly engaged in so as to display rank to the bedouin tribesmen, as well as for practical, military reasons, also had a patently transgressive character relative to his own national culture. It was in one sense "to go native," and in traditional colonial society that was the ultimate apostasy. A peculiar opprobrium was attached to the white European who chose to live and dress like the natives or who appeared to prefer their company, an opprobrium that from Conrad to Somerset Maugham found a typical literary expression in the ambivalent figure of "the outcast."

Cultural cross-dressing for Lawrence also seems to have involved that impulse to transform oneself, to embrace the concept of self as a work of art, on which Michel Foucault sought to found a modernist ethics. Clothes help make and unmake a man who is open to the experiments of masquerade. As some of the carefully posed photographs that contributed to the postwar myth of "Lawrence of Arabia" suggest, the Oxford graduate and passionate student of medieval history made himself over, in his imagination at least, into a knight in shining robes from another, more heroic age. Yet, it is typical that he himself seems only to have been half taken in by the masquerade.

If *Seven Pillars of Wisdom* turns out to be a much richer work than the campaign memoirs of generals from Caesar to Patton and Montgomery, then, it is because Lawrence offers much more than an account of military and diplomatic events or even of politics, social institutions, and manners. Lawrence also reports on the movements of his desire in a foreign adventure that exposed him at different moments to the severest forms of self-abnegation, ecstatic encounters with men and nature, death and bloodletting: "Blood was always on our hands: we were licensed to it" (*Pillars*, p. 29).

He was also frequently preoccupied with the anguish and urgency of sex in the desert, where the only women available were the prostitutes of the rare settlements: "In horror of such sordid commerce our youths began indifferently to slake one another's few needs in their own clean bodies—a cold convenience that, by comparison, seemed sexless and even pure. Later, some began to justify this sterile process, and swore that friends quivering together in the yielding sand with intimate hot limbs in supreme embrace, found there hidden in the darkness a sensual co-efficient of the mental passion which was welding our souls and spirits in one flaming effort" (*Pillars*, p. 28).

In spite of that distancing pronoun "some," the personal note in this rapturous and tender evocation of remembered passion—"quivering together . . . yielding sand . . . hot limbs in supreme embrace"—is unmistakable. The complex character of Lawrence's erotic sensibility is even more obvious in the way in which the references to lust are combined with the affirmation of purity and virtual sexlessness. Moreover, the passage ends with the suggestion of a self-chastising, masochistic frenzy that recalls the representation of perversion in the desert to be found in Flaubert; Lawrence, too, had a recognizably late-romantic sensibility: "Several, thirsting to punish appetites they could not wholly prevent, took a savage pride in degrading the body, and offered themselves fiercely in any habit which promised physical pain or filth" (*Pillars*, p. 28).

That this last remark reads like an example of projection is confirmed from Lawrence's commentary on the notorious incident at Deraa. And in this context the accuracy of the account is less significant than his way of representing it. Lawrence was clearly putting himself at risk by entering the Turkish-occupied town incognito, although he could clearly not have anticipated the bizarreness of the sexual assault to which he was subjected when picked up by the Turkish soldiers and delivered into the hands of the bey of Deraa. In the unpublished "Oxford version" of the incident, Lawrence makes poignantly clear after the fact his recognition of the self-destructive force of the drive:

> I was feeling very ill, as though some part of me had gone dead that night in Deraa, leaving me maimed, imperfect, only half myself. It could not have been the defilement, for no one had ever held the body in less honour than I had myself. Probably it had been the breaking of the spirit by that frenzied nerve-shattering pain which had degraded me to beast level when it made me grovel to it, and which had journeyed with me since, a fascination and terror and morbid desire, lascivious and vicious, perhaps, but like the striving of a moth towards its flame.[6]

Lawrence here reveals a capacity for auto-analysis that the other Perverse Traveler discussed in these pages nowhere rises to on his Mideastern journey. Moreover, that final image suggests that along with the discovery of the unsuspected and inhuman depths within—"lascivious and vicious"—there is a strangely satisfying self-destructive beauty.

If such passages are an indication of the powerful drives that were at work in the author, they also combine with other similar passages to reveal the kind of overdetermined cultural object that the *Seven Pillars of Wisdom* is. Lawrence's work has as its model not one literary genre but several. And it is in part because the author shifts abruptly from genre to genre that further dissonances emerge. They are present as a radical, stylistic heterogeneity, as a variety of contents, as shifting authorial distance and point of view.

Lawrence's book is the tale of a sexual and a political coming of age as well as a war story and a travel book. Passages that reproduce a generalized Orientalist discourse alternate with those that recall the intensity and tedium of war, the rare camaraderie of battle, the confusions of desire, spiritual aspiration, and self-disgust, and a sense of wonder at the natural beauty of the desert. The late-romantic pursuit of adventure and intense sensation at the limit, which I have called *jouissance*, conflicts with the Victorian code of chivalry and service to country that was mediated in particular by the public schools. The modern epic material of battles and preparation for battle, of bedouin camps by night, of councils of war and

---

[6] Quoted by Brown and Cave, *Touch*, p. 107.

the clash of wills and purposes, of strategy and tactics, is joined to the romance theme of personal quest, of self-testing and self-discovery. Moreover, the romance theme is also linked to the peculiarly modern theme of the divided self, of the split between public and private, between the man of action and the guilt-ridden, self-castigating man of desire.

Lawrence's eclectic text echoes the themes and employs the narrative techniques of a variety of genres of the Western literary tradition from as far back as the Homeric epic—he was later to translate *The Odyssey*— Xenophon's *Anabasis*, Caesar's *Commentaries*, and chivalric romance down through the Victorian poets and Charles Doughty's *Travels in Arabia Deserta*. Along with the campaign literature of Caesar, Napoleon, and others, one of the rare works he mentions by name is, significantly enough, the *Morte d'Arthur*. Perhaps even more important were the literary models implied by what Lawrence called his "Titanic" books, among them *The Brothers Karamazov, Thus Spake Zarathustra* and, above all, *Moby Dick*. That Lawrence's work makes a systematic use of the poetic function of language is finally most evident in certain passages of apparently documentary reportage.

A paragraph that describes Ashraf camel drivers suggests the qualities of Lawrence's frequently purple yet astringent prose:

> They wore rusty-red tunics henna-dyed, under black cloaks, and carried swords. Each had a slave crouched behind him on the crupper to help him with rifle and dagger in the fight, and to watch his camel and cook for him on the road. The slaves, as befitted slaves of poor masters, were very little dressed. Their strong black legs gripped the camels woolly sides as in a vice, to lessen the shocks inevitable on their bony perches, while they had knotted up their rags of shirts into the plaited throng about their loins to save them from the fouling of the camels and their staling on the march. Semna water was medicinal, and our animals' dung flowed like green soup down their hocks that day. [*Pillars*, p. 157]

On the level of its signified, this is obviously the Eastern Other of Western ideological representation. The color of the costumes signifies Oriental brilliance, the weapons warlike ferocity, the slaves despotic practices, the camels' diarrhea barbaric crudeness. In the play of difference and identity by means of which we report back on the alien to our culture of reference, such a passage insists on Near Eastern difference. Yet, the very vividness of this group portrait and the verbal precision of its detailing are designed to reverberate in a reader's mind and body, stimulating at the same time a *frisson nouveau* and a shock of recognition. On the one hand, it is striking for the libidinal investments located in the sharp particularity of its images. On the other, if this is the East, it is an East that recalls the heroic age of Greece; it is a reminder of the classical European past. The Near East here appears in the guise of an ally, not as an enemy, admired for the strength of its primary colors and the wholeness of its energies.

The desert Arab becomes, in part, an expression of the age-old nostalgia for the supposed lost harmony of the primitive world, a modern Noble Savage, who is different not only from the half-Europeanized and decadent Turks but also from city Arabs. From such a point of view, the scene is noteworthy because it appears against the implicit background of a contemporary European muteness of tone, world-weariness, and cynicism. Thus, it is far from clear that in the hierarchical opposition between Western civilization and Eastern barbarism—the fundamental Orientalist trope—the good is on the European side.

Finally, perhaps the most significant feature of the passage is that it demonstrates how *Seven Pillars of Wisdom* is a self-conscious work of literature in a positive sense. Because Lawrence is preoccupied by the weight and shape of the paragraph on the page as an order of words under the pressure of desire, he is diverted from the reproduction of a discourse. Consequently, the passage illuminates the potential ideological irresponsibility of language wherever an eroticized fantasy is granted the freedom to indulge itself in a literary space. From the first line to the last, the passage displays its concern for phrasing and for energizing combinations of monosyllables and alliterative patterns, as well as for an arresting anal simile. Such foregrounding of verbal signifiers releases, through association, forces that have a capacity for producing the unexpected. It is clearly writing of this kind that Roland Barthes must have had in mind when he, in effect, defined "literature" as antidiscourse.

The notion of new possibilities as inherent in previously untried combinations of words, as a utopian potential emerging within the play of language, is perhaps best illustrated by a short sentence, shortly after the passage just quoted, in which is concentrated so much of what Arabia had meant to Lawrence: "We got off our camels and stretched ourselves, sat down or walked before supper to the sea and bathed by hundreds, a splashing, screaming mob of fish-like naked men of all earth's colours" (*Pillars*, p. 159). Such a sentence reminds us that we are in the presence of "the literary" because its significance is not at all in what it asserts, in any generalizing thought it expresses about East or West, but in the hallucination of a homoerotic mingling in which all categories are collapsed back into something primordial or yet unrealized—"a splashing, screaming mob of fish-like naked men of all earth's colours." The power of this visionary scene resides in a newly minted verbal impression that suggests an untapped potential in the world. And it is a potential for which there is no support in the dominant hegemonic discourse. The imagery of baptism and of a fresh emergence from the sea as a collectivity of races constitutes a politically utopian idea as well as a homoerotic fantasy. It is, in any case, an unexpressible thought within the discourse of Orientalism as defined by Said.

o   o   o

THERE IS little in André Gide's early fiction that would seem to destine him for the kind of public role in the affairs of the French state assumed at different times by eminent French men of letters from Voltaire and Diderot to Victor Hugo, Emile Zola, Romain Rolland, and Jean-Paul Sartre. From his first works of the early 1890s through those of the First World War, Gide was associated with literary symbolism, with the late-nineteenth-century *culte du moi*, and with the forging of a highly individualist ethic that insisted on the emancipation of the senses and sexual liberation. In opposition both to the moral interdictions of the Christian religion and to the social constraints of French bourgeois life, Gide championed the ethics of *disponibilité*, or "openness." One might even say that in his novels he undertook the investigation of what Baudelaire had called for in *My Heart Laid Bare*: namely, "the study of the great sickness of the horror of home."[7] Not surprisingly, therefore, the theme of travel with all that it implies in terms of flight, displacement, and the possibility of individual renewal is a central motif in Gide's work.

He had traveled widely in Europe with his mother's blessing even before his first trip to North Africa in 1893, visiting in turn Switzerland, Belgium, Holland, Germany, and Spain. Moreover, as his biographers and critics have pointed out, he was familiar with the abundant literature of the early decades of the Third Republic in which various forms of travel writing catered to the French public's imagination. The works in question run the gamut from the reveries of symbolist and decadent poetry and the fantastic adventures of Jules Verne to frank apologies for exploration and colonial conquest, the facile exoticisms of a Pierre Loti or the expansive meditations on place of the early theorist of earth, blood, and rootedness, and Gide's *bête noire*, Maurice Barrès.

What one finds in Gide's works with reference to travel right down to *The Counterfeiters* of 1926 is, in fact, an individual code that is constructed out of a series of interlocking oppositions between, on the one hand, *famille* (family), *foyer* (home), *province* (region), and *patrie* (homeland), and, on the other, *voyage* (travel), *vagabondage* (vagabondage), *errance* (wandering), and *déracinement* (uprootedness). And connected to that are the motifs of rebellion against the paternal Law, which is often embodied in the

---

[7] *Œuvres complètes* (Paris: Pléiade, 1951), p. 1209.

figure of the bastard son, hostility to a domesticity ruled by women, and a preference for cosmopolitain male companions who initiate the young hero into the pleasures of a new life elsewhere. Not surprisingly, therefore, the young Gide preferred the resolution of Novalis's tale of a wanderer, *Heinrich von Öfterdingen*, over that of Goethe's *Wilhelm Meisters Wanderjahre* with its affirmation of social responsibility over the cultivation of inwardness.[8]

The early writing that is the richest working-through of the characteristic Gidean themes and that also comes closest to being a travel book is the 1902 novel *The Immoralist*. In that novel, the various oppositions out of which it is constructed—oppositions between home and abroad, the young husband Marcel and the young wife Marceline, between sickness and health, the life of the mind and the life of the body, Christianity and paganism, heterosexuality and homosexuality—depend for their resolution, equally as much as "Death in Venice," on the narrative structure of a journey south. Unlike Thomas Mann's Auerbach, however, Gide's Marcel pushes the exploration of his instincts even farther south than Italy. Marcel's immoral education follows his migrations on the map from Paris to Normandy to the Italian peninsula and, finally, outside Europe altogether to North Africa.

In brief, Gide's novel expresses that same impulse to go beyond the sphere of a European civilization centered on the idea of Rome and Christianity which is found in Flaubert's as well as D. H. Lawrence's travel writings. In place of Freud's archaeological metaphor for the superimposed layers of the self, Gide in *The Immoralist* substitutes the image of the palimpsest. It is, in any case, in North Africa that Marcel learns to throw off all the constraints of his northern Protestant education and, like Auerbach, pursues desire to the point of death.

Gide never wrote a travel book proper that matches *The Immoralist* for its sustained attention to place and to the power of place to activate repressed desire. From the point of view of theme and writing, the work that comes closest is *Amyntas*, a collection of short travel pieces written in journal form that records the impressions of a number of journeys to North Africa between 1896 and 1904. To the extent that it sets itself the task of finding a literary language that is precise and refined enough to register the sharpness of sensations and the movements of a desire aroused by the North African scene, it is an example of *fin de siècle* exoticism. The peculiar combination of preciousness and ecstasy that is its characteristic tone is suggested by a single, overripe sentence: "Oh! to be

[8] See Jean Delay, *La Jeunesse d'André Gide* (Paris: Gallimard, 1956–1957), 2 vols., for an account of Gide's early life; and Pierre Masson, *André Gide: Voyage et ecriture* (Lyons: Presses Universitaires de Lyon, 1983), for a helpful, if somewhat diffuse account of the theme of travel in Gide's work as a whole.

a plant and experience, after months of drought, the rapture of a little water."[9]

The two travel works that are also among his most sustained contributions to the political debate of his time, *Travels to the Congo* and *Back from the USSR; followed by, Afterthoughts to My Back from the USSR*, appeared relatively late in his career and were published at an interval of almost a decade, in 1927 and 1936/1937 respectively. They appeared, that is, at a time when Gide had been captured by his own image as grand old man of French letters and as intellectual conscience of French society at a peculiarly threatening moment of its history.

Of the two works, the former reads much more like a traditional piece of nonfictional, "literary" travel writing in which the author records his impressions of a journey to a foreign country, dates his arrivals and departures, and respects the order of the itinerary that he actually took. *Travels to the Congo* has, in fact, the form of a diary maintained more or less day by day during the eight months or so that Gide spent, between July 1925 and February 1926, in what was then French Equatorial Africa. At a time when the vogue of "primitivism" in art and literature was at its height in Paris—including the so-called *art nègre* that encompassed American jazz as well as African artifacts—and when well-equipped French anthropological expeditions were traversing Africa and creating the collections that were to form the *Musée d'Ethnographie du Trocadéro*, Gide found the Congo both shocking and disappointing.

The surprise for him was in the discovery of the hidden Conradian face of French colonialism: "I couldn't foresee that these disturbing social questions, which I was able only to glimpse, of our relations with the native populations would soon occupy me to such an extent as to become the principal concern of my journey nor that I would discover in investigating them my very reason for being in that country."[10] As the publication of Michel Leiris's *Afrique fantôme* in 1934 reminds us, however, Gide was by no means alone in his expressions of guilt and cultural self-doubt.

Back from the USSR is a much slimmer and much more focused volume than *Travels to the Congo* and concerns questions of even greater moment

---

[9] (Paris: Editions Crès, 1928), p. 120. Masson writes: "One finds a stylistic hunger that is not composed of overabundance, as in the case of Colette, but of a mixture of precision and discretion; the intoxication is supposed to arise from both an absence of the usual details and an extreme exactitude in the search of a sensation—it is not so much the object of pleasure as the pleasure itself" (*Voyage*, p. 54).

[10] *Œuvres Complètes d'André Gide* (Paris: NRF, 1937), vol. 13, p. 105; hereafter, referred to as *O.C.* See James Clifford's suggestive descriptions of the Parisian cultural climate: "On Ethnographic Surrealism" and "Tell about your Trip: Michel Leiris," in *The Predicament of Culture: Twentieth Century Ethnography, Literature, and Art* (Cambridge: Harvard University Press, 1988).

for European politics of the time. It belongs to the category of twentieth-century works written by what Paul Hollander has called "political pilgrims." In several short chapters of observations and generalizing commentary, it attempts to offer a summary of the material, political, moral, and intellectual conditions of life in the Soviet Union twenty years after the October Revolution on the basis of a visit there of a few weeks. Since, of Gide's two travel works, the Russian journey is a more single-minded example of that limit of travel writing I have called political witness, I will direct my comments here mostly to that book.

Admirers of Gide's fiction are likely to find both works disappointing. Part of the reason is given by Gide himself, in a footnote that he added to *Travels to the Congo* once he was back in France preparing his work for publication. He points there to a problem with which readers of the present study are by now thoroughly familiar. The trouble with travel writing, especially when it takes the form of a journal proper, is that it tends to lack focus: "A traveler newly arrived in a country in which everything is new to him is arrested by indecision. Since he is interested in everything to the same degree, he is unable to cope and begins by noting nothing down because he cannot note everything down. How fortunate is the sociologist who is interested only in mores, the painter who consents only to capture the look of a country, the naturalist who choses to concentrate on insects or plants. How fortunate is the specialist."[11]

It is a problem Gide solves in *Back from the USSR* by becoming a specialist himself and focusing almost exclusively on social and political life. But in his encounter with the Soviet Union of the Stalinist dictatorship, to his great credit he does not renounce those critical positions, founded on individualistic ethical values, that he had previously articulated in his fiction from *Fruits of the Earth* (*Les Nourritures terrestres*) in 1897 down through *The Cellars of the Vatican* in 1914.

By 1936, when he published his account of the journey to the Soviet Union, Gide's involvement in the political debates of his time had grown substantially. In the age of the consolidation of Soviet communism and the spread of fascism throughout continental Europe, Gide, like many of his literary peers in the Western democracies, had taken to signing petitions, writing pamphlets, attending rallies, and even making speeches. And his sympathetic interest in the development of the Russian Revolution made him, for a short time at least, one of the literary celebrities of the French Left.[12] *Back from the USSR* is, therefore, a much more self-conscious political intervention even than *Travels to the Congo*. Russia was

[11] *O.C.*, vol. 13, p. 106.
[12] See Herbert R. Lottman's discussion of the involvement of French literary intellectuals in the political arena in *The Left Bank: Writers, Artists, and Politics from the Popular Front to the Cold War* (Boston: Houghton Mifflin, 1982).

neither geographically remote nor an example of a culture still close to nature. Yet, if it was not "prehistoric," it did in its way claim to be post-historic, to be a utopian society rebuilt from scratch in the cause of universal justice and universal well-being, once the painful period of transition had been overcome.

Against that background, it is significant that Gide begins his Russian travel book with a reference to classical myth. He narrates the story of Demeter and the infant Demophon. Disguised as a nurse and inspired by love, Demeter sought to raise the child to the level of the gods by exposing his naked body to live coals. The child in Gide's telling seemed to respond well to the treatment, but Demeter is interrupted in her experiment by the child's mother and, as a result, Demophon never achieves the divinity of which he seemed capable. Gide comments: "I imagine the great Demeter bent over this radiant child as if he were a future humanity. He withstands the burning coals and the test strengthens him. Something superhuman is preparing itself in him, something powerful and unbelievably glorious. If only Demeter had been allowed to continue her bold initiative and carry her challenge through to the end" (*Back*, p. 13).

In the light of the story Gide goes on to tell of his journey through the new Russia, in the company of five French writers and intellectuals who were sympathetic to the revolutionary cause, the myth is not without its ambiguity. What one cannot avoid reading into Gide's choice of text for the times, however, is the notion of an interrupted experiment. Something that promised so much for the future of humanity and at the greatest possible cost in human suffering—those "burning coals"—had been brought to a premature end. His theme, in short, will be that of lost opportunity, although whether the opportunity is lost forever or might be seized again, if the appropriate initiatives are quickly taken, is never fully resolved in the body of the text.

The preface that follows is less categorical and more sanguine. Yet, when one reads it over after having completed *Back from the USSR; followed by, Afterthoughts to My Back from the USSR*, the latter part of which appeared in June 1937, one realizes that it was part of Gide's strategy to emphasize all the positive feelings at the beginning. For some time before his journey, he had regarded the Bolshevik Revolution and the emergence of a new Russia with a great deal of hope: "Three years ago I affirmed my admiration and my love for the USSR. Over there an experiment without precedent was being carried out, an experiment that caused our hearts to swell with hope, an experiment from which we expected immense progress, a vital energy capable of bearing the whole of humanity in its wake" (*Back*, p. 15). Whether such love was the "real thing" or merely Freud's "transference love" is, in its way, what Gide's journey was designed to test.

To begin with, it is soon clear from the context that this opening reaffirmation of Gide's enthusiasm is a rhetorical strategy designed to give greater weight to the subsequent expression of his concern about recent developments in the Soviet state. It remains his intention to give the Soviet experiment the benefit of the doubt, but he insists that in the long run the cause of the Revolution will be best served if he represents what he saw in the course of his travels without dissimulation. And he reminds his readers that the Gidean ethic places "sincerity" above "loyalty." Gide's challenge to the leftist political discourse of his time and country is founded on his insistence that it is more important to remain open to the changing feelings and responses one experiences than to remain loyal to some abstract principle or cause. Understanding for alien circumstances can once again be seen to begin at home in individual psycho-political needs.

Given all that has been disclosed concerning the repressive, totalitarian character of the Soviet state over the fifty years since the publication of Gide's travel book, it is perhaps worth reemphasizing the kind of hope that was invested in the October Revolution by so many intellectuals of Gide's generation, a hope that he had already partly distanced himself from in the very tenses of his sentences: "Who will say what the USSR has meant to us? It has been more than the homeland of choice; it has been an example, a guide. What we dreamed of, what we scarcely hoped for but what our will and our strength worked toward, had taken place over there. There was, then, a land in which Utopia was in the process of becoming a reality" (*Back*, p. 18). Here, as elsewhere, it turns out that the discourse of political observations on place shares a vocabulary with the fantasies of our psychic life—"dream," "homeland," "hope," "utopia."

The main body of the slender work that follows—just over ninety pages for *Back from the USSR* and as many more for the *Afterthoughts*—is devoted to a generalized summary of impressions of Gide's travels and contacts, with virtually none of the evocations of place and scene or of character and incident that are usually associated with the travel writings of novelists. *Back from the USSR* is a consciously political intervention that speaks directly and with considerable urgency to contemporary political issues.

In the six short chapters of the original 1936 work, Gide touches on a variety of aspects of life in the new Russia in a more or less random order. Each chapter tends to concentrate to some extent on one or more features of that life, but there is significant overlapping and backtracking. A mere summary of the contents is, however, enough to confirm the acuteness of Gide's perceptions.

Chapter 1 largely consists of praise for the Russian people, for their human warmth and the successes of their collective life. After paying tribute to the beauty of Leningrad, chapter 2 concentrates on the ugliness of Moscow and the deficiencies of Soviet consumer goods and food, of their unavailability and poor quality. Chapter 3 expresses disquiet at the ignorance of the outside world displayed by Russians of all kinds and at the often grotesque sense of superiority they feel; it also calls attention to the emergence of a new privileged class of party bureaucrats. The following chapter is specific in the warning it issues concerning the cult of Stalin and the dangers of the dictatorship of one man. Chapter 5 emphasizes the concern Gide felt for the fate of those writers and artists in the Soviet state who wanted to remain an oppositional force, like so many of their colleagues in the West, and who refused to conform to the official line in their aesthetic practices; there are references, for example, to the repression of the Formalists. The briefest of final chapters does little more than underline the degree of his ambivalence.

In committing himself to the idea of going public in order to express his concern about dangerous political developments in the Soviet Union, Gide was clearly being consistent with his earlier book on the Congo. The intellectual tradition of *engagement* that made *Back from the USSR* possible was clearly one that goes back to the French Enlightenment. Yet, the historical conjuncture of the late twenties and early thirties in Europe was such that there was a significant internationalization of political involvement by writers and artists as well intellectuals in general.[13] With the publication in 1932 of extracts from his journal that praised the Soviet Union, Gide had been drawn in to support such organizations as the Association of Revolutionary Writers and Artists and the International Writers' Association for the Defense of Culture, and even to chair international congresses set up to organize against fascism and the threat of war. Such circumstances help to explain the two contradictory impulses at work in *Back from the USSR*. Because of the political conjuncture, his task was a delicate one.

On the one hand, if Gide is often guarded in his comments, this is because he was under considerable pressure from friends and allies not to undermine the prestige of the Soviet Union at the very moment when it was the only major power supporting the Loyalist cause in the fight against fascism in Spain. At the same time, he also did not want to give too much succor to the powerful forces of the far right in France itself, nor to discourage reform from within the communist movement at home

---

[13] Lottman refers to Romain Rolland and Henri Barbusse as "the founding fathers of engagement" and "the first to see the crisis of their times as universal" (*Left Bank*, pp. 47–48). The two novelists were also the chief organizers of the First International Congress Against War, held in Amsterdam in 1932.

and abroad by judgments that were too sweeping. On the other hand, there is no denying the frequent firmness of his expressions of disappointment and even shock at certain ominous developments within the Soviet state. Gide's position seems to be that, in spite of the spread of fascism, the threat of war, and the continuing crisis of the Western capitalist democracies, the times demanded the reassertion, even the extension, of the rights of man and of the goal of social justice for all, wherever those ideals seem to be threatened.

Thus, on his Russian journey Gide had no time for impressions of landscape or atmosphere or the more exotic aspects of the human scene that take up so much space in *Travels to the Congo*. The distance from the sharply realized, sensuous impressionism of *Amyntas* is even more remote. The Soviet Union, it seems, offered none of the pleasures of travel associated with southern Europe or North Africa. "What interests me in the USSR," he notes, "is man, men, what can be made of them and what one has made of them" (*Back*, pp. 30–31)." And in the *Afterthoughts* it is the victims of Stalinist persecution whom he invokes to justify his accusations: "I can see them, those victims, I can hear them, I feel them all around me. It is their stifled cries which woke me last night; it is their silence which dictates these lines to me today. It was in thinking of these martyrs that I wrote the lines against which you [his critics] protested" (pp. 145–146).

Among Gide's "ghosts," then, are those voices he hears crying in the night once he is back home in France. Once again, this time as a man in his late sixties, he has returned from a journey abroad with a guilty conscience. It was the times that required him to bear witness, and it was a responsibility he was determined not to shirk, even if it meant denouncing the one country in increasingly fascist Europe that, for many, still represented man's last best hope.

Not all Gide has to say is negative, of course. Some of the more memorable passages in the early chapters express his enthusiasm for the evidence of progress and for the people he met at old people's homes, children's camps, or "culture parks"—"The children in all the pioneer camps that I saw are beautiful, well nourished (five meals a day), well taken care of, even spoiled, happy. . . . The same expression of expansive happiness was also found among their elders, who were equally as beautiful and as strong. . . . Everywhere one breathed in a kind of joyous fervor" (*Back*, pp. 22–23).

More than anything, he was impressed by the collective leisure activities of the "culture parks" he visited in Moscow and Leningrad, by the folk dancing and singing, the organized sports and games, and the outdoor theater. The assumption of a plenitude of being, combined with such innocence suggests, indeed, that we are wholly in the register of the imaginary and of transference love that has "place" as its object. One finds in such passages echoes of the comments frequently made about the Russian people by Western visitors from the mid-1920s on and summarized by Paul Hollander: "good mental and physical health, strong communal feeling, commitment to public affairs, kindness, generosity, wisdom, and simple authenticity."[14]

The fact that, along with his fellow travelers, Gide arrived in the Soviet Union predisposed to admire and was welcomed unambiguously as a friend goes a long way to account for the positive transference of which at certain moments he was evidently the dupe: "Also nowhere as much as in the USSR does one make contact with anyone and everyone so easily, immediately, deeply, warmly. A single glance is sometimes enough to establish bonds of violent sympathy" (*Back*, p. 27). It should be noted that such bonds of sympathy are established between people who do not even speak the same language, for Gide knew no Russian and communicated with ordinary Russians, if at all, through an interpreter. His choice of words is revealing. There is no Other. "Communication" exists between human beings in a kind of specular fullness of the image. It is wholly visual, unmediated, and nonverbal; it is what, in other contexts, is known as a *coup de foudre*.

Yet, after the early dithyrambic comments, Gide has relatively little to add that is positive and, in the *Afterthoughts* at least, he goes on to cast some doubt on what he had previously found praiseworthy, notably in regard to the use of model institutions for propaganda purposes and with respect to the expressions of happiness he had so frequently observed—to appear unhappy was politically suspect. The sense one sometimes has in reading *Back from the USSR*, that Gide was holding himself back from expressing the full force of his disquiet, is confirmed in the *Afterthoughts*.

The latter is an even more consciously polemical piece of writing. It takes the form of a response to those critics who had reproached him for representing Soviet reality in too negative a light and for failing to take into account the great difficulties the Revolution had to overcome in such a backward country. Gide's reaction is to be even more forthright in his condemnation of much that he had encountered. His observations here are more thoroughly documented with new information culled from official reports, statistical analyses, and the accounts of other witnesses of Soviet life at firsthand, read only after his return to France. Thus, to the extent that the *Afterthoughts* reveals a hardening of his position, it makes even clearer the extent of his loss of faith.

[14] *Political Pilgrims: Travels of Western Intellectuals to the Soviet Union, China, and Cuba* (New York: Harper Colophon, 1983), p. 135.

The list of charges contained in the two volumes is long and familiar into the age of Mikhail Gorbachev. They concern the extremely harsh material conditions of life for Soviet workers and peasants, the scarcities and endless waiting in queues, the depressing ugliness, standardization and lack of choice of consumer products, the depersonalization of domestic interiors, the laziness and inertia of the Soviet workforce, the harsh legislation against homosexuals, a lack of freedom not only of speech and opinion but also of employment and movement, and the absence of genuinely democratic forms of government at all levels, such that elections are stage-managed from above and give rise to the dictatorship of the party bureaucracy and not of the proletariat.

Perhaps most offensive to Gide's ethical sensibility, however, are the profound moral failures that the regime cynically promotes. Spying and informing on one's fellows have been institutionalized as integral to the Soviet way of life—"The practice of denunciation is an excellent means of promotion"; "informing on one's fellows is one of the civic virtues" (*Afterthoughts*, pp. 116, 117). Furthermore, to the horror of the great champion of individual rights, the price of happiness in the USSR has come to mean a total integration into the collective life, a massive conformism: "The happiness of all is achieved only through the 'disindividualizing' of everyone. The happiness of all is achieved only at the cost of everyone. If you want to be happy, conform" (*Back*, p. 41).

In retrospect, it is clear that Gide's denunciation of the collective pursuit of happiness in a totalitarian state anticipates, for example, the fuller evocations one finds in Milan Kundera's fiction of the use of folk music and folk traditions in national political celebrations, of a manipulated togetherness that tolerates no taste for marginality. Gide, in any case, sums up the anxiety he felt in a brief lament: "of this heroic and admirable Russian people, there will soon remain only executioners, profiteers, and victims" (*Afterthoughts*, p. 119).

Probably the most damning chapter of the *Afterthoughts*, however, concerns the official art of seduction practiced by the Soviet regime on intellectuals, writers, and artists, both Russian and non-Russian. Gide's awareness of what was going on anticipates Hollander's comments on "techniques of hospitality." It was, above all, the way in which he and his companions were received and feted throughout their visit that opened Gide's eyes to the privileges that accrue to writers who conform to the Party line: "I had never traveled in such sumptuous circumstances. In special railway carriages or in the best cars, always the best rooms in the best hotels, the best quality and the most abundant food possible. And what a welcome! What care! What thoughtfulness! Acclaimed everywhere, adulated, coddled, feted." Yet, in Gide's case, the calculated effort to woo him ends up only by disgusting him for the cynicism it implies: "I assure you that there is something tragic in my Soviet adventure. I arrived as an enthusiast and a believer to admire a new world, and I was offered *with the purpose of seducing me* all the privileges that I abominated in the old" (*Afterthoughts*, pp. 138, 140).

Gide's last important contribution to the literature of travel could not help but contribute to its demythification in his own time just as Claude Lévi-Strauss's *Tristes Tropiques* was to do in the late 1950s. What Gide's loss of political faith in the Soviet future leads to in the end, in fact, is a reaffirmation of values that had guided him throughout his entire career as a writer and a moralist. The most important thing for the individual is to try to remain open to life's possibilities and complexities, and to be honest in the representation of one's feelings in spite of the temptation of orthodoxy or the solicitations of convention—"There is no commitment that is binding, I mean binding on me, no commitment that can make me prefer the Party over truth. As soon as it is a question of lying, I am uneasy; my task is to denounce it. I am attached to truth; if the Party gives up truth, I immediately give up the Party" (*Afterthoughts*, p. 147).

If, unlike so many intellectual visitors to the USSR from the 1920s on, Gide was able to overcome his predisposition to admire and was able to resist the blandishments of official Soviet hospitality, that was probably because of the self-interrogating habits of his lifetime as a writer—a writer, moreover, who in the French tradition of the *moraliste* was particularly alert to the ruses of human narcissism and hypocrisy in himself as well as in others. The rebel who had distanced himself from his own culture, beginning in adolescence, remains true to his early emancipatory impulses in rejecting the repressive apparatuses of Soviet life.

As his chapter on the treatment of intellectuals makes especially clear, Gide found much in the Soviet Union that was morally and intellectually reprehensible from the point of view of his individualist ethic of *disponibilité* and personal responsibility. In the age of totalitarianisms of the right and of the left, *Back from the USSR; followed by, Afterthoughts to My Back from the USSR* seems by implication, like the work of Gide's British contemporary E. M. Forster, to be raising two cheers for the democracy of his homeland. By representing dystopian bleakness wherever it was to be found, Gide's work sets the example for a kind of travel writing that will become increasingly common down through the following decades, not least among such intellectuals as Lévi-Strauss and V. S. Naipaul.

Chapter X

TRAVEL FOR SCIENCE'S SAKE: MALINOWSKI AND LÉVI-STRAUSS

IF ONE limit of travel writing is what I have called political witness, another is that branch of anthropology known as ethnography; that is, a writing that has peoples and their cultures as its object. The former typically involves a "political pilgrim," who travels in order to observe an alternative, often recently established, political order to which he is drawn on ideological grounds. The latter has traditionally represented its travel as disinterested, value-free, and professional. From roughly the turn of the century on, it presupposed a new and ascetic breed of traveler who left his Western homeland not to explore, conquer, trade, convert, complete an education, or pursue strange gods but, oddly enough, to observe native peoples in their often remote homelands and to put their collective behaviors on record for the benefit of posterity.

He or she traveled, or so in its self-representations the new academic discipline would have had us believe, for science's sake. Curiosity was, so to speak, detached from its libidinal origins, disciplined and institutionalized in the cause of knowledge. Its final legitimation was the authoritative, bound tome that contained the results of the participant-observer's field study. The ethnographer was pursuing the work of civilization on a global scale that was launched by the Enlightenment.

The eighteenth-century beginnings of the human science of anthropology have been touched on in an earlier chapter. In an important sense, scarcely two hundred years later we are witnesses to its end—at least as traditionally conceived—for reasons that have been the subject of a number of recent books[1] but that are already evoked in the work of the two eminent anthropological thinkers with whom I am concerned in this chapter. There are already signs in Bronislaw Malinowski's writings, during what was in many ways the heroic age of Western ethnography, that a singular and complex intellectual adventure was coming to an end. And Claude Lévi-Strauss in the 1950s became the chronicler of the cultural

[1] Two important books appeared as I was completing my manuscript. See Clifford Geertz, *Works and Lives: The Anthropologist as Author* (Stanford: Stanford University Press, 1988); and James Clifford, *The Predicament of Culture: Twentieth Century Ethnography, Literature, and Art* (Cambridge: Harvard University Press, 1988).

loss, associated with modernism, that put an end to the dream of a universal science of man by destroying its object. The dialectic of Enlightenment had run its course.

Malinowski's *Argonauts of the Western Pacific* is a classic text of early-twentieth-century ethnography that is based on what, according to Clifford Geertz, is "probably the most famous, and certainly the most mythicized, stretch of field work in the history of the discipline: the paradigm journey to the paradigm elsewhere" (*Works*, p. 75). Its claim on my attention derives from the fact that it is also, in spite of itself, a work of Western travel literature. It is an especially rich example of the form taken by the verbal representation of alien cultures at a time when Western social science could still regard itself as detached from power relations, as universalist in its methods and commitments.

More than any other work discussed in the present book, Malinowski's illuminates the intellectual revolution that occurred when travel writing ceased to be the exclusive province of amateurs—who were primarily explorers, traders, colonial administrators, missionaries, or literary intellectuals—and became a "human science" with a specific object and increasingly codified methods of research. In *Argonauts of the Western Pacific* we encounter travel writing struggling to become self-consciously scientific and, as a result, raising questions of ethnographic authority, of responsibility for its own discourse and its own rhetoric, or of "the anthropologist as author"—questions that over the past few years have obliged anthropologists to go to school with the literary theorists at least as often as literary theorists have gone to school with anthropologists. As the focus of attention has shifted from the problematics of fieldwork to the problematics of discourse, or from the task of "participant observation" to that of "participant description" (*Works*, p. 83), in the work of the current generation of anthropologists one is almost as likely to encounter references to Roland Barthes and Mikhail Bakhtin as to other anthropologists.

Yet, although the example of Malinowski went a long way toward establishing the norms, from the 1920s on, of modern, university-based, ethnographic fieldwork, he was also aware of many of the contradictions and tensions embodied in the role of the participant-observer, and in the report he or she fabricates for consumption in the homeland. It is the effort, in a canonical text, to overcome such contradictions and to found a valid "scientific method" that is my chief interest here. My more general purpose is to distance ethnographic reportage from itself by reading it not so much as a break *from* as in continuity *with* that Western literary tradition which had long since engaged in the representation of otherness.[2]

[2] On the whole, of course, academic anthropologists have traditionally been more

It is possible to interpret the founding gesture of modern Western ethnography as a double denial. The first denial relates to the ethnographer's role, the second to the work he or she produces. On the one hand,
once the ethnographer reaches the site of the fieldwork, he or she implicitly invokes the corporate article of faith: "We are not like other authoritarian whites (soldiers, administrators, priests). Nor are we like other
pleasure-seeking whites (tourists)." On the other hand, as far as the finished product is concerned, the ethnographer is equally emphatic: "This
is not travel writing"—with equal emphasis placed on "travel," which is
potentially synonymous with "tourism," and "writing," which is inevitably
contaminated with literary associations.

Moreover, the implicit denial of writing has as its corollary the avoidance of narrative, given all that narrative connotes in terms of the fictional and the anecdotal. The rhetoric of the ethnographic monograph
is commanded in no small measure by the will to affirm, "We are not
storytellers, fabricators of fictions." As synchronic descriptions of cultural
systems, field studies ought, in fact, to belong to Jurij Lotman's category
of "plotless" texts. Yet, the example of *Argonauts* goes a long way toward
demonstrating the structural resistances to such avoidance in any verbal
representation of human beings that seeks to promote understanding of
alien peoples. In any case, it is an increasing awareness of such problems
over the past decade or so that has led to the search for "other ways of
telling" in the field.

Malinowski himself frequently acknowledges the theoretical and methodological problems that are attached to the idea of a "human science,"
especially when compared with the experimental sciences. As he reaf-
firms in some summarizing judgments a page or so from the end of *Argonauts*, in fact, the precise object and purpose of ethnographic studies,
the research methods to be adopted, and the appropriate way of setting
the results before a reader cannot be taken for granted. In each new
study, the researcher must explain and justify his choices anew. Thus it
is that he refers back at the end to the task he had set himself: "At the

---

interested in the master texts of their field than have literary theorists. Geertz, for
example, makes frequent references in his latest work to connections in practice between ethnographers and literati. The interrelations between the literary avant-garde
and the anthropological enterprise in the 1920s and 1930s in France is one of the
important themes of James Clifford's book (see n. 1, above). His chapter 3, "On Ethnographic Self-Fashioning: Conrad and Malinowski," is a subtle and elaborate attempt
to establish analogies between the two Anglo-Polish authors' writing practices as part
of a more general view of "culture" as a collective self-fashioning. And George Stocking has also given a helpful account of the rhetorical strategies in ethnographic writing: "The Ethnographer's Magic: Fieldwork in British Anthropology from Tylor to
Malinowski," in *History of Anthropology*, vol. 1: *Observers Observed: Essays on Ethnographic
Fieldwork* (Madison: University of Wisconsin Press, 1983).

beginning of this book, in the Introduction, I, in a way, promised the reader that he should receive a vivid impression of the events, enabling him to see them in their native perspective, at the same time without for one moment losing sight of the method by which I have obtained my data. I have tried to present everything as far as possible in terms of concrete fact, letting the natives speak for themselves, perform their transactions, pursue their activities before the reader's mental vision."[3]

In our critically self-conscious age, almost every other phrase of this statement of purpose gives rise to a problem. Probably the two most important issues that Malinowski touches on, issues that are frequently raised in the body of the text, are those of scientificity and representation, and of the relation between them. On the one hand, he expresses the determination to put on record in all its fullness the relevant "data" observed in the field; on the other hand, there is the kind of consciousness of the reader and of the need to present the material with a telling precision that one associates with works of literary art—"vivid impression," "the reader's mental vision." And Malinowski complicates his task still further in that his ultimate object is to represent an alien point of view—"in their native perspective"—and an alien voice—"letting the natives speak for themselves." An ethnographer, it seems, is someone who seeks "to go native" with at least part of himself on methodological grounds. In other words, Malinowski defines his task as encompassing a number of roles. He is at once a scientist, scrupulously attentive to the collection of "data" and self-conscious concerning his research methods; an interpreter of culturally distant psyches; and an author determined to produce a peculiarly concrete reading experience for his reader. No wonder a modern theorist of culture such as James Clifford is able to assert, with Malinowski very much in mind, that "in the 1920s the new fieldworker-theorist brought to completion a powerful new scientific and literary genre, the ethnography, a synthetic cultural description based on participant observation" (*Predicament*, pp. 29–30).

In any case, Malinowski chose to narrativize his material, but it is not clear from his text that he was aware of all the implications of such a choice. As Hayden White has demonstrated in connection with the representation of historical events, narrative is a solution that is also often a problem.[4] The fact is, that systems, which are static, do not in themselves constitute the raw material of stories, unlike those events which mark the transitions between systems. Malinowski made the decision to describe the alien way of life of certain South Sea island peoples, organized

[3] References are to the reprint edition (Prospect Heights, Ill.: Waveland Press, 1984), pp. 516–517.

[4] "The Value of Narrativity in the Representation of Reality," in *On Narrative*, ed. W.J.T. Mitchell (Chicago: University of Chicago Press, 1981).

around the peculiar form of socioeconomic exchange known as the Kula, in the form of a narrative. But, as it turns out, he does not tell a story of a traditional kind; that is, one characterized by a unique set of events that happened in the more or less distant past. He substitutes instead a pseudonarrative, whose chief defining characteristic is the use of the present of repeated action or what, after Gérard Genette, might be called the iterative present.[5] It is also frequently the tense of myth.

Moreover, although pseudonarrative as practiced by Malinowski in *Argonauts* gives an occasional proforma recognition to the narrator's role, it mostly effaces the present of narration and the particular circumstances of the writing. In the role of homodiegetic narrator (i.e., narrator/protagonist), he chooses to offer only brief impressions of his public or professional face. If we know that the text of the *Argonauts* is not the whole story of his field work experience, however, that is because, unlike the vast majority of ethnographers, he also maintained a record of his private feelings and attitudes during much of the time that he was gathering material for his major study. Malinowski wrote not just one but two travel books concurrently.

The official work—that of the professional anthropologist—was first published in English in 1922; however, it was accompanied by an apparently scandalous shadow text, largely in Polish, that appeared in English translation only in 1967. *A Diary in the Strict Sense of the Term*[6] is in two parts, divided by a two-year interval. The first part, which runs from September 1914 to August 1915, concerns Malinowski's first experience of fieldwork among the Mailu of New Guinea. The second part begins in August 1917 and covers a period when he was living among the Trobriand islanders. It was into this *Diary* that Malinowski put much of the uncensored material that the professional codes of the discipline would not allow him to incorporate into his wonderfully exhaustive ethnographic work. The focus of this second book is not outward on the world but inward on a psyche. It emphasizes what Roman Jakobson called the "emotive function" of language, language that calls attention to its human source. The repressed narrator of *Argonauts* puts himself extravagantly on display in the *Diary*—for the pleasure and the pain of his own self-imaging.

One may regret that the Anglo-Polish anthropologist did not find a way to combine *Argonauts* with the *Diary* in a single work that would have been, at least until quite recently,[7] virtually without precedent in the

---

[5] See his chapter entitled "Frequency," in *Narrative Discourse: An Essay in Method*, trans. Janet E. Lewin (Ithaca: Cornell University Press, 1980).

[6] Trans. Norbert Guterman (New York: Harcourt, Brace and World, 1967).

[7] See Geertz's discussion of the work of Paul Rabinow, Vincent Crapanzano, and Kevin Dwyer in "I-Witnessing: Malinowski's Children," *Works*.

whole field of ethnographic writing—a kind of ethnographic equivalent of Joyce's *Ulysses*, focusing both on the inner man, who records, and on the outer world, on the doubts, passions, rage, and ennui of the ethnographer as well as on his community of native people. One may regret it, but one should nevertheless be grateful that the *Diary* exists at all. The narrative of the anthropologist's ambivalences and disconcerting shifts of humor gives a dimension to fieldwork that is usually repressed. No "scientist" is "scientific" with more than part of himself for part of any day.[8] And nowhere does this seem to be truer than with an ethnographer in the field.

That the *Diary* has generated great interest since its publication is confirmed by Geertz's discussion, after Barthes, of "the *Diary* Disease" (*Works*, pp. 89–91). Moreover, as Geertz points out, it is of interest not simply for its own sake but for its complex relationship to *Argonauts*: "The Trobriand field experience is not exhausted by *Argonauts* or the *Diary* or by their combination. The two texts are partial refractions, specific experiments in writing" (*Works*, p. 97). In any case, if it were still needed in our suspicious age, we have the testimony of Albert Camus's *The Fall* to remind us that self-castigating "confessions" are no more to be taken at face value than "diaries." Yet, whether written for publication or not, there is no doubt that Malinowski's shadow text knowingly provided an opening that problematizes his own scientific work. As in some cunningly plotted modern novel, the *Diary* has the force of an appendix that constitutes an invitation to read the canonical text against its own professional grain.

Probably the most important question the *Diary* implicitly raises, however, is a celebrated psychoanalytic one; namely, What does the ethnographer want? What drives him away from home and homeland and, in Malinowski's day certainly, away from the comforts of civilization? What are the satisfactions and rewards sought? After Jacques Lacan we have become habituated to the notion of the "analyst's desire." In his *Diary*, Malinowski was in his own way already probing the question of the "ethnographer's desire." Yet, it is a question that has only rarely been addressed. Its importance appears with even greater obviousness when one acknowledges its connection to ethics. "The ethics of ethnography" is as crucial an issue as Jacques Lacan showed "the ethics of psychoanalysis" to be in a seminar of that title which he gave in 1959–1960.

---

[8] Edward Said's comment on this point seems incontrovertible: "No one has ever devised a method of detaching the scholar from the circumstances of life, from the fact of his involvement (conscious or unconscious) with a class, a set of beliefs, a social position, or from the mere activity of being a member of a society." *Orientalism* (New York: Vintage Books, 1978), p. 10.

o   o   o

OUTSIDE the field of literature proper there was, until very recently, no habit of rereading "the classics" of an academic discipline for their own sake, but like *The Voyage of the Beagle*, Malinowski's 1922 book has a value that is "literary," partly in Barthes's sense, as well as scientific and documentary—although the *Diary* does help to make us realize this fully. Whatever its present status among professionals in the field, *Argonauts* is still capable of raising in a lay reader questions of continuing intellectual import and of generating local textual excitements. Consequently, it amply repays the kind of close reading of its discursive practices, rhetorical strategies, insistencies, repressions, and intertextual allusions traditionally reserved for works of literary art and, until recently, largely avoided by anthropologists.[9]

A reader's first impression is likely to be that *Argonauts* is a "big book." It is an authoritative piece of bookmaking as well as text-building, and it affirms its scientific seriousness of purpose both in its bulk and in the familiar dress of scholarly research that it wears. The reader is warned, so to speak, that "this is not a travel book" well before he reaches the first page of the text proper. There are the characteristic signs that establish authority through the affirmation of an academic succession, including the high accolade of a preface by Sir James G. Frazer and the dedication to another major figure in early-twentieth-century anthropology: "My Friend and Teacher, Professor C. G. Seligman, F.R.S." The author's brief foreword is followed by two pages of acknowledgments to the eminent philanthropists, institutions, and individuals who made the research possible, by an elaborate table of contents, and by a list of the sixty-six photographic illustrations plus maps, tables, and figures. In short, the book knowingly displays those signs whose secondary or connoted meaning is "scientificity."

Throughout the opening sections the questions of a responsible "human science" are addressed: the author raises serious issues concerning the discipline, the historical moment of its emergence, the methodology and ethics of fieldwork, the situation of the ethnographer in his isolation, and the way in which ethnography is justified by the results thus far obtained. Yet it is characteristic of the historical moment if the author's foreword manages to combine a certain scientific triumphalism with a note of elegy. A newly acquired confidence in research methods in the field is affirmed alongside the ironic acknowledgment that the object of

[9] This is, of course, an expanding area of research at the limit of academic anthropology, as the work of Clifford, Geertz, and Stocking, among others, suggests. See also *Writing Culture: The Poetics and Politics of Ethnography*, eds. James Clifford and George E. Marcus (Berkeley: University of California Press, 1986).

scientific inquiry itself is rapidly disappearing: "Ethnology is in the sadly ludicrous, not to say tragic, position, that at the very moment when it begins to put its workshop in order, to forge its proper tools, to start ready for work on its appointed task, the material of its study melts away with hopeless rapidity" (*Argonauts*, p. xv). The achievements lend both urgency and nostalgia to the situation; it is as if the new science had reached its maturity when it was almost too late. This was indeed a case where the owl of Minerva first took flight at midnight.

One of Malinowski's important themes from the beginning is the difficulty of the ethnographer's task and the formidable personal and methodological problems posed for an individual who suddenly finds him or herself alone among an alien people and who does not know the language. Malinowski's reflections on the topic begin in the introduction, entitled "The Subject, Method and Scope of this Enquiry." And he outlines something like an ethics of the discipline in asserting the need for a complete disclosure of the procedures adopted by the researcher.

As he clearly foresaw and as the recent Freeman/Mead controversy showed,[10] the problem of "trustworthiness" seems to return to haunt the ethnographer's work far more frequently than it does that of the experimental scientist—although recent cases of fraudulent "scientific practice" have suddenly reopened the question. As a result, in comparing the fieldworker's task with that of the natural scientist, on the one hand, and the historian, on the other, Malinowski asserts the need for equal rigor without ignoring the important differences between the materials with which they are working: "In Ethnography, the writer is his own chronicler and the historian at the same time, while his sources are no doubt easily accessible, but also supremely elusive and complex; they are not embodied in fixed, material documents, but in the behavior and in the memory of living men" (*Argonauts*, p. 3).

The sum of Malinowski's observations is, in effect, that if one is to avoid being just another white man in the tropics, with all the prejudices and cultural self-assurance that implied in his time even more than in ours, one has to submit oneself to a special discipline and a special practice. Ethnography must define itself in opposition to travel writing, in the popular sense at least; the ethnographer's work is a vocation that imposes a difficult life of long cohabitation with one's subjects and the adoption of a number of techniques for distancing oneself from one's own cultural habits of thought and behavior.

In fact, Malinowski's practice in *Argonauts* goes a long way toward vin-

---

[10] See my article "Anthropological Tales: Unprofessional Thoughts on the Mead/Freeman Controversy," in *Notebooks in Cultural Analysis* 1 (Durham: Duke University Press, 1984).

dicating the kind of understanding of otherness at which he aimed: "As always happens when scientific interest turns towards and begins to labor on a field so far only prospected by amateurs, Ethnology has introduced law and order into what seemed chaotic and freakish. It has transformed for us the sensational, wild and unaccountable world of 'savages' into a number of well ordered communities, governed by law, behaving and thinking according to consistent principles" (*Argonauts*, pp. 9–10). Malinowski's perception of the order, regularity and, on its own terms, reasonableness of behavior that characterize the beliefs and practices of the Kula—of that apparently irrational, communally organized, circular exchange of red shell necklaces and white shell bracelets over wide stretches of ocean—demonstrates for him the truth of the judgment expressed here.

Moreover, the success of his representation is to be found in the mapping of the complexity and coherence of a complicated system functioning over a broad geographic space and over long periods of time in ways that even the participants themselves were unaware of. It is also to be found in the detailing and patient tracing of ramifications that leave the reader with a sense of wonder at the rich intricacies of an alternative form of human cultural life. In place of the visceral response of the colonial adventurer, caricatured by Malinowski in the phrase "Customs none, manners beastly" (*Argonauts*, p. 10) one finds, after all, respect and a kind of love.

Yet, as soon as one moves from the theoretic issues of the introductory sections to the body of the text, the questions of narrativization and of ethnography as a writing, in the strong sense of that word, become apparent. Malinowski himself, in effect, acknowledges in spite of himself that an "art" of representation was called for that was a verbal art. The intention was to combine objective, scientific analysis and its attention to the whole with the "plasticity" and "vividness" he found in the writings of certain talented amateurs. Frequently associated with this, moreover, was the question of trying to incorporate "the native perspective." In fact, he defines the "final goal" of ethnography as "the need to grasp the native's point of view, his relation to life, to realise his vision of the world" (*Argonauts*, p. 25).

Furthermore, the latter is particularly important when it is a question of representing what Malinowski calls "the imponderabilia of actual life" (*Argonauts*, p. 18), by which he means the routines of daily life, of work and leisure, of care of the body and cooking, general social intercourse, emotional bonds, antipathies or personal ambitions. His "imponderabilia" are, in effect, the materials on which literature has traditionally drawn, particularly that genre which, since the seventeenth century or so, has taken as its province everyday, contemporary life: namely, the novel. It is, therefore, not surprising if Malinowski finds it necessary to adopt techniques and devices of representation that produce what James Clifford calls "realist cultural fictions" (*Predicament*, p. 109) and that are familiar to all readers of the European novel.

In brief, in spite of its air of unity and scientificity, one of the most striking characteristics of *Argonauts*, too, is its "impurity" and heterogeneity. Malinowski's discourse is no more homogeneous or self-consistent than that of most of the other writers discussed in the present book. It is, of course, in the nature of full ethnographic accounts of alien cultures to be heterogeneous in content—good ethnographers inevitably become jacks-of-all-trades— but it is far more than a matter of content here, of precise descriptions of the economic activities, social organization, crafts, techniques, ceremonial life, magic, and religious beliefs of the Western Pacific islanders (buttressed by tables, maps, and photos).

It is thus symptomatic if, along with the first impression of "scientificity" he establishes, Malinowski should have indulged in the literary flourish of his evocative title, a title that is in itself an intertextual reference to a form of travel writing that is as old as Greek legend. And the book's subtitle reinforces the implication that the South Pacific islands have a cultural life that is reminiscent of an earlier and hallowed stage of European civilization. *An Account of Native Enterprise and Adventure in the Archipelagoes of Melanesian New Guinea* manages to couple the glamor of the South Seas with the idea of Homeric epic. It is consequently not surprising if, in the body of his text itself, Malinowski goes out of his way to present his material as a coherent narrative with digressions. He was reaching for a form that suggested the beauty and excitement as well as the natural and supernatural dangers that the islanders encounter on the ocean voyages undertaken by canoe, at the time of the Kula, to relatively distant islands. The evidence of *Argonauts* is, in fact, that a sense of narrative pacing and a supple prose style suitable for the evocation of place and feeling are, along with the disciplines of the trained scientist, an essential ingredient of successful ethnographic reporting.

Central to Malinowski's representational strategy, then, is the decision to concentrate on the Kula and to present his account of it in the form of a narrative. The fact that he isolated the institution in the first place is obviously justifiable on ethnographic grounds. Not only is it a central phenomenon of the islanders' cultural, social, and economic life, it also turns out to contain important lessons about collective human behavior. Yet, by its very nature, the Kula gives Malinowski the opportunity to say what he has to say in the form of a protracted narrative of a voyage and of the sailors who undertake it. That there was also some considerable awkwardness in such a mode of presentation, however, is suggested by the frequency and length of what the author himself calls "digressions."

The chapter titles of his table of contents go a long way toward illuminating the work's organization. What they suggest is that the book does
embody the narrative of an ocean voyage but that it is a narrative which
is frequently interrupted. Alongside chapters that describe the structure,
building, and launching of canoes, departures and arrivals, sailings, ship-
wrecks, ritualized exchanges, and the journey home, there are other, intercalated chapters or parts of chapters which are more purely ethnographic or sociological. Moreover, the body of the text itself is
punctuated with the kind of deictic interpolations associated with a traditional kind of narrative art. "We have brought the narrative of the Kula
to the point where all the preparations have been made," chapter 7 begins; "the canoe is ready, its ceremonial launching and presentation have
taken place, and the goods for the subsidiary trade have been collected.
It remains only to load the canoes and to set sail" (*Argonauts*, p. 195).

The urge to write with a certain epic sweep is apparent in such formulations. One is at the same time aware of the awkwardness of a rhetorical strategy that leaves a great deal of the author's interesting data
defined as "digressions." Digressions in one form or another are by no
means alien to traditional epic, of course, where they take the form of
intercalated stories or of passages of description; they are less common
in ethnographic literature proper, where, if they occur at all, they are
likely to appear in footnotes and appendices. It is the descriptions of epic
literature that come closest to Malinowski's digressions. And constitute
traditionally an essential and peculiarly rich feature of that literature,
both for the poetic value of the concrete detailing and for the suspense
they produce.

A reading of Malinowski's text reveals that there are, in fact, two types
of descriptive writing. On the one hand, there are a great many passages
of straightforward ethnographic description in which the narrator makes
no effort to have his reader respond emotionally and sympathetically to
his words. And there are, on the other hand, a great many passages in
which he strives precisely to do that. The former have a documentary
function that is encylopedic in character. The latter are commonly vignettes of people negotiating their world; they concern a place and a
lived, emotive relationship to place. The former places the emphasis on
the referential function of language, whereas the latter gives at least
equal emphasis to the poetic and conative functions. It self-consciously
works at the level of language with a view to engaging an implied reader.

One might quote, as a more or less random example of the first kind
of description, passages that describe the building of canoes, the making
of pots, various kinds of communal activities, or the arrival of a Kula
expedition on the beach at Sarubwoyna: "The fleet halts; the sails are
furled, the masts dismounted, the canoes moored. In each canoe the

elder men begin to undo their baskets and take out their personal belong-
ings. The younger ones run ashore and gather copious supplies of leaves
which they bring back into the canoes" (*Argonauts*, p. 335). This could be
characterized as a form of reasonably objective reportage on a scene of
collective activity that another, similarly trained reporter might well have
formulated in much the same words.

It is significantly different in evocative power from a passage such as
that describing another group of islanders on a beach: "The Dobuans,
during their stay in Sinaketa, lived on the beach or in their canoes. Skil-
fully rigged up with canopies of golden mats covering parts of the craft,
their painted hulls glowing in the sun against the green water, some of
the canoes presented the spectacle of some gorgeously fantastic pleasure
boat. The natives wandered amongst them, making the Lagoon lively
with movement, talk and laughter" (*Argonauts*, p. 390). It is not simply
that the narrator has supplied a series of particularly suggestive epithets
and verbs evocative of color and light. He has also indulged in a celebratory image—"some gorgeously fantastic pleasure boat"—and made particularly positive value judgments on collective native life that call to
mind painterly, golden-age imagery from Claude Lorrain and Captain
Cook's William Hodges to Paul Gauguin.

Nevertheless, this passage still has the quality of a scene reported from
the outside by an observer. At other moments in his text, Malinowski
seems determined to force the reader's empathy for Trobriand life by
writing self-consciously from "the native perspective." Yet, the narrator
as participant-observer that results is awkwardly positioned—something
that becomes apparent in the following passage describing the Trobrianders' approach from the sea to a group of islands: "Within a day or two
these disembodied, misty forms are to assume what for the Trobrianders
seems marvellous shape and enormous bulk. They are to surround the
Kula traders with their solid wall of precipitous rock and green jungle,
furrowed with deep ravines and streaked with racing water-courses. The
Trobrianders will sail deep, shaded bays, resounding with the, to them
unknown, voice of waterfalls; with the weird cries of strange birds which
never visit the Trobriands, such as the laughing of the kookooburra
(laughing jackass), and the melancholy call of the South Sea crow" (*Argonauts*, p. 220).

The future tense of this consciously purple passage, with its emotive
verbs and adjectives, is a clue to the awkwardness. It is what might be
called a "future iterative," whose function is to suggest a mood of anticipation and lend the observations of an individual traveler on a given voyage the authority of typicality. But beyond that, the passage is an example
of interpretive, descriptive writing derived from imaginative projection.

There are also "descriptions" of another type and in a different medium: namely, no fewer than sixty-six photographic images of scenes from native life, most of which have some connection with the Kula. Like the more deliberately neutral descriptive passages, their function is documentary. Yet, unlike the prose, the photos are likely to arouse responses in a reader that Malinowski can hardly have intended and certainly could not control.

He was, of course, working with the rather crude photographic equipment of his time. This, together with the fact that he was no more than an amateur photographer, means that there can be no question of stylistic registers here, of that flexibility of choice available to him in his prose. As a consequence, the reader finds that the tight pages of print are occasionally interrupted by batches of reproduced photographs characterized by harsh black-and-white contrasts and poor definition. These images of native life are a long way from the sumptuously colored, but equally problematic, images that readers of *National Geographic* have for a long time been used to.

Their documentary value resides in the record they furnish of the island world, its inhabitants, their activities and artifacts, including the objects of the Kula exchange. But, with a few exceptions, they suggest a bleak and savage world that is in contradiction with the universe projected by the verbal text. In the skinny, crouching silhouettes in greys and blacks posed against two-dimensional drab backgrounds, one sees very little of the fascinating and heroic argonauts. The contrast between Malinowski's photos and the landscape paintings of Captain Cook's illustrators could hardly be more marked in terms of suggestivity and sensuous appeal.

In the end, it seems that in its author's eyes the chief justification for incorporating his observations into a narrative structure was in the opportunity that narrative provides for promoting reader identification. And it has been a cliché of narrative theory since Henry James that there is maximum reader identification where there is dramatic scene rather than narrative summary. Consequently, Malinowski, too, paints scenes in which the reader is invited to share a point of view not only with the narrator as protagonist but also with the islanders themselves. Malinowski's higher purpose was to communicate to his target audience in the West the kind of sympathetic understanding that an Orientalist discourse or its Oceanic equivalent specifically inhibits. It turns out, therefore, that the greatest surprise he prepares for his reader is not to be found in the exoticism of difference, but in the discovery of human solidarity.

Probably the most characteristic mode of *Argonauts* is what might be called "elegiac epic". On the one hand, the narrator celebrates a form of heroic action that is situated not in some remote past but in the present. On the other, he acknowledges between the lines that the cyclical and quasi-mythical forms of the Trobrianders' collective life are on the point of being invaded by Western technology and Western history. It is, furthermore, elegiac epic that has its moments of intimacy which the reader is invited to overhear and oversee: "Let us listen to some conversations, and try to steep ourselves in the atmosphere surrounding this handful of natives, cast for a while on to the narrow sandbank, far away from their homes, having to trust only to their frail canoes on the long journey which faces them. Darkness, the roar of surf breaking on the reef, the dry rattle of the pandanus leaves in the wind, all produce a frame of mind in which it is easy to believe in the dangers of witches and all the beings usually hidden away, but ready to creep out at some special moment of horror" (*Argonauts*, p. 233). At such a moment of intraspecies solidarity, the narrator from the civilized West ends up sharing ghosts with men from humanity's past.

If, as Robert Darnton claims, the historian is susceptible to a kind of reverse "conversation" to the cultural past he explores, this seems to be even more likely in the case of an anthropologist in the field. And in passages such as that just quoted, Malinowski suggests how he, too, on occasion was "won over by the otherness of others."[11] Yet, in his case, there was also a powerful resistence to such seduction, as the *Diary* makes very clear.

o   o   o

FROM THE point of view of the ethnographer, the culture that is the object of his research confronts him as a system already in place. For his purposes, it does not normally have a (hi)story, although he may, like Malinowski, decide to represent his observations as pseudostory. On the other hand, the ethnographer on his field trip always has a story, even if reference to it is at best marginalized, for example, as comments in a foreword. There are always determinations and overdeterminations that can be represented as a series of unique events and that, at some point in a life in process, brought the ethnographer to the research site.[12] And

---

[11] See *The Kiss of Lamourette: Reflections in Cultural History* (New York: Norton, 1990), p. xiv.

[12] Clifford comments that Joseph Conrad and Bronislaw Malinowski were "enmeshed in complex, contradictory subjective situations articulated at the levels of language, desire, and cultural affiliation." *Predicament*, p. 102. The British historian Richard Cobb has also commented on the combination of "need" and contingency that sometimes leads historians to acquire "a second nationality, a second identity." He finds in such people "a crossing of the line that is the most important requisite for the English specialist of the history and culture of a foreign society. Perhaps, in all these cases, the need for *la seconde patrie* was already there; but which country it was to be was largely a matter of accident." See "Introduction: Experiences of an Anglo-French His-

it is this story in the kind of elliptical, fragmented journal form associated with modernist fiction that one finds in *A Diary in the Strict Sense of the Term*. In any case, the latter is as representative of a kind of European travel writing as *Argonauts* itself. It may have surprised Malinowski's professional contemporaries, but it comes as no surprise to anyone familiar with the literary tradition of the "romantic agony" or the theory of split subjectivity.

As suggested above, had Malinowski attempted to incorporate the material of *the Diary* into his ethnographic study, the result would have been a virtually unique, experimental text that straddled the domains of literature proper and social science. Its double focus on information and informant, on the alien culture and on the ethnographer who reports on it, would have problematized even more radically the status of the scientific work at the same time that it enlightened the reader as to the conditions and constraints under which such work is conducted.

Given Malinowski's historical moment and his academic discipline, it was unthinkable, however, for him not to disentangle the "private" material of the *Diary* from the "public" discourse of *Argonauts*. It seems that "human science" could not have survived intact from the incursion of so much that is messily "human," so much that threatens to undermine the authority of the investigator and the scientific high ground on which he stands. Even when it first appeared in 1967, Malinowski's widow and his translator decided that there were occasional comments in the "private" *Diary* itself that were still too private—the word used in the preface is "intimate"—to be published.

Whether one approves of the segregation of Malinowski's observations and analysis into two works in the name of science or regrets it as a discursive exclusion, to read both works side by side is to enrich our sense of the tensions that traverse all efforts at cross-cultural representation, including the fullest and best prepared. We have, for once, the writer's testimony on the activities, desires, conscious and unconscious choices, anger, frustrations, and boredom that go into the making of an academic field study. We also learn of the homesickness, guilt, and fierce self-reproaches that shadowed the "scientist" in his work.

Perhaps the most important and most disturbing lesson of the *Diary* is that the implied unity of the narrating subject in *Argonauts* is factitious, like the text in which he is located. In place of the one-dimensional man of science and the authoritative narratorial self of the latter work, the *Diary* substitutes a split subjectivity composed of abrupt mood changes, self-doubt and depression, surges of sexual desire, self-recrimination and

torian," in *A Second Identity: Essays on France and French History* (London: Oxford University Press, 1969), pp. 1–2.

declarations of love for the woman he left behind, rebellious outbursts against his work and his circumstances, and rage against his fellow colonials or the native population that was the object of his researches.

The notations span the mundane to the moral and metaphysical; they concern his health problems, bouts of fatigue, fevers, pains and infections, and his remedies against real or imagined disease, including doses of arsenic, quinine, or aspirin. A typical entry in telegram style reads: "Got up late, felt rotten, took enema" (*Diary*, p. 145). They also concern his psychic health and puzzling phobias—"Exhaustion, lack of strength, and characteristic nervousness: acrophobia, aversion for protruding objects" (*Diary*, p. 89). At the other extreme, his notations relate to moments of self-disgust and to projects for self-improvement, including the sublimation of his lusts in the direction of spiritual and artistic pursuits. Malinowski even has moments of Boswellian innocence, both in his uncensored directness and in his expression of the determination to change his conduct.

The various references to "niggers" in connection with Mailu and Trobrianders shock all the more because they come from the author of *Argonauts*. Even if the word did not in his time have all the pejorative connotations it has today, the context makes clear the racist hostility involved: "General aversion for niggers, for the monotony—feel imprisoned" (*Diary*, p. 162). There are, in fact, occasions when he sounds just like the European colonialist he himself had caricatured: "As for ethnology: I see the life of the natives as utterly devoid of interest or importance, something as remote from me as the life of a dog" (*Diary*, p. 167). Such expressions of contempt are difficult to reconcile with the appeal for intraspecies solidarity expressed in *Argonauts*.

Part of the explanation seems to reside in bouts of ill-health and a related irascibility of temperament that led him to condemn with equal vehemence at different moments both the British, who were frequently his only white companions, and the Germans, whose culture he also admired. A general propensity to fly into a rage and to insult those who were its immediate cause, including colonial administrators, missionaries, and native informants (his "boys"), is a fairly common motif of the *Diary*. At the same time, the doubly expatriate Pole seems to have lived his travels in ways that are frequently similar to those undertaken by European travelers at least since Byron. The *Diary* suggests the subterranean continuity that may exist between ethnography and the nineteenth-century literary tradition that encompassed the work of Flaubert as well as Conrad. To a minority of Europeans of all kinds, the attraction of "primitive societies" has long been in all that is connoted by the word "primitive."

Ethnographic fieldwork, in Malinowski's time at least, put the researcher in situations of risk not dissimilar from those deliberately sought out by nineteenth-century Bohemian travelers and imperial adventurers alike.[13] In retrospect, the satisfactions sought seem often to be similar, in that pleasure is not without a significant admixture of pain. In many ways, Malinowski in the *Diary* sounds much like his British contemporary T. E. Lawrence, who was waging war in the Arabian Desert at the same historical moment when the Anglo-Pole was in the Southwest Pacific. There are frequently similar elements of self-testing, and there is a similar intensity and ambivalence relative to Western civilization in its relations with what we now call the Third World.

In Malinowski's case, however, it is as if the opposition between Eros and Thanatos, between the binding, life-affirming drives and the sadistic, destructive ones, were largely split between two texts. Whereas *Argonauts* dedicates itself to the civilizing task of universal understanding between peoples, the *Diary* vents the narrator's rage against radical difference, even if he also expresses his efforts to rise above such sentiments.

As with so many male travelers, travel obliges Malinowski to come to terms with himself as sexual being. Thus, like Boswell again, he reports on the power, frequency, and occasional outrageousness of his desire— "Woke up at night, full of lecherous thoughts about, *of all the people imaginable*, my landlord's wife!" (*Diary*, p. 165). He also finds himself occasionally stirred to what he himself calls "lewdness" by the sight of native women, to the point where he finds it impossible not to "paw" the local girls. Yet, it is such impulses and such sexual fantasies that cause him to chastise himself fiercely. And the work is full of slighting references to his "violent whoring impulses" or to his "sloshing around in the mud" (*Diary*, p. 181), along with admonitions to overcome such temptations for the sake of the women he truly loves.

Part of the interest of all this for a modern reader is likely to be in the tension in the text between desire and guilt. As it happens, in both parts of the *Diary* the narrator represents himself as, on the one hand, tugged by random erotic impulses and, on the other, as drawn to two different pairs of white women he had left behind, to past affairs, and to the possibility of more durable relationships. Further, now and then he recalls with particular poignancy and longing the image of his mother back in Poland surrounded by the European war—"the only person I care for really" (*Diary*, p. 52). No other male writer analyzed in the present book expresses such reverence for his mother or judges his conduct from her perspective. The European past, including particularly his past with

[13] "Imagine yourself suddenly set down surrounded by all your gear," he asserts at the beginning of *Argonauts*, "alone on a tropical beach close to a native village, while the launch or dinghy which has brought you sails away out of sight." *Argonauts*, p. 4.

women back to his early life with his mother, persistently returns to stir and unnerve him on his remote South Pacific island.

The second part of the *Diary*, in particular, sets up the familiar moral polarity of the time between love and lust, and embodies them respectively in the figure of his Australian nurse and future wife, E.R.M., and in the native women, who occasionally excite lascivious thoughts. On the one hand, he collapses together the idea of civilization and white female skin; on the other, he refers, in a singularly revealing comment, to "a state of white rage and hatred for bronze-colored skin" (*Diary*, p. 261). The power of the attraction/repulsion exercised by the women of the islands is concentrated in a single swift vignette: "Young females, blackened, with shaven heads, one of them a *nakubukwabuya* (adolescent) with an animal-like, brutishly sensual face. I shudder at the thought of copulating with her. Thought of E.R.M." (*Diary*, p. 177). All the ambiguity of his response is in the verb, "shudder," which is associated both with the idea of horror and that of extreme sexual pleasure, *jouissance*. Typically, further fantasy is blocked by the idea of E.R.M. Yet, the notation is one among many that suggests another kind of motivation for Malinowski's travels, a motivation at the level of desire.

The protagonist of Malinowski's "private" work is, in any case, subject in his extreme isolation to the traditional temptations of the desert hermit that Flaubert had represented in *The Temptations of Saint Anthony*, including, in particular, lust and sloth. All the ambiguities of the traditional ascetic life emerge in erotic or sadomasochistic daytime reveries or dreams—Malinowski narrates several of the latter in his work. If the diarist attempts to overcome his lust with admonitions to "stop chasing skirts" (*Diary*, p. 122), he combats his laziness and ennui—that acedia of the medieval monks which Baudelaire diagnosed as reemergent in his time—with resolutions not to waste time and, in particular, to control his habit of reading fiction: "Not to read novels, not to be idle" (*Diary*, p. 133). Yet, for the most part, his taste in novels is a discriminating one, since it includes works by Thackeray, Kipling, Charlotte Brontë, Hardy, James Fenimore Cooper, Alexandre Dumas *père*, and his fellow anglicized Pole, Conrad, for whom he expresses a particular admiration. Indeed, it is impossible to avoid the conclusion that Malinowski was influenced, whether consciously or not, by his Anglo-Polish predecessor's fiction in the self-portrait of the *Diary*. The thematics of *The Heart of Darkness* are woven into Malinowski's autobiographical text as they are into Gide's *Journey to the Congo*.[14] Outside Conrad's works proper, in fact, no one more than Malinowski in his *Diary* has evoked more disturbingly

[14] See Clifford, "On Ethnographic Self-Fashioning," in *Predicament*.

what might be called "the Conrad complex"; that is, the seduction and the horror of "going native."

On the other hand, Malinowski does not deny himself the pleasure of observing with care the extraordinary tropical landscapes with which he is surrounded. And no other travelers have been more explicit than Malinowski in associating the beauty of landscape with a woman's body. In a particularly haunting paragraph, he suggests both the complexity and intensity of feelings a given landscape is capable of eliciting: "Picturesque view of a belt of pyramid-shaped hills; Domdom veiled with gray rain. The massive stone terraces glisten under the moisture. At moments I have a voluptuous feeling ('mixed identity of circumstances')—the gray sea, the mist-covered greenness of the island opposite, and the long, stone terraces have something of the air of a northern fishing village. The dark (mass) of the island rising behind (creates) a strange mood, such as I have never experienced before. The little houses in the village attract me, as well as intrigue me ethnologically" (*Diary*, p. 227).

Malinowski makes clear here how a scene may have for a traveler a mysteriously charged quality that is related to an irretrievable memory trace and is registered as sensations in the body. The double focus of his gaze is affirmed in the opposition between "attract" and "intrigue": the sentient man and the scientist share a single pair of eyes. It turns out that the ethnographer, like Darwin's naturalist, also looks twice. Further, one need look no further for the motivation of so much travel, in fact, than in the uncanny appeal exercised here on an observer; something pleasurable returns—"mixed identity of circumstances"—but the source of the pleasure—"voluptuous feeling"—remains mysterious—"strange mood."

Malinowski expresses in his *Diary* an openness to sensation that is the equal of Darwin's and encompasses other senses than that of sight; he remains restlessly attentive to the demands of his body and, like the literary travelers before him, enjoys submitting himself to the shock of the new as well as to the *déjà vu* of travel. He refers, for example, to the "materialistic" character of his "sense reactions," including his oral craving for ginger beer, brandy, and cigarettes. And he is even more explicit on the sense of smell, which, as Freud was the first to suggest, so often elicits disgust, in part because of its association with the sexual life of animals.

In a walk through the New Guinea jungle, Malinowski responds to the layers of scents and odors with all the discrimination of Huysmans's late-nineteenth-century decadent hero in *Against the Grain*. Picturesque travel here has gone morbid and focuses on the excitation of the olfactory organ: "the smell of the jungle creates a characteristic mood—the subtle, exquisite fragrance of the green *keroro* flower, lewd swelling of the burgeoning, fertilized vegetation; frangipani—a smell as heavy as incense, with elegant, sharply drawn profile. Rotting trees, occasionally smelling like dirty socks or menstruation, occasionally intoxicating like a barrel of wine 'in fermentation.' The atmosphere of the jungle is sultry, and saturated with a specific smell which penetrates and drenches you like music" (*Diary*, p. 85). Here, as elsewhere in the *Diary*, there is a movement from associations of the grosser or peculiarly pungent kind—"lewd swelling," "dirty socks or menstruation"—to a form of transcendence or aesthetic distancing that finds expression in the musical metaphor. "Sensual enjoyment of the world," he notes later, apparently without the benefit of an explicit theory of sublimation, "is merely a lower form of artistic enjoyment" (*Diary*, pp. 171–172).

Nevertheless, it is at such moments also that one is made sharply aware of the mixed motivation of even the most apparently disinterested travel. Officially, Malinowski's journey to the Southwest Pacific may have been undertaken for "science's sake"; but it was also clearly for the "scientist's sake," and the scientist turns out to be a man constituted more or less like other men. Moreover, in his encounters as a traveler, Malinowski belonged equally as much to the lineage of Byron, Flaubert, Gide, the two Lawrences, and Conrad as to that of Frazer and Seligman.

The purpose of Malinowski's narrative strategies and interpretive descriptions in *Argonauts*, then, is chiefly to elicit sympathetic understanding in a Western reader, an understanding based on a sense of human fellowship, of the unity of the species. It is assumed throughout his great classic that if ethnographic representation has something new to contribute, it is above all there. In one sense, the science is designed less for the natives than for the enlargement of Western understanding, although the natives will also benefit thereby. Ethnography is to "broaden our knowledge, widen our outlook and deepen our grasp of human nature" (*Argonauts*, p. 517). The hope is, in effect, that in its systematicity and comprehensiveness ethnography may be able to achieve what travelers' tales and impressions from the beginnings of recorded history have largely failed to do: namely, to overcome prejudice and partiality in the comprehension of alien peoples and their cultures. For Malinowski the promise of ethnography is that "overcoming of distance" which has preoccupied philosophical hermeneutics and which might realize the utopian dream of universal understanding.

With the hindsight of almost seventy years, we may find something naive as well as moving in Malinowski's formulation of the values that should ideally guide the ethnographer in his work and transform his "knowledge into wisdom": "It is in the love of the final synthesis, achieved by the assimilation and comprehension of all the items of a culture and still more in the love of the variety and independence of the various cultures that lies the test of the real worker in the true Science of Man. There is, however, one point of view deeper yet and more important than the love of tasting of the variety of human modes of life, and that is the desire to turn such knowledge into wisdom" (*Argonauts*, p. 517). The evidence that the expansion of anthropological studies over the intervening decades has spared the human species a great deal in incomprehension and suffering is, unfortunately, not conclusive.

Notable in this final peroration is, first, the dream of fixity—of the peaceful coexistence of autonomous cultures moving like stars in orbits at a given distance from each other—and, second, the idea of the anthropologist as a sage in the modern world. The *Diary* ends on a much more chastened note, however. Having taken stock of his personal losses and rejections, Malinowski concludes with the words "Truly I lack character (p. 298)." "Wisdom" may be the goal of Malinowski's public moral philosophy, but the *Diary* itself reveals rifts and tensions that underline the precariousness of all such aspirations.

In short, a reading of the *Diary* cannot avoid changing our reading of *Argonauts* in a number of ways, two of which I would like to emphasize here. The first concerns the ethics of anthropology; the second, Freud's reflections on the heroism of travel.

The question of "What does the ethnographer want?" opens up the whole matter of why and for whom he or she is there in the field. It is a question that can only be touched on here. But the beginning of an answer may be sketched by reflecting on the very concept of the participant-observer that is at the heart of the twentieth-century practice of fieldwork. Are there any limits on what one may observe or on the extent to which one participates? At what point does scientific observation become mere voyeurism, a form of looking for the sake of the subject's desire, and not for the object's or for science's sake? Should one push participation to the point of doing in the field what one would not do at home? May one, for example, make love to the local women or men as other travel writers discussed in this volume did? If so, would that, too, be for science's sake? Malinowski's *Diary* reveals how he struggled with such and similar questions without formulating any clear answers.

Clifford makes the point that one of the things Malinowski achieved in his writing was "the construction of a new public figure, the anthropologist as field worker" (*Predicament*, p. 110). That public figure, I would add, is also a modern hero, notwithstanding his self-effacing gestures. In a sense, the male ethnographer, unlike most male travel writers, including Freud, has it both ways. He contributes usefully to the sum of human knowledge in his homeland and, at the same time, by traveling to some remote place, he is able to explore the limits of his desire and go beyond his father with a vengeance. Yet, in his two radically different texts, *Ar-*

gonauts and the *Diary*, Malinowski goes one step further. He sketches the portrait of the ethnographer as both hero and antihero.

The dutiful son acknowledges the continuity of his public writing with that of his professional father figures—the French word is *maîtres*—and the rebellious son, in his private diary, conducts himself like a complex Flaubertian *voyageur maudit*, who condemns what he also craves. Extrapolating from the *Diary*, one might even conclude that the nightmarish image which haunts it is indeed that of Conrad's Kurtz. Was not Kurtz, in his way, the ultimate participant-observer, the participant-observer who "went native" within and became the most self-destructive of "outcasts"? Kurtz enacts in a fictional context the way in which desire at the frontier becomes desire of beyond-the-frontier, or the crossing over into "barbarism." If in his rages against "the natives" Malinowski manages to sound like a caricature of the white colonialist, that is in part an expression of denegation. At another level, he experienced them as a potent lure.

o   o   o

Not the least interest of Claude Lévi-Strauss's *Tristes Tropiques* from the point of view of the present study is that it begins, in a section provocatively entitled "The End of Travel," by reflecting on the nature of travel writing and on the reading public to whom it appeals. "I hate voyages and explorers," is the book's characteristically trenchant, opening sentence.[15] But it is immediately followed by an acknowledgment of the popularity of certain forms of travel writing in the modern world.

Implicit in this opening judgment is what I have called ethnography's double denial: the denial of an authoritarian, ethnocentric, or pleasure-seeking role and the denial of a writing. Yet, the explicit emphasis of *Tristes Tropiques* falls not so much on the voyages and the explorations as on the tales the voyagers and adventurers tell, on travel writings as writing and as narrative. It seems, in part, to be an expression of the general notion of writing as a derivative and flawed form of speech, responsible for the emergence of social hierarchy and exploitation, that, according to Derrida, Lévi–Strauss took over from Rousseau.[16] In any case, Lévi-

[15] (Paris: Plon, 1955), p. 13. It is almost certainly no accident that the notion of the "inauthenticity" of "adventures" was first a major theme of Jean-Paul Sartre's influential 1938 novel *Nausea*, trans. Lloyd Alexander (New York: New Directions, 1959): "for the most banal event to become an adventure, you must (and this is enough) begin to recount it" (p. 39). The opposition between the contingency and disorder of lived experience, on the one hand, and the patterns imposed by ex post facto, diachronic narrative, on the other, even suggests why an opening in the direction of the rule-governed synchrony of structuralism might subsequently have seemed so appealing.

[16] "The Violence of the Letter: From Lévi-Strauss to Rousseau," in *Of Grammatology* (Baltimore: Johns Hopkins University Press, 1974).

Strauss notes, it took him fifteen years to overcome the sense of "disgust" and "shame" he felt at the idea of writing an account of his expeditions to Brazil, with all the insipid, anecdotal details of his movements and the elements of adventure that characterize so much travel writing, but that have no place in the professional work of an ethnographer. The story of the latter on his or her journey or of the tribulations of daily life at the site of fieldwork is no more than the dross of the professional's serious activity, to be thrown away upon one's return home in favor of the scientific material collected as a contribution to the ethnographic literature. Yet, the dross of writing has a way of clinging to the pure ethnographic material in spite of all our precautions.

In order to affirm the distance between the two kinds of writing, Lévi-Strauss adroitly summarizes the content and attitudes of the books of so-called explorers, the platitudes and banalities that abound there, but that nevertheless find such favor with the reading public in his homeland: "What do we hear in these lectures, and what do we read in these books? Details about packing cases loaded, the misdeeds of the ship's dog and, mixed in with the anecdotes, bits of washed-out information that one can find in textbooks of the past fifty years" (*Tristes*, p. 14).

The thing that shocks him and that explains his guilty conscience, as he postpones his own writing—what, by analogy with Darwin, one might call "Lévi-Strauss's delay"— is the fundamental nonseriousness of a mystificatory genre that thrives on modern myths instead of dissipating them, that promotes ideological readings of others rather than challenging them. That is why he finds it necessary to begin with a denial. If the exoticism of the material seems similar, his work will nevertheless be different because it is critical, theoretic, and self-consciously interventionist at an historical moment that raises questions about the whole future of humanity. Central to the purpose of *Tristes Tropiques* is the expression of the form of engagement appropriate to a cultural anthropologist in what was, after all, the heyday of commitment in Parisian literary and philosophic circles.

Clifford Geertz finds in *Tristes Tropiques* five books in one: the travel book that the author claims to despise, a work of ethnography, a philosophic text, a reformist tract, and a symbolist literary text.[17] To which I would add an important sixth—namely, a memoir of a layered Proustian kind that shuffles back and forth between *énonciation* and *énoncé*, between the present of narrating and the various moments in the narrator's past that are called up by association or triggered by remembered sensations. Yet, in spite of the devices that problematize the writing, its self-reflexive

---

[17] See "The World in a Text," in *Works*.

false starts and reluctance to conclude, it is less polyphonic than linear
and, at best, only "moderately plural" in Roland Barthes's sense.

In fact, like a detective story, it contains two narratives in one: the story
of the narrator's search, or investigation, and the story of man on earth
that he discovers as a result of that search. Moreover, in this ironic, modern mystery story there is also a crime—the desecration of autonomous
cultures—and a criminal—modern Western civilization itself. If in one
sense the change in European attitudes toward the non-European world
between the eighteenth century and the mid-twentieth has involved the
progressive relativization of the concept of culture—from one to many—
Lévi-Strauss discovers in his lifetime the emergence of a new and de-
based global monoculture.

"The End of Travel" is made up of a rather disparate group of chapters that combine elements of personal memoir, reflections on journeys
undertaken before and during the Second World War, and commentary
on the conditions of modern life. Taken together they constitute a long
opening lament on the worn, crowded, and increasingly polluted world
that emerged from the brutal war and its settlement. This opening section is the introduction to the book of a man whose life and professional
career spanned both the heroic age of anthropology to which Malinowski
belonged and our own, more suspicious age. Although his earliest ethnographic fieldwork was conducted in Brazil in the mid 1930s, *Tristes
Tropiques* was published only in 1955. Moreover, like the travel writings
of T. E. Lawrence and André Gide, it can also be said to bear political
witness. Yet, it transcends politics (in the narrow sense at least), for it
takes the whole globe and the history of the human race as its province.
The *engagement* that it expresses has a universality of a kind that encompasses the past of our species as well as its future and, before the age of
ecology, it pays substantial attention to the natural environment.

Twenty pages into his text Lévi-Strauss, in effect, explains the apparent paradox of the popularity of contemporary travel writing with its
penchant for the secondhand and the second-rate. It is an expression of
the nostalgia felt in modern Western society for the freshness and difference of a world that is now lost: "I understand, therefore, the passion,
the madness, the deception of travel narratives. They contain the illusion
of that which no longer exists and which ought to exist still if we are to
escape from the overwhelming evidence that twenty thousand years of
history have come to an end" (*Tristes*, p. 38). Travel narratives promise
the fantasized satisfaction of demands that modernity denies. They play
a role in the modern world similar to that played by a certain romantic
fiction in the education of Flaubert's Emma Bovary. Yet, in his very formulation of the problematic, it is clear that Lévi-Strauss might well have

said of himself what Flaubert said to Zola: "You're just an old romantic, like me."

If Lévi-Strauss can be said to be haunted, therefore, in this particular text, it is by images of a plenitude that largely disappeared from the world with the Stone Age and that survived only in his time among the remote remnants of Stone-Age culture. His principal theme is the theme of loss, loss that is collective as well as personal, on the level of the species as well as of the individual psyche; the narrator moves between reflections on lost innocence, lost youth, and a lost golden age. Yet, even though he obviously shared many of the attitudes of those who diagnosed contemporary European discontents, he found no relief from his malaise outside Europe. In the age of global civilization, circumnavigation itself no longer caters to our capacity for wonder or our desire for the new. Consequently, whereas *Argonauts of the Western Pacific* has many of the characteristics of a modern epic, in which a balance is maintained between elegy and epic, *Tristes Tropiques* belongs to the mode of elegiac romance, whose referent is a world that is lost.

It is, however, an ironic fact that, even here, eighteenth-century thinkers had to some extent already anticipated the twentieth-century anthropologist. The tropics seemed sad to certain philosophes even before the object and domain of anthropology had been delimited. As I indicated in Chapter III, the *Histoire des deux Indes*, which was edited by the *abbé* Raynal and to which Diderot contributed, had evoked with a combination of guilt and pain as well as hope, the impact of several centuries of European colonization on the non-European world. And the Old Man of the *Supplement to Bougainville's Voyage* looked forward with some prescience to the fateful consequences of the visits to Tahiti of the first circumnavigators.

The meaning of the section's title, "The End of Travel," turns out to be that Western civilization has invaded even the remotest corners of the earth and has so contaminated them with its technological detritus that the experience of travel as radical estrangement and renewal has disappeared. By the 1950s it was obvious to Lévi–Strauss that we could never leave home, never put Europe behind us: "how can the proclaimed escape of travel achieve anything else but to confront us with the unhappiest forms of our historical existence?" "What our voyages chiefly show us," the melancholy reflection continues, "is our own garbage flung into the face of the world" (*Tristes*, p. 38). Thus, a central theme throughout will be "the failure of travel" in the contemporary world (*Tristes* pp. 42–43).

This is not to say that Lévi-Strauss indulged himself in the myth of a golden age of travel. He dismisses in a rhetorical question the illusions embodied in such a notion: "When should one have seen India, at which moment would the study of Brazilian savages have brought the purest satisfaction, made possible a knowledge about them of the least adulterated kind?" (*Tristes*, p. 44) But he is not above envying those Renaissance navigators who first encountered the New World. And it is here that one perceives how Lévi-Strauss himself was as open to the pleasures of travel as any of the writers discussed in the present study. The man of science thematizes, for example, the question of "firstness" in a way that eroticizes the ethnographer's practice and takes particular account of the satisfactions of seeing: "There is no more exalting perspective for an ethnographer than to be the first white man to penetrate into a native community" (*Tristes*, pp. 374–375). The narrator echoes Freud's comments on the heroism of travel in a formula that also combines features that leave him open to the charge, by the current generation of critical theorists, of ethnocentrism and sexism alike.

The question of the ethnographer's desire is once again foregrounded here. Not only is he assumed to be both white and male, the choice of words also equates the experience involved with a virginity taken. To come after is always to encounter a world deflowered. The rush of excitement associated with that moment of seeing and being seen first, of surveying otherness with Western eyes, and of knowing that one is in one's turn the object of a startled, answering gaze is something to which even Lévi-Strauss was clearly not immune—any more than the explorers and adventurers that he claims to despise. Yet, there is clearly implicated in the exchange of looks a complex mirroring that fixes cultural and racial identifications in a narcissistic moment of self-recognition and self-congratulation.

Unlike the vast majority of travelers, however, Lévi-Strauss acknowledges the fatal irony of a vocation that disciplined looking, that made a duty of a pleasure. Along with the powerful appeal of looking goes the possibility of pain; under certain conditions, scopophilia may give way to its opposite, scopophobia: "Victim of a double infirmity, everything I see wounds me, and I reproach myself with not looking hard enough" (*Tristes*, pp. 44–45). Unlike the tourist, the ethnographer is duty-bound not to look away.

In the last section of his book, "Return," the narrator pursues his theme of the attraction and deception of travel narratives by quoting from a play he had written in the Brazilian rain forest as an expression of his generalized mood of despair and of his inability to dissuade the reading public in his homeland from glamorizing the realities of exotic travel: "It wouldn't help if I expressed in my discourse all the emptiness, all the insignificance of every one of these events; it is enough to turn it into a narrative for it to dazzle and to set people dreaming. Yet, there was nothing to it; the earth was just like this earth and the grass just like this field" (*Tristes*, p. 440). These comments on the melancholy of travel echo Flaubert's.

Lévi-Strauss is, in effect, claiming here that narrativization functions under the auspices of the imaginary register in Jacques Lacan's sense. It invites narcissistic identifications and projects images of wholeness and plenitude of a kind that elude us in our experience, including the experience of world travel. It is in the nature of ex *post facto* narrative, as frequently of language in general, to "dazzle" and to "set people dreaming." But it has no capacity to realize those dreams. The word may be the death of the thing, as Lacan asserted, but it remains a potent lure.[18]

In the light of the sentiments expressed here, Lévi-Strauss's deep-rooted ambivalence concerning his own account of his journeys to the tropics is understandable. Yet, *Tristes Tropiques* itself is a narrative in the double sense suggested above. It has the advantage over *Argonauts*, however, in that it also contains much of the material that Malinowski relegated to his *Diary*; Lévi-Strauss collapsed his two books into one. As a result, his work goes a long way toward performing the kind of demythifying function implied by its title—a title so attentive to the poetic function of language and so resonant with nostalgia that it was retained for the English version. Paradoxically, however, it does so against the background of a myth or Western master narrative whose origins we associate, in its modern form, with the eighteenth–century philosophes, with Rousseau and Diderot. The story Lévi-Strauss tells of the human race is a retelling.

In his discussion of "lost authenticities," James Clifford claims that "modern ethnographic histories are perhaps condemned to oscillate between two metanarratives: one of homogenization, the other of emergence; one of loss, the other of invention" (*Predicament*, p. 17). Lévi-Strauss clearly falls into the former category. He makes no attempt to disguise the fact that he is a sophisticated, modern Rousseauist who deplores the passing beyond, several millennia ago, of what might be called the Rousseauist moment. The evidence for such a view is to be found, in part, in the scattered references to Rousseau throughout the text, but also, in a more interesting form, in the accounts of the Brazilian Indians

[18] This is not to say that the work offers no evidence of the pleasures of contemporary travel of a traditional kind, including that agreeable sensation of a rhythmic motion and an accompanying noise associated with a number of modern forms of locomotion, including especially ships and trains: "Finally, I remember the satisfaction and the pleasure, I might even say the placid happiness, that is the consequence of sensing in the middle of the night the throbbing of machines and the swishing of the water against the hull. It is as if such movement enabled one to achieve a kind of stability whose essence is more perfect than that of movement." *Tristes Tropiques*, p. 66. The pleasure evoked here is that of homeostasis, of a quietude and an inertia that yet knows itself.

that constitute the core of the work, particularly, in the descriptions of the neolithic culture of the Nambikwara.

o   o   o

THE variety and range of *Tristes Tropiques* is suggested by its table of contents. The book is divided into nine sections with several chapters in each. The first four sections narrate the discovery of the author's vocation in the mid-1930s, his Parisian intellectual world and mentors, his preparation, departures, early encounters with Brazil, and reflections from a global perspective on relations between the human population and its physical environment. There follow four sections devoted to describing the cultures of four different groups of Brazilian Indians with whom Lévi-Strauss lived over the years leading up to the Second World War—the Caduveo, the Bororo, the Nambikwara, and the Tupi-Kawahib—and a concluding section entitled "Return." This last section takes up many of the themes touched on here and there throughout, concerning the conditions of human life in the contemporary world and the complexity of the ethnographer's vocation. The chronology is vague throughout, and the author does not hesitate to move backward and forward in time from the moment of his writing in 1954–1955 to his earliest experiences in the field or laterally in space from Paris to Brazil to the Indian subcontinent and back.

It is of obvious significance that the two sections which come before the descriptions of Brazilian Indian cultures in his text are entitled "The New World" and "The Earth and the Human Race." Before encountering ethnography, Lévi-Strauss, like so many French intellectuals then and since, had been drawn to philosophy, and in its survey of the globe from on high *Tristes Tropiques* does have something in common with the eighteenth-century philosophic voyage.

"The New World" begins by affirming the uniqueness of the discovery of the New World by the European explorers. In retrospect, however, it appears to the narrator as the most perfect embodiment of the dream of travel at a certain privileged moment: "A continent barely touched by man was offered to men whose avidity was no longer satisfied with their own" (*Tristes*, p. 81). The key word in this sentence is "avidity," for it is difficult not to read into it a projection onto Renaissance explorers and adventurers of the impulses that drew Lévi-Strauss to the ethnographic voyage. Yet, in his telling, the opportunity given Europeans by the discovery of the New World was lost. As with his own approach to the coast of Brazil, the promise of fresh beginnings is followed by anticlimax; the tropics are not so much "exotic" as out of date.

The function of "The Earth and the Human Race" is to take up some of the themes touched on up to this point, develop them, and move away from the Brazilian situation in order to offer a global perspective on the huge problems faced by contemporary human populations in accommodating themselves to their environment. The themes involved are those of the uneven distribution of the world population across the globe, underpopulation, overpopulation, exploitation and spoliation. They can be summed up in the idea of "the absurdity of the relations that man agrees to maintain with the world" (*Tristes*, p. 142), so long as one adds "the absurdity of the relations men maintain with each other.

The distance may seem great between underpopulated Brazil and the Indian subcontinent to which Lévi-Strauss shifts in a chapter entitled "The Flying Carpet." Yet, in spite of appearances, he perceives a symmetry in the attitudes and forces that are forever pushing back the frontiers of the wilderness in that South American country and "the garbage, disorder, promiscuity, constant touchings; the ruins, huts, mud, filth; the miasmas, droppings, urine, pus, secretions, fevers" (*Tristes*, p. 150) that he finds in India's mass urban life. As later for V. S. Naipaul, India represents for Lévi-Strauss the failure of a civilization that is in large part caused by the great density of a population in a circumscribed space and by the consequent "systematic devalorization of man by man" (*Tristes*, p. 169)—a "devalorization" expressed most obviously in the Indian caste system.

As Lévi-Strauss himself notes, to travel is to move through time as well as through space, to experience aspects of the historical past as well as anticipations of our collective future. That is why, on the one hand, he maps the world and its human possibilities in the form of a grid or structuralist *combinatoire*—and why, on the other hand, he thinks in terms of quasi-mythical cycles in history. Thus, he affirms that the development of a civilization that had begun in the Indus basin several millennia ago and had subsequently spread to Europe, and that was exported to the Americas in the age of discovery, was returning to Asia once again via Japan. With the ragged industrialization and urbanization of modern India and Pakistan, the cycle was coming to an end: "Thus I saw arising before my eyes an Asia of workers' towns and high-rise, subsidized housing estates that will be the Asia of tomorrow, an Asia which rejects all exoticism and is catching up with the kind of modern, efficient life that it perhaps invented in the third millennium B. C." (*Tristes*, p. 143).

The surprise is in the philosophic traveler's choice of the word "exoticism." It registers the fact that the sharp loss for the anthropologist, as for more casual tourists, was in the disappearance of novelty, or forms of radical difference that are pleasurably disorienting. "Exoticism" is what drew nineteenth-century romantics and Bohemians to foreign travel and is associated with spectacle. It is, in effect, something the anthropologist seeks to reduce, for it implies the point of view of the outsider and is an attribute particularly of first encounters. To understand, as Malinowski indicates in *Argonauts*, is to adopt the native point of view; it is to "de-exoticize." Such and similar passages justify Geertz's charge that Lévi-Strauss's attitude to the consequences of modernity is one of "aesthetic repugnance" (*Works*, p. 41).

It is the alternative to the new Asia suggested by the relationship, in neolithic cultures, between earth and man, on the one hand, and between men themselves, on the other, that Lévi-Strauss is concerned with in the crucial middle sections of his book. Thus, before going backward in time, he issues a warning: "What frightens me in Asia is the image of our future that they have anticipated. With America's Indians I prize the reflection, however fleeting it may be even there, of a period when our species and its universe were in a state of balance and when a satisfactory relationship existed between the exercise of liberty and its signs" (*Tristes*, p. 169). After the long preamble, the transition to the ethnographic descriptions of surviving, pre-Columbian native peoples carries with it a burden of remorse and cultural self-doubt similar to that which hung over the beginnings of the long intellectual adventure of Western anthropology among the eighteenth-century philosophes. If, as Lévi-Strauss claims, Rousseau was indeed "the father of anthropology," his legacy has proved to be a heavy one.[19]

o   o   o

As ONE reads through the accounts of Lévi-Strauss's sojourns among different groups of Indians, presented in the chronological order of their occurrence, one is conscious through the first three at least of a rising scale of excitement that is, in effect, dependent on an increasing level of exoticism. His first significant lesson in the undeniably exotic occurs when, as a neophyte anthropologist, he meets the Caduveo—"I made my first contact with savages" (*Tristes*, p. 174). But he soon discovers that they are, in reality, neither "savages" nor "true Indians." The Bororo of the following section, on the other hand, are referred to in a provocative chapter title as "Noble Savages." Finally, the Nambikwara are defined as creatures from a "Lost World" who, in comparison with "the learned societies" of the Caduveo and the Bororo at least, give the appearance of "the childhood of humanity" (*Tristes*, p. 312).

Among the works discussed in the present study, apart from *Argonauts*, only *Tristes Tropiques*, in its properly ethnographic sections at least, reveals the thoroughness and systematicity one would expect from a professional ethnographer. Nevertheless, as Lévi-Strauss moves from de-

---

[19] See Robert Darnton's discussion of this: "History and Literature," in *The Kiss of Lamourette: Reflections in Cultural History* (New York: Norton, 1990), pp. 326–327.

scriptions of the layout of a village and the construction of huts to the physique of the natives, their clothing, ornaments, tools, and utensils, and on to their economy, language, myths, religious beliefs and practices, kinship systems, social and family relations, and sex roles, it becomes apparent that certain motifs recur with a peculiar insistence. And they do so partly in spite of such reigning Parisian discourses of the time as Marxism, psychoanalysis, and structuralism and partly because of them. As Lévi-Strauss implies, along with the science of geology that he also took as his model, those three bodies of theory posited an opposition between manifest content and latent content, ideology and relations of production, *langue* and *parole*. And it was Lévi-Strauss's ambition to plot such latent patterns in human cultural behavior, to produce order out of apparent contingency.

If *Tristes Tropiques* reads so often like an elegy, that is because of the sadness its narrator expresses both for the destruction of the natural environment and for the diminution of human diversity—all those endangered cultures which had developed their own diverse and complex solutions to the problems of collective living, under widely varying conditions, from a virtually infinite number of possibilities available. Lévi-Strauss argues passionately for balance and conservation, however, for reasons that are not solely humanistic or altruistic. His reasons are also deeply personal and aesthetic.

One gets a vivid sense of this in the narrator's descriptions of the facial and body paintings of the Caduveo. It is in such passages that one is reminded of the specifically Parisian connection between the artistic and literary avant-garde and ethnographic fieldwork. Lévi-Strauss finds among the Caduveo a form of graphic art that is in his experience without comparison among American Indians—recalling nothing so much as the stylizations of our playing cards. In the intricate arabesques and symmetrical patterns inscribed on faces and bodies, often deliberately athwart natural lines and features, Lévi-Strauss discovers a sophisticated logic and an artistic taste that, although he does not say so, is in some ways comparable to the aesthetics of the modernist movement in art and the reaction against realism. The pleasure for the ethnographer was clearly in observing and in recording his observations in precisely detailed descriptions. Moreover, he describes the same thing not in one medium but two, for he also reproduces particularly vivid photographs and sketches.

Such graphic effects have a fetishistic charge—all of them are of women—that is either centered in one way or another on the mouth or eye, or on substitutes for them on cheek or forehead in the form of altogether displaced and unrecognizable painted organs. Whether or not one explains their appeal to the male eye as a denial of castration and of a sexual difference founded on the phallus, they constitute powerful stimulants to sexual fantasy. In words and images, in any case, such transgressive asymmetry constitutes an invitation to scopophilic play of a kind that European men so often traveled to remote regions for. This is something the narrator himself is especially aware of as he looks at the painted bodies of the women: "These delicate and subtle contours, which are as sharp as the lines of the face and which sometimes underline them and sometimes betray them, lend the women something deliciously provocative. This pictorial surgery grafts art onto the human body. . . . No doubt the erotic effect of makeup has never been as systematically and consciously exploited" (*Tristes*, pp. 214–215). Like Malinowski in his *Diary*, Lévi-Strauss here implicitly calls attention to his sexuality as white male observer.

Body painting, however, had another meaning for the Caduveo. It was, in Lévi-Strauss's interpretation, their way of asserting that they are human and not animal, that they belong to culture and not to nature, equally as much as our Western ancestors or ourselves. Yet, the lesson he draws from his observations of the Brazilian Indians is, in the end, that of a lived harmony between the two spheres, a kind of recognition that even in culture mankind is still part of nature and denies it to his peril. Perhaps the most striking example of what this might mean is offered in a description that defamiliarizes the very notion of a house, transforming it from something rigid and substantial into something as flexible as a garment. A house in a Bororo village is not so much lived in as worn— "The nudity of the inhabitants seems protected by the grassy velvet of their walls and the fringe of palms; they slip out of their homes as if they were giant bathrobes made of ostrich feathers" (*Tristes*, pp. 244–245). What is being suggested here is, of course, a form of existence in which a balance has been struck, a harmony achieved, between human beings and the natural world.

It is, however, the Nambikwara who best suggest to Lévi-Strauss a condition of society that comes closest to Rousseau's ideal; if there ever was such a thing as a Rousseauist moment, it was in the stage of human social development that they had reached. The mystery of the origins of the Nambikwara, along with that of the various other Indian peoples of Northeast Brazil, is the subject of the conjectures and hypotheses of the chapter whose evocative title is "The Lost World." It is apparently difficult to determine whether or not the Nambikwara, with a culture that is significantly less elaborate than the cultures of the Caduveo or the Bororo, should be identified as having remained at a less-evolved stage of human development or as having "regressed" into it for various reasons.

What is not in doubt is the "destitution" of a collective life that at least has the appearance of "the childhood of humanity" (*Tristes*, p. 312). And

Lévi-Strauss emphasizes the penury of a material culture that is undoubtedly much closer to that of stone-age life than the far more complex Indian cultures of Middle and North America. As the wonderfully suggestive photographs reveal—the contrast with Malinowski's is marked—not only do the Nambikwara go about entirely naked except for rudimentary ornaments, but they sleep in the dirt, build only the crudest kinds of shelter, and during the nomadic dry season are reduced to gathering a heterogeneous collection of insects, roots, and berries in order to survive at all. Yet, it is with the Nambikwara that the committed Rousseauist reached the goal of his quest: "I had sought a society reduced to its simplest expression. The society of the Nambikwara was that, to the point where I found there simply men" (*Tristes*, p. 365). It is with these two sentences that Lévi-Strauss concludes his discussion of this most primitive of Indian bands in a section that for the narrator/protagonist is the climax of his narrative of investigation.

The Nambikwara's simplicity is undeniable. But it is interpreted as a virtue because it seems to be the condition of the generalized state of harmony he sought. The contrast is great between the barely subsistence level of their material existence and the warmth of their human relations as Lévi-Struass describes them. If from our point of view the balance between men and nature seems here tilted too cruelly on the side of nature, Nambikwara culture appears to have accommodated itself wonderfully to circumstances that are normally assumed to be especially dehumanizing—among the Ik described by Colin Turnbull, for instance.[20]

It is in their family life and in their political arrangements especially that Lévi-Strauss identifies the utopian characteristics of a stone-age culture that surprises because of its potential nearness to ourselves as well as its distance. Here, if anywhere, Lévi-Strauss allows himself to be "won over to the otherness of others." "Simply men," we are taught to acknowledge to our shame, turns out to be a very great deal. And nowhere is this more apparent than in warm and playful family relations and group dynamics generally. He singles out the humor, the caresses, the friendly wrestling, and the mutual delousing sessions among adults and adolescents as signs of superior group relations, and he observes the tenderness manifested in a form of childrearing that is accompanied neither by beatings nor by punishment of other kinds. Finally, he finds among adults a generalized tolerance of eroticism that permits amorous play in public, even if actual sexual intercourse is normally a private activity. It is an attitude he translates into the pidgin of "It's good, making love" (*Tristes*, p. 326).

The distance between what the observer finds among these most prim-

[20] See *The Mountain People* (New York: Simon and Schuster, 1972).

itive of Brazilian Indians and Western familial relations as posited by psychoanalytic theory could hardly be more marked. Culture here functions without repression and without aggression. In opposition to his contemporary Jacques Lacan, Lévi-Strauss apparently concluded that the emergence into human language and culture was not necessarily a kind of Fall, as a result of which dyadic plenitude gave way to split subjectivity and the tug of a restless desire. In effect, the pidgin just quoted suggests a barely verbal level of communication, one that is presumed to be fuller because relatively unmediated. If the narrator imples that there is an unwonted transparency of the sign, this is because it has only partly detached itself from the body of nature.

Nowhere else in *Tristes Tropiques* does Lévi-Strauss come closer to the mode of elegiac romance than in his representations of the evening scene at a Nambikwara campsite. Like Malinowski in similar circumstances on a Southwest Pacific island, he makes an appeal to intraspecies solidarity by means of an evocative little vignette that signifies innocence and vulnerability:

> On the dark savanna the campfires gleam. Around the hearth, which is the only protection against the descending cold, and behind the frail screen of palms and branches hastily stuck into the soil on the side where wind and rain are feared, next to the baskets which contain the poor objects that are all their worldly wealth, lying directly on the earth around them, haunted by other bands which are equally hostile and fearful, husband and wife hold each other tight with the realization that they are for each other the only support, comfort, help against the daily difficulties and the dreamy melancholy which sometimes invades the Nambikwara soul. [p. 335]

The lesson for the West in such a spectacle, reproduced with a novelist's eye for suggestive detail and in a long, cadenced sentence, is in the attitudes that render seemingly impossible circumstances tolerable. Eros is, for once, triumphant at the level of the community as well as of the couple.

In a final sentence, the narrator goes on to give a new meaning to the notion of "the primal scene" in which narrative is once again functioning at the level of the imaginary register: "Yet, this destitution is animated by whispers and laughter. The couples embrace as with the nostalgia of a lost unity; the caresses go uninterrupted by a stranger walking by. One assumes in all of them an immense kindness, a profound casualness, a naive and charming animal satisfaction and, gathering together all these diverse feelings, something like the most moving and the truest expression of human tenderness" (*Tristes*, pp. 335–336). The "scene" that is rendered here is Jamesian as well as Freudian; it is the focus of a scopic drive that we associate with realist description as well as with voyeurism. More-over, it is "primal" also in the sense that it is associated with origins, with the childhood and innocence of the race. As a result, the ethnographer's look itself is disculpated. "The Lost World" is prelapsarian; sex is good and is good to look at.

Nevertheless, in spite of this image of love fulfilled under circum-stances that can be described only as mythic, the narrator does acknowl-edge that there is politics in paradise. There is not space here to consider Lévi-Strauss's discussion of the political institutions of the different Bra-zilian tribes, except to note that he argues both directly and indirectly for the reaffirmation of the social contract, for communitarian bonds, for government by consent, and for a form of welfare statism. But it is im-possible in this context not to mention the attack on writing, which was the focus of Jacques Derrida's well-known critique on Western logocen-trism referred to above. Nowhere more than here does Lévi-Strauss sound more Rousseauist.

The point of his twofold attack on writing is partly missed by Derrida, however. On the one hand, the cultural anthropologist associates it not with enlightenment but with the deployment of power. He follows those who, after Rousseau, have traced the origins of writing in the fourth to third millennia B.C. and the concentration and hierarchical organization of large populations. Writing accompanied the emergence of cities and empires, and seems "to favor the exploitation of men before their illu-mination. . . . the primary function of written communication is to facili-tate enslavement. The use of writing for disinterested ends, with a view to obtaining intellectual and aesthetic satisfaction, is a secondary result" (*Tristes*, p. 344). On the other hand, he is not content to emphasize the prior investment by power of the palace of culture; he also seeks to sub-vert the smugness of a Western society that has traditionally associated the superiority of "civilization" over "barbarism" on the basis of the writ-ten word.

For that historical and epistemological break which separates cultures with writing from those without, Lévi-Strauss seeks to substitute what for him was the far more momentous one that occurred with the advent of the Neolithic Age. The "giant steps" (*Tristes*, p. 343) taken then involved the beginnings of agriculture, the domestication of animals, and the practice of such crafts as pottery and weaving. Thus, even if the Nambik-wara can give one only an incomplete idea of what collective life was like before the advent of modern forms of social organization dependent on writing, they offer enough to suggest how great has been the cost for humanity of its subsequent development.

It turns out, in fact, that in his quest for origins, "for the unshakable base of human society" (*Tristes*, p. 451), Lévi-Strauss finds himself more or less in agreement with the unfashionable Rousseauist view—unfashionable until the late 1960s that is, and the cult of a return to the land—that the best state of society for humankind was not a primitive one, but an intermediary one before writing and metallurgy and "the advent of mechanistic civilization" (*Tristes*, p. 452).[21] His argument is, of course, a sociopolitical one whose ambitions transcend politics as conventionally understood: namely, that given mid-twentieth-century circumstances, the only way back is through the science of cultural anthropology and that purposeful, disciplined travel which moves back in historical time as well as far from Europe in space.

The preeminent task of the times is the construction of a theoretic model of an alternative society that begins with observation and analysis—a human society "that may not correspond to any observable model but with the aid of which we will succeed in distinguishing 'what is originary and what is artificial in the nature of contemporary man, and to know well a state which no longer exists, which has perhaps never existed, which will probably never exist, but about which it is important to have correct ideas in order to judge properly our present state'" (*Tristes*, p. 453). Lévi-Strauss finds the quotation from Rousseau so much to his liking that he repeats it twice in the book in order to emphasize his allegiance to the task of the Enlightenment philosopher.

Perhaps the most important reason why we study alien cultures is after all for our own sakes as well as for that of others. Understanding is inseparable from self-understanding through the detour of otherness and a dialogic openness to the possibility of change. Thus, in spite of the elegiac tone that predominates throughout *Tristes Tropiques*, Lévi-Strauss does not give up on the idea that there is something to be done, that one has a choice in the present. In spite of his professed admiration for psychoanalysis, the combination of Rousseau, of a modern human science, and of contemporary existentialism leads him away from the idea of the tragic entrapment of biological *Homo erectus* in the contradictions of sociality, the kind of entrapment posited by Freud in *Civilization and Its Discontents*.

If in his theory and practice the Parisian intellectual celebrated *la pensée sauvage*, it was because it suggested an alternative and apparently superior mode of thinking. In opposition to the abstract and linear logic of Western rationalist thought, it presupposed a different relationship to the natural world and to the human body. It was concrete, analogical, sensational. Its model was in myth, and it had survived in the modern

[21] Lévi-Strauss shares with D. H. Lawrence the distinction of being one of the most eloquent critics of industrial society and its human cost in the first half of the twentieth century.

world chiefly in art and music. One of the important implicit themes of
Tristes Tropiques is, in fact, that although a return to a stone age way of
living is probably impossible for modern humanity, it is still perhaps not
too late to become "stone age" within.

Tristes Tropiques is, then, a strangely hybrid work, animated by the contradictory impulses of a sense of mission and the consciousness of an ir-
remediable loss, part personal and historical memoir, part philosophic
meditation, part ethnographic record. The promising title of the concluding section is "Return," but it turns out to be an ambivalent affair, by
no means the kind of triumphant happy ending associated with traditional voyage literature; not all returns are joyful homecomings. The fifty
pages or so of sobering commentary that the section contains include reflections on the vocation, responsibilities, and difficult role of the cultural
anthropologist. And it is in these pages that Lévi-Strauss also makes the
implicit connection between travel and transgression.

The gist of his argument is, in effect, that the ethnographer discovers
his or her vocation in dissatisfaction—if not precisely with his home, then
with his homeland. There is something within that asks for more, something that his contemporary Lacan was theorizing psychoanalytically in
the concept of "desire." In any case, it is from this sense of distance from
the customs and values of his own society that the ethnographer derives
the "patience" and "devotion" required for the study of alien cultures.
"Alienation" from one social system may find expression in an academic
discipline that legitimates the celebration of another.

No wonder Lévi-Strauss found it impossible to avoid narrative. The
ethnographer turns out to be very much one of Jurij Lotman's "dynamic
heroes" who crosses frontiers in pursuit of alternative ways of life. Such
motivation also explains in part why Lévi-Strauss affirms—in a passage
that once again reminds us of Freud on "transference love"—that the
value the ethnographer attaches to exotic societies does not necessarily
bear any relation to "objective reality": it is "without true foundation; it
is rather a function of the disdain and even the hostility that the customs
of his own milieu inspire in him" (*Tristes*, p. 443). The disturbing implication is clearly that the understanding of otherness typically begins with
"misunderstandings" at home. Without that difficult assumption of one's
subjectivity, one would never be energized to lead the difficult life of the
ethnographic traveler at all.

It is, in any case, in the light of such reflections that the reader is likely
to read the narrative of Lévi-Strauss's own journey. And in this connection, perhaps the most surprising assertion in the whole rich and disturbing work concerns the imaginary plenitude of beginnings. The ambition
of the ethnographer, the narrator notes unexpectedly, is "to return to
the origin. Man only truly creates on a grand scale at the beginning; in

any field whatsoever, only the first step is integrally valid" (*Tristes*, p. 472). One recognizes in such an assertion how Lévi-Strauss's own voyage was inspired by the discourse of myth. The desire expressed both here and in the scenes he paints of Nambikwara life, in particular, are an expression of the desire to go home again. But the home is far from Europe, and the journey is philogenetic rather than ontogenetic. Historically situated in the peculiarly cruel decades that stretch from the 1920s through the 1950s, the European ethnographer appears to be nourished by recollected images of a neolithic Indian tribe as he looks back to a mythic past and forward to a potentially utopian future.

In fact, he concludes *Tristes Tropiques* with an atheistic profession of faith that, in effect, defines the anthropologist's vocation as that of a memorialist of dying cultures: "The world began without man and will end without him. The institutions, manners, and customs that I will have spent my life cataloguing and understanding are an ephemeral efflorescence of a creation in relation to which they have no meaning, except perhaps that of allowing humanity to play a role in it" (*Tristes*, p. 478). The language of this passage, along with that of the last few pages of the book, suggests nothing less than the discourse of "the absurd" that was the common currency of intellectual Paris during the 1950s.

It is in any case a way of defining the "human condition" that leaves the anthropologist with the Sisyphean role, made fashionable by Albert Camus, of repeating endlessly a task rendered futile by a universe that serves no purpose outside itself. Lévi-Strauss puts his own peculiar gloss on that role when he substitutes the resonant neologism "entropologist" for "anthropologist." Not only does he find in the universe a process of progressive disintegration from an originary moment of plenitude and order, but he also concludes that humankind itself functions as a machine which accelerates the decay. Thus, if "entropology" seems to him a more suitable name for his academic field than "anthropology," that is because all human creativity is fundamentally entropic. "Entropology," he notes, is "the name of a discipline devoted to the study of this process of disintegration in its highest manifestations" (*Tristes*, pp. 478–479). The master narrative of humanity's life on earth, which the investigator uncovers in the course of telling the story of his own travels, seasons elegiac romance with irony. The aim of life, in *Tristes Tropiques* as in Freud's *Beyond the Pleasure Principle*, turns out to be death. And in both cases humanity appears to be the unwitting agent of the ruse of history.

Nevertheless, down to his concluding paragraphs Lévi-Strauss can be seen, in retrospect, to be implicated in the discourse of his historical moment even as he struggles to effect a break with it. At the time of writing *Tristes Tropiques*, he still allows the ethics and the metaphysics of existentialism to cohabit in his text with the "superrationalism" of an emergent structuralism.[22] In his vocabulary of personal human "choice" and of human solidarity in the face of an ineluctable destiny, in fact, we are reminded of nothing so much as the existentialist humanism of Jean-Paul Sartre. Given the choice between "us" and "nothing," he opts understandably for the former: "I assume thereby my human condition" (*Tristes*, p. 479).

As is clear from the preceding discussion, this generalized commitment leads Lévi-Strauss to adopt positions that may be characterized as politically progressive, socially interventionist, democratic, and broadly socialist. Yet, from the perspective of the species, all such positions have to be understood as probably only temporary palliatives; they function against a background of scission and tragic loss. A world stripped of wonders and monsters is no longer adequate to the human imagination; otherness has grown banal and the future will never be the equal of the past. Thus, it turns out that the attitude Lévi-Strauss recommends is contemplative rather than active, the stance of the sage. It is an expression of the will to suspend the destructive forward rush of our species, "its beehive activity" (*Tristes*, p. 479), in order to enjoy on his way up the hill, like Camus's boulder-pushing Sisyphus once again, the spectacle of the created world.

[22] This does not prevent Lévi-Strauss from referring disparagingly to existentialism. He objects to "the complacency it shows toward the illusions of subjectivity," a complacency that gives rise to "a metaphysics of the typing pool." *Tristes Tropiques*, p. 63.

PART FOUR

Postcolonial Dilemmas

Chapter XI

WRITING THE ORIENT:
BARTHES

THE FIRST PART of Claude Lévi-Strauss's *Tristes Tropiques* proclaims "The End of Travel." Yet, in spite of its author's opinions on the subject, it does not announce the end of travel writing. Though not without some discomfort, Lévi-Strauss himself goes on to tell the story of his travels around the world in a work that, like Bougainville's voyage, provoked its own supplement by a contemporary critical philosopher in the person of Jacques Derrida. The burden of the latter's critique is that Lévi-Strauss, by failing to posit a structure without "a transcendental signified" or a globe without a center, did not practice systematically his own structuralist theory: "As a turning toward the presence, lost or impossible, of the absent origin, this structuralist thematic of broken immediateness is thus the sad, negative, nostalgic, guilty Rousseauist face of the thinking of freeplay of which the Nietzschean affirmation—the joyous affirmation of the freeplay of the world without truth and without origin, offered to an active interpretation—would be the other side. *This affirmation determines then the non-center as otherwise than a loss of the center.*"[1]

Some fifteen years after Lévi-Strauss, in a France that had finally, if painfully, brought to an end its long colonial adventure, Roland Barthes, on the other hand, pursued the logic of Derrida's argument in his own foray into travel writing. *The Empire of Signs* of 1970 was Barthes's attempt to go beyond essentialism in the European relation to otherness through a practice of "writing" that was intransitive.[2] Although he emerged from the same Parisian intellectual matrix as Lévi-Strauss—one that included prominently the discourses of Marxism, existentialism, structuralism, and psychoanalysis—Barthes's career in theory led him to a kind of poststructuralist beyond of theory. In later works such as *Roland Barthes by Roland Barthes* and *Fragments of a Lover's Discourse*, he developed a practice of writing that broke decisively with the tradition of realism, scientific representation, or the high theoretic model building that still characterizes *Tristes Tropiques*, in spite of its gestures toward modernism.

[1] "Structure, Sign, and Play in the Discourse of the Human Sciences," in *The Languages of Criticism and the Sciences of Man*, eds. Richard Macksey and Eugenio Donato (Baltimore: Johns Hopkins University Press, 1970), p. 264.
[2] *L'Empire des signes* (Geneva: Skira and Paris: Flammarion, 1970).

As a result, Barthes's account of his visit to Japan turns out to be one of the most radically different travel books ever written, one that was not designed to please the area specialists. The man who first came to public attention as the analyst of the myths of modern French life could hardly be expected to respect convention in a genre that, like Lévi-Strauss before him, he recognized as more ideologically saturated than almost any other form of verbal representation outside propaganda proper.

In this respect, Barthes clearly shared the peculiar nausea associated with the vast majority of works in the field. And in the case of French writing on Japan, it involved a whole colonial literature going beyond that late-nineteenth and early-twentieth-century period in which such figures as Pierre Loti (*The Last Days of Peking*, *Madame Chrysanthemum*) and Pierre Claudel (*The Black Bird in the Rising Sun*) figured so prominently. The nausea tended to be aroused by multiple signs of a generalized cultural smugness in relation to the foreign, of partiality for the stereotype and the ready-made formula, and of the self-confident assumption of an identity that enables one to speak the truth of the Other. In run-of-the-mill travel writing of the kind Lévi-Strauss had in mind, one encounters a more or less turgid ethnocentric discourse triumphant. But Barthes was able to overcome the latter's attack of bad conscience chiefly on two grounds. On the one hand, travel was practiced by Barthes as another mode of displacement that allowed him to explore the nature of his own desire by means of a detour through otherness; the aim was the kind of shock (*secousse*) to the preconstituted self he elsewhere associated with *jouissance*. On the other hand, travel writing also became an opportunity to reconceptualize and problematize the question of representation itself.

As a result, his Japanese travel book has a salutary subtlety and abrasiveness that is in its own way antihegemonic, even though it makes no overt reference to the political or socioeconomic scene. Its strength is, in part, that through its example and the questions it raises, it challenges the journalistic reports, diplomatic memoirs, and monographs by area-studies experts that are the main current forms through which our Western knowledge of Japan is mediated and that recirculate the Orientalist discourse which Edward Said has denounced. It challenges such works to acknowledge their own status as texts, their being as writing, especially where they claim to speak with the impersonal authority of a human science: "what is fundamentally unacceptable from my point of view is scientism; that is to say, a scientific discourse that thinks of itself as science and censures the need to think of itself as discourse."[3]

Such a formula may serve to remind us that Barthes's travel book ap-

[3] "Sur *S/Z* et l'*Empire des signes*," in *Le Grain de la voix* (Paris: Le Seuil, 1981), p. 80.

peared right at the beginning of the 1970s at a time when (in the avant-garde of literary theorists at least) literature of a certain kind was taken to be the model of antidiscursivity among discourses. In this respect, Terry Eagleton's acerbic comment on Yale deconstructionism applies, in part, to its influential French precursor: "literature becomes the truth, essence or self-consciousness of all other discourses precisely because unlike them, it knows that it does not know what it is talking about."[4] The difference is that Barthes, unlike most deconstructionists, celebrates the emancipatory play of a written word that has bracketed its referent.

Therefore, not only does *The Empire of Signs* consciously avoid the kind of sense-making that is characteristic of traditional forms of travel writing, it also seeks to put into question two millennia of Western verbal representation that took for granted the metaphysical presuppositions of the mimetic tradition, including particularly the relationship between world and language. In a context where there is typically an indecent rush to assign meaning to the manifold phenomena of alien cultures, Barthes's deliberate suspension of meaning production attempts to distance the reader both from a presumed reality and from the medium of representation itself. And he finds in Japanese culture a wonderfully complicit ally. Japan furnishes for Barthes a model that justifies his own antirepresentational aesthetic, an aesthetic summed up from the late 1960s on in the concepts of *écriture* and of textuality.

Japan also enables him to indulge in the impossible dream of a linguistic revolution against his language that, after Jacques Lacan, he characterizes as paternal. The goal is to immerse oneself in untried linguistic possibilities "to the point where the whole Occident within us is shaken to its foundations and the rights of paternal language wobble, the language of our fathers, the language that makes us in our turn, fathers and owners of a culture that history transforms into 'nature' " (*Empire*, p. 11). Like so many other male travelers before him, Barthes exploits the opportunity afforded by a foreign journey to play the interventionist intellectual in the sexual-political debate in his homeland. He, too, has no intention of taking up a prescribed paternal function on his return.

The result of such attitudes is in any case a perversely antihermeneutical reading of a country in which a whole culture is construed as a text in the strong sense and attention is deliberately arrested at the surface, at the level where signs are produced and circulate in their seductive materiality. Japan is plural and beyond interpretation. The clear corollary of such an attitude is that the traveler himself becomes a reader who has learned to read from such poststructuralist works as Barthes's own *Plea-*

---

[4] *The Function of Criticism: From the Spectator to Poststructuralism* (London: Verso Editions and NLB, 1984), p. 104.

sure of the Text.[5] Japan provides the occasion for the discovery of the comparable pleasure of a new, delicately hedonistic art of travel and travel writing. Thus, the narrator here makes no secret of the relationship between travel and desire. In his Asian text Barthes openly pursues pleasure on the two registers of *plaisir* and *jouissance* described in his theoretic book on the subject.

The title of Roland Barthes's book on Japan may be *The Empire of Signs.* Yet, unlike all those empires with which we are familiar, the one he has in mind is paradoxically an empire without emperor or site of power, centerless. Barthes's *Empire of Signs* is an empire of empty signs, not fullness but difference, not Baudelairean *correspondances* but signs without secret equivalences, the dream world not of a nineteenth-century symbolist but of an early-1970s poststructuralist.[6] The Japan he produces corresponds to what he described elsewhere as his own particular "ethic of the sign and of meaning"; that is to say, an "ethic of the empty sign."

It is, in other words, a privileged space in which signifiers are exchanged in the virtual absence of signifieds—especially the final transcendental signified, which founds all meaning and arrests semiosis; the transcendental signified that monotheistic religions call God: "Japan offers the example of a civilization in which the articulation of signs is extremely refined and highly developed, in which nothing is left over as non-sign; but this semantic level which is characterized by extraordinary finesse in the treatment of the signifier does not mean anything, in a way does not say anything. It does not refer to any signified, certainly not to any final signified. It therefore expresses, in my view, the utopia of a world that is strictly semantic and strictly atheist" ("Sur *S/Z*," p. 82). In "Japan," his "Japan," Barthes finds already in place the practice of his poststructuralist theory, a culture that functions as a writing.

From the start, Barthes makes clear that he rejects the Western representational aesthetic which opposed an Occidental knowing subject to an Oriental object of knowledge. His Japan will be no more than a fantasmatic construct, therefore, notes inspired by a system of signs that enables one Western observer, at least, to distance himself provisionally from his own culture: "The Orient and the Occident are not to be taken for 'realities,' then, that one would attempt to approach and to oppose historically, philosophically, culturally, and politically. I do not look lovingly toward an Oriental essence; the Orient is a matter of indifference

[5] Trans. Richard Miller (New York: Farrar, Straus, and Giroux, 1975).

[6] In an astute review of Barthes's book, Hide Ishiguro comments: "The country depicted, with the recognizable images and several interesting truths, is a fantasy world, just like the one in *The Mikado* which the Japanese would not think of as being Japan" (*Times Literary Supplement*, 12 August, 1983). It is, however, a point that Barthes himself had already made.

to me; it simply furnishes me with a stock of features whose combination or invented play allow me to try out the idea of an unheard-of symbolic system, one that is wholly remote from our own" (*Empire*, p. 7).

In effect, it is precisely the suspicion of the dogmatic claims empowered by an aesthetics of representation that led Barthes to write a travel book unlike any other. His work will not take up the task of assigning meanings but will instead be consciously experimental, play with a utopian potential—"try out the idea of an unheard-of symbolic system." If he can be said to have discovered a form of utopia on his extra-European journey, therefore, it is very different from the kind sought out by political pilgrims. Barthes's book is, in its way, symptomatic of his generation's break with *engagement*. In his ironic and fragmentary self-portrait of 1975, *Roland Barthes by Roland Barthes*, he notes about himself in the third person, "because of a perverse disposition to see forms, languages, and repetitions, he gradually became a political misfit."[7]

The attitude of openness is apparent in the first place at the level of composition. *The Empire of Signs* is not organized as a narrative, although it is not entirely "plotless" in spite of itself. In that polarity between mimesis and diegesis, it is much closer to the latter, since the narrator foregrounds his sentient, searching presence in all its encounters. But it a presence that is often curiously depersonalized, written in as an intermittent register of sensations felt and thoughts provoked.

Empire of Signs does not, unlike traditional travel books, tell the story of a journey whose identifiable narrator emerges on his return home as the hero or antihero of a difficult journey. No "I" sets forth, arrives and, in a series of episodes, encounters Japan in its landscapes, cities, architecture, monuments, and people. There is no chronology and no itinerary, no dates and relatively few place names. Nor are there those scenes, characters, or dialogues that travel writing in modern times adapted from the realist tradition in fiction. The narrator eschews the production of a traveling personality who is enriched by his experiences so as to offer at the end the sum of a completed journey and a self chastened or renewed.

Like his subsequent works, Barthes's *Empire of Signs* admits a plurality of entries. It can be opened at any section and read without difficulty or loss because, after a few pages of opening remarks, there is no development, middle, or end. It is a text traversed by other texts, claiming to be without origin or closure, acknowledging its openness. No effort is made to offer a synoptic totalizing view of the country, Japan. We learn almost nothing about the Japanese economy, its political and social life, or its geography and history. At the most, Barthes does uncover a certain systematicity in the codes of Japanese social behavior, and a sympathy is

[7] Trans. Richard Howard (New York: Farrar, Straus, and Giroux, 1977), p. 170.

acknowledged between the author's poststructuralist ethic of the empty sign and the refinements of sign production in Japan.

If Barthes offers a Japan that can be said to teach his reader something, then, it is not in the form of usable truths or of a transportable moral. Rather, it is that of the experience of a limit case, of a country that offers the experience of euphoria which Barthes sought primarily in certain forms of art, music, and literature. Travel turns out to have for him a comparable capacity to disorient and to produce a thrilling disruption of sense. The exotic forms of Japanese daily life are themselves incitements to enjoyment on the various registers between pleasure and *jouissance*. Japan responds in an exemplary fashion to what, as he indicated in an interview, travel at its best meant to him: "travel for me is an adventure or series of possible adventures of great intensity. It is obviously related to the heightened receptivity of love."[8] In the meaning he attaches to adventure here, Barthes gives explicit acknowledgment to the opportunities travel affords for libidinal play.

As with several of Barthes's mature works, *The Empire of Signs* is set out as a collection of random reflections of roughly two to six pages in length. These reflections are interspersed with a variety of images: photographs of people and scenes; reproductions of Japanese paintings, maps, and manuscripts; pages from handwritten notebooks; handwritten phrases in French; Japanese ideograms. In both the original Skira edition and in the paperback form, *The Empire of Signs* has, in fact, the appearance of an "art book" that speaks in turn to the different senses. The quality of the paper and of the illustrations, as well as their quantity, oblige the reader to hesitate in assigning priority to the printed text or to the images.

It is a hesitation that Barthes undoubtedly intended to promote, as the very form of the book takes one to the heart of the question concerning the relationship between painting and writing. The point for him is that whereas the two seem to constitute easily identifiable oppositional categories in the West, in the East that opposition is problematized. "Where does writing begin?" / "Where does painting begin?" are two parallel questions posed beneath a haiga painting-inscription entitled "Collecting Mushrooms." A form of description is involved that combines signs which have become figurative with a painting that tends toward the abstraction of signs.

In short, both in the sphere of the ideogram and in its tradition in painting, Japanese artistic practice suggests that the division between a representational and supposedly natural art such as painting and a

---

[8] See the interview with Bernard-Henri Lévy, "What Are Intellectuals For?" in *Le Grain de la voix*, p. 249.

wholly conventional sign system such as writing is far less obvious than it appears to the Western eye. The poststructuralist conviction that there is no "before" of writing, that all systems of communication are already a writing and involve the operation of conventional codes without anchors in an anterior referential order, finds a warrant for its stand in an Oriental practice that might be called "sign painting." Japan offers the example of a paintbrush that writes.

Moreover, such an Oriental practice is, in Barthes's view, virtually co-extensive with Japanese culture.[9] That is why his travel book may be said to be as much about writing as about Japan. It is also why Barthes is able to avoid the traps of "Orientalism" in Said's sense. His Japan is not posited as an essence but as a difference that merely serves to throw light on the peculiar ideology of the sign to which we cling in the West. It shares with modern literary discourse a combination of aesthetic poise and the will to put an end to metaphysics, for it knows that it does not know and relishes the play of its signs for their own sake.

Barthes himself made the point succinctly in a passage that is quoted on the back cover of the French paperback edition: "Why Japan? Because it is the land of writing; of all the countries the author has come to know, Japan is the one where he encountered the work of the sign closest to his convictions and his fantasms or, if one prefers, the farthest removed from the disgust, the irritation, and the refusal that Western semiocracy arouses in him. The Japanese sign is strong; admirably controlled, executed, displayed, it is never naturalized or rationalized."

That is why, in retrospect, his Japanese travel book can be seen to perform operations that are both continuous with and, in an important sense, the antithesis of those of an early work such as *Mythologies*.[10] The short essays of that book constituted in their own way a form of travel writing in his native culture: Barthes attempted to analyze contemporary French myths by making himself a stranger in his own land and by showing how, through ideological practice, history comes to be transformed in consciousness into nature. Yet, where Barthes's France is represented as the country of the naturalized sign that required the work of ideological demystification—or what, in the context, amounts to the same thing, rehistorization—Barthes's Japan simply offers the endlessly renewed moves of its exquisite signifiers to his enthralled and henceforth provocatively ahistorical eye. In the East he experiences the emptiness of lan-

---

[9] Ishiguro observes that the difference between Europeans and the Japanese in their attitude to nature is by no means as great as Barthes supposes: "As a result we have Barthes, for whom 'nature' and 'natural' have tended to be dirty words, expressing his fascination with a people whose traditional self-image involves being close to nature and cherishing emotive responses" (see n. 6 above).

[10] Trans. Annette Lavers (New York: Hill and Wang, 1972).

guage and the excitement that induces, not just in the sphere of Japanese words he can neither read nor understand, but in all the signifying practices of the culture.

How this operates in practice may be seen in the three short sections devoted characteristically to Japanese cuisine and to eating. The sections are entitled "Water and Flake," "Chopsticks," and "Food Decentered." Barthes's writing here cannot help but remind us that one of the most celebrated pieces of *Mythologies* was entitled "Steak and French Fries." For Barthes, the extraordinary thing about Japanese meals is that the various logics of Western cuisine and Western eating practices are subverted. Our culturally consecrated oppositions between the raw and the cooked, (*pace* Lévi-Strauss), between preparation and consumption, between kitchen and dining room, for example, are deconstructed in Japan.

Thus, in Barthes's reading, a Japanese meal is not placed before a diner like a series of paintings to be contemplated with all their elements already in place, according to a compositional scheme that imposes a logico-temporal order which, like the order of classic narrative, is destroyed in the course of its consumption. In a Japanese restaurant, a tray arrives covered with its many delicate dishes and its condiments, and although it has the appearance of a painting, it is nevertheless destined to be unmade and remade a great many times before the meal is over. It is less something stable and finished to be observed and consumed than an activity to be engaged in or a game to be played. The original tray with its variety of precious dishes is thus not so much a painting as a palette. The diner is free to engage in the eating art, to swoop and choose with his chopsticks according to the shifting whims of his palate. No protocol obliges him to consume the dishes in a fixed order or to respect any given compositional rules. Like a postmodernist text, a Japanese meal is characterized by its multiplicity of potential entrances. One does not have to begin at a beginning imposed by a cook/author and consume what is in front of one passively, in the sequential order of classic Western narrative; one is, in one's own right, a producer, painter, cook, and player of the eating game.

Rightly or wrongly, what characterizes Japanese food for Barthes is finally, like everything else he encounters in Japan—see "Town Center, Empty Center"— its decenteredness, as the section entitled "Decentered Food" makes clear. Unlike the red wine or the steak of France, in his reading Japanese food bears within it no precious substance; it contains in its hidden depths no equivalent to that essential Frenchness which Barthes discovered in certain traditional foods of his homeland: "Entirely visual . . . the food thus indicates that it is not deep; the comestible substance is without a precious heart, without buried power, without a vital secret; no Japanese dish is provided with a *center* (an alimentary center that is implied with us by the rite which consists in giving order to a meal, in surrounding a dish or covering it with a sauce). Everything is the ornament of another ornament; first of all because on the table, on the tray, the food is never anything more than a collection of fragments among which none is privileged by an order of ingestion" (*Empire*, pp. 32–33). What one recognizes here—"ornament of another ornament"—is the logic of supplementarity that was so important in Derrida's early thought.

The poststructuralist theme of decenteredness appears at its most provocative from the point of view of Western consciousness in the final section, entitled "The Cabinet of Signs." In evoking his experience of the Japanese delineation of space, Barthes once again describes that perilous euphoria which we now call *jouissance* and which he associates with the sudden loss of selfhood, of cultural identity and an ideologically fixed positionality. Traveling about the country, he is invariably struck by the paradox that one encounters a combination of discontinuity and openness in the landscape. There are no barriers—but, at the same time, none of those distant horizons, so dear to the romantics and to our continuing romantic taste in landscapes, that flatter pride in our own constituted subjecthood: "no desire to swell my lungs, to stick out my chest in order to assert my ego or to turn myself into the receptive center of infinity; obliged to recognize the evidence of empty limit, I become limitless with no sense of grandeur, without metaphysical reference" (*Empire*, p. 144). In such passages one sees the kind of "adventure" Barthes sought out in his travels. In effect, he records here the experience of living, momentarily at least, that beyond of metaphysics which we can only speculate about in the West.

Further, what is true of Japanese space on the level of its landscapes is equally true for Barthes in the configurations and disposition of its cities and of the domestic sphere. At the heart of Tokyo where one would expect to find an imperial palace or the monumental architecture of power for which, in the West, Rome provides the model, Barthes finds instead the emptiness of a park. In the Japanese house and its concept of furniture, he discovers a flexibility and a deconstructibility that is antithetical to all mystifications of the human subject. There is none of that complicity between property and the affirmation of selfhood which characterizes arrangements in Western houses: "in the [Shikidai] corridor, as in the ideal Japanese house, without furniture (or with very little furniture), there is no place that designates the least proprietorship, neither seat nor bed nor table where the body can transform itself into the subject (or master) of a space; a center is denied (a burning frustration for Western man, who is everywhere provided with his armchair, his bed, the proprietor of a domestic place)" (*Empire*, p. 146).

The disruptive force of Barthes's work for a Western reader is obvious in such passages. It is a force that draws its energy, on the one hand, from the poststructuralist critique of a Western rationality and a Western common sense that is egocentric in a Cartesian sense, a pursuit of knowledge founded on self-presence and personhood. On the other hand, it is a force that proceeds from a restless critical intelligence that was peculiarly Barthes's own in its hostility to received ideas and its sensuous openness to the play of the new. It is, for example, characteristic that in a discussion of the Japanese practice of bowing, unlike almost all other Western observers, he discovers not the submissiveness to authority of an unregenerate hierarchical society, but the cultural formalism of a nation of semioticians that recognizes in that act nothing more than a form of writing in which bodies take on the graphic function—"Form is empty."

The significance of the Japanese codification of gestures in this instance is that it provides Barthes with the opening to reevaluate our Western politics of politeness. And what he finds in that politics is a suspicion of all learned codes that is based, once again, on a metaphysics of the self or a "mythology of the 'person' ". It is our habit, in the United States even more than in France, to assume that a social "exterior" overlays a natural "interior," and it is this inner, authentic self which in the popular imagination simply betrays its true nature whenever it conforms to the codes learned by the factitious outer self.

The capacity for the critical reading of social myth and of the process of "naturalization" that produces it, already apparent in *Mythologies*, allows Barthes to raise the possibility that bowing in Japan is far from having the meaning we usually attribute to it: "it is not the sign of an observed, condescending, and precautionary communication between two autarchies, two personal empires (each of which reigns over its ego, over the small realm of which it has the key); it is only the indication of a network of forms in which nothing is arrested, tied, deep. *Who is saluting whom?*" (*Empire*, p. 88). That question justifies for Barthes the whole practice of bowing; it enables him to realize that what is involved is not sense but "graphism." It is a gesture from which "every signified is inconceivably absent."

o   o   o

BARTHES'S travel book is, then, continuous with almost all his writings after the period of programmatic structuralism. In its way, it is an "essay," in the sense that Barthes gave to that word: "I can accept the word if it has the kind of meaning of a phrase such as 'trying on' (*faire l'essai*) a language relative to an object, a text; one tries on a language as one tries on an article of clothing; the closer it fits, that is, the further it goes, the happier one is" ("Sur *S/Z*," p. 77). *The Empire of Signs* is an "essay" in this sense. It is experimental, fragmentary, willfully open-ended, playful. However, it takes as its object not a "text," but a culture or cultural text. As a result, its relationship to Japanese culture is not that of a subject of knowledge to its object, but that of experimental openness and pleasurable anticipation. The question it embodies is not, then, What can I know about Japan? Rather, it is, What does Japan enable me to discover by distancing me from myself and from my culture? It offers its reader not science but a highly self-conscious verbal art, not knowledge but the play of intelligence associated with the poetic function of language; it offers also that peculiarly poststructuralist pleasure of demonstrating, with panache and all manner of verbal sleights of hand, how unfounded are truth claims that are congealed in discourse.

The eroticism that is associated with travel writing from the beginning becomes verbal in the play of the language that Barthes tries on for his Japanese journey, but not exclusively verbal. As noted in a passage quoted above, travel for Barthes connoted "adventure," as it has for so many travelers—"adventure," moreover, in the libidinal rather than the heroic sense. It is not that Barthes narrates episodes which evoke his sexual encounters; he, in fact, repudiates the kind of "dirty plunge" that Flaubert, for example, engaged in during his time or, in a different way, Piero Paolo Pasolini did during ours.[11] Barthes's taste goes to a more generalized sensuous encounter with a foreign world that solicits him in the piquant diversity of its signs. As he acknowledged in the Lévy interview quoted above, he pursued in travel, "the sensation of plunging into a simple and opaque world (for the tourist everything is simple). Not a dirty plunge but the voluptuous immersion in a language, for example, whose sounds I don't understand. It is amazingly relaxing not to understand a language. It eliminates all vulgarity, all stupidity, all aggression" ("Intellectuals," p. 249).

The distinction made here goes a long way toward characterizing the refined hedonism of the mature Barthes's sensibility. It is similar to the distinction made in *Camera Lucida* between "heavy desire, that of pornography" and "light or good desire, that of eroticism."[12] In any case, one

[11] In the account of a journey he took to India in 1961, Pasolini projects in his narrator the persona of the *flâneur* who explores the nocturnal streets of India's swarming cities. The scent of his title is largely that of putrefaction and feces, that odor of death associated with the romantic agony. See *The Scent of India* (London: Olive Press, 1984). Barthes, in fact, comes closest to what he seems to mean by "the dirty plunge" not abroad, but when he turns himself into a kind of nocturnal tourist at home, in his accounts of cruising the bars and streets of Paris in the posthumously published "Soirées de Paris," in *Incidents* (Paris: Le Seuil, 1987).

[12] *Camera Lucida*, trans. Richard Howard (New York: Farrar, Straus, and Giroux, 1981), p. 93.

recognizes in such passages the discourse, not of the *voyageur maudit*, but of the aesthete.

Such a suspension of meaning also implies the suspension of sexual meaning. Japan affords Barthes the pretext for interrogating once again fixed gender identities and for engaging verbally in fantasies of decentered, nonphallic sexuality. The whole section entitled "Chopsticks," is an example of the kind of witty, allusive poetic writing that is, in fact, the *raison d'être* of *The Empire of Signs*. There is no more readily available exoticism than the exoticism of foreign food. Food is something we can see, smell, taste and, in our mouth at least, touch. Food is a more or less piquant form of foreign substance that we openly admit into our own body, normally with the expectation of a new pleasure.[13] Consequently, that classic question of the male traveler—What are the women like?— is, if anything, less common than What is the food like? Eating in a foreign land is an "adventure" in the mouth that, under certain conditions, may stir memories of our remotest psychic past.

In the section on chopsticks, however, Barthes is not concerned with the art of cooking but with the relationship to food implied by the instruments of eating. The narrator here plays knowingly with a series of erotic associations that attach themselves to the use of chopsticks in opposition to Occidental knives and forks. The purpose of the former is claimed to be multiple. They are used to point to the food, to pinch it delicately, to divide it and to transport it to the mouth; but in all these activities they avoid the brutal, predatory crudeness of the knife and fork we have designed for ingestion. They are celebrated instead as a quasi-magical instrument that transforms solid food into a rare form of nourishment: "because of the chopstick, food is no longer a prey to which one does violence . . . but a substance harmoniously transferred; it transforms the previously divided matter into a food for birds and the rice into a stream of milk" (*Empire*, pp. 27–28).[14]

The fantasm embodied in such a carefully wrought and knowingly precious passage is, of course, that of nonphallic sexuality—there is no display of power, no aggression, no penetration. It suggests rather the image of a maternal solicitude that is always sufficient and tenderly equal to each fresh demand. Chopsticks reawaken in Barthes the pleasures of

[13] Abdelkebir Khatibi comments: "Every foreign dish that defies our customs liberates our body from its earliest habits. It expatriates it to the sphere of the unknown. That is why I enjoy the foreigner, male and female." *Figures de l'étranger dans la littérature française* (Paris: Denoël, 1987), pp. 78–79.

[14] The English word "chopstick" attaches the implement to a wholly different semantic field from the French word "baguette." Because the latter is the word for both a conductor's baton and a magician's wand, it suggests the play of a sensibility entirely absent from the aggressively workaday resonances of "chopstick."

orality and of the mother's body from which we are separated at the moment of our weaning and our entry into paternal language or the symbolic order: "the chopstick . . . introduces into the practice of eating not
an order but fantasy and a sensation of laziness" (*Empire*, p. 25). A fantasy, one might add, of dyadic plenitude and a breast that is always
there.[15]

The effect of such and similar passages is to transform our Western
discursive understanding of Japan by associating it with a certain idea of
maternity. Japan in *The Empire of Signs* is as effectively maternalized by
Roland Barthes as was Rome by Stendhal in *Promenades dans Rome*.

Erotic satisfaction of a different but equally nonphallic order is also
suggested in the section that evokes the Japanese version of the slot machine, "Pachinko." Whereas the Western slot machines embody "a symbolism of penetration," because one is invited to possess "at one stroke"
the pinup whose body is illuminated on the machine, the Japanese game
offers no sex, as Barthes disingenuously puts it, before he goes on to
evoke the kind of reward that the Japanese player may expect from his
electronic play: "It is easy to understand, then, the importance of a game
that to the constrictions of capitalist wealth and the constipated parsi-
mony of salaries opposes this voluptuous rout of silver balls which suddenly fills the player's hand" (*Empire*, p. 42). The jubilant anality of the
surge of pleasure involved here hardly needs highlighting.

For the most part, the multiple pleasures with which Japanese culture
is invested have for Barthes a less startling, more diffused quality of a
kind that is evident, for example, in his evocation of packages. He finds,
for example, in Japan a peculiar "sensuality of the package" that is also
unknown in the West. On many occasions there is a reversal of our un-
questioned hierarchical opposition which assumes the priority of the contained over the container, of message over its envelope: "One might say
that it is the box that is the object of the gift and not what is inside it."

All the art, in short, is in the wrapping, and for the recipient of the gift
all the pleasure is there, too—between the wrapping and the unwrapping
of what has been so exquisitely put together. One recognizes here the
celebrated Barthean theme of the pleasure of the text transported from
the literary sphere to the practical arts of everyday life, from the play of
verbal signifiers to that of the futile signifiers of colored paper and card-
board. In both cases, the reader/player enjoys the excess engendered
when the signified is banished: "from one wrapping to the next the signified flees, and when one finally finds it (there is always a little some-

[15] Barthes notes in the Lévy interview that food was significant for him in three different ways, the first of which has to do with "the prestige or taste of the maternal
model, one's mother's food as she prepares it and conceives it; that's the food that I
like." "Intellectuals," p. 250.

thing in the package), it seems insignificant, derisory, vile. Pleasure, which belongs to the realm of the signifier, has already been taken; the package is not empty but emptied" (*Empire*, pp. 60-61). It is impossible not to read the metaphor of phallic sexuality and the structure of strip-tease into Barthes's negative language here. The reward for the recipient of a Japanese package, as for the reader of a postmodernist text, on the other hand, is not in the final act of possession, the revelation of its hermeneutical secret, but in the more or less elaborate detours that take you toward it.

What eating practices, Pachinko players, the art of packaging, and so many other features of Japanese life do for Barthes is precisely to stimulate the play of his fantasy. They open up new possibilities, new vistas to be explored in his (and therefore our) intellectual and aesthetic, as well erotic, life. Moreover, in Barthes's case, they take him increasingly in the direction of trying out the new and/or repressed pleasures of the ungendered body, of the before and after of gender differentiation. They take him, that is, toward polymorphous sexuality and infinitely protracted play, toward the uncharted and finally unchartable territory that, after Lacan, he gestured toward in enlarging the associations of that already untranslatable French word, *jouissance*.

It is finally the genre of the haiku that summarizes Barthes's whole experience of Japan. It is a literary genre that is alien to those of us who are familiar only with Western literature. In Barthes's view, it offers the paradox of a text that is perfectly readable yet resistant to the imposition of meaning; it is intelligible but meaning-less. In spite of its apparent simplicity, it suspends the effort of sense making and cuts off the kind of commentary that is an ingrained expectation of our literary life; the work of reading haiku is "to suspend language, not to provoke it." Barthes, in fact, refers to haiku as the literary branch of Zen, one of whose fundamental practices is "to stop language" (*Empire*, p. 97).

If he finds haiku so exciting, that is because it suggests the kind of liberation associated in Zen thought with the state of "a-linguisticality." Thus, the shortness of the haiku is not a mere matter of form—"the haiku is not a rich thought reduced to a short form, but a short event that suddenly finds its proper form" (*Empire*, p. 98)—but one of "rightness," of adequation between signifier and signified, and not of an exact representation of reality as in Western "description." Haiku is articulated on "a metaphysics without subject and without God" (*Empire*, p. 101); it has the character of an event or of an adventure in language. Furthermore, each individual haiku opens out onto the virtually infinite and collective corpus of other haikus, without origin or end in an unstoppable series of referrals—a case of universal semiosis that recalls nothing so much as a dictionary: "Thus, the haiku reminds us of what has never happened to us; in it we *recognize* a repetition without a source, an event without a cause, a memory without a person, a word without moorings" (*Empire*, p. 104).

In sum, the haiku for Barthes is emblematic of a nonrepresentational, nondidactic, nonnarrative art that manages to embody what he admires most in Japanese culture. It provides in the textual sphere proper an example of the aesthetic of the fragmentary and the discontinuous that, in Japan at least, is combined with an unequaled sureness of touch and of refinement in sign production. A haiku recognizes its own writerly status and, in the instantaneousness of its appearance acts out its own eventful and incomplete character.

Given all this, it is not surprising if one recognizes in haiku a model of the textual art that Barthes sought to practice at book length in *The Empire of Signs* itself, namely, "vision without commentary." Like haiku, Barthes's travel book may be partly defined in negatives; it seeks not to teach, nor to express, nor even to describe or entertain in the way of a traditional travel book. It seeks instead to be writing on a writing, a work of brilliant formal evanescence that opens onto nothing beyond itself. To the extent that it foregrounds the emotive and poetic functions of language to the detriment of the referential, it is also empty of content of a conventional kind. That is why those critics who claim that Barthes misunderstood various aspects of Japanese culture and society are misguided. The book does not claim to be about a country on the map, but a possible country—what, after Italo Calvino, might be called an "invisible country."

The challenge of Barthes's "Japan" is precisely that it mocks the truth claims of Western philosophy, social science, and literature. *The Empire of Signs* evokes the brilliant surface of Japanese culture in order to reflect back, for a Western reader, all the myths of interiority and expressivity and referentiality, of nature and depth and spontaneity, of body and soul, of the self and imaginary plenitude, of property and identity that were indeed so conducive to nausea in a poststructuralist of Barthes's generation and sensibility.

What Barthes's book tries to write is the way in which Japanese culture, like Bunraku theater, is endlessly and consciously antinaturalist, coded, citational. By means of a detour through otherness, he seeks to distance himself and his reader, for the time of a reading at least, not only from the attitudes and values of his own culture, but also from the literary genre by means of which it had traditionally represented otherness to itself: namely, travel writing. Barthes's position is resolutely antihermeneutical. There will be no understanding through the overcoming of distance—although there is a great deal of praise—no production of the truth of the Other, just the perception of a nonfixable difference.

Barthes's short sections, in their more or less random order, offer neither depth nor totality, but the more or less disconnected and more or less systematic play of cultural parts that tells us more about ourselves than about the Japanese. It is in all of these senses that *The Empire of Signs* marks an end of travel literature as we have known it in the West. Under the circumstances, it is disturbing, if inevitable, to record that Barthes's example is one that has gone largely unfollowed. It does not share haiku's power to stop language.

o   o   o

YET, should we so be disturbed after all? Why is it so important to pay attention to a work that in spite of its obvious enthusiasm treats Japan with casual irresponsibility, that simply seems to use it, in fact, for its own aesthetic-hedonistic purposes? In short, can a work that practices a form of dehistoricization even more radical than that of the New Criticism be thought of as a work of general ethical or social significance, let alone as a political intervention? In implying that Japanese culture acknowledges no source and no center, no *archē* and no *telos*, Barthes is affirming that the writing of history or of social analysis as we know it is merely another mode of mythic production. Poststructuralism can have no truck with history, if history means the perception of order in time, the mapping of change, of beginnings, developments, continuities, endings, phases and periods, the narration of revolution and reaction, conflict and cooperation between identifiable entities or human groups, cause and effect.

The question is at bottom one that has been frequently raised in connection with the relationship between poststructuralist thought and politics, especially in the light of the broadly leftist and even Maoist positions adopted by the majority of Parisian intellectuals in the late 1960s and early 1970s. In the case of *The Empire of Signs*, the question might be interpreted as taking a more specific form: Can there be a politics in the absence of a history? It is a question to which Barthes's book can hardly be said to offer a satisfactory answer. It does do something else, however, something that has its own importance.

Because it consciously takes responsibility for its own language, it is above all an extensive reflection on representational discourses and, by implication, on the writing of history, geography, and ethnography as travel writing. And since these various disciplines are themselves intimately bound up with the exercise of power in ways that both Foucault and Said, among others, have shown, *The Empire of Signs* constitutes in its own way a meditation on power and on the activity of representation that articulates and reproduces it. One remembers that what Barthes called "literature" in his inaugural lesson at the Collège de France is a site of "powerlessness." It is the place where knowledge is uncoupled from power precisely because no truth claims are made.

It is in this connection that Barthes returns so often and in a variety of contexts to the question of decenteredness. The different manifestations of such a condition in Barthes's Japan serve by contrast to remind us of that ruse of power which in Western ideology posits a center that stands outside semiosis and fixes the system. So it is with our religions, our empires, and our families as it is with our towns. The center is always the site of truth: "in conformity with the very movement of Western metaphysics, for which a center is always the place of truth, the center of our towns is *full*" (*Empire*, p. 43). It is to the center that we look for spirituality (churches), power (offices), money (banks), commerce (the big stores), and our intellectual life (the various sites of verbal exchange). In Barthes's reading, centeredness is the myth that sustains all our myths of identity and continuity, of self and other, as well as our various discourses of power.

In the briefest of essays, published in book form in 1975 and entitled *Whither China?*[16] Barthes did follow up on the example of *The Empire of Signs* and raise once again the question of travel writing and its problematic discursive practices. Are there, he asked, any limits to what one can and cannot say? And he did so at a time when it was still common among French intellectuals to make their political pilgrimage to China in order to celebrate Mao's model of revolution—Julia Kristeva's *On Chinese Women* is a typical example of the style of engagement of the time. Writing about himself in the third person in a work that came out in the same year as *Whither China?* Barthes makes clear the kind of postpolitical politics he had come to embrace: "His place (his milieu) is language: that is where he accepts or rejects, that is where his body *can* or *cannot*. To sacrifice his life-as-language to political discourse? He is quite willing to be a political *subject*, but not a political *speaker*" (*Barthes*, p. 53).

Barthes's eight pages on China, therefore, are in their way a brief, anti-Kristevan manifesto in which he declines to respond to the question posed in his title, since such questions are, in effect, a symptom of the problem. He even, in effect, declined André Gide's role in *Back from the USSR*, for Gide undertook the task of representing the dystopian features of a Soviet society that so many of his friends and colleagues had praised.

Since then, of course, contemporary Western travelers have once again been swarming over the immense body of China in search of answers to the many and various question that our Western knowledge industry generates. Thus, unlike Kristeva, for example, Barthes returned from

---

[16] (Paris: Christian Bourgois, 1975).

China not with lessons for the West, but with "nothing," not full but "empty." Proclaiming once again "the end of hermeneutics," he proposed instead what in his last paragraph he calls "a negative hallucination."

The meaning of the phrase is made apparent earlier, when in a speculative vein Barthes refers to the "desire" of a human subject for a nonexistent grammatical mood that neither affirms nor negates, neither doubts nor questions, but simply "suspends enunciation without for that matter eliminating it" (*Whither*, p. 13). The apparently paradoxical goal sought is a form of commentary on otherness whose tone is "No comment." In practice, this leads him to make a series of affirmations—China is said to be "without flavor (*fadeur*)," "colorless," "flat," "calm"—that, in their guarded neutrality, sound like negations.

Barthes does acknowledge in the Lévy interview that China, for some unexplained reason, failed to captivate him in the way that Japan did—"I found no opportunities for erotic, sensual, or sentimental investment there" ("Intellectuals", p. 250). In the context of the China essay proper, however, the apparently negative attributes to which he refers have a certain celebratory force, since they point for Barthes to a cultural way of being that blurs constituted differences, including sexual ones. China, in another way than Japan, suggested to him the nonphallic, diffused sexuality of motherhood itself, a sense of peace and of strength that overwhelms fixed meanings. Thus, the brief Chinese travel sketch as a whole can be seen as an attempt to substitute an antidogmatic and apolitical "hallucination" for its more familiar opposite, a neither/nor for the either/or of various hegemonic discourses in place.

Given the massive misrepresentations of foreign places and peoples to which we are still subjected—what Barthes might have called with characteristic irony "positive hallucinations"—it is difficult to deny that there is a need, not so much for silence as for a writerly ethics of "No comment." Thus, in its way, *The Empire of Signs* itself is Barthes's contribution to the endeavor to go beyond Orientalism. Moreover, in my reading it also implies, like *Tristes Tropiques*, that we would all be better off, if the great majority of the world's travel books had never been written at all.

Chapter XII

ORIGINARY DISPLACEMENT
AND THE WRITER'S BURDEN:
V. S. NAIPAUL

IN SPITE OF Claude Lévi-Strauss, travel to remote places is not likely to end soon; nor, in spite of Barthes's writerly ethics of "No comment," is travel writing of a more or less representational kind. We may have given up the dream of an encounter with a pristine world—that "coral island" of adolescent fantasy—and grown suspicious of a use of language that remains blind to any but the referential function. Given the important, if frequently unacknowledged, place they occupy in our individual and collective psyches, however, neither travel nor travel writing are about to disappear. Thus, even our most skeptical and critically self-regarding contemporaries go on engaging in both, even if they claim to "take responsibility for their discourse" and produce their observations "under erasure."

A writer who did not spend his formative years in Paris and who has, therefore, been less inhibited by "theory" in producing a substantial body of travel literature is V. S. Naipaul. By common consent one of the most important writers of travel books in English to have emerged since the Second World War, he is a "man of letters" in a traditional sense. Yet, he has nevertheless addressed many of the issues that preoccupied the Lévi-Strauss of *Tristes Tropiques*, in particular. And, in recent years at least, he has succeeded in going beyond the French anthropologist in rejecting contemporary, global monoculturalism as mere entropic process. If, as James Clifford has suggested,[1] the two metanarratives that dominate current thinking in the field are those of homogenization and loss or emergence and invention, then in his latest works at least—*Finding the Center, The Enigma of Arrival,* and *A Turn in the South*[2]—Naipaul is drawn to the

---

[1] *The Predicament of Culture: Twentieth Century Ethnography, Literature, and Art* (Cambridge: Harvard University Press, 1988).

[2] In what has become a characteristically low-key style, Naipaul's recent U.S. travel book, *A Turn in the South* (New York: Knopf, 1989), blends interview and description of place with historical commentary in order to uncover the tortuous bonds that unite the southern states to the Caribbean colonial world. It is in many ways far less a new departure than the English travel book and, in order to avoid repetition, I will not comment on it here.

latter. It is in his English book in particular, *The Enigma of Arrival*, in a so-called novel which is largely personal memoir and meditation, that he goes a long way toward deconstructing some of the oppositions that had dominated his travel writing up to that point. In the process, he recognizes that change is not necessarily decay, nor the existence of tradition the sign of continuity or centeredness.

From many points of view, Naipaul's travel works provide a fitting end to this exploration of European travel writing, not least because he is European only by adoption. That European-male gaze which from the eighteenth century on could claim virtually the whole globe and its peoples for its object finds in Naipaul's latest observations an answering gaze. Yet, not the least paradox of the Trinidadian-born Hindu's career is that, although he settled in England in the early 1950s, it is only recently that he has come to observe closely his adopted homeland. Up to that point, with a gesture that comes close to the kind of disavowal Freud discovered in himself on the Acropolis, Naipaul as writer has averted his gaze from his English surroundings.

Although *The Enigma of Arrival* is not, strictly speaking, a work of travel literature and claims to be fictional, it is an important document in this context for several reasons. First, it problematizes the opposition between "traveling" and "dwelling" and thereby supports Clifford's notion that, from a modern ethnographic point of view, they are less and less distinct (*Predicament*, p. 9). Its focus is on the writer's relationship to that place in Wiltshire that has been his home for a great many years. Second, its very title, with the implied reference to the mysterious attraction and threat of travel, confirms after the fact the appropriateness of my own. It is taken, as the narrator explains, from one of Giorgio de Chirico's surrealistic dreamscapes that represents two robed figures in some Mediterranean port with the top of a ship's sail appearing above a city wall. Not only does the subject of the painting come to be woven into the writer's own dreams, it also suggests to him the idea for a story that is resonant with his own past and future, a story of the impossibility of return— "There was no ship of antique shape to take us back."[3] Third, among all the writers discussed in the present book, none is more conscious than Naipaul of both ontogenetic and philogenetic forces at work within him as he moves through alien worlds: "It is as if we all carry in our makeup the effects of accidents that have befallen our ancestors, as if we are in many ways programmed before we are born, our lives half outlined for us" (*Enigma*, p. 77). It is for such and similar reasons that Naipaul can state that, whether traveler or dweller, no one ever has an innocent eye

---

[3] *The Enigma of Arrival* (New York: Knopf, 1987), p. 352.

for place: "Not an observer merely, a man removed; but a man played on, worked on, by many things" (*Enigma*, p. 103).

Like other expatriates from the New World before him, Naipaul's flight is to Europe, not from it. He comes from a part of the globe that has been recategorized in his own lifetime as Third and has transmigrated to one that is designated First. Since the Second World War, we have taken to counting the countries on the map of the world that were formerly colored pink, blue, or green. Yet, the numerical signs are also, like the colors of the colonial age, the code of a geopolitics, of a globe mapped, divided, and temporarily recentered once again. As a result of that change and of the changed relationships between countries it implies, travel and travel writing have been for Naipaul, too, consciously and disturbingly political activities. In one way or another, the essays and books that report on his journeys are preoccupied both with power—its passage from one set of rulers to another, its abuse, its spectacular failures and its lack—and with the newly forged discourses of power, even if the word "discourse" is never used.

This does not, of course, mean that Naipaul is a political pilgrim in Paul Hollander's sense; if anything, he would be better described as a political ironist and anatomist of national independence movements. His journeys, in any case, have given rise to accounts that evoke the same dystopian spaces described by André Gide and Lévi-Strauss and, in particular, the same spectacle of "our own garbage flung in the face of the world" the West first colonized and then quit. The difference between the French anthropologist and the Trinidadian-born, British-educated Hindu is in that personal adjective, that "our." Given the place and circumstances of his birth, the "garbage" can hardly be said to be "his." Moreover, it soon becomes apparent that much of his travel writing will turn on that question of ownership. From Naipaul's postcolonial vantage point, in any case, "the West's" responsibility in the matter is by no means as obvious or as complete as it apparently was for Lévi-Strauss in the mid-1950s. And it is largely for this reason that Naipaul is such a controversial figure.

As much as those of any other contemporary writer, his travel works, then, are exemplary of our modernity; and final confirmation of this is provided by his English "dwelling book." Because it tracks local, incremental change and movements of people between two of England's most sacred sites, Stonehenge and Salisbury Cathedral, it is as if Naipaul, too, finally discovers that the center cannot hold. In his confrontation with a modern, desacralized England, displacement comes to appear originary. All places are "the wrong place." Moreover, it is as if all his previous writings in the genre had pointed in the direction of this fateful discovery in spite of themselves.

In any case, the recurring motifs and obsessions of his travel writings in general offer peculiarly disturbing testimony to the tensions and contradictions of our time, tensions and contradictions in which the private and the public spheres intersect. Naipaul has found himself caught up in geopolitical, historical, and cultural movements that place a peculiar burden on the writer. And nowhere more than in travel writings, which call up his own past as he moves through the world, is his consciousness of that burden more apparent.

o   o   o

THE TITLE OF Naipaul's penultimate travel work proper, *Finding the Center: Two Narratives*,[4] suggests immediately the distance between his deeper purposes and those of his structuralist and poststructuralist contemporaries across the English channel. In the author's foreword he explains in connection with the first of his two narratives, "Prologue to an Autobiography," how it took him eight years to find the right approach to writing an account of his beginnings as a writer, to find "the center of the narrative" (*Center*, p. VIII). By way of introduction to the second, a travel essay on the Ivory Coast entitled "The Crocodiles of Yamoussoukro," he discusses the significance of travel for a modern writer with his particular background. And he goes on to affirm what he has in common with the people to whom he had been attracted in that West African country: "They too were trying to find order in their world, looking for the center" (*Center*, p. IX). The contrast with Barthes's reflections on the topic could hardly be more marked. According to Barthes's *Empire of Signs*, of course, "centeredness" is the problem, not the solution; it is precisely "decenteredness" that is to be strived for.

The repetition of the metaphor of the center in the title of Naipaul's work, as well as in two widely divergent contexts within it, is important because it confirms something that a reading of Naipaul's previous contributions to the literature of travel already point to. A preoccupation with "center" and "periphery" at all levels was in the decades of decolonization after the Second World War, crucial to the experience of the former colonial subject and to his formation as a writer. In a world that, even from the point of view of his backward, remote, native Trinidad, was visibly changing shape, Naipaul found himself drawn to take up once again the old questions of social order and anarchy, civilization and barbarism, history and origins, but from a global perspective. It is as if in his geopolitical imaginary the center were giving way before the assault of barbarian hordes of a different kind. By his own admission, the only

4 (New York: Knopf, 1984).

writer who under those circumstances proved to be of any help in his own work was Joseph Conrad.

A short article written in 1974 and entitled "Conrad's Darkness"[5] is particularly illuminating in this respect, as it takes us to the core of those intertextual weavings which enabled a Caribbean-born, Hindu immigrant to Britain to think about the world with the help of a Polish-born immigrant to the same island of an earlier generation. The piece is by turns autobiographical, confessional, and critical. It chiefly concerns what Conrad had meant to Naipaul at different moments in his life, starting with his hearing "The Lagoon" read to him at age ten by his father. And that voice, too, has its importance. The earliest mediator of the Conradian oeuvre was, in fact, to prove at least as important as that oeuvre itself.

The tenor of the essay is that in spite of the reservations he was to have about Conrad as a novelist, especially in his longer works, Naipaul found himself drawn to him on account of the themes and settings. He discovered that "Conrad—sixty years before, in the time of a great peace—had been everywhere before me" (*Return*, p. 216). That is to say, Conrad had traveled through a world largely unknown to the major practitioners of the English novel—the "Great Tradition" from Jane Austen to Henry James— all of whom had written about "highly organized societies" (*Return*, p. 213). Conrad had been to places like the Trinidad in which Naipaul was born—"one of the Conradian dark places of the earth" (*Return*, p. 214)—and it was because Conrad projected in his fiction a special vision of such places that he apparently made such an impression on Naipaul.

It is significant that, along with *The Heart of Darkness*, it is the short story "An Outpost of Progress" that Naipaul singles out for special praise— "the finest thing Conrad wrote" (*Return*, p. 215). That slim tale concerns two very ordinary Belgian ivory traders who unwittingly involve themselves in slave trading, are consequently ostracized by the local inhabitants, and go mad. Its theme of the collapse of supposedly civilized Europeans into barbarism, familiar from Conrad's most celebrated novella, is rendered with a telling simplicity. It is in this connection typical that the scene in *The Heart of Darkness* itself which most appealed to the younger Naipaul is the one that evokes the discovery of a tattered old book in a hut by the river. The book's title is, of course, *An Inquiry into Some Points of Seamanship*, and the sentences Naipaul quotes in order to specify the nature of its appeal stress not only the ideas of dedication,

[5] The Conrad article appears in *The Return of Eva Perón* (New York: Knopf, 1980) along with the title article, "Michael X and the Black Power Killings in Trinidad," and "A New King for the Congo: Mobutu and the Nihilism of Africa."

singleness of purpose, and honest work, but something that has to do with the very concept of civilization. The book is declared by Conrad's narrator to be "luminous with another than a professional light," the light of civilization itself against the background darkness. The significance of the brief episode for Naipaul is summed up in a resonant phrase; it expressed "something of the political panic I was beginning to feel" (*Return*, p. 216).

Naipaul's "political panic" derived, of course, from the historical given of his being the member of a nonwhite ethnic minority on a colonial island in the era of decolonization. In this respect, the importance of Naipaul's essay on Conrad for an understanding of the peculiar conditionedness of all Naipaul's writings is vastly out of proportion to its short length. On the one hand, it suggests how Conrad's work played an important mediating role in helping Naipaul to locate and develop his themes in a tradition of fiction writing that offered no other model appropriate to his needs: "Conrad's value to me is that he is someone who sixty to seventy years ago meditated on my world, a world I recognize today. I feel this about no other writer of the century" (*Return*, p. 219). On the other hand, the essay is even more important in this context because of the perspective Naipaul offers on the other side of independence, the negative side.

Whether in Africa or the Caribbean, the descendants of the Hindu diaspora could hardly be expected to regard decolonization with the same untroubled enthusiasm as the black majority. In what for Naipaul is a singularly confessional vein, in fact, he suggests with great cogency the psychic cost represented by independence for someone about to experience the shift from minority colonial administration to rule by indigenous politicians of a different race:

> To be a colonial was to know a kind of security; it was to inhabit a fixed world. And I suppose that in my fantasy I had seen myself coming to England as to some purely literary region, where, untrammeled by the accidents of history or background, I could make a romantic career for myself as a writer. But in the new world I felt that ground move below me. The new politics, the curious reliance of men on institutions they were not yet working to undermine, the simplicity of beliefs and the hideous simplicity of actions, the corruption of causes, half-made societies that seemed doomed to remain half-made: these were the things that began to preoccupy me. They were not things from which I could detach myself. [*Return*, p. 216]

The image of an earthquake reinforces the earlier notion of a "political panic"; it translates the fear associated with a sudden loss of faith in the earth's fixity, even if that fixity derived from the British imperial system.

At the same time, Naipaul is fully aware of the romantic idyll that was his dream of a writer's life in the homeland of empire. The England he had previously fantasized about but that, unlike Henry James in *English Hours*, he could hardly call "our old home," was precisely "some purely literary region." Moreover, the lesson of his subsequent career as a writer has been that one never lives "untrammeled by the accidents of history or background."

The passage is also interesting from another point of view, for it provides an introduction to the lexicon of concepts that Naipaul has joined together to form a self-consistent discourse of his own. Probably the most important single phrase in the passage concerns the former colonial territories themselves; Naipaul refers to them as "half-made societies that seemed doomed to remain half-made." The notion of "half-made societies" is repeated in the sentence following the passage quoted above, and it recurs in one form or another in all of Naipaul's travel writings. It is also used in the Conrad essay in order to specify the way in which the Anglo-Polish writer had preceded him. In words that apply with equal force to his own works, Naipaul affirms that what Conrad offered was "a vision of the world's half-made societies as places which continuously made and unmade themselves, where there was no goal, and where always something inherent in the necessities of successful action . . . carried with it the moral degradation of the idea" (*Return*, p. 216). Responsibility here is placed squarely on the societies themselves—they "made and unmade themselves." And from his early "Return of Eva Perón" essay to the March 1984 piece in *Harper's* on the invasion of Grenada, the appositeness of his Conradian text goes virtually unchallenged.

The implications of Naipaul's comments are troubling as well as fascinating. What the notion of a "half-made society" suggests, of course, is the possibility of its opposite, of a "fully made society," although this is not a concept that Naipaul himself ever uses. Nor, until his most recent works, does he cite an example of such a society. In the travel writings of the early 1970s, it is only through its negative Other—there are, in fact, a number of examples —that one can conceive of what a "fully made society" might be like.

Prominent among Naipaul's "half-made societies" is the one to which he devoted one of his earliest and most controversial of travel essays: namely, Argentina. As published in book form, "The Return of Eva Perón" comprises five relatively short pieces written between 1972 and 1977. These evoke Argentine life and reality at distinct moments in its recent history down into the years of what Naipaul calls the Terror; but throughout there runs the theme of arrested development in spite of early independence from the Spanish motherland, an arrested development that, in his analysis, finds its original cause in the character of Span-

ish colonialism itself. It is symptomatic that the words used by Joseph
Conrad to describe the attitudes of Belgian imperialists in Africa are chosen by Naipaul to suggest what he finds half a globe away and some sixty
years later: "Their talk was the talk of sordid buccaneers: it was reckless
without hardihood, greedy without audacity, and cruel without courage;
there was not an atom of foresight or of serious intention in the whole
batch of them, and they did not seem aware that these things are needed
for the work of the world" (*Return*, p. 149).

After what has been said above, it is perhaps not surprising that the
harshness of Conrad's judgments concerning those who made the Belgian Congo should seem to Naipaul to apply with equal force to the Argentineans in the early 1970s. What is surprising is the continuity of a
moral condemnation between two historical eras that are normally considered to be distinct, between the most expansive moment of European
colonialism and the age of postcolonialism. The homage Naipaul pays his
predecessor and fellow expatriate under radically changed historical circumstances is, then, the expression of a persistent will to reassert order
amid the perceived emergence of world anarchy, to affirm the need for
an enlightened, critical tradition under siege. Like Conrad, he has assumed in his writings the burden of bearing witness to the threats to civilization in "the outposts of progress." But, subsequent to the withdrawal
of the European colonizers, the spotlight is no longer ironically turned
on the Europeans themselves.

It is difficult to imagine a more negative view of a society, in fact, than
the one Naipaul paints of Argentina as a consequence of his visits there—
difficult but, as Naipaul's travel works on Zaire, India, or Iran show, not
atypical in his nonfictional oeuvre. Proceeding sometimes as a realist novelist, sometimes as a reporter, and sometimes as a general moral or social
commentator, in "The Return of Eva Perón" Naipaul offers vignettes
from contemporary Argentine life, snatches of reported speech, resonant phrases or slogans in Spanish, paraphrases of conversations and interviews, and descriptions of places and types, all of which are designed
to encapsulate the meanings he locates in Argentine reality. Such episodes function as illustrative metonyms of the general themes to which
he returns with an almost weary insistence—namely, the fatal flaws of
Argentine history that have made contemporary society what it is, the
sins of the colonial fathers and their perpetuation in the brutal present,
and the collective amnesia: "In Argentina, unmade, flawed from its conception, without a history, still only with annals, there can be no feeling
for a past, for a heritage, for shared ideals, for a community of all Argentines" (*Return*, p. 151).

The reference to an unwritten history is important: the question of a
society's failure to complete a full historical narrative of the past recurs

with the insistence of a leitmotiv throughout Naipaul's travel writings. In his reading, in any case, the half-obscured history of Argentina is a history of conquest, expropriation, and extermination of the indigenous Indian population, of the exploitation of a rich land by the conquerors and their descendants, of a population explosion with the importation of an immigrant workforce, and of the emergence of Argentina into the world commercial system of late-nineteenth-century imperialism: "Vast *estancias* on the stolen, bloody land: a sudden and jealous colonial aristocracy. Add immigrants, a labor force: in 1914 there were eight million Argentines. . . . A vast and flourishing colonial economy, based on cattle and wheat, and attached to the British Empire; an urban population as sudden as the *estancia* aristocracy; a whole and sudden artificial society imposed on the flat, desolate land" (*Return*, p. 103).

The passage is a typical example of Naipaul's swift, authoritative judgments and of the captivating, insistent rhythms of his prose; this is not "scene" but the kind of narrative summary in which authorial omnipotence goes unchallenged. The words that go furthest to help us understand his geopolitical phobias and fantasies, as well as his own less-than-critical history, are the repeated "sudden" and "artificial." They or their synonyms recur in many different passages, punctuating the various essays with the insistence of a complaint—"an artificial, fragmented colonial society made deficient and bogus by its myths" (*Return*, p. 115)—and inviting a deconstructionist reduction of the hierarchical opposition they imply.

The significance of "sudden" as a pejorative adjective applied to a society is apparent if one considers its implied opposite. A "gradual society" would presumably be one whose origins are remote, if not prehistoric, one that has developed slowly over the centuries without interference from without. When "sudden" is coupled with the equally pejorative "artificial," it becomes clear that Naipaul's ideal society would in some sense be a "natural" or "organic" one—an oxymoronic concept that points to an underlying mystification. Moreover, other passages suggest that what Naipaul means by an "artificial society" is, in fact, an immigrant society composed of a heterogeneous population, brought together in an empty or emptied land over a relatively short period of time by the accidents of history and economic need.

For Naipaul, the problem with Argentina can, in effect, be summarized in the ideologically charged concept of "transplantation," a concept that occurs in the text only in its adjectival form, in phrases such as "a transplanted people" (*Return*, p. 156). The word is clearly in a metonymic relation to the ideas of "suddenness," "artificiality," and "fragmentation" already referred to, for like them (as its derivation from the biological sphere suggests) it implies the notion of an uprooting that has the char-

acter of an arbitrary and fatal intervention in a natural process. It is
"transplantation" that explains for Naipaul the Argentineans' alienated
relationship to their land as well as to each other, their lack of "natural
bonds."

If as Naipaul claims, the politics of a country can be only "an extension
of its idea of human relationships," then Argentina's politics is epito-
mized for him by the code of the macho, the brothel, and the sodomizing
of women. An agressively heterosexual culture that tolerates a high degree of sadomasochism in relations between the sexes has as its correlative a particularly brutal politics. No higher good is served by Argen-
tinean-style politics. Instead, there are such substitutes as Peronist
national-populism, *espiritismo*, institutionalized machismo, and the victim-
ization of women—"For men so diminished there only remains machismo" (*Return*, p. 153)—or the cult of Eva Perón herself. Thus, although Argentina has the appearance of an open, educated, and civilized
society with newspapers and magazines, publishing houses, and even a
film industry, "it has as yet no idea of itself": "Streets and avenues are
named after presidents and generals, but there is no art of historical analysis; there is no art of biography. There is legend and antiquarian romance, but no real history. There are only annals, lists of rulers, chroni-
cles of events" (*Return*, p. 144). Or, as he comments elsewhere: "There
are no archives; there are only graffiti and polemics and school lessons"
(*Return*, p. 114).

The failure of Argentina, the failure of a country that has always
seemed so equipped by nature to be prosperous and successful, is, in
effect, largely attributed by Naipaul to a propensity to national self-de-
ception and a lack of national self-accounting that has never allowed it to
come to terms with its sordid colonial origins. Thus he is, in effect, able
to conclude that the primary problem is a lack of "writers"—of historians,
biographers and, one might add, realist novelists, who do not write legends or romances, but who offer critical, historically grounded narratives. He interprets Argentina's need, like that of the newly independent
nations in general, in terms of an opposition between a politicized discourse—"graffiti and polemics and school lessons"—and a socially responsible writing that is full, complex, and disturbing.

As for the travel writer, the stranger who is only passing through, one
might extrapolate from Naipaul's practice to conclude that his role
should be that of a critical but enlightened observer. His task, too, is to
record and provoke through the practice of a verbal art that moves between summary and concentrated, suggestive anecdotes. Not only is this
stance remote from the hedonistic disengagement implied by the Barth-
ian notion of "No comment," it is also different from the different

modes of "participant observation" practiced by the two Lawrences, Bronislaw Malinowski, and Lévi-Strauss. There is always a distance.

The final essay of Naipaul's book ends, for example, with a narration of the visit of a simple woman from Mendoza, accompanied by her polio-stricken daughter, to the site where Eva Perón's embalmed body lies, to the shrine of Argentina's unlikely, red-lipped saint. The visit is the result of a vow made fifteen years before. Told with the evocative precision that characterizes Naipaul's fiction at its best, the episode is designed to illustrate the simple faith, tantamount to belief in magic, that is the only recourse of ordinary people in a land without visible moral purpose or stable institutions. The theme it illustrates, with the power of an ironic genre painting, is that of "abandonment." "Without faith," the narrator had noted earlier, "these abandoned Spaniards and Italians will go mad" (*Return*, p. 104).

Another revealing word in Naipaul's lexicon is "simplicity": "Argentina is a simple materialist society, a simple colonial society created in the most rapacious and decadent phase of imperialism" (*Return*, pp. 152–153). And, as the sentence just quoted suggests, the concept stands in a metonymic relation, not to "innocence" but to "barbarism," to an unreflecting capacity for action of the bloodiest kind. Furthermore, as he meditates on the "disappearances" and the systematic practice of torture that characterized Argentine life under the military junta, that opposition between barbarism and civilization, which Conrad dramatizes as a conflict within isolated Europeans in colonial territories, is projected by Naipaul onto a whole culture. It is a barbarism that he locates with pointed irony in the nation's cosmopolitan capital: "Barbarism, in a city which has thought of itself as European, in a land which, because of that city, has prided itself on its civilization . . . the civilization of Europe divorced from any idea of an intellectual life and equated with the goods and the fashions of Europe: civilization felt as something purchasable" (*Return*, p. 161). It is to that absence of "any idea of an intellectual life" that Naipaul will return with the insistence of an obsession in his subsequent writings.

The point made here in connection with Buenos Aires—the "imported metropolis"—is of a piece with what has been said above about "artificiality" and political discourse. In regard to the latter, it is notable that an important part of Naipaul's representational technique in the various travel writings collected under the title of *The Return of Eva Perón* involves the stylized reporting of conversations with representative individuals whom the narrator encounters—conversations that are usually summarized in indirect speech, except for a particularly resonant phrase or sentence that is highlighted in quotation marks.

Written speech, for the most part, imitates spoken speech in Naipaul's texts in order to foreground a code that is abstracted from social and human reality and imported from elsewhere. The consequences are held to be devastating. "So, in sinister mimicry, the south twists the revolutionary jargon of the north" (*Return*, p. 112), the narrator notes in connection with the national popular discourse of Peronism. And it is against that "sinister mimicry," as well as against the native tendency to treat the national past as myth and romance, that Naipaul directs what is most interesting in his energetic polemic.

Argentina's colonial past is, so to speak, still to be written. All that has occurred so far is a form of discourse production, calculated to repress the originary trauma of genocide and expropriation of a native people. The repeated efforts at erasure and mythic narrativization are, therefore, interpreted as no more than the symptoms of a return of the national repressed.[6]

o   o   o

AMONG THE other three pieces in *The Return of Eva Perón*, only "A New King for the Congo: Mobutu and the Nihilism of Africa" can be legitimately described as travel writing. The piece on Conrad is, as mentioned earlier, a critical essay with an important autobiographical component. The essay on Michael Abdul Malik, the "Michael X" of the title, combines reportage on a bloody news event in Trinidad—which was followed with some interest by the British press—with critical reflection on what might be called "Thirdworldism" and Western liberal attitudes toward it. Some elements of travel writing appear only in certain evocations of the island of Trinidad; yet, like "The Return of Eva Perón" which, as we have seen, is a consciously political travel piece, the "Michael X" story is also the account of a place.

In spite of their rather disparate character, then, there are nonetheless significant continuities between these different essays, as Naipaul acknowledges in a brief "Author's Note." He himself speaks of "the intensity of some of the pieces, and their obsessional nature" and adds: "The themes repeat, whether in Argentina, Trinidad or the Congo" (*Return*, "Author's Note"). And, one might add, in India, Iran, or Grenada. All

---

[6] Support for Naipaul's contention of a fatal Argentine tendency to mythify the national past may be found in a recent article by Luisa Valenzuela, entitled "A Legacy of Poets and Cannibals: Literature Revives in Argentina" (*New York Times Book Review*, 16 March, 1986). Her opening sentence acknowledges the propensity Naipaul describes: "I am afraid that my country from the moment of its discovery has been faithful to a literary tradition that has promoted misrepresentation and fantasy." She then goes on to narrate the founding myth of discoverers who were forced to eat their dead but who included a poet, author of the ode "The Argentina." This anecdote is then used, in lieu of analysis, to explain the terror of the military junta: "That is why I believe we are descendants of poets and cannibals. And every so often the cannibals get hold of power, and silence the poets."

four essays in the book concern, in one way or another, former colonial countries which are now independent nation states and belong to that loose configuration of nations commonly referred to as the Third World. The three countries directly involved all have markedly different histories, different records of economic development, different political systems, and different racial mixes in their populations. One of them, the ex-Belgian Congo, now Zaire, has essentially the same racial stock as the one that existed there before the whole colonial enterprise began; the two countries of the Western hemisphere, on the other hand, have populations descended virtually in their entirety from people who arrived from elsewhere. Yet, the thing that seems to strike Naipaul most is what these countries have in common and not their differences. What they most obviously have in common is an imported national political discourse.

There is considerable bitterness in Naipaul's cautionary tale of a Trinidadian Black Power leader in Notting Hill, London, of his commune in Trinidad, the murders associated with it, and Michael X's own death. This brief political biography is a portrait of the new, composite man of the postcolonial age: "Malik's Negro was, in fact, a grotesque: not American, not West Indian, but an American caricatured by a red man from Trinidad for a British audience" ("Michael," pp. 31–32). Michael X is another example of a fabricated identity that, as in the case of Argentina and its myths, relies on a discourse to produce a convenient past: "With words he remade his past; words gave him a pattern for the future" ("Michael," p. 14).[7]

The story of Michael X, however, though not a piece of travel writing, does confirm Naipaul's "obsession," that central preoccupation with politics and the discourse of politics which characterizes all his writings. In "A New King for the Congo" such a preoccupation is once again directly related to travel. Given the importance of Conrad's example, it was perhaps inevitable that Naipaul would sooner or later travel to the country in which the Anglo-Polish novelist set his most famous novella as well as the short story that had meant the most to Naipaul personally. With the withdrawal of the colonizing power, the problems challenging the newly

---

[7] Naipaul concludes his short article on Grenada after the U.S. invasion with the following statement: "The revolution was a revolution of words. The words had appeared as an illumination, a short-cut to dignity, to newly educated men who had nothing in the community to measure themselves against and who, finally, valued little in their own community. But the words were mimicry. They were too big; they didn't fit; they remained words. The revolution blew away; and what was left in Grenada was a murder story" ("Grenada: An Island Betrayed," *Harper's*, March, 1984). Once again Naipaul finds that his anatomy of postcolonial revolution fits the situation on the ground.

independent nation of Zaire were, of course, different from those encountered by both Argentina and Trinidad. Whatever cultural and intellectual traditions the latter possessed at the time of independence were
derived from elsewhere, whether from the colonial homeland or from
the legends and practices that had survived among the descendants of
slavery and immigration.

The difficult task among the decolonized nations of Africa, on the
other hand, was to forge new unities out of the frequently arbitrary col-
locations of tribes and peoples inherited from the colonial era and, in one
way or another, to reaffirm their ties with their native cultural heritage
at the same time that they sought economic and social development according to Western models. Naipaul's assessment of the result in the case
of Zaire might be summed up once again in the antithetical concepts of
"authenticity" and "mimicry," seen against the background of what he
defines as a peculiarly African nihilism—except that, now, even the "authenticity" is made to appear factitious. Behind the façade of the institutions of a modern bureaucratic state, the "eternal" Africa of Conrad's
nightmare persists. In spite of the name change to Zaire, the confused
etymology of which Naipaul refers to at the beginning of his essay, the
original "dark place" remains.

As in the essay on Trinidad, the question of renaming seems to strike
Naipaul as symptomatic. Of course, in the case of Zaire, it is as part of the
effort to re-Africanize that the former Joseph Mobutu is now known as
Mobutu Sese Seko Kuku Ngbendu Wa Za Banga. Although Naipaul, with
the instincts of a novelist, witholds comment from such notations, the
context makes clear that this renaming, like other emblems of African-
ness such as the leopardskin cap and the elaborately carved stick Mobutu
always carries, is part of the new hegemonic discourse of power. It is an
aspect of the campaign for "authenticity," which in itself is a sign of distance from the African cultural past.[8]

Naipaul finds "mimicry" in the reliance made on Western political
thought to explain the history of Africa since colonization and to fantasize about the prospects of a nobler future: "So the borrowed ideas—
about colonialism and alienation, the consumer society and the decline of
the West—are made to serve the African cult of authenticity; and the
dream of an ancestral past restored is allied to a dream of a future of
magic power" (*Return*, pp. 198–199). In effect, the narrator identifies the
same absence of intellectual life and of critical historical thought, the
same substitution of myth for history, that he encountered in Argentina.

[8] The critical articles in *The Invention of Tradition*, eds. Eric Hobsbawm and Terence
Ranger (Cambridge: Cambridge University Press, 1983), show a similar reinvention of
the past much closer to home.

Yet, on this occasion, the narrator does note that the current regime in Zaire is merely following in the footsteps of the Belgians. The difference is that instead of beginning the history of the Congo with the late-fifteenth-century European navigators and then jumping to the nineteenth century, the Zairois now restore Africans to African history: "but it is no less opaque: a roll call of tribes, a mention of great kingdoms" is all that precedes a leap forward to the founding of the Congo Free State. In the beginning was "le bon vieux temps de nos ancêtres," a golden age of tribal oneness and black patriarchy. The problem, in part, is that for climatic reasons the past is easily obliterated in such a country; if a systematic effort is not made to preserve the memory of it, the bush is unforgiving: "Bush has buried the towns the Arabs planned, the orchards they planted, as recently, during the post-independence troubles, bush buried the fashionable eastern suburbs of Stanleyville. . . . In 1975 some of the ruins still stand, and they look very old, like a tropical, overgrown Pompeii" (*Return*, p. 190).

The lesson of Zaire for Naipaul in the postcolonial age, therefore, is in the end not very different from the one Conrad had drawn from his experience of the Belgian Congo. But in Naipaul's version it is a lesson for blacks as well as for whites, for Third World nations as well as for the West. It concerns preeminently the notion of the perishability of civilizations and the immense human commitment required for their preservation, that "work of the world" and that action redeemed by "the idea" to which Conrad referred. If Stanleyville remains for Naipaul "the heart of darkness" that it was for his predecessor, that is because it is the great anti-Rome or anti-London. It is the center of civilization's barbarous Other, the place in which, far from being preserved in great monuments and images, the memory of civilization is annihilated.

The "African nihilism" referred to in the piece's title is indeed the central theme of the journey to Zaire. The meaning Naipaul confers on the term appears in such a quick portrait as that of Simon, the manager of a nationalized company and a kind of black, postcolonial Kurtz. Educated, money-making, but "adrift and nervous in this unreal world of imitation," men like him are interpreted as having frustrated ambitions that are easily converted into "a wish to wipe out and undo, an African nihilism, the rage of primitive men coming to themselves and finding that they have been fooled and affronted" (*Return*, p. 195).

Once promoted to positions of national leadership, such men end up indulging in the savagery of an Idi Amin or in the autocratic kingship of Mobutu himself, "the great African nihilist" (*Return*, p. 196). In effect, Naipaul—and it is here that one recognizes the origins of his "obsession" in his "political panic"—identifies in such men a complicity with the bush, the will to erase and destroy that is the death instinct on the level of a culture. The attraction he discerns in the heart of darkness is not simply that of a regression to primitive savagery, but also that of the promise of extinction; its darkness is the solicitous darkness of the void. In the Congo once again, a Westernized writer politicized by his own past finds that the elemental struggle between life and death, civilization and barbarism, appears at its starkest. But as Naipaul's other travel works testify, this phenomenon is by no means unique to the Congo. Moreover, throughout his career as travel writer, Naipaul enlists his talent in the cause of the former, of life and civilization; he is the antithesis of the *voyageur maudit*, a "useful traveler" of a kind Dr. Johnson would hardly have recognized, who returns from each fresh voyage outside his adopted, European homeland with disturbing reports of a world under siege.

Naipaul's account of Zaire is much richer in suggestive detail and narrative incident than I have space to take stock of here. There are the familiar political ironist's references to its ceremonial, to its hostile officialdom and petty inefficiencies, to its party-line newspapers, to its overelaborate and often tawdry modern conference centers and athletic facilities, to its ambitions to create a new national literature, and to the "outpost civilization" of acquisitions and imported artifacts that, as in Argentina, serves only to underline the absence of the real thing.

There are also reminders of the country's continuity with its nineteenth-century past in its river steamers and river towns, the former "outposts of progress." If Naipaul is successful in persuading his reader of the accuracy of his version of the sad tropics, it is largely because of the sharpness of the concrete impressions he evokes and because of his eye for the ironies of modern Third World life. His best travel writing is constituted by descriptive passages rich in montage effects.

The promiscuity and squalor of a steamer, for example, is rendered as in a realist novel in order to suggest a modern African place: "In the forward part of the steamer, beyond the second-class w.c., water always running off their steel floors, and in the narrow walk beside the cabins, among the defecating babies, the cooking and the washing and the vacant girls being intently deloused, in a damp smell of salted fish and excrement and oil and rust, and to the sound of gramophone records, there are stalls: razor blades, batteries, pills and capsules, soap, hypodermic syringes, cigarettes, pencils, copybooks, lengths of cloth" (*Return*, pp. 183–184).

Furthermore, along with such sordid heterogeneity in which the mass-consumer products of modern industrial society are juxtaposed with the unchanged habits of African village life on a nineteenth-century ship, Naipaul offers his readers the sharper exoticism of butchered monkeys hung out for sale among the merchandise. It is an example of what, after Said, might be called "Africanism": "basins of slugs in black earth, fresh fish, and monkeys, monkeys ready-smoked, *boucane*, charred little hulks, or freshly killed, gray or red monkeys, the tips of their tails slit, the slit skin of the tail tied around the neck" (*Return*, pp. 183–184). In such passages, as in so many other places, Naipaul behaves like the novelist he is. Unlike the ethnographer who seeks to overcome cultural distance through some effort at totalization—through the integration of such episodes into the economy and mores of a society's life—Naipaul promotes a calculated shock for his reader. His purpose here is not to awaken a sense of intraspecies solidarity, but to proclaim Africa's irreducible otherness.

o   o   o

GIVEN Naipaul's Hindu ancestry and the powerful attraction of travel, it was probably inevitable that sooner or later he would go to India and report his findings there. Moreover, a peculiar interest also attaches itself to the results of such an encounter to the extent that it is necessarily charged by the relationship to his parents in a way that is much less obvious in the case of a more "neutral" country. If ever a journey were likely to be haunted in Naipaul's case, it would, therefore, probably be the one that took him to his "old home," the land of his ancestors.

It is in India especially that he acknowledges the weight of a past that is individual as well as collective. A recurrent theme of his writings is, as has already been noted, the need to assume one's history at all levels. And Naipaul himself has worked in the various fictional and nonfictional genres that are in one way or another devoted to such a purpose, from the novel to history, biography, autobiography, and travel writing itself. Moreover, the journey in space turns out to be a painful, if rewarding, journey back in time. Throughout Naipaul's writings one finds an implicit ethics of full disclosure, whether or not he himself is able to practice it fully.

There are, in fact, not one but two Indian travel books, the first of which has the Conradian title *An Area of Darkness* and was published in 1964. The second, which for reasons of space I shall concentrate on here and which was written in the same year as "A New King for the Congo," is entitled *India: A Wounded Civilization*.[9] In many ways, it is a less disciplined piece of writing than either of the two principal travel sketches of *The Return of Eva Perón*, less sharply evocative in its descriptions, but it is equally disturbing in the conclusions it draws.

The "wounded civilization" of the title is, in Naipaul's analysis, self-wounding. India is, of course, like Zaire rather than Argentina, to the extent that after independence the colonial power simply withdrew and

9 (New York: Vintage Books, 1981).

left behind an indigenous population equipped with Western-style institutions. Yet, unlike Zaire or Argentina, the Indian subcontinent is the site of one of the world's oldest, most elaborate, and most enduring civilizations. Nevertheless, in 1975 as in 1964 it, too, is represented as one of the dark places of the earth, in its different way equally "unmade." Although he does not use the word, the state of India suggests "entropy" to Naipaul just as much as it did to Lévi-Strauss. But it does not lead him to complain of a lack of "exoticism."

At the moment Naipaul arrived there in 1975, in fact, the new India was facing a crucial test: its "borrowed" institutions were under challenge, and it was not at all clear what would emerge to replace them. The so-called Emergency, proclaimed by Indira Gandhi, had meant the suspension of the constitution left behind by the British. Naipaul, wrongly as it turns out, reads into the Emergency a sign of the imminent dissolution of the new state, a dissolution that for him has its causes in the nature of Hindu thought itself and in the Gandhism which, as a political philosophy, is wholly inadequate to India's real needs.

In this respect, his judgment is categorical and repeated in a number of different formulations throughout. The problem, says Naipaul, does not derive from the legacy of British imperialism, but from the indigenous religion that turns its back to the world: "Hinduism hasn't been good enough for the millions. It has exposed us to a thousand years of defeat and stagnation. It has given men no idea of a contract with other men, no idea of the state. It has enslaved one quarter of the population and always left the whole fragmented and vulnerable. Its philosophy of withdrawal has diminished men intellectually and not equipped them to respond to challenge; it has stifled growth" (*India*, p. 50). The social unity and civilized order he had failed to find in Trinidad, Argentina, or Zaire also eludes him in India. And if he does not find "barbarism" as such, there are nevertheless multiple signs of it left over from the past and of its potential reemergence in the future.

Because *India: A Wounded Civilization* is largely designed to illustrate such themes, it turns out to be even less of a conventional travel book and even more of a work of explicit political witness than Naipaul's other writings in the genre. The author himself called it "an inquiry about India" (*India*, p. IX). But it is an inquiry that begins with the narrator's recognition that India is not just another country for him, to be observed, described, and left behind like those countries which are the object of his other writings. On the one hand, it is the homeland of his ancestors; on the other, it is not his home. What strikes him most about it, in fact, is its "strangeness." And the context makes clear that "strangeness" here is virtually synonymous with the "uncanny" encountered by other travelers, for it is a "strangeness" produced by the experience of something once familiar and since forgotten: "I am at once too close and too far" (*India*, p. IX). The particular *déjà vu* of India for Naipaul is derived from the circumstance that it is mediated through the memories it stirs of familial relations during his early years in Trinidad. More obviously than in his other travel books, the journey to a remote land here overlaps with an inner journey into his own past.

In the space of two pages of his foreword, in fact, Naipaul makes that set of conditions coincide which in Freud's essay are defined as productive of the two different forms of the uncanny. It will be remembered that, in social life, the "uncanny" is hypothesized by Freud as occurring whenever a previously surmounted system of belief returns—he cites magic, animism, and the omnipotence of mind as examples of this in the modern world. On the level of the individual psyche, "the uncanny" is associated with the return, in some form, of repressed material from early childhood.[10]

Thus, on the one hand, as Naipaul himself acknowledges, his inquiry into Indian attitudes and Indian civilization is also an inquiry into himself and into past beliefs he thought he had overcome: "Because in myself, like the split-second images of infancy which some of us carry, there survive, from the family rituals that lasted into my childhood, phantasmal memories of old India which for me outline a whole vanished world" (*India*, p. X). On the other hand, he also dredges up the specific, forgotten memory of a ritual that probably comes as close as any recorded to the symbolic enactment of castration. Having noted that the pebbles brought from India by his grandfather were "phallic emblems," he goes on to wonder, without himself making anything of the connection, "why it was necessary for a male hand to hold the knife with which a pumpkin was cut open." He simply notes that at the time it did seem to him "because of the appearance of a pumpkin halved downward—that there was some sexual element in the rite" (*India*, pp. X–XI).

One does not need to be very familiar with psychoanalysis to recognize in the appearance of a halved pumpkin a metaphor for the female genitals and for the very sight/site of castration. The savagery of the Law of the Father has rarely been suggested more graphically than in this reference to the ritual cutting of the pumpkin in the bosom of the family and the "necessity" of a male hand on the knife. No wonder Naipaul is able to conclude that although he is a "stranger" in India, "the memories of that India which lived on into my childhood in Trinidad are like trapdoors into a bottomless past" (*India*, p. XI).

Furthermore, if one substitutes the word "barbarism" for "savagery" in

[10] See "The Uncanny," in *The Standard Edition of the Complete Psychological Works* (London: Hogarth, 1955), vol. 17.

connection with the ritual, it helps us understand Naipaul's lifelong preoccupation with the threat it constitutes in the cultural and geopolitical
sphere. And it will come as no surprise that patriarchal India—India the
fatherland—is associated with the threat of "barbarism" in his imagination at least as much as less familiar countries. What is wrong with modern India turns out to be largely what is wrong with the other lands surveyed in his travels, in spite of their different historical itineraries.

Naipaul illustrates the problem and himself draws the parallel with the
situation in Africa by condemning "the ultimate Hindu retreat" as portrayed in a novel by R. K. Narayan entitled *The Vendor of Sweets*. Unlike
his predecessor, Naipaul defines the retreat negatively as a "retreat from
civilization and creativity, from rebirth and growth, to magic and incan-
tation, a retrogression to an almost African night, the enduring primitivism of a place like the Congo" (*India*, p. 39). In short, if modern India is
still so susceptible to blood cults like the Anand Marg, it is because the
hegemony of Gandhi's Hinduism has turned its back on the world and
on civilization, thus leaving the country defenseless against the return of
a barbarism of the knife.

o   o   o

A DECADE after the travel essays on Zaire and India, in the second narrative of *Finding the Center* ("The Crocodiles of Yamoussoukro"), Africa
at least is made to appear in a far less negative light. The interest of the
work is less in the narrative itself than in a certain ambivalence it allows
us to perceive retrospectively in the fierce negations of the earlier works.
Thus, the reasons for the partial change of perspective are only partly to
be found in the objective conditions of life that make one African country
seem to Naipaul superior in important ways to another.

The narrator does explain that he chose the Ivory Coast partly because
it was in West Africa and partly because it was a former French colony,
but above all because it was politically and economically successful in "the
mess of black Africa" (*Center*, p. 79). It, therefore, becomes part of Naipaul's task in what is for him a characteristic piece of geopolitical investigation to explain that success. And he does so in such a way that he ends
up writing something like a celebration of Africa. Nevertheless, what also
appears in Naipaul's penultimate travel book, on a country entirely separated from the familial, cultural, and literary traditions in which he was
raised, is a partial conquest of the fears that characterized the Indian
essay and the reappearance of the "uncanny" in Freud's first, or social,
sense; that is, the return of a previous system of belief.

In the light of that central concept from Naipaul's earlier travel writings, "the half-made society," it is significant that on more than one occasion in his narrative of the Ivory Coast he proclaims Africa "complete":

"Africa . . . has always been in its own eyes complete, achieved, bursting with its own power" (*Center*, p. 78). Such an imaginary vision of wholeness is justified by the end, on the grounds that in the Ivory Coast the two worlds—the old Africa and the new—have been joined under the benevolent rule of President Houphouet-Boigny. The Ivory Coast's president is interpreted as the embodiment of an African ideal of kingship founded on the principle of the visibility of power and of reconciliation.

In what is perhaps the single memorable episode in this otherwise perfunctory piece of writing, in fact, Naipaul focuses on the new city of Yamoussoukro as the overcoming of the contradictions between the old and the new. Yamoussoukro was constructed by foreign technicians in the bush on the site of the president's native village, and it is reached by a 150-mile superhighway. It has wide, straight avenues, modern international hotels, swimming pools, and a splendid golf course. It also has an artificial lake stocked with the president's man-eating crocodiles, crocodiles that may be observed by visiting tourists during daily ritual feedings that include a live chicken. Yamoussoukro, then, is a paradox.

On the one hand, it is the embodiment of a "pharaonic" ambition to build one of the great modern cities of Africa and the world, a developmentalist's dream. On the other hand, it uses totemic symbolism and magic in order to affirm the chief's power in ways that are described as characteristically African and impossible to analyze. Yet, in place of the irony with which Naipaul illuminates such incongruities in earlier works, he is on this occasion (for unexplained reasons) ready to believe. Against the background of the failed and violent nation-states that surround the Ivory Coast—Liberia, Ghana, Guinea—Naipaul suggests with something like awe that, in spite of the "artificiality" of the mix, it works.

In fact, Naipaul finds in the Ivory Coast something he is familiar with from West Indian stories about slave culture: namely, the coexistence of two separate worlds, a Night world of spirits, magic, ritual, and crocodiles in an artificial lake and a prosaic Day world of progressive peasant agriculture, technological planning, and the metropolis of Yamoussoukro. Naipaul, it seems, has come to terms with that uncanny which involves the return of a previously discarded system of belief. We are, in any case, a long way here from the thematics of the heart of darkness, for at least equal homage is paid to the truths of the Night as to those of the Day, to traditional African culture as well as to imported Western civilization. Thus, it is this time the white technicians encountered in a bar who strike the narrator with their futility: "phantoms, preparing plans for things that are one day bound to perish" (*Center*, p. 174).

Whatever one thinks about the "wisdom" Naipaul projects on the old Africa in its attitudes toward the new—and this reader at least finds a disturbing bathos in the high lighting of such comments as "But the world is sand. Life is sand" (*Center*, p. 175)—Naipaul's attempt to achieve a new understanding of African reality seems in part to be a function of distance of a different kind, the kind that has liberated him, at least temporarily, from some of his obsessions. Like one of the many expatriates whose life stories he tells and whose comments he reports, Naipaul's new and more sympathetic understanding derives from "a correct distancing of himself from the continent and its people" (*Center*, p. 154). He is disturbed neither by the recourse to magic of many more enlightened Ivoiriens nor by the tales of human sacrifice. Such cultural phenomena are no longer fastened on as signifiers of a persistent barbarism. The fundamental hierarchical opposition between civilization and barbarism of the earlier travel writings is, in fact, deconstructed here.

On this occasion, Naipaul seems to have been more mellow, more willing—like those other transplanted souls he encounters, who in the era of postcolonialism are also in search of a "center"—to allow his ideas and values to be questioned by Africa. This is, in part, a consequence of the blurring of the opposition referred to; it is also a function of the purpose he now attributes to travel: "I travel to discover other states of mind. . . When my curiosity has been satisfied, when there are no more surprises, the intellectual adventure is over and I become anxious to leave" (*Center*, p. 90). "Other states of mind" are hardly what had interested him before in any positive sense. He, too, now recognizes that he is in search of the new, but he distances himself from the tradition of romantic sensation-seekers with the characteristic move of defining his adventures as "intellectual."

The other narrative of *Finding the Center*, "Prologue to an Autobiography," is more illuminating as to why a middle-aged, Hindu expatriate from Trinidad might find Africa more spiritually congenial than he had previously found it. The sketch also makes explicit certain fantasies of cultural wholeness and of the "fully made society" that had been merely implicit before. This narrative of his early years in Trinidad, of his extended Hindu family, of his father's struggle to write, of his own discovery of his vocation as a writer, and of the writing of his first story, is one of the forms of that historical accounting to which he has affirmed his commitment; in this case, it is self-accounting or autobiography. But personal and collective history are shown to intersect. He brings a highly politicized consciousness to bear on the human problem of growing up a colonial subject in a minority culture that was cut off from its roots in another continent.

The focus he gives his narrative is that of learning to write and of the discovery through writing of the complexity of his Caribbean material.[11]

---

[11] See the discussion of this autobiographical material in *The Enigma of Arrival*, in a chapter entitled "The Journey."

The piece also emphasizes the racial and ethnic diversity of the different communities that cohabit the circumscribed space of the island of his birth, and the particularity of each of their different histories. But in order to understand this fully, he had first to go away to England and become something of a scholar himself: "True knowledge of geography, and with it a sense of historical wonder, began to come sixteen years after I had left Trinidad, when for two years I worked on a history of the region" (*Center*, pp. 35–36). Abetted by time, travel with its radical *dépaysement* helped provide the distance for retrospective auto-analysis. But it is only through narrative that Naipaul was able to recover the past and fill in the troubling gaps. Instead of the denial of narrative that characterizes modern ethnography, narrative is implicitly celebrated as the work of civilization. It is through narrative that one precipitates meaning and order from a chaotic past, and comes to terms with one's present.

Seen from the vantage point of middle age, Naipaul's childhood appears to him to be characterized by a series of upheavals and moves, by "disorder within, disorder without" (*Center*, p. 27). The "political panic" associated with decolonization was preceded by a familial one, by the discovery of originary displacement; and it is the function of his brief autobiographical sketch to overcome that experience of dispersion and fragmentation. The goal is to uncover the hidden directionality of his past, to find its "center" now that the world of his childhood has disappeared. For the individual as for a country, the struggle to constitute an "identity" presupposes a history and a point of origin for Naipaul. Moreover, he finds this center, in effect, through the contrast between his father's career and his own. The power of place comes to be intimately connected to the power of paternity.

Naipaul's father had been a journalist off and on throughout his life, and was the writer of a number of unpublished stories, but his own story in the end is summarized by the son in a phrase: "poverty, cheated hopes, and death" (*Center*, p. 31). In effect, Naipaul's explanation of the failure relates to the intellectual impoverishment of the colonial conditions in which his father as an aspiring, isolated intellectual found himself. As is made even more evident in a 1975 paper that the novelist offered as an introduction to a conference proceedings entitled *East Indians in the Caribbean*,[12] Naipaul senior is described as a writer of romance who, once the tightly integrated Hindu community of his early stories began to disintegrate, found it impossible to become a critical recorder of change. What Naipaul finds in his father's stories is an idyllic vision of Indian village life and of the Hindu rituals that gave "a grace and completeness to that

---

[12] *East Indians in the Caribbean: Colonialism and the Struggle for Identity* (Millwood, N.Y.: Kraus International Publications, 1982).

life" (*Center*, p. 29)—that very "completeness" which in the countries Naipaul has surveyed in his previous travel works is notably lacking.

Consequently, the world of the stories haunts him with a sense of what the idea of "homeness" might be: "to me they gave a beauty (which in a corner of my mind still endures, like a fantasy of home) to the Indian village life I had never known" (*Center*, p. 29). In the light of this nostalgia for the lost home of the traditional Hindu community, of Naipaul's "fantasy of things as they were at the very beginning" (*Center*, p. 37), it is not difficult to understand the sympathy he might come to feel for African village life, for its rituals and its magical relatedness to the earth— something he had missed in Argentina, in particular, and virtually denounced in India, but that he now asserts as essential in the foreword to *Finding the Center*.

Nevertheless, it is Naipaul himself who, rather late in his career, also designates such desire for wholeness and immersion in a ritualized communal life as a "fantasy" for someone in his position. And he emphasizes that fact with a brief but terrible anecdote from the past. In this anecdote, previously repatriated Indians living in Calcutta storm a passenger ship, newly arrived from Trinidad, in their desperation to return to that Caribbean island: "India for these people had been a dream of home, a dream of continuity after the illusion of Trinidad. All the India they had found was the area around the Calcutta docks" (*Center*, pp. 48–49). One finds here a transposition to an Eastern port scene of the theme of *The Enigma of Arrival*.

The whole burden of the introduction to *East Indians in the Caribbean* is precisely that such "a dream of home" is doomed to remain a dream; once a break has been made, there can be no going back. Once one has entered the space of global geopolitics and experienced the cultural pluralism of the modern world as a birthright, one is condemned to live otherwise—if one is to avoid the debilitating mythification of the past that Naipaul encountered in Argentina, Zaire, and India itself.

The only tenable approach to the past under such circumstances is the approach of the intellect and of critical inquiry—of what he calls civilization. And both the introduction and "Prologue to an Autobiography" argue for the crucial importance in former colonial countries of a fully developed intellectual life, for cultural self-knowledge through collective self-examination. Moreover, in the task of substituting history for fantasy and myth, on the one hand, and self-deluding political discourse, on the other, writers and intellectuals must play a role alongside historians and scholars of all kinds.

The central theme of "Prologue to an Autobiography" is similar to that of his earlier, harsher book on India in which he refers contemptuously to "That Indian past! That fantasy of wholeness and purity" (*India*, p.

154). Yet, even more significant and provocative is the fact that the obscurantist attitude is associated with Gandhi and Gandhism, which, as noted above, Naipaul equates with an instinctive, inward-turned, nonintellectual life. The chapter devoted to Gandhi in *India: A Wounded Civilization* is, in fact, entitled "A Defect of Vision." Naipaul, in effect, interprets this defect as scopophobia; and evidence for it is to be found in the total lack of attention Gandhi pays, in his autobiography, to the countries and places in which he lived. What goes unstated in Naipaul's reasoning here is the notion that there is a responsible kind of looking as well as a driven, erotic kind. Scopophilia is susceptible to socially useful sublimation and is potentially the foundation of the writer's vocation.

Although Naipaul does not say so, Gandhi as Hindu sage is, in effect, the embodiment of the anti-novelist and a fortiori of the anti–travel writer. There are in Gandhi's autobiography no descriptions of the landscapes, cities, sites, and people of the England and South Africa in which he lived for so many years. He thus solved the dilemma of having violated the taboo on foreign travel, affirmed by his merchant caste, by not looking at the world in which he found himself, by, so to speak, repressing his scopic drive. Thus it is that the habit of observation and of social inquiry which characterizes the novel in the West is, in fact, affirmed by Naipaul to be "outside the Indian tradition" (*India*, p. 10). But it is a habit that, in spite of his Hindu ancestry, Naipaul made his own in a way that he is able to explain only in retrospect.

Moreover, the taboo on travel passed on by modern India's founding father is a prohibition that Naipaul broke at birth and that he has continued breaking with a symptomatic frequency over the years since—not only by traveling widely throughout the world, but by writing about it. Yet, the transgressive force of travel is not directed against his own father here, but against the ancestral Father. Perhaps that is why he does not associate travel, in whole or in part, with pleasure. For him, as for an eighteenth-century paterfamilias, it is ostensibly undertaken as a duty, as work.

Naipaul's account of the discovery of his vocation turns out to be crucially implicated in his relationship to his father. The position he seems to posit for his father is an intermediary one between himself and Gandhi. On the one hand, under the peculiar colonial circumstances of the 1920s and 1930s in Trinidad, it is odd that the son in a Hindu family would become a journalist and writer; it already implies a certain detachment from the beliefs of his ancestors. On the other hand, Gandhi notwithstanding, there was a partial precedent for that choice of career in the Hindu tradition itself. After all, on both sides of Naipaul's own family tree, there were ancestors who had been traditional Hindu pundits, and his grandparents had intended his father for such a vocation. A life dedicated to the study of Sanskrit, to philosophy, religion, and jurisprudence is also, in its way, a life dedicated to the word and to the preservation of the past through reading and commentary, the life of a writer in the sense that Naipaul apparently prefers. And it was this calling that Naipaul senior had, in effect, attempted to practice, alongside romance, in such a nontraditional or Western mode as journalism.

The mere mention of these two kinds of writing, journalism and romance, is, however, enough to suggest the contradiction at the level of the writing itself. Whereas the former is associated with the idea of the investigation and reporting of contemporary events, the latter suggests ritual, magic, and traditional values as well as the narrativization of experience. The genres of the novel and of travel writing, on the other hand, may be said to overcome the contradiction, since they fuse the two; they investigate and narrativize. But Naipaul's father never wrote novels or travel books. Like Gandhi, he also sought to avoid the pollution of foreign travel; he did so, however, not by the hysteric's solution of refusing to see, but by renouncing travel as such. He never left the Caribbean island of his birth.

The cultural and intellectual transition that, virtually unassisted, Naipaul senior attempted to make in colonial Trinidad was apparently too much for one man in one generation. The contradiction he lived seems, in fact, to have isolated him to the point that Naipaul the son locates therein the cause of the "madness" that overcame him toward the end of his life.

The single significant episode that is evoked as a symptom of his father's condition also concerns "a defect of vision" of a different kind. He suddenly became incapable of seeing his own reflection. "He looked in the mirror one day," Naipaul's mother reports, "and couldn't see himself. And he began to scream" (*Center*, p. 70). He had become an invisible man, invisible to himself. Concentrated in these two sentences one finds the idea of a regression back beyond the mirror stage and that first narcissistic perception of the self in its jubilant but illusory wholeness. Standing between a disintegrating culture and a more complex, emergent one, Naipaul senior seems to have experienced the refragmentation of imaginary identity, loss of selfhood. And it is such a fear of extinction that, at the end of the "Prologue," Naipaul claims to have inherited as a "gift" from his father alongside the vocation of writer. What he also finds is that the only way to conquer the fear is in writing itself: "That was his subsidiary gift to me. That fear became mine as well. It was linked with the idea of vocation: the fear could be combated only by the exercise of the vocation" (*Center*, p. 72). Thus, writing is for Naipaul both a matter of personal survival and, for the traveler who went so far beyond his father, an act of filial piety in Freud's sense.

Moreover, what Naipaul claims to be true for himself on a personal level can be extrapolated to the life of societies. Where there is no writing and—what is virtually synonymous with writing for Naipaul—no developed intellectual life, there is the experience of a collective loss of continuity with the past and of identity in the present or, in other words, of extinction on the level of a culture—that sense of "abandonment" he has diagnosed among European immigrants to Argentina or the "cultural destitution" he found among the surviving Mayan Indians of Belize.

In "Prologue to an Autobiography," then, one finds the outline of a relationship between Naipaul and his father that has some similarity with that described by Freud in connection with Rome. In the solicitude of the tribute Naipaul pays his father, there is the implication of guilt at having gone so far beyond him, of having traveled widely in a world the latter could only read about. But in Naipaul's case there is also a powerful element of identification and of heroic commitment to take up his father's uncompleted work. Moreover, the work concerned is reinterpreted as both "the work of the world," in Conrad's Western sense, and, in spite of Gandhi, the work of the Hindu pundits among his own ancestors. That is why in *Finding the Center* Naipaul is able to interpret his extensive travel and the writing that results from it as a vocation accepted as an obligation.

In the same way that Naipaul sees himself as both an historian and a novelist—he is, in fact, the author of a straightforwardly historical work, *The Loss of El Dorado*—he is also in his travel writings the scribe as cultural geographer and political analyst, the critical observer who remembers. And all these activities embody a commitment to writing understood as a taking of bearings, as a mapping in space as well as in time. In going backward in history from a given cultural location in the present, one is writing the critical biography of a society, and in leaving one's birthplace to go out into the world one is attempting to map diversity. In both cases, the writer is involved in a form of narrativization that, as Naipaul himself recognizes in his "Author's Note," is a centering as well as a deciphering and a recording—the kind of narrativization and centering that Roland Barthes condemned. In his double exile, however, Naipaul is clearly searching for a way of preserving continuity. Only through the reestablishment of broken connections, apparently, is it possible for this particular former colonial subject to overcome the fear of invisibility, once he emerged from the innocence of his colonial condition.

There is a sense in which Naipaul's abundant travel writings may be interpreted, like Lévi-Strauss's *Tristes Tropiques*, as a long and bitter lament for worlds that are lost and systems of belief that are overcome— the Indian village community and all those other traditionalist, so-called organic cultures that developed independently of one another or even the security of an assigned place within an imperial order. At the same time, his writings also embody a plea for social inquiry and a protest against forgetting, against loss and extinction. Naipaul at his best is, therefore, one of our most alert chroniclers of difference, who has learned from his earlier years in colonial Trinidad to treat the land as a cultural palimpsest. He strives to disassociate what former colonizers and contemporary ideologues alike carelessly lump together in their different discourses.

Perhaps nowhere more than in his travel writings has the wandering Hindu remained more faithful to the vocation of the pundit, in fact. In overcoming "the dread of the unknown" (*Center*, p. 69) that he attributes to his father, Naipaul in his more recent travel books has sought to confront the questions of transplantation, displacement, and homelessness in the postcolonial world—"the great movement of peoples" that, as he notes in *The Enigma of Arrival* (p. 141), he paradoxically first became aware of in the center of the former British imperial order, London itself. The work of Naipaul's life, therefore, has involved the effort to overcome his personal fear of extinction in socially profitable ways.

A poignant symbol of the distance that this former colonial subject has traveled, while remaining loyal to his paternal heritage, is the unused British passport he found among his father's personal effects. The passport has in its textual context the evocative power of *An Inquiry into Some Points of Seamanship* in Conrad's *Heart of Darkness*. It is in its own way a talisman that is "luminous with another than a professional light," but it is a talisman that Naipaul's father, unlike the son, never put to use. The hold of Hindu culture was apparently too strong. In the fragment of autobiography, the passport affirms the indispensability and fragility of the civilizing function as a task learned and passed on. And for Naipaul, the Westernized writer, it is associated now with a Hindu as well as a Western tradition, though not with Hinduism itself. What is important to him is the idea of a past and of a connectedness with it as well as of a paternal inheritance that places him under an obligation.

Thus, Naipaul is both an anti-Foucault and an anti-Barthes, an anti-genealogist and an anti-poststructuralist, who asserts his preference for continuity over discontinuity, identity through time over dispersal, linearity over a broken periodicity. He affirms not the pleasure of travel and of the text, but the work of travel and its narrativization. One is, after all, freer to dehistoricize the national past if one's homeland is France than if one is born in Trinidad. Two such countries are out of phase and are likely to remain so for the foreseeable future. Yet, there are intimations in Naipaul's more recent writings that the "fully made society" is always a fantasized construct, even if he still affirms obstinately the oppositions between journalism and romance, history and myth.

When Naipaul observes England close up, as he does in *The Enigma of Arrival*, the centerpiece of the colonial system and motherland of empire itself begins to look strangely like a colony. Yet, the experience is interpreted positively to the extent that change is redefined as flux and is no longer held to be synonymous with decay. Even in the English heartland of Wiltshire, between those potent signifiers of tradition and continuity that are Stonehenge and Salisbury Cathedral, Naipaul encounters not an imaginary permanence but a form of transience that proves to be the opposite of disabling. Even there, it turns out, the past is continually erased and reinvented; in Thomas Hardy country itself, people come and go.

The discovery that the narrator now attributes to himself and his family—that "the sacred world has vanished" (*Enigma*, p. 354)—is, in fact, the emblematic experience of modernity. Unlike his Hindu ancestors in Trinidad, who were lured by the image of India, Naipaul has come to recognize that we are all from somewhere else and that the place in which we find ourselves is always "the wrong place" (*Enigma*, p. 130).

Modern world societies, except where they are artificially isolated by power from the outside, are always in process. It follows, therefore, that there is for Naipaul no possibility of a return to the innocence of communitarian romance, no "home" to go back to. He is left instead, like a quintessential poststructuralist, with his writing. But it is writing without the latter's sense of Nietzschean free play; it is writing as filial piety and burden. In sum, like his stories of the collective past, Naipaul's travel sketches are obsessive efforts to recenter a decentered world. His latest work, however, offers the belated recognition that such a task is Sisyphean. There is "no ship of antique shape to take us back."

journal form, 31–32, 38–39, 138, 148.
See also diary
jouissance, 11, 81, 103, 105, 175, 216,
232, 263, 288, 290, 292, 295, 300
Joyce, James, 118, 251
Jung, Karl, 204

Kuchak Hanem, 176–177
Khatibi, Abdelkebir, 292n
Kipling, Rudyard, 263
Kristeva, Julia, 303
Kuhn, Thomas, 147n, 152
Kundera, Milan, 244

La Boëtie, Etienne de, 91
Lacan, Jacques, 8, 11, 20, 251, 272, 279,
282, 289
Lahontan, Louis Armand, *baron* de, 26
Lamartine, Alphonse de, 126, 154, 165
Lavater, Johann, 149
Lawrence, David Herbert, 13, 155, 199,
202–222, 223, 236, 264, 281n, 315
Lawrence, Frieda, 206, 213, 219, 220
Lawrence, Thomas Edward, 155, 199,
223–235, 262, 264, 269, 315
Leiris, Michel, 237
Le Vasseur, Thérèse, 45, 46
Lévi-Strauss, 12, 16, 17, 21, 47, 67, 91,
101, 155, 161, 199, 245, 246, 267–284,
287, 288, 294, 305, 306, 315, 322, 331;
Lévi-Strauss's delay, 268
Locke, John, 27, 28, 69, 92, 155
Lopez, Barry, 158, 201n
Lorraine, Claude, 257
Loti, Pierre, 165, 235, 288
Lotman, Jurij, 88, 106, 126, 152, 198,
248, 282
Lottman, Herbert R., 238n
Lough, John, 76n
Luciros, Ferdinandes de, 93
luxury, 78–79
Lyell, Charles, 160

Maclean, Donald, 226
Malinowski, Bronislaw, 199, 246–267,
275, 277, 315
Malthus, Thomas Robert, 150
Mann, Thomas, 236
Mannheim, Karl, 122

Mansfield, Katherine, 214
Marcuse, Herbert, 141
Masson, Pierre, 236n, 237n
Maugham, Somerset, 231
Mead, Margaret, 36n, 91, 253
melancholy: of tourism, 182–183; of
travel, 33, 217, 269–270; of travel
writing, 269
Melville, Hermann, 91
Mercier, Louis Sébastien, 26
Michael X, 316
Miller, Christopher L., 3n
Mobutu, Joseph, 318, 319
Montaigne, Michel Eyquem de, 16, 73n,
80, 91
Montesquieu, Charles-Louis de Secon-
dat, 26
More, Sir Thomas, 91
motivation of travel, 10, 13, 147, 150,
175, 188–192, 196–197, 214–215, 224,
251, 259, 259n, 264, 265, 273, 282,
289, 292, 321. *See also* father/son relations, Freud
Murry, John Middleton, 214, 216

Naipaul, V. S., 12, 201, 245, 274, 305–
333
nakedness, 12–13, 27, 94–95, 96, 110,
113–114. *See also* body painting, tattooing
Napoleon (Napoleon Bonaparte), 128,
133, 194, 197, 233
Narayan, R. K., 324
narcissism, 33–39, 42, 45–46, 139, 155,
162, 197, 271, 272, 295. *See also* heroism
narrative, 74, 138, 145, 255–256, 258,
268–269, 272, 283, 291, 308–309,
320–321, 326–327; as critical task,
312–313, 330, 331, 332; denial of,
249, 267; and description, 157; and
journal, 32–33, 39, 148–149; and letters, 59–60; metanarratives, 305–306;
and narrators, 117–118, 152, 159,
260–261; plotted, 88, 106, 126, 198,
282; pseudo, 249–250
negative hallucination, 304
Nerval, Gérard de, 165, 170
Newton, Sir Isaac, 89
Nietzsche, Friedrich, 4, 6, 127, 208
Novalis, Friedrich, 236